INTERMEDIATE ANCIENT GREEK LANGUAGE

INTERMEDIATE ANCIENT GREEK LANGUAGE

DARRYL PALMER

PRESS

Published by ANU Press
The Australian National University
Acton ACT 2601, Australia
Email: anupress@anu.edu.au

Available to download for free at press.anu.edu.au

ISBN (print): 9781760463427
ISBN (online): 9781760463434

WorldCat (print): 1241230170
WorldCat (online): 1241230169

DOI: 10.22459/IAGL.2021

This title is published under a Creative Commons Attribution-NonCommercial-NoDerivatives 4.0 International (CC BY-NC-ND 4.0).

The full licence terms are available at
creativecommons.org/licenses/by-nc-nd/4.0/legalcode

Cover design and layout by ANU Press

This edition © 2021 ANU Press

Contents

Abbreviations and Symbols		xiii
Introduction		1
1.	Time and Aspect of the Indicative Mood	5
	1.1. Tense	5
	1.2. Forms and Functions	5
	1.3. Time and Aspect (Summary)	8
	EXERCISE 1	9
2.	Aspect in the Imperative, Subjunctive and Optative Moods	13
	2.1. Introduction	13
	2.2. Forms	13
	2.3. Functions	14
	EXERCISE 2	17
3.	Infinitive	21
	3.1. Introduction	21
	3.2. Forms	21
	3.3. Functions	22
	3.4. Infinitive without Article	22
	3.5. Infinitive with Article	25
	EXERCISE 3	28
4.	Participles	31
	4.1. Introduction	31
	4.2. Forms	32
	4.3. Functions	32
	4.4. Negatives	36
	EXERCISE 4	36
5.	Genitive Absolute	39
	5.1. The Usual Construction	39
	5.2. Subject Unexpressed	40
	5.3. Improper Genitive Absolute	41
	EXERCISE 5	42
6.	Accusative Absolute	45
	6.1. Introduction	45
	6.2. So-Called Impersonal Verbs	45
	6.3. Verbs Used Impersonally in the Passive Voice	46
	6.4. Neuter Adjectives	47

	6.5. Personal Accusative Absolute	48
	6.6. Note	49
	EXERCISE 6	50
7.	Verbal Adjectives Ending in -τος, -τη, -τον	53
	7.1. Introduction	53
	7.2. Formation of Verbal Adjectives Ending in -τος, -τη, -τον	53
	7.3. Meaning of Verbal Adjectives Ending in -τος, -τη, -τον	55
	EXERCISE 7	57
8.	Verbal Adjectives Ending in -τέος, -τέα, -τέον	61
	8.1. Formation of Verbal Adjectives Ending in -τέος, -τέα, -τέον	61
	8.2. Usage of Verbal Adjectives Ending in -τέος, -τέα, -τέον	61
	8.3. Impersonal Construction	62
	8.4. Personal Construction	63
	8.5. Ambiguous Constructions	64
	8.6. Agent in Accusative	64
	8.7. Construction Continued with Infinitive	65
	8.8. Impersonal Passive Construction	65
	EXERCISE 8	66
9.	Voice	69
	9.1. English	69
	9.2. Greek	69
	9.3. Uses of the Middle Voice	70
	9.4. The Development of the Middle Voice	74
	EXERCISE 9	75
10.	Commands	79
	10.1. Introduction	79
	10.2. Negative Commands	79
	10.3. Virtual Commands	80
	10.4. Reported Commands	82
	EXERCISE 10	85
11.	Wishes	89
	11.1. Wishes for the Future	89
	11.2. Unfulfilled Wishes for the Present and the Past	91
	11.3. Reported Wishes	95
	11.4. Reported Wishes Instead of Direct Wishes	95
	11.5. Interrogative Wishes Combined with Deliberative Subjunctive	96
	EXERCISE 11	97
12.	Directly Reported Speech	101
	12.1. Homer	101
	12.2. Drama	102
	12.3. Historiography	102
	12.4. Prose Quotation Formulae	103
	12.5. ὅτι and ὡς as Quotation Markers	103
	EXERCISE 12	104

13.	Reported Statements with ὅτι or ὡς	107
	13.1. Introduction	107
	13.2. Reported Statements in Primary Sequence	107
	13.3. Reported Statements in Past Sequence	108
	13.4. Vivid Construction	110
	EXERCISE 13	111
14.	Reported Statements with Infinitive	113
	14.1. Aspect of the Infinitive	113
	14.2. Accusative and Infinitive Phrases	113
	14.3. Nominative and Infinitive Phrases	114
	14.4. Exceptional Accusative and Infinitive Phrases	115
	14.5. Negative	116
	14.6. Usage	116
	14.7. Passive of λέγειν	116
	EXERCISE 14	117
15.	Reported Knowledge and Perception	121
	15.1. Introduction	121
	15.2. Reported Knowledge or Perception with ὅτι or ὡς	121
	15.3. Reported Knowledge or Perception with a Participial Phrase	122
	15.4. Physical Perception	124
	15.5. Reported Knowledge or Perception with an Infinitive Phrase	125
	EXERCISE 15	126
16.	Reported Thoughts, Hopes, Promises and Oaths	129
	16.1. Reported Thoughts	129
	16.2. Reported Hopes and Promises	131
	16.3. Reported Oaths	132
	EXERCISE 16	134
17.	Questions	137
	17.1. Ordinary Questions	137
	17.2. Alternative Questions	139
	17.3. Questions with Interrogative Adjectives or Adverbs	140
	17.4. Deliberative Questions	141
	17.5. Rhetorical Questions	141
	EXERCISE 17	143
18.	Reported Questions	145
	18.1. Reported Ordinary Questions	145
	18.2. ἆρα in Reported Questions	146
	18.3. Reported Alternative Questions	146
	18.4. Reported Questions with Interrogative Adjectives or Adverbs	148
	18.5. Reported Deliberative Questions	149
	EXERCISE 18	150

19.	Conditions	153
	19.1. Introduction	153
	19.2. Open Conditions	153
	19.3. Unfulfilled Conditions	155
	19.4. Mixed Conditions	156
	19.5. The Negative in If-Clauses	158
	EXERCISE 19	159
20.	Homeric Conditions	161
	20.1. Introduction	161
	20.2. Open Conditions	161
	20.3. Unfulfilled Conditions	164
	EXERCISE 20	166
21.	Subordinate Clauses in Reported Discourse	169
	21.1. Reported Complex Sentences	169
	21.2. Reported Subordinate Clauses in Primary Sequence	169
	21.3. Reported Subordinate Clauses in Past Sequence	170
	21.4. Assimilation of Construction	171
	21.5. Vivid Construction	172
	EXERCISE 21	173
22.	Result Constructions	175
	22.1. Natural Result	175
	22.2. Comparative Result	177
	22.3. Actual Result	177
	22.4. Adjectival Clauses of Result	178
	22.5. Provisos	178
	22.6. Antecedents for Result Constructions	179
	22.7. ὥστε = 'And so'	180
	EXERCISE 22	180
23.	Causal Constructions	183
	23.1. Adverbial Clauses of Cause	183
	23.2. Adjectival Clauses of Cause	186
	23.3. Causal Participles	186
	23.4. Coordinating Use of ἐπεί and ὡς	187
	EXERCISE 23	188
24.	Constructions with Verbs of Effort and Caution	191
	24.1. Introduction	191
	24.2. Primary Sequence	191
	24.3. Past Sequence	193
	24.4. Variations of the Constructions in §§24.2 and 24.3	196
	24.5. Infinitive Constructions	196
	24.6. Omission of Main Clause	197
	EXERCISE 24	198

25.	Adjectival Clauses	201
	25.1. Introduction	201
	25.2. Definite Clauses Introduced by ὅς	201
	25.3. Indefinite Clauses Introduced by ὅς	202
	25.4. Indefinite Clauses Introduced by ὅστις	204
	25.5. Coordinating Use of the Relative Adjective or Pronoun	206
	25.6. Parenthetic ὅστις Clause	206
	25.7. Special Uses of ὅστις and ὅς ἄν	207
	EXERCISE 25	208
26.	Concessive Constructions	211
	26.1. Introduction	211
	26.2. Concessive Participial Phrases	211
	26.3. Concessive Clauses	212
	EXERCISE 26	215
27.	Purpose Constructions	217
	27.1. Prepositions	217
	27.2. Infinitive	218
	27.3. Participles	218
	27.4. Adjectival Clauses of Purpose	218
	27.5. Adverbial Clauses of Purpose	219
	EXERCISE 27	221
28.	Clauses of Comparison	223
	28.1. Introduction	223
	28.2. Definite Comparison	223
	28.3. Indefinite Comparison	224
	28.4. Potential, Conditional and Temporal Constructions	224
	28.5. Other Correlative Adjectives and Adverbs	226
	EXERCISE 28	227
29.	Expressions of Hindering, Forbidding, Denying and Failing	229
	29.1. Introduction	229
	29.2. Direct Object	230
	29.3. Genitive of Separation	230
	29.4. Infinitive after a Positive Expression	231
	29.5. ἐμποδών	232
	29.6. Infinitive after a Negative Expression	233
	29.7. Result Construction	235
	29.8. Effort Construction	236
	29.9. Conditional Construction	236
	29.10. Participial Construction	236
	29.11. Passive Constructions	236
	EXERCISE 29	237

30.	Temporal Constructions 1: Clauses in Primary Sequence	239
	30.1. Introduction	239
	30.2. Contemporaneous Action in Temporal Clause	240
	30.3. Prior Action in Temporal Clause	241
	30.4. Subsequent Action in Temporal Clause: Indefinite	242
	EXERCISE 30	243
31.	Temporal Constructions 2: Clauses in Past Sequence	245
	31.1. Introduction	245
	31.2. Contemporaneous Action in Temporal Clause	245
	31.3. Prior Action in Temporal Clause	246
	31.4. Subsequent Action in Temporal Clause	247
	EXERCISE 31	248
32.	Temporal Constructions with πρίν	251
	32.1. Introduction	251
	32.2. πρίν with an Infinitive Phrase	251
	32.3. πρίν with a Finite Verb	253
	EXERCISE 32	256
33.	Adverbial Clauses of Place and Manner	259
	33.1. Adverbial Clauses of Place	259
	33.2. Adverbial Clauses of Manner	262
	33.3. Adverbial Clauses of Place Expressing Purpose	263
	33.4. Adverbial Clauses Distinguished from Noun Clauses	264
	EXERCISE 33	265
34.	Noun Clauses with Expressions of Emotion	269
	34.1. Introduction	269
	34.2. Verbs of Emotion	270
	34.3. εἰ Clause as Subject	273
	34.4. Negatives with ὅτι and εἰ Clauses	275
	34.5. General Comments	276
	EXERCISE 34A	278
	EXERCISE 34B	279
35.	Expressions of Fearing	281
	35.1. Introduction	281
	35.2. Verbs of Fearing with Noun or Pronoun as Object	281
	35.3. Verbs of Fearing with Infinitive Phrase as Object	282
	35.4. Verbs of Fearing with a μή Clause as Object	283
	35.5. Fears that Something is (etc.) Actually Happening	285
	35.6. Fears Expressed with Other Conjunctions	286
	35.7. Introductory Noun Phrases	289
	35.8. Note	290
	EXERCISE 35A	291
	EXERCISE 35B	292

36.	Nominative and Vocative Cases	295
	36.1. Nominative as Subject	295
	36.2. Nominative as Complement	295
	36.3. Predicate Nominative with Passive Verb	296
	36.4. Quoted Nominative	296
	36.5. Nominative Address	297
	36.6. Nominative Exclamation	297
	36.7. Vocative	298
	36.8. Hanging Vocative	299
	EXERCISE 36	301
37.	Accusative Case	305
	37.1. Accusative as Direct Object	305
	37.2. Adverbial Uses of the Accusative	310
	37.3. Accusative in Apposition to a Sentence	312
	EXERCISE 37	312
38.	Genitive Case 1	315
	38.1. Introduction	315
	38.2. Simple Possessive Genitive	315
	38.3. Subjective Genitive	315
	38.4. Objective Genitive	316
	38.5. Partitive Genitive	316
	38.6. Genitive of Definition (or Apposition)	316
	38.7. Genitive of Description (or Quality)	317
	38.8. Genitive of Material	317
	38.9. Genitive of Measure	318
	38.10. Genitive of Price or Value	318
	EXERCISE 38	318
39.	Genitive Case 2	321
	39.1. Introduction	321
	39.2. Possessive Genitive	321
	39.3. Partitive Genitive	323
	39.4. Genitive of Separation	327
	39.5. Genitive with Compound Verbs	328
	EXERCISE 39	329
40.	Dative Case 1	331
	40.1. Introduction	331
	40.2. Dative of Interest	331
	40.3. Dative of Accompaniment (or Sociative Dative)	334
	EXERCISE 40	336
41.	Dative Case 2	339
	41.1. Locative	339
	41.2. Means or Instrument	343
	EXERCISE 41	346

42.	Prepositions	349
	42.1. Adverbs	349
	42.2. Compound Verbs	349
	42.3. Prepositions	349
	42.4. Case Functions	350
	42.5. Possessive Genitive with Preposition	351
	42.6. Compound Verb with Preposition	351
	42.7. Metaphorical Use of Prepositions	352
	42.8. Accent and Position of Prepositions	353
	42.9. Adverbial Accusative as Preposition	353
	42.10. Pregnant Construction	354
	42.11. 'Proper' and 'Improper' Prepositions	354
	42.12. Hellenistic and Later Developments	355
	EXERCISE 42A	355
	EXERCISE 42B	357
43.	Correlative Clauses	359
	43.1. Introduction	359
	43.2. Adjectival Clauses	359
	43.3. Adverbial Clauses	360
	43.4. Interrogative Antecedent	362
	43.5. Mixed Adjectival and Adverbial Construction	362
	43.6. Pronominal Idioms	363
	43.7. Note	363
	EXERCISE 43	364
44.	Exclamations	367
	44.1. Exclamatory Cries	367
	44.2. A Cry with First Person Singular Pronoun	368
	44.3. An Exclamation with a Causal Genitive	368
	44.4. Exclamatory Infinitive Phrases	369
	44.5. Exclamatory Sentences Introduced by οἷος, ὅσος or ὡς	370
	44.6. Interrogative Adjective or Adverb	371
	44.7. Reported Exclamations	372
	EXERCISE 44	374
Bibliography		377
Index of Passages Quoted in the Lessons		379

Abbreviations and Symbols

abs.	absolute	Intr.	Intransitive
Acc.	Accusative	lit.	literal(ly)
Act.	Active	masc.	masculine
adj.	adjective	Mid.	Middle
adv.	adverb	neut.	neuter
Aor.	Aorist	Nom.	Nominative
(B)CE	(Before) the Common Era	Opt.	Optative
		Partc.	Participle
Dat.	Dative	Pass.	Passive
fem.	feminine	Perf.	Perfect
Fut.	Future	pers.	person
Gen.	Genitive	pl.	plural
Hist.	Historic	Pres.	Present
Imperf.	Imperfect	sg.	singular
Impv.	Imperative	Subj.	Subjunctive
Indic.	Indicative	Voc.	Vocative
Infin.	Infinitive		

Angular brackets enclose words supplied in translation: <…>.

Square brackets enclose either brief explanatory notes or words not needing to be translated in Exercises: […].

Introduction

This series of Lessons and Exercises is intended for students who have already covered all or most of an introductory course in the ancient Greek language. It aims to broaden and deepen students' understanding of the main grammatical constructions of Greek. Further attention is given to grammatical forms only to the extent necessary to illustrate their functions. With one exception, all Greek passages in the Lessons and Exercises (including English to Greek translation) are direct quotations from Greek authors. Some quotations are modified by the omission of a few words (marked by ellipses) for the sake of brevity, but without affecting the grammatical structure. In Lesson 19 on Conditions, brief model sentences have been employed to demonstrate more clearly the variety of conditional sentences.

In the Lessons, all Greek passages are translated into literal but reasonably idiomatic English. For the most part, passages in both the Lessons and the Exercises are drawn from main genres of the classical period (fifth to fourth centuries BCE)—tragedy, comedy, historiography (together with biography), oratory and philosophy. Non-dramatic lyric is not often used, since it is more difficult to understand a single sentence out of context in this genre. Didactic poetry (Hesiod) also appears seldom. Homer receives attention at particular points, mainly Homeric conditions (Lesson 20) and Homeric similes (Lesson 28 on clauses of comparison). In general, the focus is on the classical Attic dialect. Where Epic or Ionic forms occur, they are explained if necessary. Occasionally there are references forward to the Hellenistic period.

The first few Lessons have an emphasis on Time and Aspect in the Greek verbal system. After the Moods of the finite verb in Lessons 1 and 2, Infinitives and Participles are treated in Lessons 3 and 4. The absolute constructions of the Participles in the Genitive and Accusative Cases follow in Lessons 5 and 6. The verbal adjectives ending in -τος, -τη, -τον are treated in Lesson 7, and those ending in -τέος, -τέα, -τέον in Lesson 8. Lesson 9 is primarily concerned with the use of the Middle Voice in the classical period. Lesson 10 deals with commands and Lesson 11 with wishes. These two Lessons expand the concise treatment of Imperative,

Subjunctive and Optative Moods in Main clauses in Lesson 2. In addition to the most basic constructions, Lessons 10 and 11 present the variety of ways in which commands and wishes may be expressed. These two Lessons also cover the subordinate constructions for reported commands and reported wishes.

Lesson 12 provides a brief and basic presentation of directly quoted statements. This leads on to the range of subordinate constructions, which begins with reported statements in Lessons 13 and 14, and extends to Lesson 35. This sequence is interrupted at two points. Lesson 17 on questions is followed by Lesson 18 on reported questions. Lesson 21 on subordinate clauses in reported discourse is placed intentionally in the midst of the sequence of subordinate constructions.

Discussion of the Cases has been deliberately placed late in the series at Lessons 36 to 41. By this stage, students will be better prepared to analyse the Case usage with which they are now familiar. For the classical period, the consideration of prepositions in Lesson 42 naturally follows the treatment of the Cases. Lesson 43 on correlative clauses has numerous links with adjectival and adverbial constructions in previous Lessons. Finally, Lesson 44 deals with exclamations.

The majority of the Exercises comprise several passages for translation from Greek to English and one or more passages (depending on length) for translation from English to Greek. It is intended that students should use the full and most recent edition of *A Greek–English Lexicon* originally compiled by H. G. Liddell and R. Scott. Alternatively, *The Brill Dictionary of Ancient Greek*, originally compiled by F. Montanari for Italian readers, is now available with American-English spellings (see Bibliography for both dictionaries). However, to save time for students, some vocabulary is provided for specific passages in each of the Exercises. Exercises 7 to 9 and Exercises 36 to 42 involve translation from Greek to English only, but do require brief analytical comment. Exercise 20 on Homeric conditions involves translation from Greek to English only, but requires no further comment. Alternative Exercises (A and B) are provided for Lessons 34, 35 and 42. Exercises are of approximately equal length.

Accent marks indicate how a pitch accent was probably pronounced in Classical Greek. No separate Exercises are provided for this purpose. But the books of Allen (1987) and Probert (2003) are recommended. The table near the end of Lesson 1 and the accompanying list of Tenses largely correspond to those of the Joint Committee on Grammatical Terminology (1911) as modified by Masterman (1962). Masterman (1962, p .72) began his article with the following words:

> It is over fifty years now since the formation of the Joint Committee on Grammatical Terminology, and the presentation of its *Report*; and it seems to be high time that teachers of languages considered, first, how successful they have been in carrying out its recommendations, and secondly, what modifications are called for in the light of more recent knowledge.

Since Masterman's article was published, over 50 more years have passed, and it seems high time that a new intermediate Greek language textbook be made available. The grammars of Ancient Greek by Goodwin (1889) and Smyth (1956) remain the most convenient in English, despite their age.

LESSON 1
Time and Aspect of the Indicative Mood

1.1. Tense

Tense may be regarded as the combination of the Time and Aspect of a Greek verb. In classical usage, there are three Times—Present, Past, Future—and three Aspects—Imperfect, Perfect, Aorist.

The main functions of the Aspects are as follows:

- Imperfect expresses continuous or repeated action.
- Perfect expresses completed action or the state resulting from completed action.
- Aorist expresses momentary action or sums up a whole period as a single action.
- Aspect is not inherent in an action but expresses the point of view of the speaker or writer.

(Palmer regards 'durative' as an inadequate description of the function of the Imperfect Aspect and prefers to think of it as the 'eye-witness aspect'.)

The combination of three Times and Aspects would give a theoretical nine Tenses. But Greek does not have separate forms for each of the nine theoretical possibilities.

1.2. Forms and Functions

By way of illustration, the first person singular forms of the Indicative Active are given in the following list. The Active Voice of παύειν is normally used transitively (i.e. with a direct Object).

1.2.1. Present Time

Present

παύω	*I am stopping*
	I stop (repeatedly or regularly)

This Tense form is properly Present Imperfect. However, there is no separate form for Present Aorist. So παύω also covers the meaning 'I stop' (momentarily), and the Tense is usually called simply 'Present'. The Aorist function of the Present is most obvious in the Historic Present usage, where a Present Indicative vividly expresses a past action.

Present Perfect

πέπαυκα	*I have stopped*

It is generally agreed that, at the earliest stage of its development, the Perfect Aspect expressed a state resulting from previous action. In the classical period, this is especially noticeable with the Present Perfect forms of certain verbs used with Present meaning, for example: οἶδα, 'I have come to know', hence 'I know'; or ἕστηκα, 'I have taken my stand', hence 'I am standing'. By the later classical period, the emphasis on *completed action* had become more prominent and new Perfect forms with this resultative force were invented. But this emphasis had declined again by the first century CE. The Present Perfect and the Past Aorist Indicatives became increasingly interchangeable during the first three centuries CE. By the fourth century CE, the Present Perfect had been superseded by the Present (replacing its stative force) and by the Past Aorist (replacing its resultative force).

1.2.2. Past Time

In the classical period, all three Past Tenses were marked by the augment ε and had endings different to the Present and Future Tenses. Verbs with an initial short vowel in the Present Tense (e.g. ἱκετεύω with short ι) regularly lengthened the vowel in Past Tenses (ἱκέτευον, ἱκέτευσα with long ι).

Past Imperfect

ἔπαυον	*I was stopping, I used to stop*

Past Perfect

ἐπεπαύκη	*I had stopped*
ᾔδη	*I had come to know, (hence) I knew*
εἱστήκη	*I had stood, (hence) I was standing*

Past Aorist

ἔπαυσα	*I stopped*
ἐπολέμησα	*I fought*

'Stopping' is by nature a momentary action. 'Fighting' a battle or a war is by nature a continuous action. In the following passage, neither the composition of the account of the Peloponnesian war nor the actual fighting of the war was a momentary action. But both actions are summed up by the complexive use of the Past Aorist Indicatives (ξυνέγραψε, ἐπολέμησαν).

Θουκυδίδης Ἀθηναῖος ξυνέγραψε τὸν πόλεμον τῶν Πελοποννησίων καὶ Ἀθηναίων, ὡς ἐπολέμησαν πρὸς ἀλλήλους ... (Th. 1.1.1.)

Thucydides the Athenian wrote an account of the war of the Peloponnesians and the Athenians, how they fought against each other ...

1.2.3. Future Time

Future

παύσω	*I shall stop* (Aor. Aspect)
	I shall be stopping (Imperf. Aspect)

There are not separate forms for Future Imperfect and Future Aorist. The Future is primarily Aoristic in function. Some scholars explain the Future Indicative as derived from an Aorist Subjunctive with a sigma suffix. παύσω is an ambivalent form: 'I shall stop' (Fut. Indic.); 'I am to stop', 'let me stop' (Aor. Subj.). Palmer (1980) prefers to explain the

Future as a desiderative Mood in origin. Alternatively, the Future could be regarded as an Intentive Aspect in function. (Cf. the other common English idiom for expressing futurity: 'I am going to stop'.)

Future Perfect

πεπαύξω	*I shall have stopped*
πεπαυκὼς ἔσομαι	*I shall have stopped* (periphrastic, the usual form)

Actual forms of the Future Perfect Active are rare; they occur especially in two verbs that are regularly used in the Perfect with an Imperfect meaning.

ἑστήξω	*I shall have stood*, (hence) *I shall stand*
τεθνήξω	*I shall have died*, (hence) *I shall be dead*

Those verbs that form a regular Future Perfect Middle/Passive mostly prefer *either* a Middle *or* a Passive meaning. The Passive meaning is more common.

Emphatic reduplicated Futures such as δεδέξομαι 'I shall certainly receive' (Hom.*Il.* 5.238) constituted a model for the formation of Future Perfects from the Present Perfect base. Conversely, Future Perfect forms can sometimes be translated appropriately as emphatic Futures.

1.3. Time and Aspect (Summary)

	Aspect		
Time	**Imperfect**	**Perfect**	**Aorist**
Present	παύω	πέπαυκα	(παύω)
	I am stopping	*I have stopped*	*I stop*
Past	ἔπαυον	ἐπεπαύκη	ἔπαυσα
	I was stopping	*I had stopped*	*I stopped*
Future	(παύσω)	πεπαύξω	παύσω
	I shall be stopping	πεπαυκὼς ἔσομαι	*I shall stop*
		I shall have stopped	

LESSON 1. TIME AND ASPECT OF THE INDICATIVE MOOD

In the Lessons and Exercises, the following terminology will be used for the Tenses of the Indicative Mood (Cf. Masterman, 1962, 76).

παύω	Present
πέπαυκα	Present Perfect
ἔπαυον	Past Imperfect
ἐπεπαύκη	Past Perfect
ἔπαυσα	Past Aorist
παύσω	Future
πεπαύξω	Future Perfect
πεπαυκὼς ἔσομαι	Future Perfect (periphrastic)

References

Goodwin (1889), *Syntax of the moods and tenses of the Greek verb*, §§19–84.

Masterman (1962), On grammatical terminology and aspect in particular, *Greece and Rome*, 9, 72–86.

Palmer (1980), *The Greek language*, pp. 261, 292–307, 310–311.

Smyth (1956), *Greek grammar*, §§355–380, 1850–1858, 1875–1965.

EXERCISE 1

Translate the following passages into English or Greek as appropriate, giving particular attention to the Time and Aspect of the Indicative verbs.

1. αἰτοῦμαι οὖν ὑμᾶς, ὦ ἄνδρες, εὔνοιαν πλείω παρασχέσθαι ἐμοὶ τῷ ἀπολογουμένῳ ἢ τοῖς κατηγόροις …

αἰτεῖν (Act. and Mid.)	to ask, to request
εὔνοια, -ας, ἡ	goodwill
παρέχεσθαι (Mid.)	to show, to display
ἀπολογεῖσθαι (Mid.)	to defend
κατήγορος, -ου, ὁ	accuser

2. τὰ μὲν γενόμενα ἠκούσατε, ὦ ἄνδρες, καὶ ὑμῖν οἱ μάρτυρες μεμαρτυρήκασιν·

μέν	Anticipates a following δέ and should not be translated.
μαρτυρεῖν	*to testify (to)* (+ Dat.)

3. μετὰ δὲ τὴν δευτέραν ἐσβολὴν τῶν Πελοποννησίων οἱ Ἀθηναῖοι, ὡς ἥ τε γῆ αὐτῶν ἐτέτμητο τὸ δεύτερον καὶ ἡ νόσος ἐπέκειτο ἅμα καὶ ὁ πόλεμος, ἠλλοίωντο τὰς γνώμας ...

δεύτερος, -α, -ον	*second*
ἐσβολή, -ῆς, ἡ	*invasion*
ὡς	*as* (Temporal + Causal)
τε	Anticipates the following καί and should not be translated.
τέμνειν	*to ravage*
νόσος, -ου, ἡ	*plague*
ἐπικεῖσθαι (Mid.)	*to have been laid upon* (The Imperf. Mid. is equivalent to the Perf. Pass. of ἐπιτιθέναι.)
ἅμα καί	*at the same time as*
ἀλλοιοῦν	*to change* (here Pass. + Acc. of Respect)
γνώμη, -ης, ἡ	*attitude*

4. οὐ μόνον ἐγὼ ἀλλὰ καὶ ὁ πατὴρ δόξει ἄδικος εἶναι καὶ τῶν ὄντων ἁπάντων στερήσομαι.

δοκεῖν	*to seem*
ὄντα, -ων, τά	*possessions, property* (Partc.)
στερεῖν	*to deprive* (here Fut. Mid. in Pass. sense)

5. καὶ μάχῃ τῇ μὲν πρώτῃ νικᾶται ὑφ' ἡμῶν, τῇ δ' ὑστεραίᾳ ἱππεῦσί τε πολλοῖς καὶ ἀκοντισταῖς βιασθέντες ἀνεχωρήσαμεν ἐς τὰ τείχη.

μάχη, -ης, ἡ	*battle*
μέν	Cf. 2 above

νικᾶν	to beat, to defeat
ὑστεραῖος, -α, -ον	next
ἱππεύς, -έως, ὁ	horseman; (pl.) cavalry (here personal Dat. of Means)
τε	Cf. 3 above
ἀκοντιστής, -οῦ, ὁ	javelin-thrower
βιάζειν	to overpower
ἀναχωρεῖν	to withdraw (Intr.)
ἐς	inside, within (+ Acc. of motion)
τεῖχος, -ους, τό	fortification

6. πλεῖστον δή, οἶμαι, ἀληθοῦς ἡδονῆς καὶ οἰκείας ὁ τύραννος ἀφεστήξει, ὁ δὲ ὀλίγιστον.

πλεῖστον (neut. Acc.)	most (i.e. furthest) (adv.)
δή	so, therefore
οἰκεῖος, -α, -ον	genuine
τύραννος, -ου, ὁ	absolute ruler
ὁ δέ	and he (referring to the philosopher-king)
ὀλίγιστον (neut. Acc.)	least (i.e. least far away)

7. And yet what was I intending, if I informed against my father, as these [men] say, but was entreating my father to stay and suffer something from me?

and yet	καίτοι
to intend	βούλεσθαι
to inform against	μηνύειν κατά (+ Gen.)
[men]	Words in square brackets need not be translated.
to entreat	ἱκετεύειν (+ Acc. and Infin.)
to stay	μένειν
to suffer	πάσχειν
from	ὑπό (+ Gen.)

LESSON 2
Aspect in the Imperative, Subjunctive and Optative Moods

2.1. Introduction

As a general principle, the Moods of the Greek verb other than the Indicative have Aspect but not Time. This generalisation is valid, provided that the so-called 'Future' Optative is treated as belonging to a fourth, 'Intentive' Aspect. (This will also apply to the 'Future' Infinitive and Participle.) At any rate, there are forms for Imperative, Subjunctive and Optative Moods in the Imperfect, Perfect and Aorist Aspects. There are no forms for Imperative and Subjunctive Moods in Present, Past or Future Time. The 'Future' or 'Intentive' Optative is mostly limited to reported discourse in Past sequence, where it represents an original Future Indicative of direct discourse. It is occasionally used in the same way after verbs of effort. The terminology 'Present' Imperative, Subjunctive and Optative has often been used (misleadingly) for what is in fact the Imperfect Aspect of these Moods.

2.2. Forms

The usual paradigms for Imperative, Subjunctive and Optative in the Active Voice begin as follows.

Imperfect Aspect

Imperative	παῦε	2nd pers. sg.
Subjunctive	παύω	1st pers. sg.
Optative	παύοιμι	1st pers. sg.

Perfect Aspect

	Regular Form		**Periphrastic Form**	
Imperative	πέπαυκε	2nd pers. sg.	πεπαυκὼς ἴσθι	(possible)
Subjunctive	πεπαύκω	1st pers. sg.	πεπαυκὼς ὦ	(usual)
Optative	πεπαύκοιμι	1st pers. sg.	πεπαυκὼς εἴην	(usual)

Aorist Aspect

Imperative	παῦσον	2nd pers. sg.
Subjunctive	παύσω	1st pers. sg.
Optative	παύσαιμι	1st pers. sg.

'Future'/Intentive Aspect

Optative	παύσοιμι

2.3. Functions

This section gives a brief survey of the uses of the non-Indicative Moods. Most of these uses will receive further attention in later Lessons on particular topics.

2.3.1. Imperative

The Imperative expresses commands. Imperfect Aspect expresses continuing or repeated action. Aorist Aspect expresses momentary action. Perfect Aspect is less common in the Imperative. It generally emphasises the state resulting from a completed action. (See Lesson 10 on Commands.) However, as with the Indicative Mood, some verbs by their very meaning express a momentary action. Thus παῦε, although an Imperative form of the Imperfect Aspect, may express a command requiring instant action.

παῦε, παῦε, μὴ λέγε· (Ar. V. 37.)
Stop, stop, do not say <any more>.

Imperfect Aspect
καί μοι κάλει τούτων τοὺς μάρτυρας. (And. 1.28.)
Now please summon the witnesses of these <matters>.

LESSON 2. ASPECT IN THE IMPERATIVE, SUBJUNCTIVE AND OPTATIVE MOODS

The Imperfect Imperative (2nd pers. sg. Act.) κάλει suggests that the summoning may take a while. However, it would not be idiomatic to translate it as 'be summoning'.

Aorist Aspect

... φωνήσατ', εἴπερ ὡς φίλοι προσήκετε. (S.Ph. 229.)
... *speak, if indeed you have come as friends.*

The Aorist Imperative (2nd pers. pl. Act.) φωνήσατ(ε) suggests that the speaking should be brief and prompt.

Perfect Aspect

νῦν δ' εἰς ἀναιδὲς ἡμέρας μέρος βραχὺ
δός μοι σεαυτόν, κᾆτα τὸν λοιπὸν χρόνον
κέκλησο πάντων εὐσεβέστατος βροτῶν. (S.Ph. 83–85.)

But for the present please give yourself to recklessness
for a brief part of a day, and then for the rest of time
be called the most pious of all mortals.

The Perfect Imperative (2nd pers. sg. Pass.) κέκλησο, lit. 'have been called', implies 'have the ongoing reputation of'. This stative force, expressing the result of completed action, is emphasised by the adverbial phrase 'for the rest of time'.

2.3.2. Subjunctive

Despite differences of terminology, the following usages are all basically of the same type, expressing an exhortation or command. The negative for each usage is μή, except that οὐ may negate a particular word other than the Subjunctive verb.

Hortatory

The hortatory use occurs in the first person, usually plural.

χωρῶμεν δὴ πάντες ἀολλεῖς,
Νύμφαις ἁλίαισιν ἐπευξάμενοι
νόστου σωτῆρας ἱκέσθαι. (S.Ph. 1469–1471.)

Now let us go all together
(after) praying to the Nymphs of the sea
that they come as guarantors of our return.

Jussive

In the classical period, this construction occurs primarily in the negative with the second person singular or plural of the Aorist Subjunctive. Hence, the usage is often called 'Prohibitive'. The positive use at S.*Ph.* 300 is exceptional in the classical period, although further positive examples occur in the Hellenistic period. (See Lesson 10 on Commands.)

ὃ μὴ πάθῃς σύ· (E.*Ba.* 341.)
And you *are not to suffer this.*

ὃ is a coordinating relative pronoun: 'And ... this'.

The third person of the Aorist Subjunctive used in a prohibition is usually indefinite and equivalent to the second person. (The Imperfect Subjunctive is rare in this usage.)

καὶ μηδεὶς ὑπολάβῃ με δυσκόλως ἔχειν, ὅτι τραχύτερον τούτων ἐμνήσθην ... (Isoc. 4.129.)

And let no one suppose that I am discontented, because I recounted these points rather harshly ...

Deliberative

The Deliberative Subjunctive is an interrogative use of the Hortatory Subjunctive. Instead of stating 'Let us do this', a Deliberative question asks 'What are we to do?'. Deliberative questions occur in Imperfect or Aorist Aspect, primarily in the first person, rarely in the second person (repeating a question) and in the indefinite third person. (See Lesson 17 on Questions.)

... εἴπω Ἀθηναίοις ἅπερ ἤκουσα Εὐφιλήτου αὐτοῦ τοῦ ποιήσαντος; (And. 1.51.)

... am I to tell the Athenians what I heard from Euphiletus himself who did <it>?

2.3.3. Optative

Wishes

Without ἄν, the Optative in a Main clause expresses a wish for the future. Often, such wishes are introduced by εἰ γάρ or εἴθε; the negative is μή. (See Lesson 11 on Wishes.)

LESSON 2. ASPECT IN THE IMPERATIVE, SUBJUNCTIVE AND OPTATIVE MOODS

ἐχθρούς γε μέντοι μὴ φίλους δράσειέ τι. (E.*Med.* 95.)
However, may she do something to her enemies, not to her friends.

Potential

With ἄν the Optative in a Main clause is potential; the negative is οὐ.

Ιω	οὔκουν πόροις ἂν τήνδε δωρειὰν ἐμοί;
Πρ.	λέγ᾽ ἥντιν᾽ αἰτῇ· πᾶν γὰρ ἂν πύθοιό μου. (A.*Pr.* 616–617.)
Io	Would you not, then, grant this gift to me?
Pr.	Say what \<gift\> you are requesting; for you would learn everything from me.

References

Goodwin (1889), *Syntax of the moods and tenses of the Greek verb*, §§233–242, 250–293, 720–728.

Smyth (1956), *Greek grammar*, §§1795–1811, 1814–1842, 1859–1864, 2212.

EXERCISE 2

Translate the following passages. Give particular attention to the Aspect of the non-Indicative verbs, so far as idiomatic translation allows. The Exercise is concerned with the use of non-Indicative verbs in Main clauses.

1. τούτῳ μέντοι τῷ νόμῳ σκέψασθε ὡς ἐναντίος ἐστὶν ὃν οὗτος τέθεικεν.

μέντοι	*so* (Progressive)
σκέπτεσθαι	*to consider, to examine*
ὡς	*how* (Modifies ἐναντίος.)
ὅν	Understand νόμος as antecedent.
τιθέναι	*to propose* (a law)

2. μέμνησθε δέ, ὦ ἄνδρες, ὅτι καὶ ταῦθ' ὑμῖν προσομολογεῖται ἅπαντα.

μέμνησθε	Perf. Impv. with Imperf. meaning: *remember*
προσομολογεῖν	*to admit, to confess* (here Pass.)

3.   τὸν θεὸν δ' ἐς γῆν δέχου
καὶ σπένδε καὶ βάκχευε καὶ στέφου κάρα.

στέφειν (Act. and Mid.)	*to wreathe*
κάρα, τό (irregular)	*head*

4. ... περὶ δὲ τῆς εἰρήνης πρῶτον διαλεχθῶμεν, καὶ σκεψώμεθα τί ἂν ἐν τῷ παρόντι γενέσθαι βουληθεῖμεν ἡμῖν.

διαλέγεσθαι (Mid.)	*to discuss* (Aor. Pass. in Act. sense)
παρόν, -όντος, τό	*the present <situation>* (neut. Partc.)

5. ἀλλ' εὖ ς' ὁ Μαίας παῖς ἐκεῖσε καὶ πάλιν πέμψειεν Ἑρμῆς, ὅς γε φηλητῶν ἄναξ.

ἀλλ(ά)	*well* (introducing a prayer: Denniston, 1954, p. 15)
Μαῖα, -ας, ἡ	*Maia* (mother of Hermes)
πέμπειν	*to escort*
φηλήτης, -ου, ὁ	*thief*

6. ... πολὺ ἂν μᾶλλον καταφρονηθεῖμεν καὶ μισηθεῖμεν τῶν ταῖς ἄλλαις πονηρίαις ἐνόχων ὄντων.

καταφρονεῖν	*to despise*
μισεῖν	*to hate*
πονηρία, -ας, ἡ	*wickedness*
ἔνοχος, -ον	*liable (for)* (+ Dat.)

LESSON 2. ASPECT IN THE IMPERATIVE, SUBJUNCTIVE AND OPTATIVE MOODS

7. ποῖ γὰρ τράπωμαι πατρίδος ἐκβεβλημένη;

τρέπεσθαι (Mid.)	*to turn* (Intr.)
πατρίς, -ίδος, ἡ	*fatherland*
ἐκβάλλειν	*to cast out*

8. ἀλλ', ὦ ξέν', ἴσθι τοῦτο πρῶτον, οὕνεκα Ἕλληνές ἐσμεν.

ἀλλά	*well* (assentient: Denniston, 1954, p. 18)
οὕνεκα	*that*

9. τίς ὁδῷ, τίς ὁδῷ; τίς μελάθροις; ἔκτοπος ἔστω, στόμα τ' εὔφημον ἅπας ἐξοσιούσθω

μέλαθρον, -ου, τό	*hall*
ἔκτοπος, -ον	*out of doors*
στόμα, -ατος, τό	*speech*
εὔφημος, -ον	*holy*
ἐξοσιοῦν (Act. and Mid.)	*to keep pure*

10. And who would try to learn from another these [things], which he knows from his own nature?

to try	ἐπιχειρεῖν
to learn	μανθάνειν
from	παρά (+ Gen.)
to know	ἐπίστασθαι
nature	φύσις, -εως, ἡ

LESSON 3
Infinitive

3.1. Introduction

The Infinitive is the verbal noun, that is, the name of the verb. The Infinitive expresses Aspect but not Time. The apparent exception is the so-called 'Future' Infinitive. As with the 'Future' Optative, the 'Future' Infinitive may be regarded as expressing an Intentive Aspect rather than Future Time.

3.2. Forms

By way of illustrating the Aspect of Infinitives, only Active forms are listed here.

Imperfect

παύειν	*to be stopping*

Perfect

πεπαυκέναι	*to have stopped*

Aorist

παῦσαι	*to stop*

'Future'/Intentive

παύσειν	*to be going to stop*

A 'Future Perfect' Infinitive form μεμνήσεσθαι (Mid./Pass.) occurs in Homer and in Attic prose. But that is the 'Future' of a Perfect verb with Imperfect meaning; it means 'to be going to remember' (Intentive).

3.3. Functions

As a verb, the Infinitive may take any construction which finite parts of the verb may take.

As a noun, the Infinitive may be used without the definite article:

- as the Subject or Object of another verb
- in dependence on certain adjectives, adverbs and even nouns (especially when these parts of speech denote ability or suitability)
- to express Purpose with certain verbs.

The Infinitive with the neuter definite article (or 'articular Infinitive') may also be used in the Nominative or Accusative Case respectively as Subject or Object of a verb. In addition, the Infinitive with the definite article may be used in various constructions in the Genitive or Dative Cases, and after prepositions governing Accusative, Genitive or Dative Cases. (See further the Lessons on the Cases.)

The negative for all Infinitive constructions in this Lesson is regularly μή. There are three examples in §§3.5.3 and 3.5.4 below.

The use of the Infinitive in reported speech and thought and in Temporal and Result constructions will be treated in other Lessons.

3.4. Infinitive without Article

3.4.1. Infinitive as Subject

οὐκ ἄξιον περὶ τούτων, Ἀπολλόδωρε, νῦν ἐρίζειν. (Pl.*Smp.* 173 E.)
To quarrel about this now, Apollodorus, <is> not worthwhile.

ἐρίζειν is Subject; ἄξιον is Complement (predicate Nom.). ἄξιον is neuter Gender in reference to the Infinitive as a neuter singular noun. The more usual form of English expression for this sentence is: 'It is not worthwhile quarrelling about this now, Apollodorus'. 'It' is in anticipatory apposition with 'quarrelling'. As in this example, the verb 'to be' is not always expressed in Greek.

τὴν πεπρωμένην μοῖραν ἀδύνατα ἐστὶ ἀποφυγεῖν καὶ θεῷ· (Hdt. 1.91.1.)

It is impossible even for a god to escape one's appointed fate.

(lit. 'To escape one's appointed fate is impossible even for a god'.) Here, the neuter plural form ἀδύνατα is used as Complement of the Nominative Infinitive phrase; and the verb 'to be' (ἐστί) is expressed.

σχέτλια γὰρ
ἐμέ γε τὸν μακρῶν ἀλάτων πόνων
οὐρίῳ μὴ πελάσαι δρόμῳ,
... (S.*Aj.* 887–889.)

For <it is> wretched
that I the wanderer through lengthy labours
should not approach a favourable course
...

(lit. 'For that *I* the wanderer through lengthy labours should not approach a favourable course <is> wretched...'.) Here, the Subject is an Accusative and Infinitive phrase; and the verb 'to be' is not expressed in Greek. Within the Accusative and Infinitive phrase, ἐμέ ... τὸν ... ἀλάταν is the Subject of the Infinitive πελάσαι. And the neuter plural adjective σχέτλια is the Complement of the Infinitive phrase.

3.4.2. Infinitive as Object

μᾶλλον δ' ἐξ ἀρχῆς ὑμῖν, ὡς ἐκεῖνος διηγεῖτο, καὶ ἐγὼ πειράσομαι διηγήσασθαι. (Pl.*Smp.* 173 E–174 A.)

But rather, as he was relating <the matter>, I too shall attempt to relate <it> to you from the beginning.

διηγήσασθαι is direct Object of πειράσομαι.

3.4.3. Infinitive Expressing Purpose

The use of the Infinitive with certain verbs, nouns, adjectives and adverbs reflects its Indo-European background as a Dative verbal noun expressing Purpose.

3.4.3.1. Infinitive with Verbs

The Infinitive may express Purpose, mostly with verbs used transitively, and in prose especially with verbs of giving, receiving and choosing.

οἱ δ' ἄρ' ἀπ' ὤμοιιν Σαρπηδόνος ἔντε' ἕλοντο
χάλκεα μαρμαίροντα, τὰ μὲν κοίλας ἐπὶ νῆας
δῶκε φέρειν ἑτάροισι Μενοιτίου ἄλκιμος υἱός.
(Hom.*Il*. 16.663–665.)

But then from the shoulders of Sarpedon they took the shining bronze armour, which the brave son of Menoitius gave to his companions to carry to the hollow ships.

The Infinitive φέρειν expresses the Purpose of the verb δῶκε (without augment).

3.4.3.2. Infinitive with Nouns

μὴ δῶμεν αὐτοῖς σχολὴν μήτε βουλεύσασθαι μήτε παρασκευάσασθαι ἀγαθὸν αὐτοῖς μηδέν, μηδὲ γνῶναι πάμπαν ὅτι ἄνθρωποί ἐσμεν ... (X.*Cyr.* 4.2.22.)

let us not give them leisure for deliberating or preparing any benefit for themselves, nor for realising at all that we are humans ...

The Infinitives βουλεύσασθαι, παρασκευάσασθαι and γνῶναι express the Purpose of the noun σχολήν.

3.4.3.3. Infinitive with Adjectives

ἅμα μὲν γὰρ αὐτῷ ὁ χῶρος ἐπιτήδειος ἐφαίνετο ἐνστρατοπεδεῦσαι ... (Th. 2.20.4.)

For at the same time the place appeared to him suitable for encamping ...

The Infinitive ἐνστρατοπεδεῦσαι expresses the Purpose of the adjective ἐπιτήδειος.

3.4.3.4. Infinitive with Adverbs

οὕτω χαλεπῶς ἂν ἐδόκουν οἱ στρατιῶται τοὺς Μαντινέας ἐφηδομένους τῷ δυστυχήματι θεάσασθαι. (X.*HG* 4.5.18.)

The soldiers would be thinking it so difficult to look upon the Mantineans exulting over their misfortune.

The Infinitive θεάσασθαι expresses the Purpose of the adverb χαλεπῶς. (The adverb has been translated as an adjective for the sake of English idiom. But English idiom itself sometimes allows an adverb where an adjective would be expected: 'all is *well* that ends well'.)

3.5. Infinitive with Article

3.5.1. Infinitive as Subject (Nominative)

τὸ γὰρ φιλότιμον ἀγήρων μόνον, καὶ οὐκ ἐν τῷ ἀχρείῳ τῆς ἡλικίας τὸ κερδαίνειν, ὥσπερ τινές φασι, μᾶλλον τέρπει, ἀλλὰ τὸ τιμᾶσθαι. (Th. 2.44.4.)

For love of honour alone <is> unaffected by age, and in the ineffective <stage> of life <it is> not making a profit, as some say, <which> gives more enjoyment, but being honoured.

τὸ κερδαίνειν and τὸ τιμᾶσθαι are (contrasted) Subjects of τέρπει.

3.5.2. Infinitive as Object (Accusative)

πρὸς μὲν οὖν τὸ ἐμπειρότερον αὐτῶν τὸ τολμηρότερον ἀντιτάξασθε, πρὸς δὲ τὸ διὰ τὴν ἧσσαν δεδιέναι τὸ ἀπαράσκευοι τότε τυχεῖν. (Th. 2.87.5.)

Therefore, against their greater experience set <your> greater daring, and against <your> being afraid because of <your> defeat <set> the fact that you happened to be unprepared then.

τὸ ... τυχεῖν is a second Object of ἀντιτάξασθε, parallel to the first Object τὸ τολμηρότερον. Although τὸ ... τυχεῖν is in the Accusative Case, ἀπαράσκευοι ('unprepared'), within the Infinitive phrase, is Nominative, because it refers to the Subject of the Main verb ἀντιτάξασθε. The sentence also contains a prepositional phrase with articular Accusative Infinitive phrase (for this usage see §3.5.5 below).

3.5.3. Genitive

The following examples illustrate the main ways in which the Genitive of the articular Infinitive is used.

Objective
πολλὰ δὲ καὶ ἄλλα ἔχω ἐς ἐλπίδα τοῦ περιέσεσθαι ... (Th. 1.144.1.)

And I have many other <arguments> relevant to the hope of being successful ...

Partitive
... καὶ νῦν οὐδὲν οὔτ' ἀναιδείας οὔτε τοῦ ψεύδεσθαι παραλείψει. (D. 37.45.)

... even now he will leave out no <aspect> of shamelessness nor of being deceitful.

Comparative
τὸ μὴ γενέσθαι τῷ θανεῖν ἴσον λέγω,
τοῦ ζῆν δὲ λυπρῶς κρεῖσσόν ἐστι κατθανεῖν. (E. Tr. 636–637.)

*Not to be born I count as equal to dying,
but dying is better than living in grief.*

Separation
εἰ γὰρ οἴεσθε ἀποκτείνοντες ἀνθρώπους ἐπισχήσειν τοῦ ὀνειδίζειν τινὰ ὑμῖν ὅτι οὐκ ὀρθῶς ζῆτε, οὐκ ὀρθῶς διανοεῖσθε· (Pl. Ap. 39 D.)

For if you think that by putting people to death you will prevent anyone from criticising you because you do not live properly, you do not think properly.

Purpose
καὶ φρούριον ἐπ' αὐτοῦ ἦν καὶ νεῶν τριῶν φυλακὴ τοῦ μὴ ἐσπλεῖν Μεγαρεῦσι μηδ' ἐκπλεῖν μηδέν ... (Th. 2.93.4.)

And there was a fort on it and a protective force of three ships, so that nothing might sail in nor sail out for the Megarians ...

αὐτοῦ ('it') refers to the point of the island of Salamis.

This construction is usually left unexplained in Greek grammars. And to say that the Genitive articular Infinitive has been separated from any governing noun or verb does not clarify the usage. The idiom occurs first and especially in Thucydides and is often negative. As in the present example, a number of instances in Thucydides and Xenophon are close to a construction of 'preventing' with Genitive of Separation. (Cf. Lesson 29.6.8.)

καὶ πρῶτον μὲν περιεσταύρωσαν αὐτοὺς τοῖς δένδρεσιν ἃ ἔκοψαν τοῦ μηδένα ἐπεξιέναι ... (Th. 2.75.1.)

And in the first place they [= Spartans] stockaded them [= Plataeans] with trees which they had felled

a. *<to prevent> any one from going out against <them>...* [Prevention]
b. *<so that> no one might go out against <them>...* [Purpose]

οὓς δὲ μὴ δύναιντο λαμβάνειν, ἀποσοβοῦντες ἂν ἐμποδὼν γίγνοιντο τοῦ μὴ ὁρᾶν αὐτοὺς τὸ ὅλον στράτευμά σου ... (X.*Cyr.* 2.4.23.)

and those whom they could not catch, they would scare off

a. *and get in the way of their seeing your whole contingent ...* [Prevention]
b. *and get in their way, so that they might not see your whole contingent ...* [Purpose]

3.5.4. Dative

The Dative articular Infinitive is especially used to express Cause, means or instrument.

σαφῶς γὰρ ἄν, εἰ πείθοιμι ὑμᾶς καὶ τῷ δεῖσθαι βιαζοίμην ὀμωμοκότας, θεοὺς ἂν διδάσκοιμι μὴ ἡγεῖσθαι ὑμᾶς εἶναι ... (Pl.*Ap.* 35 D.)

For clearly, if I were to persuade you and by begging were to force you when you have sworn an oath, I would be teaching you not to believe that gods exist ...

τῷ δεῖσθαι is Dative of Means.

3.5.5. Prepositions

οὕτω γὰρ πρὸς τὸ ἐπιέναι τοῖς ἐναντίοις εὐψυχότατοι ἂν εἶεν, πρός τε τὸ ἐπιχειρεῖσθαι ἀσφαλέστατοι. (Th. 2.11.5.)

For in this way they would be most courageous with regard to assaulting their opponents, and most steadfast with regard to being attacked.

References

Goodwin (1889), *Syntax of the moods and tenses of the Greek verb*, §§741–750, 758–775, 788–814.

Palmer (1980), *The Greek language*, p. 314.

Smyth (1956), *Greek grammar*, §§1966–2015, 2025–2037.

EXERCISE 3

Translate the following sentences. Give particular attention to the Aspect of the Infinitives, so far as idiomatic translation allows.

1. ἀλλὰ γὰρ οὐδὲν εἶχε σαφὲς λέγειν.

   | ἀλλὰ γάρ | *but really* |
   | ἔχειν | *to be able* (+ Infin.) |

2. οὐδενὶ γὰρ ἐπιμελὲς ἦν σκοπεῖν ταῦτα.

   | ἐπιμελής, -ές | *<a matter> of concern* |
   | σκοπεῖν | *to examine* |

3. καὶ ὁπόθεν ποτὲ ταύτην τὴν ἐπωνυμίαν ἔλαβες τὸ μανικὸς καλεῖσθαι, οὐκ οἶδα ἔγωγε·

ἐπωνυμία, -ας, ἡ	*name, reputation*
μανικός, -ή, -όν	*mad*
τὸ μανικὸς καλεῖσθαι	in apposition with ταύτην τὴν ἐπωνυμίαν

4. ὁ δὲ Χαλκιδεὺς καὶ ὁ Ἀλκιβιάδης πλέοντες ὅσοις τ' ἐπιτύχοιεν ξυνελάμβανον τοῦ μὴ ἐξάγγελτοι γενέσθαι …

Χαλκιδεύς, -έως, ὁ	personal proper name
πλεῖν	*to sail*
τ(ε)	Omit: anticipates a following καί.
ἐπιτυγχάνειν	*to encounter* (+ Dat.)

ξυλλαμβάνειν	*to arrest*
ἐξάγγελτος, -ον	*reported*

5. τῷ δὲ ἐμπειρότεροι εἶναι θρασύτεροί ἐσμεν.

ἔμπειρος -ον	*experienced*
θρασύς, -εῖα, -ύ	*bold, confident*

6. καὶ νῦν τοὺς Ἀθηναίους ... ἐγγὺς ὄντας περιορᾶτε, καὶ ἀντὶ τοῦ ἐπελθεῖν αὐτοὶ ἀμύνεσθαι βούλεσθε μᾶλλον ἐπιόντας ...

περιορᾶν	*to overlook* (here Indic.)
ἀντί (+ Gen.)	*instead of*
ἐπιέναι (Aor. ἐπελθεῖν)	*to attack*
ἀμύνεσθαι (Mid.)	*to ward off* (+ Acc.)

7. ἀδύνατον δὲ καὶ ὑμῖν ἐστι, περὶ τοιούτου πράγματος φέρουσι τὴν ψῆφον, ἢ κατελεῆσαι ἢ καταχαρίσασθαι Ἀνδοκίδῃ ...

δὲ καί	*and indeed*
ἀδύνατος, -ον	*impossible*
φέρειν	*to cast* (here Dat. pl. Partc.)
ψῆφος, -ου, ἡ	*vote*
κατελεεῖν	*to pity* (+ Acc., not expressed here)
καταχαρίζεσθαι (Mid.)	*to show favour (to)* (+ Dat.)
Ἀνδοκίδης, -ου, ὁ	*Andocides*

8. ὥστε μὰ τὸν Δία οὐ ῥᾴδιόν ἐστιν ὑμῖν αὐτῷ οὐδὲν χαρισαμένοις παρὰ τὸ δίκαιον λαθεῖν τοὺς Ἕλληνας.

ὥστε	*and so* (used as coordinating conjunction)
μὰ τὸν Δία	*by Zeus* (oath formula)
ῥᾴδιος, -α, -ον	*easy*
παρά (+ Acc.)	*contrary to*
λανθάνειν	*to escape the notice of someone* (Acc.) *in doing something* (Partc.)

9. ἤδη τεθνάναι καὶ ἀπηλλάχθαι πραγμάτων βέλτιον ἦν μοι.

ἀπαλλάσσειν	*to free, to release*
πρᾶγμα, -ατος, τό	*trouble, problem*
βελτίων, -ον	*better*

10. For you are the most appropriate [person] to be reporting your companion's discussions.

appropriate	δίκαιος, (-α,) -ον
to report	ἀπαγγέλλειν
companion	ἑταῖρος, -ου, ὁ
discussion	λόγος, -ου, ὁ

11. having expelled those [people], they did not dare to expropriate their lands …

to dare	τολμᾶν
to expropriate	ἐξιδιοῦσθαι (Mid.)
land	χώρα, -ας, ἡ

LESSON 4
Participles

4.1. Introduction

Participles are verbal adjectives. As a verb, a Participle may take any construction that finite parts of the verb may take. As an adjective, a Participle may be used in any appropriate Case, Gender and Number.

As a general principle, Participles express Aspect but not Time. The Aspect of the Participle expresses the type of action in relation to the verbal form to which it is subordinate. Most simply, a Participle may be subordinate to a finite verb in the Indicative Mood. But it may also be subordinate to a finite verb in a non-Indicative Mood, or to an Infinitive, or even to another Participle. The subordination of a Participle to another verb form applies more readily to the adverbial functions of circumstantial and supplementary Participles than to the adjectival function of attributive Participles.

The Imperfect Participle expresses continuous or repeated action contemporary with the action of the verbal form to which it is subordinate.

The Perfect Participle expresses (the state resulting from) action which is completed in relation to the verbal form to which it is subordinate.

The Aorist Participle expresses momentary action, which may be either prior to or contemporary with the action of the verbal form to which it is subordinate. If the context allows it, an Aorist Participle may (but need not) be translated 'after stopping' or 'having stopped'. But such a phrase as γέγωνε βοήσας (Hom. *Od.* 5.400) clearly means 'he calls out with a shout', not 'having shouted he calls out'.

The so-called 'Future' Participle expresses an intention and may be subordinated to any Tense of an Indicative verb. The Participle has no Time reference in itself but is subordinate to the Time reference of the Indicative verb, whether Present, Past or Future. Thus, the 'Future' Participle needs to be regarded as an Intentive Participle, analogous to the Intentive ('Fut.') Optative and Infinitive (Lessons 2.1 and 3.1). Like other Participles, this Intentive Participle may be subordinated not only to a finite Indicative verb, but to a non-Indicative verb, an Infinitive or another Participle.

4.2. Forms

The usual paradigms for the Participles in the Active Voice begin as follows (Nom. masc. sg.).

Imperfect

παύων	*(while) stopping*

Perfect

πεπαυκώς	*having stopped*

Aorist

παύσας	*stopping*

'Future'/Intentive

παύσων	*going to stop*

The only certain example of a Future Perfect Participle in classical Greek is the Passive form διαπεπολεμησόμενον 'going to have been fought out' (Th. 7.25.9.)

4.3. Functions

4.3.1. Attributive Participle (Adjectival)

Like other adjectives, a Participle may be used attributively; it is then normally placed between the definite article and the noun to which it refers.

πρὸς τὴν παροῦσαν ὄψιν (Th. 2.88.3.)
in face of the present sight

LESSON 4. PARTICIPLES

A longer Participial phrase may sometimes be placed only partly between article and noun.

... καὶ αὐτά γε δὴ ταῦτα ... δηλοῦται τοῖς ἔργοις ὑποδεέστερα ὄντα τῆς φήμης καὶ τοῦ νῦν περὶ αὐτῶν διὰ τοὺς ποιητὰς λόγου κατεσχηκότος· (Th. 1.11.2.)

... *and* this *<campaign> itself* [the Trojan war] ... *is shown by the actions <undertaken> to be inferior to its reputation and to the assessment which has now come to prevail concerning it on account of the poets.*

The attributive Participle κατεσχηκότος stands outside article and noun, τοῦ ... λόγου.

The Participle may be used attributively after the definite article even without a noun.

ὁ διηγούμενος (Pl.*Smp.* 172 C.)
the <person> narrating, the narrator

4.3.2. Circumstantial Participle (Adverbial)

A Participle may be used to express the circumstances under which an action takes place, usually the action of the Main verb of a sentence. A circumstantial Participle expresses an adverbial relation such as Time, Cause, Condition, Concession, Manner, Means or Purpose. Such a Participle is not used with its own definite article. If it agrees with a noun which has an article, the Participle stands in the predicate position, before the article or after the noun. καίπερ or just καί may precede Participles expressing concession (see also Lesson 26). ὡς may precede Participles expressing Cause (Lesson 23) or Purpose (Lesson 27).

ἡ δὲ βουλὴ ἐξελθοῦσα ἐν ἀπορρήτῳ συνέλαβεν ἡμᾶς ... (And. 1.45.)
And the council, <after> adjourning, secretly arranged to arrest us ...

ἐξελθοῦσα expresses time.

καὶ οἱ παρὰ θάλασσαν ἄνθρωποι μᾶλλον ἤδη τὴν κτῆσιν τῶν χρημάτων ποιούμενοι βεβαιότερον ᾤκουν ... (Th. 1.8.3.)

and the people by the sea, <since they were> now, rather, achieving the acquisition of resources, were living more securely ...

ποιούμενοι expresses Cause.

δείσαντες μή τι διὰ τὴν ξυμφορὰν νομίσαντες ἐλασσωθήσεσθαι καὶ ὄντες ἐπίτιμοι νεωτερίσωσιν, ἤδη καὶ ἀρχάς τινας ἔχοντας ἀτίμους ἐποίησαν ... (Th. 5.34.2.)

fearing that, if they thought that they would be downgraded because of the disaster and if they remained enfranchised, they would revolt, they disenfranchised them, even some currently holding office ...

νομίσαντες and ὄντες express condition.

ἆρα λογίζεταί τις ὑμῶν, ὦ ἄνδρες Ἀθηναῖοι, καὶ θεωρεῖ τὸν τρόπον δι' ὃν μέγας γέγονεν ἀσθενὴς ὢν τὸ κατ' ἀρχὰς Φίλιππος; (D. 1.12.)

Does any one of you, O men of Athens, take account and observe the means through which Philip, though being weak at first, has become great?

ὤν expresses concession.

ἦ κἀπαπειλῶν ὧδ' ἐπεξέρχῃ θρασύς; (S.Ant. 752.)
Do you thus boldly go to extremes in actually making threats?

ἐπαπειλῶν expresses manner.

Κρ.	ταύτην ποτ' οὐκ ἔσθ' ὡς ἔτι ζῶσαν γαμεῖς.
Αι.	ἥδ' οὖν θανεῖται καὶ θανοῦσ' ὀλεῖ τινα. (S.Ant. 750–751.)
Creon:	*It is not possible that you will ever marry this girl while she is still living.*
Haemon:	*She will therefore die and by dying she will destroy someone.*

θανοῦσ(α) expresses means.

πόλιν τε νομίσαι χρὴ ἐν ἀλλοφύλοις καὶ πολεμίοις οἰκιοῦντας ἰέναι ... (Th. 6.23.2.)

And <we> should acknowledge that we are going in order to found a city among foreign and hostile <people> ...

οἰκιοῦντας ('Fut.'/Intentive Partc.) expresses Purpose, as may the Imperfect Participle.

ὥστε τῷ ὑμῶν πιστὸν ὡς ἐγὼ πρότερον μὲν ἐξέπλευσα ἐκ τῆς πόλεως ἔχων τὸ μειράκιον ... (Lys. 3.32.)

And so to which one of you <is it> credible that I previously sailed out from the city having the boy <with me...?

ἔχων expresses attendant circumstances in general.

4.3.3. Supplementary Participle (Adverbial)

A supplementary Participle is regularly used in idiomatic phrases with a significant number of verbs such as the following. Although the Greek construction is adverbial, the corresponding English idiom most often uses a gerund (verbal noun) as direct Object of the finite verb.

ἄρχεσθαι	*to begin (doing something)*
διατελεῖν	*to continue (doing something)*
ἥδεσθαι	*to enjoy (doing something), to be pleased (to do something)*
παύεσθαι	*to stop (doing something)*
τυγχάνειν	*to happen (to be doing something)*

ἀλλ' ἥδομαι μὲν σ' εἰσιδὼν παρ' ἐλπίδα
ἀνώδυνον βλέποντα κἀμπνέοντ' ἔτι· (S.*Ph.* 882–883.)

*Well, I am pleased to see you contrary to expectation
free from pain <and> still alive and breathing.*

εἰσιδών is Aor. Partc. with ἥδομαι.

καὶ γὰρ ἐτύγχανον πρῴην εἰς ἄστυ οἴκοθεν ἀνιὼν Φαληρόθεν· (Pl.*Smp.* 172 A.)

For I happened to be going up during the early morning to town from home at (lit. 'from') *Phalerum.*

ἀνιών is Imperfect Participle with ἐτύγχανον.

4.4. Negatives

In the classical period, οὐ negates a Participle with factual force and μή negates a Participle with indefinite or conditional force. In the Hellenistic period, μή is increasingly used with all types of Participial phrase.

ἄνδρες Πέρσαι, οὕτω ὑμῖν ἔχει· βουλομένοισι μὲν ἐμέο πείθεσθαι ἔστι τάδε τε καὶ ἄλλα μυρία ἀγαθά, οὐδένα πόνον δουλοπρεπέα ἔχουσι· μὴ βουλομένοισι δὲ ἐμέο πείθεσθαι εἰσὶ ὑμῖν πόνοι τῷ χθιζῷ παραπλήσιοι ἀνάριθμητοι. (Hdt. 1.126.5.)

Men of Persia, this is the situation for you: if you are willing to obey me, there are these and ten thousand other benefits for you while having no slave labour; but if you are not willing to obey me, there are unnumbered labours like yesterday's for you.

οὐδένα ... ἔχουσι: Temporal or general circumstantial Participle.

μὴ βουλομένοισι: conditional Participle.

πείθεσθαι here takes the Genitive Case by analogy with ἀκούειν. ἐμέο (Ionic) = ἐμοῦ (Attic).

References

Goodwin (1889), *Syntax of the moods and tenses of the Greek verb*, §§138–153, 213–217, 224, 821–846, 877–901.

Smyth (1956), *Greek grammar*, §§1166–1167, 2039–2056, 2060–2069, 2079–2105, 2110–2119, 2123–2148, 2720–2734.

EXERCISE 4

Translate the following passages. Give particular attention to the Aspect of the Participles, so far as idiomatic translation allows.

1. ὅταν γὰρ μάλιστα σίτου τυγχάνητε δεόμενοι, ἀναρπάζουσιν οὗτοι καὶ οὐκ ἐθέλουσι πωλεῖν ...

μάλιστα	*especially, precisely, just* (Modifies ὅταν.)
σῖτος, -ου, ὁ	*grain*

δεῖσθαι	to be in need (of) (+ Gen.)
ἀναρπάζειν	to snatch up
(ἐ)θέλειν	to be willing (+ Infin.)
πωλεῖν	to sell

2. ἡγούμενος δὲ ἐγὼ δεινὸν εἶναι τοιαῦτα ἐθίζεσθαι ποιεῖν τὴν βουλήν, ἀναστὰς εἶπον ὅτι μοι δοκοίη κρίνειν τοὺς σιτοπώλας κατὰ τὸν νόμον ...

ἡγεῖσθαι (Mid.)	to think (+ Acc. and Infin.)
δεινός, -ή, -όν	terrible
ἐθίζειν	to accustom; (Pass.) to become accustomed (+ Infin.)
δοκεῖν	to seem (right)
κρίνειν	to judge
σιτοπώλης, -ου, ὁ	grain-seller

3. κατέβην χθὲς εἰς Πειραιᾶ μετὰ Γλαύκωνος τοῦ Ἀρίστωνος, προσευξόμενός τε τῇ θεῷ καὶ ἅμα τὴν ἑορτὴν βουλόμενος θεάσασθαι τίνα τρόπον ποιήσουσιν, ἅτε νῦν πρῶτον ἄγοντες.

καταβαίνειν	to go down
χθές	yesterday
Πειρα(ι)εύς, ὁ, Acc. -ᾶ	Piraeus
τοῦ Ἀρίστωνος	the <son> of Ariston
προσεύχεσθαι	to pray (to) (+ Dat.)
ἑορτή, -ῆς, ἡ	festival
θεᾶσθαι (Mid.)	to see
ἅτε (+ Partc.)	inasmuch as (doing something), since (they are/were doing something)
ἄγειν	to celebrate (a festival)

4. οἱ δ' αὖ, μαρτυρήσαντες τὰ ψευδῆ ἀδίκως ἀνθρώπους ἀπολέσαντες, ἑάλωσαν παρ' ὑμῖν ψευδομαρτυρίων, ἡνίκ' οὐδὲν ἦν ἔτι πλέον τοῖς πεπονθόσιν.

οἱ δ(έ)	but others
ἀπολλύναι	to destroy

ἁλίσκεσθαι	to be convicted of (+ Gen.; Intr. 2nd Aor. ἁλῶναι)
ἡνίκ(α)	when

5. τόδε ἐνθυμητέον, ὅτι πολλοὶ ἤδη πολλὰ καὶ δεινὰ κατηγορήσαντες παραχρῆμα ἐξηλέγχθησαν ψευδόμενοι οὕτω φανερῶς, ὥστε ὑμᾶς πολὺ ἂν ἥδιον δίκην λαβεῖν παρὰ τῶν κατηγόρων ἢ παρὰ τῶν κατηγορουμένων·

ἐνθυμητέον	<it is> necessary to keep in mind (+ Acc.)
ὅτι	that (expanding τόδε)
καί	When joining an adj. of size or number with a descriptive adj., καί is regularly omitted in English translation.
δεινός, -ή, -όν	serious (here internal Acc. with κατηγορήσαντες)
παραχρῆμα (adv.)	promptly, immediately
ἐξελέγχειν	to prove someone (Acc.) guilty (of doing something) (+ Partc.)
ψεύδεσθαι (Mid.)	to speak falsely, to lie
φανερῶς (adv.)	openly, obviously
δίκην λαμβάνειν	to exact punishment

6. For since these [men] were attributing the responsibility to those [men], we, having summoned the magistrates, were questioning [them].

to attribute .... to	ἀναφέρειν (+ Acc. and εἰς + Acc.)
responsibility	αἰτία, -ας, ἡ
to summon	παρακαλεῖν (Imperf.), παρακαλέσαι (Aor.)
magistrate	ἄρχων, -οντος, ὁ (Partc. as noun)
to question	ἐρωτᾶν
these [men]	Refers to grainsellers
those [men], [them]	Refer to magistrates

LESSON 5
Genitive Absolute

5.1. The Usual Construction

A Participle may be used with its own Subject in the Genitive Case, where that Subject does not normally appear elsewhere in the same clause. The Participles in a Genitive absolute have a more restricted range of meaning than a circumstantial Participle agreeing with a noun in any Case or agreeing with the unexpressed Subject of a verb (as indicated by the ending of the verb).

5.1.1. Time

ὑμεῖς οὖν καὶ αὐτοὶ ὕστερον, κακῶν οὐκ ἐλαττόντων ἢ ἐκείνοις γεγενημένων, ἀγαθοὶ ἐξ ἀγαθῶν ὄντες ἀπέδοτε τὴν ὑπάρχουσαν ἀρετήν· (And. 1.109.)

So subsequently, when troubles no less serious had happened than <had happened> to those <men>, you yourselves, being good <men> descended from good <ancestors>, displayed their traditional virtue.

Negative οὐκ.

5.1.2. Cause

ἀντιλέγοντος δὲ Ἀλκιβιάδου πολλὰ καὶ ἐξάρνου ὄντος ἔδοξε τοῖς πρυτάνεσι τοὺς μὲν ἀμυήτους μεταστήσασθαι ... (And. 1.12.)

And since Alcibiades was speaking at length in opposition and was denying <the accusation>, the members of the standing committee decided to remove the uninitiated ...

5.1.3. Condition

ταῦτα μὲν οὖν ἦν ἐμοῦ μὴ εἰπόντος· (And. 1.59.)
Well then, this was <the situation>, if I did not speak.

Negative μή.

5.1.4. Concession

… νῦν ἐγὼ ἥκω οὐδεμιᾶς μοι ἀνάγκης οὔσης παραμεῖναι … (And. 1.2.)
… now I have come, although there is no compulsion for me to stay here …

Negative οὐ (compound).

5.1.5. Attendant Circumstances in General

νῦν γὰρ ἐμὲ μὲν λόγον δεῖ διδόναι τῶν ἐμοὶ πεπραγμένων μετὰ τῆς ἀληθείας, αὐτῶν παρόντων οἵπερ ἥμαρτον καὶ ἔφυγον ταῦτα ποιήσαντες … (And. 1.55.)

For now I must truthfully give an account of what has been done by me, when there are present the very <men> who did wrong and went into exile after doing this …

5.2. Subject Unexpressed

A Participle is sometimes used in the Genitive absolute without an expressed Genitive Subject. This may occur when the Subject is easily understood from the context, or is general (and sometimes deliberately vague), or when the Participle is used impersonally with a ὅτι clause or an Accusative and Infinitive phrase as its Subject.

πεφασμένου δὲ τίς ποθ' ἡ προθυμία; (S.*OT* 838.)
And when <he> has appeared, what at such time <will be> your desire?

The unexpressed Subject of πεφασμένου is 'the herdsman' of the previous line, τὸν ἄνδρα τὸν βοτῆρα (S.*OT* 837.)

στένει πόλισμα γῆθεν ὡς κυκλουμένων. (A.*Th.* 247.)
The city groans from the earth, since <people> are surrounding <it>.

Those who are besieging Thebes are more generally indicated solely by the Participle κυκλουμένων (understood as Mid.).

τελουμένων εἴποιμ' ἄν· (S.*El.* 1344.)
When <things> are being brought to an end, I would tell <you>.

Here, the neuter Participle contains a deliberately vague reference to the plan to kill Clytemnestra and Aegisthus.

σημανθέντων δὲ τῷ Ἀστυάγει ὅτι πολέμιοί εἰσιν ἐν τῇ χώρᾳ, ἐξεβοήθει καὶ αὐτὸς πρὸς τὰ ὅρια σὺν τοῖς περὶ αὐτόν ... (X.*Cyr.* 1.4.18.)

But when it was indicated to Astyages that there were enemy in the country, he himself went out to the borders with his attendants to help ...

In this impersonal construction, the ὅτι clause is the Subject of the neuter plural Participle σημανθέντων. Often, in such constructions, the Participle is artificially plural in keeping with a plural Subject of the ὅτι clause.

5.3. Improper Genitive Absolute

Improper Genitive absolute constructions occur where the Subject of the Genitive phrase is the same as a Nominative, Accusative or Dative of the main construction. An improper Genitive absolute usually precedes the Main verb. This irregular construction, which emphasises the idea expressed by the Genitive absolute, became more common in the Hellenistic period.

ὅμως δὲ οὔτε ξυνοικισθείσης πόλεως οὔτε ἱεροῖς καὶ κατασκευαῖς πολυτελέσι χρησαμένης, κατὰ κώμας δὲ τῷ παλαιῷ τῆς Ἑλλάδος τρόπῳ οἰκισθείσης, φάνοιτ' ἂν ὑποδεεστέρα. (Th. 1.10.2.)

Nevertheless, since the community had not been combined into a single <city>, and did not have the use of temples and expensive structures, but had been settled as a group of villages in the early manner of Greece, it would appear rather deficient.

The 'community' of Sparta is the Subject of three successive Participles in an improper Genitive absolute construction, but then becomes the Nominative Subject of the Main verb φάνοιτο.

References

Goodwin (1889), *Syntax of the moods and tenses of the Greek verb*, §§847–850.

Smyth (1956), *Greek grammar*, §§2058, 2070–2074.

EXERCISE 5

Translate the following passages.

1. … βουλόμενοι δὲ τὸ Πάνακτον παραλαβεῖν ὡς τὴν Πύλον ἀντ' αὐτοῦ κομιούμενοι, … ἐποιήσαντο τὴν ξυμμαχίαν τοῦ χειμῶνος τελευτῶντος ἤδη καὶ πρὸς ἔαρ.

παραλαμβάνειν	*to acquire*
κομίζειν	*to obtain* (with Fut. Mid.)
χειμών, -ῶνος, ὁ	*winter*
ἔαρ, ἦρος, τό	*spring*

2. ἐγὼ τῶν ἀρχόντων κελευόντων συνεπριάμην.

ἄρχων, -οντος, ὁ	*magistrate* (as in Exercise 4.6)
συμπρίασθαι (Aor.)	*to buy up* (Understand 'the grain' as Object.)

3. … Ἄνυτος δ' ἔλεγεν ὡς τοῦ προτέρου χειμῶνος, ἐπειδὴ τίμιος ἦν ὁ σῖτος τούτων ὑπερβαλλόντων ἀλλήλους καὶ πρὸς σφᾶς αὐτοὺς μαχομένων, συμβουλεύσειεν αὐτοῖς παύσασθαι φιλονικοῦσιν …

χειμών, -ῶνος, ὁ	*winter*
τίμιος, (-α,) -ον	*expensive, at a high price*
ὑπερβάλλειν	*to outbid*
μάχεσθαι	*to fight*
συμβουλεύειν	*to advise* (+ Dat. and Infin.)
φιλονικεῖν	*to squabble* (here Dat. pl. Partc. with αὐτοῖς)

LESSON 5. GENITIVE ABSOLUTE

4. ὥστ' ἐνίοτε εἰρήνης οὔσης ὑπὸ τούτων πολιορκούμεθα.

ἐνίοτε (adv.)	*sometimes* (Modifies πολιορκούμεθα.)
πολιορκεῖν	*to besiege*

5. καὶ ἄλλου οὐδενὸς ἐθέλοντος βαδίζειν ... ἐγὼ τὸν ἀκόλουθον τὸν ἐμαυτοῦ πέμπειν ἕτοιμος ἦ·

βαδίζειν	*to go*
ἀκόλουθος, -ον	*attendant* (adj. used as noun)
ἕτοιμος, (-η,) -ον	*ready, prepared*

6. ὅ τι δὲ μέλλετε, ἅμα τῷ ἦρι εὐθὺς καὶ μὴ ἐς ἀναβολὰς πράσσετε, ὡς τῶν πολεμίων τὰ μὲν ἐν Σικελίᾳ δι' ὀλίγου ποριουμένων ...

μέλλειν	*to intend*
ἅμα (adv.)	*at the same time as* (+ Dat.), *at the beginning of*
εὐθύς (adv.)	*immediately*
ἐς ἀναβολάς	*with (respect to) delay(s)*
τὰ ... ἐν Σικελίᾳ	*the <forces> ... in Sicily*
δι' ὀλίγου	*within a short <time>, shortly*
πορίζεσθαι (Mid.)	*to procure*

7. ... ὅτε ἦν ἀφανὴς ὁ ἀνήρ, οὐδεὶς ᾐτιάσατό με ἀνθρώπων, ἤδη πεπυσμένων τούτων τὴν ἀγγελίαν.

ἀφανής, -ές	*unseen, missing*
αἰτιᾶσθαι (Mid.)	*to blame*
πυνθάνεσθαι (Mid.)	*to learn (by inquiry)*

8. For they make most profit then, when, after something bad has been reported to the city, they sell the grain at a high price.

most	πλεῖστα (neut. Acc. pl.)
to make profit	κερδαίνειν
when (indef.)	ὅταν (+ Subj.)
after ... reported	Use Gen. abs.

LESSON 6
Accusative Absolute

6.1. Introduction

Instead of a Genitive absolute, an Accusative absolute is used:

1. with Participles of so-called impersonal verbs
2. with Participles of verbs which are used impersonally in the Passive Voice
3. with neuter adjectives which are used with the Participle of the verb 'to be'
4. and sometimes with a Participle which has an explicit Subject other than an Infinitive phrase.

These four categories will be treated separately in the following sections.

The Participles in the Accusative absolute have the same restriction of meaning as those in the Genitive absolute. καίπερ is not used with the Accusative absolute constructions, although they may have a Concessive force.

6.2. So-Called Impersonal Verbs

Some common verbs, which are usually designated 'impersonal', are δεῖ, meaning 'it is necessary'; and ἔξεστι and πάρεστι, both meaning 'it is possible', 'it is permissible'. Such verbs are often described as being 'followed by' an Infinitive. These verbs are not 'impersonal' in the sense that they do not have a grammatical Subject. Rather, they may have an Infinitive or Infinitive phrase as Subject. Thus, ἔξεστιν ὑμῖν φίλους γενέσθαι (Th. 4.20.3) may be translated 'it is possible for you to become friends'. But in grammatical structure, the phrase φίλους γενέσθαι is Subject of ἔξεστιν, 'to become friends is possible for you'. (Cf. Lesson 3.4.1.)

Such verbs use a neuter singular Accusative absolute of the Participle instead of a Genitive absolute. The construction is first attested in Herodotus (Ionic) and in Attic prose writers of the fifth century BCE. The Participles are most often used in the Imperfect Aspect. Apart from δόξαν and τυχόν (and their compounds), the Aorist Participle rarely appears.

τί παρθενεύῃ δαρόν, ἐξόν σοι γάμου
τυχεῖν μεγίστου; (A.*Pr.* 648–649.)

Why do you so long remain a virgin, when it is possible for you to obtain the greatest marriage?

However, an impersonal verb does not always have an Infinitive phrase as Subject, either with a finite verb form or in an Accusative absolute.

ἀλλὰ γὰρ ἐμοὶ τούτων, ὦ ἄνδρες Ἀθηναῖοι, οὐδὲν μέτεστιν. (Pl.*Ap.* 19 C.)

But really, O men of Athens, I am not involved in these matters [lit. *there is no share for me of these matters*].

οὐδέν, not an Infinitive, is Subject of the finite verb μέτεστιν.

... ἐκέλευον Κορινθίους τοὺς ἐν Ἐπιδάμνῳ φρουρούς τε καὶ οἰκήτορας ἀπάγειν, ὡς οὐ μετὸν αὐτοῖς Ἐπιδάμνου. (Th. 1.28.1.)

... they were ordering the Corinthians to withdraw their garrison members and colonists in Epidamnus, on the grounds that they had no claim to Epidamnus [lit. *there not being a share for them of Epidamnus*].

There is no Subject for the neuter Accusative Participle μετόν. ὡς emphasises that the grounds are alleged by the Corinthians, not by the writer Thucydides.

6.3. Verbs Used Impersonally in the Passive Voice

The Accusative absolute construction also occurs with the Participles of verbs which are used impersonally in the third person singular Indicative Passive. Some of the more common examples are in the Perfect Aspect; the Aorist Passive Participle occurs more rarely.

... προύλεγον τὸ περὶ Μεγαρέων ψήφισμα καθελοῦσι μὴ ἂν γίγνεσθαι πόλεμον, ἐν ᾧ εἴρητο αὐτοὺς μὴ χρῆσθαι τοῖς λιμέσι τοῖς ἐν τῇ Ἀθηναίων ἀρχῇ μηδὲ τῇ Ἀττικῇ ἀγορᾷ. (Th. 1.139.1.)

... they declared <to them> that a war would not occur, if they rescinded the decree about the Megarians, in which it had been stated that they were not to use the ports in the control of the Athenians nor the Athenian market-place.

εἴρητο is impersonal third person singular Past Perfect Indicative Passive. However, the whole Accusative and Infinitive phrase αὐτοὺς ... ἀγορᾷ, is the Subject of εἴρητο. Compare §6.2 above. (The negatives in the passage are μή, because προύλεγον represents an ultimatum and εἴρητο refers to a decree.)

The following example uses the Perfect Passive Participle of the same verb in the neuter singular Accusative absolute.

προπέπεμπται δ' ὡς αὐτούς, καὶ ἀπαντᾶν εἰρημένον καὶ σιτία ἅμα κομίζειν. (Th. 7.77.6.)

And <instructions> have been sent ahead to them, since it has been stated both that <they> are to meet and that <they> are to bring provisions at the same time.

The whole Infinitive phrase καὶ ἀπαντᾶν ... καὶ σιτία ἅμα κομίζειν, representing a command, is the grammatical Subject of εἰρημένον.

... Ἡσίοδος ὁ ποιητὴς λέγεται ὑπὸ τῶν ταύτῃ ἀποθανεῖν, χρησθὲν αὐτῷ ἐν Νεμέᾳ τοῦτο παθεῖν ... (Th. 3.96.1.)

... Hesiod the poet is said to have been killed by the people here, when it had been prophesied to him that he <was to> suffer this in Nemea ...

The Infinitive phrase ἐν Νεμέᾳ τοῦτο παθεῖν is the grammatical Subject of the Aorist Passive Participle χρησθέν.

6.4. Neuter Adjectives

Some neuter adjectives are used impersonally with the Indicative of the verb 'to be', for example: αἰσχρόν ἐστι, 'it is disgraceful', and δυνατόν ἐστι, 'it is possible'. Such adjectives may be used in an Accusative absolute construction with the Participle of the verb 'to be'.

τοὺς δὲ λόγους μακροτέρους οὐ παρὰ τὸ εἰωθὸς μηκυνοῦμεν, ἀλλ' ἐπιχώριον ὂν ἡμῖν οὗ μὲν βραχεῖς ἀρκῶσι μὴ πολλοῖς χρῆσθαι, πλέοσι δὲ ἐν ᾧ ἂν καιρὸς διδάσκοντάς τι τῶν προύργου λόγοις τὸ δέον πράσσειν. (Th. 4.17.2.)

And we shall prolong our words at greater length not contrary to our custom, but because it is characteristic for us not to use many <words> when few are sufficient, but to achieve what is necessary when there is opportunity by explaining something of what is useful in more words.

In this passage, the whole section οὗ μὲν ... χρῆσθαι is the grammatical Subject of ὄν and ἐπιχώριον is its Complement.

In this construction, the adjective and the Participle are in the neuter singular, but in the following example, the adjective and Participle are plural, despite the fact that the grammatical Subject of the Participle is the (singular) Infinitive phrase παντὶ ... πιστεῦσαι.

τὰ μὲν οὖν παλαιὰ τοιαῦτα ηὗρον, χαλεπὰ ὄντα παντὶ ἑξῆς τεκμηρίῳ πιστεῦσαι. (Th. 1.20.1.)

Well then, I found the early <events to be> such, although it was difficult to rely on every inference along the way.

6.5. Personal Accusative Absolute

Sometimes, a personal construction is used in the Accusative absolute: the Participle has an Accusative Subject other than an Infinitive phrase. ὡς or ὥσπερ generally introduces this construction. The Participle is usually in the neuter Gender and is often derived from a verb which is used impersonally. But this personal construction may occur with any Gender or Number.

6.5.1. With ὡς or ὥσπερ

ὁ δ', ὡς καθ' ἡμᾶς ἔσθ' ὁ πληθύων λόγος,
τὸ κοῖλον Ἄργος βὰς φυγὰς προσλαμβάνει
κῆδός τε καινὸν καὶ ξυνασπιστὰς φίλους
ὡς αὐτίκ' Ἄργος ἢ τὸ Καδμείων πέδον
τιμῇ καθέξον ἢ πρὸς οὐρανὸν βιβῶν. (S. *OC* 377–381.)

*But he, as the current story among us is,
having gone as an exile to the valley of Argos, is taking on
a new relationship and companions in arms as friends,
on the understanding that presently Argos either will occupy the Cadmeans'
land in honour or will exalt it to heaven.*

ὡς is used with Ἄργος as Accusative Subject of the Intentive ('Fut.') Participles καθέξον and βιβῶν (neut. sg. contracted α).

6.5.2. Without ὡς or ὥσπερ

ὁ δέ, εἴτε καὶ διὰ τὸ ἐπιβόημα εἴτε καὶ αὐτῷ ἄλλο τι ἢ κατὰ τὸ αὐτὸ δόξαν ἐξαίφνης, πάλιν τὸ στράτευμα κατὰ τάχος πρὶν ξυμμεῖξαι ἀπῆγεν. (Th. 5.65.3.)

But he, whether actually on account of the shout or rather because some other <course of action> than the one he was currently following suddenly seemed right to him, began to lead the army away again in haste before making contact with <the enemy>.

The whole Accusative absolute phrase runs from αὐτῷ to ἐξαίφνης.

ἀλλό τι (ἢ κατὰ τὸ αὐτό) is the Subject of the Aorist Participle δόξαν.

καί reinforces εἴτε in each occurrence of the phrase εἴτε καὶ: 'actually … rather'.

κατὰ τὸ αὐτό means literally 'in accordance with the same'.

6.6. Note

In the Hellenistic period, the Accusative absolute is partly replaced by the Genitive absolute—papyri frequently have ἐξόντος for ἐξόν—and partly drops out of use altogether.

References

Goodwin (1889), *Syntax of the moods and tenses of the Greek verb*, §§851–854.

Smyth (1956), *Greek grammar*, §§2059, 2076–2078, 2086d, 2087, cf. 905, 932–935 (impersonal verbs).

EXERCISE 6

Translate the following passages.

1. ὃ δ' ἐς τοσοῦτον μωρίας ἀφίκετο,
   ὥστ', ἐξὸν αὐτῷ τἄμ' ἑλεῖν βουλεύματα
   γῆς ἐκβαλόντι, τήνδ' ἀφῆκεν ἡμέραν
   μεῖναί μ' ...

ὅ	he
ἐς τοσοῦτον	to so great (a degree of) (+ Gen.)
μωρία, -ας, ἡ	foolishness
τἄμ'	τὰ ἐμά
ἑλεῖν (Aor.)	to destroy, to ruin
βούλευμα, -ατος, τό	purpose, intention
ἀφιέναι	to allow
μ'	με

2. Ἀλκιβιάδης δ' ἐτόλμησεν ἀναβῆναι, ... ὡς οὐκ ἐξεσόμενον τῇ πόλει δίκην παρὰ τῶν ἀδικούντων λαμβάνειν.

ἀναβαίνειν	to mount (a horse)
ἀδικεῖν	to do wrong

3. προσταχθὲν γὰρ αὐτῷ τεττάρων μηνῶν ἀναγράψαι τοὺς νόμους τοὺς Σόλωνος, ... ἑξέτη τὴν ἀρχὴν ἐποιήσατο ...

προστάττειν	to give instructions (Acc.) to someone (Dat.) to do (Infin.)
μείς or μήν, μηνός, ὁ	month
ἀναγράφειν	to write up/out, to record
ἑξέτης, -ες	(here) lasting six years; (usually) six years old
ἀρχή, -ῆς, ἡ	office, appointment

4. ... καὶ ἄδηλον ὂν ὁπότε σφίσιν αὐτοῖς ξυρράξουσι, ... πῶς οὐκ εἰκότως ἠθύμουν;

ξυρράσσειν	*to fight with, to clash with* (+ Dat.)
εἰκότως	*reasonably, with (good) reason*
ἀθυμεῖν	*to be disheartened* (here 3rd pers. pl.)

5. ὃς πρῶτον μὲν μεθ' ἡμέραν ἐξέκοπτον τὸν σηκόν, ὥσπερ οὐ πάντας λαθεῖν δέον, ἀλλὰ πάντας Ἀθηναίους εἰδέναι.

ὅς	*For ... I* (coordinating relative pronoun)
πρῶτον	*in the first place*
μεθ' ἡμέραν	*by day, in the day-time*
ἐκκόπτειν	*to cut out*
σηκός, -οῦ, ὁ	*olive-stump*
ὥσπερ	*as if*
πάντας λαθεῖν	πάντας is Object of λαθεῖν.
πάντας Ἀθηναίους	Subject of εἰδέναι

6. δόξαντα δὲ ταῦτα καὶ περανθέντα, τὰ μὲν στρατεύματα ἀπῆλθε ...

περαίνειν	*to bring to an end, to finish*

7. σοὶ γὰρ παρὸν γῆν τήνδε καὶ δόμους ἔχειν
κούφως φερούσῃ κρεισσόνων βουλεύματα,
λόγων ματαίων οὕνεκ' ἐκπεσῇ χθονός.

ἔχειν	*to inhabit, to live in*
κούφως	*lightly*
μάταιος, -α, -ον	*rash*
οὕνεκα	*because of* (after Gen.)
ἐκπίπτειν	Used instead of Pass. of ἐκβάλλειν.

8. But if *we* are taking revenge later, although it was necessary to take revenge long ago, he gains the time during which he was living, although it was not appropriate for him [to do so] …

to take revenge	τιμωρεῖσθαι (Mid.)
later	ὕστερον
although it was necessary	Use Acc. abs.
long ago	πάλαι
time	χρόνος, -ου, ὁ
during	Use Acc. of extent.
he was living	ἔζη
to be appropriate (for)	προσήκειν (+ Dat.) Use Acc. abs.

LESSON 7
Verbal Adjectives Ending in -τος, -τη, -τον

7.1. Introduction

In addition to Participles, which are a standard component of the Greek verbal system, there are two other sets of verbal adjectives. These sets use the endings of the first and second declensions. The forms are listed separately in dictionaries. Lesson 7 deals with verbal adjectives ending in -τος, -τη, -τον. These forms appear already in Homer. Verbal adjectives ending in -τέος, -τέα, -τέον will be treated in Lesson 8.

7.2. Formation of Verbal Adjectives Ending in -τος, -τη, -τον

The letter τ was often used as a suffix to form adjectives, for example, ἀ-γερασ-τος, 'without a prize' (Hom.*Il.* 1.119.). It was usually added to the shortest form of the root of a word. Thus, θε-τός ('placed') is cognate with the verb τι-θέ-ναι ('to place') and the noun θέ-σις ('placing'), all incorporating the root θε. And verbal adjectives, which are related to verbs with reduplicated Imperfect stems, have the short form of the root. Thus, δο-τός is cognate with δι-δό-ναι. However, for contracted verbs, -τος is usually added after the lengthened form of the theme vowel. Thus, ἀγαπητός is cognate with the contracted α verb ἀγαπᾶν ('to tolerate', 'to accept', 'to desire'), which has η in Tenses other than Present and Past Imperfect (ἀγαπήσω, ἠγάπησα, etc.). But some contracted verbs use the short form of the theme vowel in some Tenses. And this short theme vowel may appear in the related verbal adjective. Thus, αἱρετός is cognate with αἱρεῖν ('to take'), which has η in some Tenses (e.g. Fut. Act. αἱρήσω) but ε in other Tenses (e.g. Past Aor. Pass. ᾑρέθην).

But contracted α verbs, whose base ends in ρ or a short vowel ∈ or ι (and sometimes ο), often retain α in the Tenses other than Present and Past Imperfect. Examples are περᾶν ('to cross'; περάσω, ἐπέρασα, etc.), θεᾶσθαι ('to look at'; θεάσομαι, ἐθεασάμην, etc.) and αἰτιᾶσθαι ('to censure'; αἰτιάσομαι, ᾐτιασάμην, etc.). Verbal adjectives cognate with these verbs also retain α: περατός, θεατός, αἰτιατός. (The α of the root is long in all the forms cited, both in the verbs and in the verbal adjectives. But there are some exceptions to this pattern; cf. Smyth, 1956, §488.)

Following the regular pattern, φιλητός ('likable') is cognate with the contracted ∈ verb φιλεῖν ('to like'), which has η in Tenses other than Present and Past Imperfect (φιλήσω, ἐφίλησα, etc.). And δηλωτός ('able to be shown') is cognate with the contracted ο verb δηλοῦν ('to show'), which has ω in tenses other than the Present and Past Imperfect (δηλώσω, ἐδήλωσα, etc.).

In practice, the stem of the verbal adjectives (both in -τος and in -τέος) is usually most easily recognisable from the Aorist Passive of the cognate verb. For example, σπαρτός ('sown') is cognate with the verb σπείρειν ('to sow'), whose (second) Aorist Passive is σπαρῆναι ('to be sown'). The θ at the end of the base of first Aorist Passive verbs does not appear in the cognate verbal adjectives. But where a verb has σ before θ in first Aorist Passive verbs, this σ appears before τ in the verbal adjective: παυσθῆναι, 'to be stopped'; ἄπαυστος, 'unceasing' (Active, Intr.) or 'unstoppable' (Passive). The insertion or omission of σ may vary with different occurrences of the same verb or verbal adjective (e.g. γνωτός or γνωστός), and different manuscripts may vary in the spelling of the same term in the same context (e.g. γνω(σ)τός [A.*Ch.* 702; S.*OT* 396]). (In the 1st Aor. Pass. of τιθέναι, the root θε has been modified to τε before the following θ; thus, τε-θῆναι instead of θε-θῆναι.)

Verbal adjectives ending in -τος, which are uncompounded (as φιλητός) or are prepositional compounds (as δια-βατός, 'fordable'), are generally accented on the final syllable and often (but not always) have all three gender endings: -ός, -ή, -όν. Other compound verbal adjectives regularly have recessive accent and use the ending -ος for both masculine and feminine genders. Thus, νυκτί-πλαγκτος, -ον ('causing to wander at night') is formed from the root of πλάζειν ('to cause to wander'; 1st Aor. Pass. πλαγχθῆναι). Negative α is common in these compounds. Simple α- precedes a consonant (ἄ-φυκτος, 'unable to escape' [Act.]; 'inescapable'

[Pass.]), ἀν- precedes a vowel (ἀν-έγκλητος, 'blameless') and when ἀ- precedes ρ, the ρ is doubled (ἄρ-ρηκτος, 'not broken', 'not to be broken'; cf. Smyth, 1956, §80).

7.3. Meaning of Verbal Adjectives Ending in -τος, -τη, -τον

It is likely that originally these verbal adjectives were not specifically Active or Passive but merely indicated relevance to the sphere of meaning of the verb. Thus, μεμπτός (cognate with μέμφεσθαι, 'to blame') would have indicated relevance to blaming. In the classical period, this word may have had either Active or Passive force. (Cf. ἄπαυστος in §7.2 above.)

ὥστ᾽ εἴ τι τὠμῷ τ᾽ ἀνδρὶ τῇδε τῇ νόσῳ
ληφθέντι **μεμπτός** εἰμι, κάρτα μαίνομαι, ... (S. *Tr.* 445–446.)

*And so, if I am **blaming** my husband at all for getting caught by this disease, I am surely mad, ...*

Active meaning. τὠμῷ = τῷ ἐμῷ. τ(ε) anticipates ἤ in the following clause.

τί δὴ τὸ Νείλου **μεμπτόν** ἐστί σοι γάνος; (E. *Hel.* 462.)
*Just why is the bright-water of the Nile **blamed** by you?*

Passive meaning.

The Passive force of these verbal adjectives is more common. But verbal adjectives with Passive force can be used to indicate either what is (already) done or what may or must be done. Some verbal adjectives are used in only one of these ways in extant Greek literature, but others are used in both ways. Thus, ῥητός, -ή, -όν may indicate either what has been stated or what may be stated.

τέλος δὲ παντὸς τοῦ λόγου ψηφίζονται ἥκειν τοὺς ἱερομνήμονας πρὸ τῆς ἐπιούσης πυλαίας ἐν **ῥητῷ** χρόνῳ εἰς Πύλας ... (Aeschin. 3.124.)

*And as the conclusion of all the discussion they voted [Hist. Pres.] that the representatives should come to Thermopylae at a **stated** time before the next amphictyonic-meeting ...*

The verbal adjective indicates what has been done.

Πρ.	γαμεῖ γάμον τοιοῦτον ᾧ ποτ' ἀσχαλᾷ.
Ιω	θέορτον ἢ βρότειον; εἰ **ῥητόν**, φράσον. (A.*Pr.* 764–765.)
Pr.	*He will make such a marriage, by which one day he will be distressed.*
Io	*Divine or mortal? If it **may be stated**, tell me.*

The verbal adjective indicates what may be done.

When an Infinitive phrase is the Subject of the verb 'to be' (expressed or understood), a neuter verbal adjective may be Complement, mostly singular as in the preceding examples (E.*Hel.* 462; A.*Pr.* 765), but sometimes plural. (Cf. Lesson 3.4.1.)

συγγνωστὰ μέντἄρ' ἦν σε λυπεῖσθαι, γύναι. (E.Med. 703.)
It was understandable, therefore, that you should be upset, lady.

Lit. 'That you should be upset, therefore, was understandable, lady'. Here, an Accusative and Infinitive phrase is the Subject of ἦν. Within the Accusative and Infinitive phrase, σε is Subject of the Passive Infinitive λυπεῖσθαι. And the neuter plural συγγνωστά is the Complement of the Infinitive phrase. (The crasis of μέντοι ἄρα accounts for the apparent double accent.)

A Dative of Interest, implying Agency, may be used with verbal adjectives in their Passive sense.

... οἱ δὲ τοὺς μύθους εἰς ἀγῶνας καὶ πράξεις κατέστησαν, ὥστε μὴ μόνον **ἀκουστοὺς ἡμῖν** ἀλλὰ καὶ **θεατοὺς** γενέσθαι. (Isoc. 2.49.)

*... but they put the stories into conflicts and actions, so as to become not only **heard by us** but also **seen**.*

(The passage refers to early tragedians, by contrast with Homer who put into stories the conflicts and wars of the demigods.)

References

Palmer (1980), *The Greek language*, pp. 256–257, 314.

Smyth (1956), *Greek grammar*, §§80, 358, 425.c, 471–472, 488, 1003.a, 1052, 1488.

LESSON 7. VERBAL ADJECTIVES ENDING IN -τος, -τη, -τον

EXERCISE 7

1. Translate the following passages.
2. For each passage:
   a. write down the Nominative masculine singular of any verbal adjectives whose Nominative ends in -τος, -τη, -τον
   b. indicate any negative ἀ(ν)- prefixes by inserting a hyphen
   c. write the Imperfect Infinitive of the verb to which the verbal adjective is etymologically related
   d. mark accents and breathings correctly.
3. Montanari (2015), *The Brill dictionary of Ancient Greek*, or the full edition of Liddell and Scott (1996), *A Greek–English lexicon*, should be used.

Example

Ἀριστόδημος ἦν τις, Κυδαθηναιεύς, σμικρός, ἀνυπόδητος ἀεί. (Pl.*Smp.* 173 B.)

It was a certain Aristodemus of Kydathenaeum, a small <man>, always unshod [i.e. barefoot].

ἀν-υπόδητος related to ὑποδεῖν.

1. δοκῶ μοι περὶ ὧν πυνθάνεσθε οὐκ ἀμελέτητος εἶναι.

   | δοκῶ μοι | lit. *I seem to me* (i.e. *it seems to me that I*) |
   | περὶ ὧν (neut.) | Condensed for περὶ ἐκείνων περὶ ὧν. |

2. ἀλλ' ἄτερ γνώμης τὸ πᾶν
   ἔπρασσον, ἔστε δή σφιν ἀντολὰς ἐγὼ
   ἄστρων ἔδειξα τάς τε δυσκρίτους δύσεις.

ἄτερ (+ Gen.)	*without*
ἔστε	*until*
ἀν(α)τολή, -ῆς, ἡ	*rising*
δύσις, -εως, ἡ	*setting*

3. τοῦτο γὰρ δὴ ἐγὼ παντάπασιν οὐ διδακτὸν ᾤμην εἶναι …

παντάπασιν (adv.)	altogether
οἴεσθαι	to think (Mid. with Aor. Pass.; ᾤμην = ᾠόμην, Past Imperf.)

4. καταψηφιεῖσθε τοῦ τὰ ἐλεεινὰ ταῦτα δράματα εἰσάγοντος καὶ καταγέλαστον τὴν πόλιν ποιοῦντος …

καταψηφίζεσθαι (Mid.)	to vote in condemnation of (+ Gen.)
ἐλεεινός, -ή, -όν	pitiful, pitiable

5. ἃ δὴ λόγῳ μὲν καὶ διανοίᾳ ληπτά, ὄψει δ' οὔ·

ἅ	And these (coordinating relative pronoun)
λόγος, -ου, ὁ	reason
διάνοια, -ας, ἡ	thought
ὄψις, -εως, ἡ	sight

6. σφρηγῖδα δὲ ἕκαστος ἔχει καὶ σκῆπτρον χειροποίητον·

σφρηγίς, -ῖδος, ἡ (Ionic)	seal (Attic σφραγίς)
σκῆπτρον, -ου, τό	staff

7. τούτων δ' Ἀθηναίους φημὶ δεῖν εἶναι πεντακοσίους, ἐξ ἧς τινος ὑμῖν ἡλικίας καλῶς ἔχειν δοκῇ, χρόνον τακτὸν στρατευομένους …

τούτων	masc.
ἐξ ἧς τινος … ἡλικίας	from any age(-group) which

8. ταῦτα, ὦ Ἀθηναῖοι, καὶ ἀληθῆ ἐστιν καὶ εὐέλεγκτα.

9. οἱ δὲ Πέρσαι καταρρήξαντες τὴν κρυπτὴν γέφυραν ἔθεον ἔσω ἐς τὸ τεῖχος.

καταρρηγνύναι	*to break down*
γέφυρα, -ας, ἡ	*bridge*
θέειν (Ionic)	*to run* (Attic θεῖν)

10. ... ὁ δὲ ἀνεξέταστος βίος οὐ βιωτὸς ἀνθρώπῳ ...

Understand ἐστί.

LESSON 8
Verbal Adjectives Ending in -τέος, -τέα, -τέον

8.1. Formation of Verbal Adjectives Ending in -τέος, -τέα, -τέον

According to Palmer (1980), the verbal adjectival suffix -τεο- is derived from the action suffix *-ti- inherited from Indo-European. In Greek, this suffix becomes -σι-. Thus, for example, the action noun ποίη-σι-ς ('do-ing') is related to the verbal stem of ποιεῖν ('to do'), as it appears in Tenses other than Present and Past Imperfect: ποιήσω, ἐποίησα, etc. The corresponding verbal adjective is ποιη-τέος. Where a verb has σ before θ in First Aorist Passive, this σ appears before τ in the verbal adjective: ἐδράσθη, δραστέος. The accent is persistent on -ε-. The α of the feminine ending is long.

Verbal adjectives formed with a suffix -τεο- are listed separately in dictionaries. If only a Passive use of a particular verbal adjective occurs in extant classical Greek, the word is listed alphabetically in Liddell and Scott (1996) with the ending -τέος. If only an Active use occurs, the word is listed with the ending -τέον. Where both Passive and Active uses occur, the Active form is listed first in Montanari (2015), but there is some inconsistency in Liddell and Scott (1996) as to which form is listed first.

8.2. Usage of Verbal Adjectives Ending in -τέος, -τέα, -τέον

The verbal adjectives ending in -τέος do not occur at all in Homer. They are in general use from the fifth century BCE onwards. (The earliest extant example is γεγωνητέον, Pi. *Ol.* 2.5, 476/5 BCE.) They denote the *necessity* of the action of the cognate verb.

When these verbal adjectives are used *personally*, they may appear in any gender (-τέος, -τέα, -τέον) and they have a *Passive* meaning, indicating that something is to be done. But they are more often used *impersonally*, mainly in the neuter singular (-τέον), but sometimes in the neuter plural (-τέα). The plural occurs especially in Thucydides among prose writers. The impersonal use regularly has an *Active* meaning, indicating that it is necessary to do something; and the verb 'to be' is usually omitted ('<it is> necessary to do'). However, in reported discourse the Infinitive of the verb 'to be' may be included for the sake of clarity. And for an exceptional impersonal Passive usage, see §8.8 below.

The Agent for both personal and impersonal constructions is normally expressed in the Dative Case. Examples are given in §§8.3 and 8.4.1 below.

In both personal and impersonal constructions, the verbal adjective generally appears in the Nominative Case in direct discourse. In reported discourse, the verbal adjective regularly appears in the Accusative Case with Infinitive or Participle as appropriate. For a usage with the definite article in any Case, see §8.4.2 below.

In so far as these verbal adjectives regularly occur in statements (direct or reported), the negative used with them is οὐ. However, in the impersonal Active construction, οὐ ποιητέον means not '<It is> not necessary to do', but '<It is> necessary not to do'. Although negative α is common as a prefix to verbal adjectives ending in -τός, -τή, -τόν, it appears as a prefix to verbal adjectives ending in -τέος, -τέα, -τέον only in some 11 forms cognate with verbs which contain the negative α. Alphabetically, the first and last examples are ἀδικητέον cognate with ἀδικεῖν (Plato) and ἀσιτητέον cognate with ἀσιτεῖν (Galen).

8.3. Impersonal Construction

In the following example, the relation of the form of the verbal adjective to the cognate verb is indicated by citing the verbal adjective itself, the Imperfect Active Infinitive and the Aorist Passive Infinitive.

ὥσθ' ὁμοίως ἡμῖν **φιλονικητέον** ὑπὲρ τῶν ἐνθάδε ψηφισθησομένων, ὥσπερ ὑπὲρ τῶν ἐν τοῖς ὅπλοις ἀγώνων. (Isoc. 6.92.)

And so in a similar way <it is> **necessary** *for us* **to campaign** *for what is going to be voted on here, just as for contests under arms.*

| φιλονικη-τέον | φιλονικεῖν | φιλονικη-θῆναι |

ἡμῖν is Dative of Interest implying Agency: the 'campaigning' is to be done 'by us'.

... καὶ ὡς ᾔσθοντο τῶν λόγων, ἔδοξεν αὐτοῖς **παριτητέα** ἐς τοὺς Λακεδαιμονίους **εἶναι** ... (Th. 1.72.1.)

*... and when they had heard the speeches, it seemed to them **to be necessary to appear** (lit. 'to come forward') before the Spartans ...*

The neuter plural verbal adjective παριτητέα is used here (in Thucydides); and the Infinitive εἶναι is included in the reported discourse. (ἰτητέον is equivalent to ἰτέον in function and meaning.)

8.4. Personal Construction

8.4.1. Regular Usage

ταῦτα μὲν οὖν, ὦ ἄνδρες δικασταί, τούτοις **ποιητέα ἦν** ... (And. 1.136.)

*Well then, O men of the jury, **this was (bound) to be done** by these <men> ...*

In the personal construction, ποιητέα is Nominative neuter plural in agreement with ταῦτα. τούτοις is Dative of Interest implying Agency.

8.4.2. Usage with Article

The personal usage of the verbal adjective occasionally appears with the definite article to form a noun phrase. This idiom is not restricted to the Nominative Case.

περὶ μὲν δὴ **τῶν** ὑμῖν **πρακτέων** καθ' ὑμᾶς αὐτοὺς ὕστερον βουλεύσεσθε, ἂν σωφρονῆτε· (D. 6.28.)

*Indeed, concerning **what is to be done** by you, you will subsequently deliberate by yourselves, if you are sensible.*

8.5. Ambiguous Constructions

When the entire verbal adjectival phrase is neuter, it is often difficult to decide whether a neuter noun or pronoun is Subject of a personal construction or Object of an impersonal construction.

… ἡ ἄλλη Πελοπόννησος ἐς θροῦν καθίστατο ὡς καὶ σφίσι **ποιητέον τοῦτο** … (Th. 5.29.2.)

… *the rest of the Peloponnese was getting into a discussion, that <it was>* **necessary** *for them too* **to do this** … [OR: *that* **this** *<was>* **to be done** *by them too* …]

τοῦτο may be either Object of ποιητέον (used impersonally) or Subject of ποιητέον (used personally). But the absence of the verb 'to be' makes it more likely that the construction should be understood as impersonal here.

ἢ τοίνυν δεινότερόν **τι** τούτου **δέος εὑρετέον ἐστὶν** ἢ τόδε γε οὐδὲν ἐπίσχει … (Th. 3.45.4.)

Either, therefore, **some cause-of-fear** *more fearsome than this* [= death] **is to be found** *or* this [= cause-of-fear] *restrains nothing* …

[OR: *Either, therefore,* **it is necessary to find some cause-of-fear** *more fearsome than this or* this *causes no restraint* …]

δέος may be either Subject of εὑρετέον (used personally) or Object of εὑρετέον (used impersonally). But the presence of ἐστίν makes it more likely that the construction should be understood as personal here.

8.6. Agent in Accusative

Sometimes, the Agent of a verbal adjective appears in the Accusative Case instead of the Dative, apparently by analogy with δεῖ or χρή with the Accusative (and Infinitive).

οὐ μὴν **δουλευτέον τοὺς** νοῦν **ἔχοντας** τοῖς οὕτω κακῶς φρονοῦσιν … (Isoc. 9.7.)

<It is> certainly **necessary that those who have** *sense (should) not* **be subject** *to people with so bad an attitude* …

8.7. Construction Continued with Infinitive

The construction of verbal adjectives becomes more closely assimilated to the pattern of δεῖ or χρή, when an initial verbal adjective is followed by a second phrase with an Infinitive, which is dependent on the notion of necessity contained in the verbal adjective. In the following sentence, ποιητέον is continued by πείθειν.

... ἀλλὰ καὶ ἐν πολέμῳ καὶ ἐν δικαστηρίῳ καὶ πανταχοῦ **ποιητέον** ἃ ἂν κελεύῃ ἡ πόλις καὶ ἡ πατρίς, ἢ **πείθειν** αὐτὴν ᾗ τὸ δίκαιον πέφυκε ... (Pl.*Cri.* 51 B–C.)

... but both in war and in law-court and everywhere <it is> **necessary to do** *what the city and the fatherland commands, or* **to persuade** *it where justice lies ...*

8.8. Impersonal Passive Construction

Contrary to the usual practice, an impersonal construction with Passive meaning occurs with ἡσσητέα (neut. pl.). The cognate verb ἡσσᾶσθαι occurs only in the Middle/Passive in the classical period. The Genitive of Comparison, which is used with the verb and the verbal adjective, implies Agency: 'to be inferior (compared with)', 'to be defeated (by)'.

κοὔτοι γυναικὸς οὐδαμῶς **ἡσσητέα**. (S.*Ant.* 678.)
And <it is> certainly **necessary** *by no means* **to be defeated** *by a woman.*

But the impersonal Passive construction is not limited to verbal adjectives cognate with verbs which are used only in the Passive Voice. In the following quotation, ἀπολειπτέον illustrates the point.

ἆρά γε, ὦ γύναι, διὰ τοιαύτας τινὰς προνοίας καὶ τῆς ἐν τῷ σμήνει ἡγεμόνος αἱ μέλιτται οὕτω διατίθενται πρὸς αὐτήν, ὥστε, ὅταν ἐκείνη ἐκλίπῃ, οὐδεμία οἴεται τῶν μελιττῶν **ἀπολειπτέον εἶναι**, ἀλλ᾽ ἕπονται πᾶσαι; (X.*Oec.* 7.38.)

(Is it), O wife, on account of some such caring-actions even of the leader in the hive (that) the bees are so disposed towards her, that, when she quits <the hive>, none of the bees thinks that **it is necessary to be left behind**, *but they all follow?*

References

Goodwin (1889), *Syntax of the moods and tenses of the Greek verb*, §§920–926.

Palmer (1980), *The Greek language*, pp. 257, 314.

Smyth (1956), *Greek grammar*, §§358, 425.c, 471, 1003.a, 1052, 1488, 2149–2152.

EXERCISE 8

1. Translate the following passages.
2. For each passage:
   a. write down, in the form in which they appear, any verbal adjectives of the type whose Nominative singular ends in -τέος, -τέα, -τέον
   b. write the Imperfect Infinitive of the verb to which each of these adjectives is related
   c. state whether the particular use is personal Passive or impersonal Active
   d. if the construction appears to be ambiguous, indicate whether there are grounds for preferring an Active or Passive interpretation
   e. mark accents correctly.
3. Montanari (2015), *The Brill dictionary of Ancient Greek*, or the full edition of Liddell and Scott (1996), *A Greek–English lexicon*, should be used.

Example

κωλυτέον δὲ τοὺς ὑβρίζειν βουλομένους … (X.*Hier.* 8.9.)

and <it is> necessary to prevent those wanting to act violently …

κωλυτέον related to κωλύειν. Impersonal Active.

LESSON 8. VERBAL ADJECTIVES ENDING IN -τέος, -τέα, -τέον

1. περὶ γὰρ τῶν αὐτῶν οὐχ ὁμοίως ἅπασι βουλευτέον, ἀλλ' ὡς ἂν ἐξ ἀρχῆς ἕκαστοι τοῦ βίου ποιήσωνται τὴν ὑπόθεσιν.

τῶν αὐτῶν	neut.
ὡς ἄν	Introduces a clause of indefinite comparison.
ἕκαστοι (pl.)	*each group*
ὑπόθεσις, -εως, ἡ	*basis* (qualified by τοῦ βίου)

2. ... καίπερ τοσοῦτον πλεονεκτούσης τῆς ποιήσεως, οὐκ ὀκνητέον, ἀλλ' ἀποπειρατέον τῶν λόγων ἐστίν ...

πλεονεκτεῖν	*to have an advantage*
ποίησις, -εως, ἡ	*poetry*
οἱ λόγοι	*prose* (lit. *the words*)

3. ... ὑμᾶς δὲ ὁσίως ὁρᾶν προσήκει τὰ πραχθέντα· ἐκ τῶν λεγομένων γὰρ ἡ ἀλήθεια σκεπτέα αὐτῶν ἐστίν.

ὁσίως	*conscientiously*
προσήκειν	*to be appropriate* (here with Acc. and Infin.)
ἐκ	*on the basis of*
λεγομένων	neut. Pass.
αὐτῶν (neut.)	Refers to τὰ πραχθέντα.

4. ἀλλὰ σὺ πρῶτον μὲν ἡγῇ παρασκευαστέον τὸ μή ποτε κινδυνεῦσαι;

ἡγεῖσθαι (Mid.)	*to think*
κινδυνεύειν	*to run a risk, to be in danger*

5. πρῶτον μὲν οὖν οὐκ ἀθυμητέον, ὦ ἄνδρες Ἀθηναῖοι, τοῖς παροῦσι πράγμασιν ...

6. ἄλλου λόγου μέμνησθε, τόνδε δ' οὐδαμῶς
   καιρὸς γεγωνεῖν, ἀλλὰ συγκαλυπτέος
   ὅσον μάλιστα.

λόγος, -ου, ὁ	subject, topic
μεμνῆσθαι (Mid.)	to make mention of (+ Gen.; Perf. with Imperf. meaning; here Impv.)
τόνδε	Understand λόγον.
γεγωνεῖν	to declare
ὅσον μάλιστα	so far as possible

7. καὶ τῶν μὲν πλεόνων ἐπὶ τὸ αὐτὸ αἱ γνῶμαι ἔφερον, ... πολεμητέα εἶναι ἐν τάχει·

φέρειν (Intr.)	to tend (to), to incline (to)

8. ... ἐκεῖνο μάλιστα φυλακτέον, ὅπως μηδὲν ἀνάνδρως φανησόμεθα διαπραττόμενοι μηδὲ συγχωροῦντες τοῖς πολεμίοις παρὰ τὸ δίκαιον.

φαίνεσθαι (Pass. + Partc.)	to be clear(ly doing something)
διαπράττειν (Act. and Mid.)	to manage
συγχωρεῖν	to yield (to) (+ Dat.)
παρά (+ Acc.)	contrary to

LESSON 9
Voice

9.1. English

Both in classical Greek and in modern English, Voice is a function of the verb including not only finite forms of the verb but also Infinitives (verbal nouns) and Participles (verbal adjectives). In English, there are two Voices: Active and Passive. The Active forms are simple, being expressed by a single form of a verb; Passive forms are compound, being expressed with the help of auxiliary verbs.

*He **had** a good time.* (Act.)
*A good time **was had** by all.* (Pass.)

Active verbs may be used transitively or intransitively, that is, with or without a direct Object.

*He **turned the handle** of the lounge-room door.* (Transitive)

*I **turned**, and saw below
The same shape twisted on the banister …* (Intr.) (T. S. Eliot, *Ash Wednesday*, III.2–3.)

The (grammatical) Subject *performs* the action expressed by an Active form of a verb. The Subject *experiences* (suffers, receives) the action expressed by a Passive form of a verb.

*The **hoplite hurled** his spear with all his strength.* (Act.)
*The **first spear was hurled** by a hoplite in the front rank.* (Pass.)

9.2. Greek

In the classical period of Ancient Greek, there are three Voices of the verb: Active, Middle and Passive. The forms and functions of the Active Voice are relatively straightforward and will not be treated further here. In most

Tenses of the Indicative, there are not separate forms for the Middle and Passive Voices. The function of such forms needs to be determined in each context. An expressed Agent is a pointer to a Passive function: 'The spear **is hurled by** a hoplite'.

Separate forms for Middle and Passive Voices do occur in the Future and Past Aorist Tenses of the Indicative Mood, and likewise for the Aorist Subjunctive and Optative, and for the Intentive ('Fut.') Optative.

παύσομαι, *I shall stop* (Intr.) (Mid.); παυ(σ)θήσομαι, *I shall be stopped* (Pass.).

ἐπαυσάμην, *I stopped* (Intr.) (Mid.); ἐπαύ(σ)θην, *I was stopped* (Pass.).

In English, it is not appropriate to apply the category of Voice to verbs such as 'to be', 'to become', 'to seem', which may have a (Subjective) Complement. The same restriction would apply to εἶναι in Greek. But the status of γίγνεσθαι and δοκεῖν is not simply equivalent to that of εἶναι; γίγνεσθαι has a mixture of Active, Middle and Passive forms; δοκεῖν means 'to think' as well as 'to seem'.

9.3. Uses of the Middle Voice

9.3.1. In General

The Middle Voice expresses greater interest or involvement of the Subject in the action of the verb than would be expressed by the Active Voice.

αἱρεῖν (Act.)	*to take*
αἱρεῖσθαι (Mid.)	*to take for oneself, to choose*

Often verbs of emotion, thought and perception are used especially or solely in the Middle Voice.

αἰδεῖσθαι	*to be ashamed*
νοεῖσθαι	*to think*
αἰσθάνεσθαι	*to perceive*

Likewise, verbs denoting bodily activity.

| οἴχεσθαι | to go, to have gone |
| ἕπεσθαι | to follow |

Similar to the last two groups are Active verbs which use the Middle Voice in the Future Tense only, without any distinction of meaning.

| ἀκούειν, ἀκούσεσθαι | to hear, to be going to hear (perception) |
| βαίνειν, βήσεσθαι | to walk, to be going to walk (physical activity) |

9.3.2. Causative

In the following example, Croesus caused the action of 'making' to take place but did not himself 'make' the image of the lion.

ἐποιέετο δὲ καὶ λέοντος εἰκόνα … (Hdt. 1.50.3.)
And he **had** an image of a lion **made** also …

But this causative force may also be expressed by the Active Voice. In the following example, the Subject (Artaphrenes) causes something to be done but does not personally execute the Persians.

τούτων δὲ γενομένων φανερῶν **ἀπέκτεινε** ἐνθαῦτα πολλοὺς Περσέων ὁ Ἀρταφρένης. (Hdt. 6.4.)

And when <the identity of> these men became known, Artaphrenes promptly **had** many of the Persians **put to death**.

9.3.3. Reflexive

The Middle Voice in itself may have a reflexive force.

… καὶ ἐκ τῶν δένδρων τινὲς ἀπήγχοντο … (Th. 3.81.3.)
… and some hanged themselves from the trees …

The stock example of this use is λούομαι, 'I wash myself'. But here the force may rather be 'I wash' (Intr.), in the sense 'I have a wash', 'I am having a wash'. Likewise with many other such Middle forms.

A definitely reflexive construction is more often expressed by an Active verb with a reflexive pronoun as direct Object.

ἐπαινέσαντες γὰρ πολλὰ ἑαυτοὺς οὐδαμοῦ ἀντεῖπον ὡς οὐκ ἀδικοῦσι τοὺς ἡμετέρους ξυμμάχους καὶ τὴν Πελοπόννησον· (Th. 1.86.1.)

*For although **praising themselves** at length, they nowhere denied that they were maltreating our allies and the Peloponnese.*

However, this Transitive construction may also occur with a verb in the Middle Voice.

... οὐδὲ **ἐσεγράψαντο ἑαυτοὺς** οὔτε ἐς τὰς Ἀθηναίων σπονδὰς οὔτε ἐς τὰς Λακεδαιμονίων. (Th. 1.31.2.)

*... nor <had> **they enrolled themselves** either in the treaty with the Athenians or in that with the Spartans.*

9.3.4. Reciprocal

A reciprocal use of the Middle Voice has often been proposed.

... οἱ ἀθληταὶ ἠγωνίζοντο ... (Th. 1.6.5.)
... the contestants used to compete (with one another) ...

In the context of this example, however, Thucydides is discussing continuity and change in social practice, including clothing in general and for sport. He is not making a point about competition, mutuality or reciprocity. Moreover, ἀγωνίζεσθαι is used only in the Middle and occasionally the Passive (usually Perf. Pass.) Voices throughout the ancient period (apart from the Act. in an inscription of uncertain date).

μάχεσθαι (only Middle), 'to fight (with one another)' is also cited as an example of reciprocal use of the Middle Voice. But πολεμεῖν, which has a similar meaning, is not used in the Middle but only in the Active Voice apart from a few Passive instances.

Some verbs are used in both Active and Middle Voices without any significant difference regarding reciprocity.

καί περ χωόμενος παύθη χόλου, ὃν πρὶν ἔχεσκεν

οὕνεκ' **ἐρίζετο** βουλὰς ὑπερμενέϊ Κρονίωνι. (Hes. *Th.* 533–534; Middle.)

Although being angry he [= Zeus] ceased from the anger, which he previously had

because he [= Prometheus] **contended** *in his designs* **with** *the mighty son of Kronos.*

παύθη has no augment.

νόον γε μὲν οὔ τις **ἔριζε**
τάων ἃς θνηταὶ θνητοῖς τέκον εὐνηθεῖσαι. (Hes.*Sc.* 5–6; Active.)

And indeed in intellect there **contended with** *<her> no one of the <girls>, whom mortal women when brought to bed bore to mortal men.*

The Middle Voice of some verbs compounded with διά and σύν is often assigned a reciprocal force.

ἐγὼ γὰρ ὑπεθέμην οὐχ ὡς περὶ τῶν πολιτειῶν **διαλεξόμενος**, ἀλλ᾽ ὡς ἐπιδείξων τὴν πόλιν ἡμῶν πολὺ πλείονος ἀξίαν Λακεδαιμονίων περὶ τοὺς Ἕλληνας γεγενημένην. (Isoc. 12.112.)

For I proposed <my topic> not in order to **have a discussion** *about constitutions, but in order to show that our city had been worth much more than <that> of the Spartans with regard to the Greeks.*

In this example, however, any suggestion of reciprocity or mutual involvement may be due to the prefix as much as to the Middle Voice of δια-λεξόμενος.

A genuinely reciprocal expression is more clearly formed by the reciprocal pronoun as Object of an Active verb (or as another component of the predicate).

ἔφερον γὰρ **ἀλλήλους** τε καὶ τῶν ἄλλων ὅσοι ὄντες οὐ θαλάσσιοι κάτω ᾤκουν. (Th. 1.7.)

For **they used to plunder each other** *and as many of the rest as, although not being seagoing, lived on the coast.*

However, the reciprocal pronoun may also be used with the Middle Voice. ἔφερον (Act.) and ἐλῄζοντο (Mid.) are synonymous in the preceding and following sentences.

ἐλῄζοντο δὲ καὶ κατ᾽ ἤπειρον **ἀλλήλους**. (Th. 1.5.3.)
And **they used to plunder each other** *on the mainland also.*

In short, it is not clear that there is a specifically reciprocal use of the Middle Voice. Rather, in some contexts some verbs may be used in the Active Voice with the reciprocal pronoun, or in the Middle Voice with or without the reciprocal pronoun, to express reciprocity. The Middle Voice is used in a general way in such contexts to convey the interest or involvement of the Subject.

9.4. The Development of the Middle Voice

It is generally, but not universally, agreed that in Indo-European there were two Voices: Active and Middle. 'The active verb was used to present an activity proceeding from a subject outwards: when the event took place within the subject or was reflected on the subject, then the middle voice was used' (Palmer, 1980, p. 292).

In Homer, second Aorist verb forms ending in -ην in first person singular are generally Intransitive Active, not Passive. Thus, from φαίνειν, *to show*:

ἔφηνα, *I showed* (1st Aor. Act. Transitive); ἐφάνην, *I appeared* (2nd Aor. Act. Intr.).

Most (about three-quarters) of first Aorists ending in -θην in first person singular are also Active Intransitive in Epic:

ἐφάνθην, *I appeared* (Act. Intr. in Epic); *I was shown* (Pass. in Attic).

This feature is still evident in some forms which are used in Attic tragedy with Middle force.

σύθην δ' ἀπέδιλος ὄχῳ πτερωτῷ. (A.*Pr.* 135.)
And I rushed off without my shoes on a winged conveyance.

σύθην has no augment.

Future forms ending with -σομαι in first person singular may still have both Middle and Passive force in the classical period. Passive Futures ending in -(θ)ήσομαι in first person singular, which were formed on the basis of first and second Aorist Passives ending in -(θ)ην, are largely a development of the fifth century BCE. (It cannot safely be maintained that -σομαι Futures are durative or Imperfect, whereas -(θ)ήσομαι forms are Aoristic.)

In the Hellenistic period, the Active Voice tends to supplant the Middle. In particular, Active verbs with Middle Futures now begin to use Active Future forms; thus, ἀκούσω for classical ἀκούσομαι. The Future and Past Aorist Tenses of the Middle Voice, which in the classical period were distinguished from the Passive, tend to disappear. Middle verbs with Active meaning now prefer Passive forms; thus, for 'he replied', ἀπεκρίθη replaces ἀπεκρίνατο.

References

Gildersleeve (1900), *Syntax of classical Greek from Homer to Demosthenes* (Vol. 1), pp. 61–79.

Moorhouse (1982), *The syntax of Sophocles* (Mnemosyne Supplement 75), pp. 176–180.

Palmer (1980), *The Greek language*, pp. 292–293, 298–299, 302–303, 311–312.

Rijksbaron (1994), *The syntax and semantics of the verb in classical Greek*, pp. 131–160.

Smyth (1956), *Greek grammar*, §§800–821, 1703–1758.

EXERCISE 9

Identify all Middle or Passive verb forms (including Infinitives and Participles) in the passage of Euripides *Alcestis* 29–31, 42–64. (Do not include any parts of εἶναι.)

1. Write the line number in the left margin.
2. Write the form which appears in the Greek text.
3. Parse the form.

   For finite verb forms, state the person, Number, Tense (of Indicative forms) or Aspect (of non-Indicative forms), Mood and Voice (indicating *whether* Middle *or* Passive).

   For Infinitives, state the Aspect and Voice.

   For Participles, state the Aspect, Voice, Case, Gender and Number.

   Give the Imperfect Active Infinitive form of the verb (if the Active form does not occur in classical Greek, give the Middle or Passive form).

Give the English meaning of the quoted Imperfect Infinitive which is relevant to the context (not the whole range of possible meanings).
4. Montanari (2015), *The Brill dictionary of Ancient Greek* or the full edition of Liddell and Scott (1996), *A Greek–English lexicon*, should be used.

Example

πῶς δ' ἂν μᾶλλον ἐνδείξαιτό τις
πόσιν προτιμῶσ(α) ἢ θέλουσ(α) ὑπερθανεῖν; (E.*Alc.* 154–155.)

| 154 | ἐνδείξαιτο | 3rd pers. sg. Aor. Opt. Mid. | ἐνδεικνύναι | to show |

Euripides *Alcestis* 29–31, 42–64

Θ = ΘΑΝΑΤΟΣ
Α = ΑΠΟΛΛΩΝ

Θ. τί σὺ πρὸς μελάθροις; τί σὺ τῇδε πολεῖς,
   Φοῖβ'; ἀδικεῖς αὖ τιμὰς ἐνέρων   30
   ἀφοριζόμενος καὶ καταπαύων;

       *   *   *   *   *

Α. φίλου γὰρ ἀνδρὸς συμφοραῖς βαρύνομαι.
Θ. καὶ νοσφιεῖς με τοῦδε δευτέρου νεκροῦ;
Α. ἀλλ' οὐδ' ἐκεῖνον πρὸς βίαν σ' ἀφειλάμην.
Θ. πῶς οὖν ὑπὲρ γῆς ἐστι κοὐ κάτω χθονός;   45
Α. δάμαρτ' ἀμείψας, ἣν σὺ νῦν ἥκεις μέτα.
Θ. κἀπάξομαί γε νερτέραν ὑπὸ χθόνα.
Α. λαβὼν ἴθ'· οὐ γὰρ οἶδ' ἂν εἰ πείσαιμί σε.
Θ. κτείνειν γ' ὃν ἂν χρῇ; τοῦτο γὰρ τετάγμεθα.
Α. οὔκ, ἀλλὰ τοῖς μέλλουσι θάνατον ἀμβαλεῖν.   50
Θ. ἔχω λόγον δὴ καὶ προθυμίαν σέθεν.
Α. ἔστ' οὖν ὅπως Ἄλκηστις ἐς γῆρας μόλοι;
Θ. οὐκ ἔστι· τιμαῖς κἀμὲ τέρπεσθαι δόκει.
Α. οὔτοι πλέον γ' ἂν ἢ μίαν ψυχὴν λάβοις.
Θ νέων φθινόντων μεῖζον ἄρνυμαι γέρας.   55
Α. κἂν γραῦς ὄληται, πλουσίως ταφήσεται.

Θ. πρὸς τῶν ἐχόντων, Φοῖβε, τὸν νόμον τίθης.
Α. πῶς εἶπας; ἀλλ' ἦ καὶ σοφὸς λέληθας ὤν;
Θ. ὠνοῖντ' ἂν οἷς πάρεστι γηραιοὶ θανεῖν.
Α. οὔκουν δοκεῖ σοι τήνδε μοι δοῦναι χάριν;   60
Θ. οὐ δῆτ'· ἐπίστασαι δὲ τοὺς ἐμοὺς τρόπους.
Α. ἐχθρούς γε θνητοῖς καὶ θεοῖς στυγουμένους.
Θ. οὐκ ἂν δύναιο πάντ' ἔχειν ἃ μή σε δεῖ.
Α. ἦ μὴν σὺ παύσῃ καίπερ ὠμὸς ὢν ἄγαν·

LESSON 10
Commands

10.1. Introduction

Positive commands are normally expressed by the Imperative Mood. Negative commands are normally expressed by μή with the Imperfect Imperative, or by μή with the Aorist Subjunctive. The Imperfect Aspect expresses continuous or repeated action. The Aorist Aspect expresses momentary action. The Perfect Aspect is used especially with verbs, whose Perfect Aspect has an Imperfect meaning, for example, ἕστηκα, 'I have taken my stand', hence 'I am standing'; μέμνημαι, 'I have recalled', hence 'I remember'. (Cf. Lesson 2.1 and Lesson 2.3.1.)

10.2. Negative Commands

The Aorist Imperative is not normally used in negative commands; it occurs occasionally in the third person, and rarely (and only in poetry) in the second person. The Imperfect Subjunctive is not normally used in negative commands; it occurs not at all in the second person, and only rarely in the third person.

This apparently arbitrary distinction of Moods (Imperative for Imperfect action, Subjunctive for Aorist action) had already developed in the classical period and has continued through Hellenistic usage up to modern Greek.

καί, ὅπερ λέγω, μὴ θορυβεῖτε, ὦ ἄνδρες. (Pl.*Ap.* 21 A.)
And, as I say, do not be making a disturbance, O men.

Imperfect Imperative.

καί μοι, ὦ ἄνδρες Ἀθηναῖοι, μὴ θορυβήσητε, μηδ' ἐὰν δόξω τι ὑμῖν μέγα λέγειν· (Pl.*Ap.* 20 E.)

And please, O men of Athens, do not make a disturbance, not even if I seem to you to be telling something exaggerated.

Aorist Subjunctive.

It is sometimes suggested that μή with the Imperfect Imperative implies a command to *stop* doing something, while μή with the Aorist Subjunctive implies a command *not* to *start* doing something. This view sometimes suits the circumstances of a particular passage, but the basic principle seems to be the usual distinction of Aspects, as stated above. Moreover, there does not always seem to be any significant difference in function between Imperfect Imperative and Aorist Subjunctive in negative commands. An author's choice may depend partly on established idiom and partly on the meaning of a particular word, as well as on the distinction of Aspect.

10.3. Virtual Commands

Various idioms using Future Indicative, Aorist Subjunctive, and Imperfect or Aorist Optative may have the function of commands.

10.3.1. Future Indicative (Positive)

πρὸς ταῦτα **πράξεις** οἷον ἂν θέλῃς· (S.*OC* 956.)
In view of this [you will] do what you like.

10.3.2. Future Indicative (Negative: οὐ)

ξεῖνε, κακῶς ἀνδρῶν τοξάζεαι· **οὐκέτ'** ἀέθλων
ἄλλων **ἀντιάσεις**· νῦν τοι σῶς αἰπὺς ὄλεθρος. (Hom.*Od*. 22.27–28.)

*Stranger, wrongly you shoot at men; **never again [will you] take part** in other contests; now indeed your sheer destruction <is> assured.*

10.3.3. Future Indicative (Negative Interrogative: οὐ ...;)

οὐκ ἄξεθ' ὡς τάχιστα; καὶ κατηρεφεῖ
τύμβῳ περιπτύξαντες, ὡς εἴρηκ' ἐγώ,
ἄφετε μόνην ἔρημον ... (S.*Ant*. 885–887.)

*[Will you not] take <her> as quickly as possible[?] And surrounding <her> with a vaulted tomb, as I have said,
leave her alone, deserted ...*

ἄφετε (Aor. Impv.) confirms the Imperative function of ἄξεθ' (ἄξετε, Fut. Indic.).

10.3.4. Future Indicative (Double Negative Interrogative: οὐ(...)μή ...;)

ὦ δεινὰ λέξας', **οὐχὶ συγκλήσεις** στόμα
καὶ **μὴ μεθήσεις** αὖθις αἰσχίστους λόγους; (E.*Hipp.* 498–499.)

*O <you>, having said terrible things, **will you not shut up** your mouth and **not emit** most shameful words again?*

Future Indicative occurs in both coordinate clauses, which are joined by καί. The first negative (οὐκ) negates the whole sentence. The second negative (μή) is functionally subordinate to the first negative and negates the second clause: 'Will you not shut up ... and will you not not emit ...?' (i.e. 'Shut up ... and do not emit ...').

οὐ μὴ φλυαρήσεις ἔχων, ὦ Ξανθία,
ἀλλ' ἀράμενος οἴσεις πάλιν τὰ στρώματα; (Ar.*Ra.* 524–525.)

***Do not** keep on **being silly**, O Xanthias,
but pick up and carry the trappings back.*

Lit. 'Will you not not keep on being silly ..., but will you not carry ...?' Again, οὐ negates the whole sentence, μή further negates the first coordinate clause and the second clause is introduced by ἀλλά (not καί).

10.3.5. οὐ μή with Aorist Subjunctive

οὐ μὴ σκώψῃς μηδὲ ποιήσῃς ἅπερ οἱ τρυγοδαίμονες οὗτοι,
ἀλλ' εὐφήμει· (Ar.*Nu.* 296–297.)

***Do not joke nor do** what these comic poets do,
but keep silent.*

In this sentence, after an initial negative command with οὐ μή and the Aorist Subjunctive, a second negative command is added by μηδέ (also with Aor. Subj.), and a contrasting positive command follows with ἀλλά and Imperfect Imperative.

The origin and explanation of the constructions in §§10.3.4 and 10.3.5 are disputed. The issue is complicated by variant readings in manuscripts and emendations by editors, for example, -ῃς and -εις.

10.3.6. Optative with ἄν

τοῦτ᾽ **οὐκέτ᾽ ἂν πύθοιο**, μηδὲ λιπάρει. (A.*Pr.* 520.)
[You would] no longer make this enquiry, and do not persist.

The Imperative form λιπάρει in the second clause confirms the Imperative function of the Optative with ἄν in the first clause. Negative οὐ is used with this potential Optative.

Such sentences having Optative with ἄν are usually punctuated as statements, although they would often make sense as questions.

λέγοις ἂν ὡς τάχιστα, καὶ τάχ᾽ εἴσομαι. (A.*Th.* 261.)
[Would you] speak as soon as possible[?] And I shall soon know.

10.4. Reported Commands

10.4.1. Reported Commands with Infinitive

Commands, requests and exhortations are most often reported in an Infinitive phrase as direct Object of a verb of commanding. Most verbs of commanding have a second direct Object in the Accusative, denoting the person who is commanded to do something. Instead of this second direct Object, particular verbs may have a Genitive of Separation or a Dative indirect Object.

The Aspect of the Infinitive in a reported command reflects the Aspect of the Imperative in the presumed direct command. And the Number of the noun or pronoun in the Accusative Object (or Genitive or Dative) of the reported command reflects the Number of the Imperative of the presumed direct command. The negative with the Infinitive is μή.

ἤδη κελεύω τούσδ᾽ ἀπὸ γνώμης φέρειν
ψῆφον δικαίαν ...; (A.*Eu.* 674–675.)

*Do I now command these <jurors> to cast a just vote
on the basis of their judgment ...?*

Acc. (pl.) and (Imperf.) Infin.

Direct form: φέρετε.

... αὐτοῦ τε Κύρου ἐδέοντο ὡς προθυμοτάτου πρὸς τὸν πόλεμον γενέσθαι. (X.*Cyr.* 1.5.2.)

... and they begged Cyrus himself to become as enthusiastic as possible for the war.

Genitive (sg.) and (Aor.) Infinitive.

Direct form: γενοῦ.

οὐ γὰρ ὅτι τοὺς ἀδικοῦντας ἐκόλαζον, ἀλλ' ἐνίοις καὶ προσέταττον ἐξαμαρτάνειν. (Isoc. 18.17.)

For they were not only not punishing those acting unjustly, but they were actually instructing some to do wrong.

Dative (pl.) and (Imperf.) Infinitive.

Direct form: ἐξαμαρτάνετε. (For οὐ(...)ὅτι meaning 'not only not'; see Smyth, 1956, §2763.b.)

ὃ δὲ ἐπιλέξας τῶν ἀστῶν τοὺς ὑπώπτυε μάλιστα ἐς ἐπανάστασιν ἀπέπεμπε τεσσαράκοντα τριήρεσι, ἐντειλάμενος Καμβύσῃ ὀπίσω τούτους μὴ ἀποπέμπειν. (Hdt. 3.44.2.)

And he, having picked out from the citizens those whom he most suspected with respect to an uprising, sent them away on forty triremes, instructing Cambyses not to send these <men> back again.

Dative (sg.) and (Imperf.) Infinitive with negative μή.

Direct form: τούτους μὴ ἀπόπεμπε. τούς (Ionic) = οὕς (Attic).

10.4.2. Reported Commands with ὅπως

In addition to the more common Infinitive construction, some verbs of commanding may sometimes have as their Object a clause introduced by ὅπως. In Primary sequence, ὅπως is followed either by Future Indicative or by the Subjunctive (sometimes with ἄν). In Past sequence, ὅπως is followed by the Optative. Vivid constructions, using Subjunctive or Future Indicative in Past sequence, also occur. The negative is μή.

As the Object of a verb of commanding, these ὅπως clauses are noun clauses. Contrary to Smyth (1956, §2218), the ὅπως clause is best understood as merely stating the content of the command, not 'the purpose in giving it' as well. Purpose clauses with ὅπως are adverbial clauses, not noun clauses.

τοῖς οὖν ἄρχουσι καὶ πρῶτον καὶ μάλιστα **παραγγέλλει** ὁ θεός, **ὅπως μηδενὸς** οὕτω φύλακες ἀγαθοὶ **ἔσονται μηδ᾽** οὕτω σφόδρα φυλάξουσι **μηδὲν** ὡς τοὺς ἐκγόνους … (Pl.R. 415 B.)

*Therefore the god both first and foremost **commands** the rulers **to be** good guardians of **nothing** so much as the children, and to guard carefully **nothing** so much <as them>…*

ὅπως with Future Indicative and negative μή compounds in Primary sequence.

λύουσι γάρ, ἔφη, οἱ ἕνδεκα Σωκράτη καὶ **παραγγέλλουσιν ὅπως ἂν** τῇδε τῇ ἡμέρᾳ **τελευτᾷ**. (Pl.Phd. 59 E.)

*'For the Eleven', he said, 'are unchaining Socrates and **are giving orders that he is to die** on this day'.*

ὅπως with Subjunctive and ἄν in Primary sequence.

… **ἐδέοντό** τε τῶν στρατηγῶν **ὅκως ἀπάγοιεν** ὑφέας ὀπίσω … (Hdt. 9.117.)

*… and **they begged** their generals to **lead** [OR: that they should lead] them **away** <and take them> back again …*

ὅκως (Attic ὅπως) with Optative in Past sequence.

… καλέσας αὐτὸν Δημοκήδεα **ἐδέετο** αὐτοῦ **ὅκως** ἐξηγησάμενος πᾶσαν καὶ ἐπιδέξας τὴν Ἑλλάδα τοῖσι Πέρσῃσι ὀπίσω **ἥξει**· (Hdt. 3.135.2.)

*… summoning Democedes himself, **he required** of him **that**, when he had shown the way and had displayed all Greece to the Persians, **he should come back**.*

Vivid construction with Future Indicative in Past sequence.

Hom.Od. 3.327 seems to be the only instance of ἵνα + Subjunctive expressing a reported request or command prior to the later classical or Hellenistic periods.

References

Goodwin (1889), *Syntax of the moods and tenses of the Greek verb*, §§237, 250–251, 259–260, 294, 297–298, 355–357, 746–747, Appendix II (pp. 389–397).

Smyth (1956), *Greek grammar*, §§1800, 1830, 1835–1836, 1840–1841, 1918–1919, 1991–1992, 1996–1998, 2155, 2210, 2218, 2754, 2756–2757.

Goodwin (1889, Appendix II) has not convinced all his contemporaries nor all subsequent scholars.

EXERCISE 10

Translate the following passages. The Imperative function of virtual commands should be made clear in translation.

1. καί μοι τὰ μὲν παρόντα μὴ δύρεσθ' ἄχη,
   πέδοι δὲ βᾶσαι τὰς προσερπούσας τύχας
   ἀκούσαθ'…

(ὀ)δύρεσθαι	to lament (for) (+ Acc.)
ἄχος, -ους, τό	pain
πέδοι (adv.)	(on) to the ground
προσέρπειν	to approach
ἀκούσαθ'	ἀκούσατε

2. στείχοις ἂν ἤδη· καὶ γὰρ ἐξεπίστασαι
   τά γ' ἐν δόμοισιν ὡς ἔχοντα τυγχάνει.

ὡς	how (Introduces reported question after ἐπίστασαι.)

3. μή μοι θάνῃς σὺ κοινά, μηδ' ἃ μὴ 'θιγες
   ποιοῦ σεαυτῆς·

κοινά (adverbial Acc. neut.)	in common (with), jointly (with) (+ Dat.)
μηδέ	and (…) not
θιγγάνειν	to touch, to handle
ποιεῖσθαι (Mid.)	to make, to claim as; to regard as (here + Possessive Gen.)

INTERMEDIATE ANCIENT GREEK LANGUAGE

4. Euadne: ᾄσσω θανόντος Καπανέως τήνδ' ἐς πυράν.
   Iphis: ὦ θύγατερ, οὐ μὴ μῦθον ἐπὶ πολλοὺς ἐρεῖς;

ἀΐσσειν, ᾄσσειν	to move quickly, to hurry
Καπανεύς, -έως, ὁ	here Possessive Gen.
πυρά, -ᾶς, ἡ	pyre
μῦθος, -ου, ὁ	statement, announcement
ἐπί (+ Acc.)	before, in the presence of (Some editors emend to ἐς.)

5. αἱ μὲν γὰρ πλεῖσται πόλεις ἀφεῖσαι παιδεύειν ὅπως τις ἐθέλει τοὺς ἑαυτοῦ παῖδας ... προστάττουσιν αὐτοῖς μὴ κλέπτειν μηδὲ ἁρπάζειν ...

| ἀφιέναι | to allow |
| ὅπως (+ Indic.) | as |

6. καὶ Σεύθην ἐκέλευον παραγγεῖλαι ὅπως εἰς τὰ Ἑλληνικὰ στρατόπεδα μηδεὶς τῶν Θρᾳκῶν εἴσεισι νυκτός·

καί	And (Links whole sentence to preceding.)
Σεύθης, -ου, ὁ	Seuthes
ἐκέλευον	3rd pers. pl.
στρατόπεδον, -ου, τό	camp
εἰσιέναι	to go into, to enter (Pres. Indic. equivalent to Fut.)

7. Therefore, from a distance catching sight of us having set off for home, Polemarchus the son of Cephalus told his slave to run and tell [us] to wait for him. And the slave, catching me from behind by the cloak, said, 'Polemarchus tells you [pl.] to wait'.

from a distance	πόρρωθεν
to catch sight of	καθορᾶν, Aor. κατιδεῖν (+ Acc.)
to set off	ὁρμᾶσθαι
Polemarchus	Πολέμαρχος, -ου, ὁ
Cephalus	Κέφαλος, -ου, ὁ
to run	τρέχειν, Aor. δραμεῖν

to wait (for)	περιμένειν (+ Acc.)
to catch (someone) by (something)	λαμβάνεσθαι (Mid.) (+ double Gen.)
from behind	ὄπισθεν
cloak	ἱμάτιον, -ου, τό
'Polemarchus tells …'	Use direct speech in Greek.

LESSON 11
Wishes

11.1. Wishes for the Future

Wishes for the future are regularly expressed by a verb in the Optative Mood. The usual Aspects are either Imperfect for continuous action or Aorist for momentary action. The Perfect Aspect is normally limited to verbs which are used in the Perfect with an Imperfect meaning. The Intentive ('Fut.') Optative is not used for wishes. Introductory particles often occur with this construction. The negative is μή.

11.1.1. Optative Alone

στέργοι δέ με σωφροσύνα, δώρημα κάλλιστον θεῶν· (E.Med. 636.)
And **may** moderation, finest gift of the gods, **favour** me.

εἰ δ' οἶδ' ἁμαρτάνουσι, **μὴ** πλείω κακὰ
πάθοιεν ἢ καὶ δρῶσιν ἐκδίκως ἐμέ. (S.Ant. 927–928.)

But if these men are making a mistake, **may they suffer no** more harm than they are unjustly causing me.

Negative μή.

11.1.2. εἰ γάρ or εἴθε with Optative

The usual Epic spelling of these terms is αἲ γάρ and αἴθε. After Homer, εἰ γάρ is found mainly in tragedy and especially in responses.

εἰ γὰρ τύχοιεν ὧν φρονοῦσι πρὸς θεῶν
αὐτοῖς ἐκείνοις ἀνοσίοις κομπάσμασιν· (A. Th. 550–551.)

May they obtain from the gods what they intend,
by reason of those very boasts <so> impious.

ὧν = τούτων ἅ.

αἴθ' οὕτως, Εὔμαιε, φίλος Διὶ πατρὶ **γένοιο**
ὡς ἐμοί, ὅττι μ' ἔπαυσας ἄλης καὶ ὀϊζύος αἰνῆς.
(Hom.*Od.* 15.341–342.)

May you, *Eumaeus*, ***become*** *so dear to father Zeus*
as to me, because you stopped me from my wandering and my dreadful misery!

11.1.3. εἰ or ὡς with Optative

The use of εἰ or ὡς with Optative is more restricted. εἰ alone occurs mainly in poetry, including Homer. An exclamatory use of ὡς also occurs in poetry, especially Homer.

εἴ μοι **ξυνείη** φέροντι μοῖρα τὰν
    εὔσεπτον ἁγνείαν λόγων
ἔργων τε πάντων … (S.*OT* 863–865.)

May *destiny* ***be with*** *me as I attain*
    reverent purity in all
words and actions …

ὡς ἔρις ἔκ τε θεῶν ἔκ τ' ἀνθρώπων **ἀπόλοιτο** … (Hom.*Il.* 18.107.)
May *strife* ***perish*** *from among gods and men …*

11.1.4. πῶς ἄν and τίς ἄν with Optative

Sentences, which are in form questions introduced by πῶς ἄν or τίς ἄν with the Optative, may function as wishes. The question 'How would I …?' is equivalent to the wish 'May I …'. And the question 'Who would …?' is equivalent to the wish 'May someone …'. The negative in these virtual wishes is μή, not οὐ as in genuine potential Optative constructions.

ὦ Ζεῦ, προγόνων προπάτωρ,
πῶς ἄν τὸν αἱμυλώτατον,
ἐχθρὸν ἄλημα, τούς τε δισσ-
άρχας ὀλέσσας βασιλῆς,
τέλος **θάνοιμι** καὐτός; (S.*Aj.* 387–391.)

O Zeus, forefather of my forbears,
may I, *after destroying that most wily man,*
a hateful trickster, and the jointly
ruling kings, <may I>
finally ***die*** *myself.*

τίς ἂν δῆτά μοι, **τίς ἂν** φιλοπόνων
ἁλιαδᾶν ἔχων ἀΰπνους ἄγρας
    ἢ τίς Ὀλυνπιάδων
        θεᾶν, ἢ ῥυτῶν
Βοσπορίων ποταμῶν,
τὸν ὠμόθυμον εἴ ποθι
        πλαζόμενον λεύσσων
ἀπύοι; (S.*Aj.* 879–887.)

May some one, then, ***some one*** of the hard-working
fishermen maintaining sleepless searches
    or one of the Olympian
        goddesses, or of the rivers
flowing into the Bosporus,
if seeing the savage-hearted man
        wandering somewhere,
tell me.

11.2. Unfulfilled Wishes for the Present and the Past

The negative in all the following constructions is μή.

11.2.1. εἰ γάρ or εἴθε with Indicative

This Indicative construction does not yet occur in Homer.

11.2.1.1. Wishes for the Present

Unfulfilled wishes for the present with εἰ γάρ or εἴθε use the Past Imperfect Indicative.

εἰ γὰρ τοσαύτην δύναμιν **εἶχον** ὥστε σὴν
ἐς φῶς πορεῦσαι νερτέρων ἐκ δωμάτων
γυναῖκα καί σοι τήνδε πορσῦναι χάριν. (E.*Alc.* 1072–1074.)

If only I had (now) enough strength to convey
your wife to the light from the dwellings below
and to provide this favour for you.

εἴθ' εἶχε φωνὴν εὔφρον' ἀγγέλου δίκην ... (A.*Ch.* 195.)
If only it had (now) a kindly voice in the manner of a messenger ...

(Electra speaks about the lock of hair found at Agamemnon's tomb.)

11.2.1.2. Wishes for the Past

Unfulfilled wishes for the past with εἰ γάρ or εἴθε use the Past Aorist Indicative.

εἰ γάρ μ' ὑπὸ γῆν νέρθεν θ' Ἅιδου
τοῦ νεκροδέγμονος εἰς ἀπέραντον
Τάρταρον **ἧκεν** δεσμοῖς ἀλύτοις
ἀγρίως πελάσας ... (A.*Pr.* 153–155.)

If only, having savagely put me in inescapable bonds,
he had sent me under the earth
and beneath Hades, who receives the dead,
to boundless Tartarus ...

ἰὼ Λαΐειον ὦ τέκνον,
εἴθε σ' **εἴθε** σε
μήποτ' **εἰδόμαν**· (S.*OT* 1216–1218.)

Ah! O child of Laius,
if only, if only
I had never seen you.

11.2.2. ὤφελον with Infinitive

Unfulfilled wishes for the present or the past may also be expressed by ὤφελον with an Infinitive. ὤφελον is first person singular Past Aorist Indicative of ὀφείλειν 'to owe'. The idiomatic English equivalent of ὤφελον is 'I ought'. 'Ought' is itself a past form of 'owe' in English, and functions as an Imperfect Subjunctive ('would owe'). In Homer, besides the Past Aorist Indicative ὤφελον, the Past Imperfect Indicative ὤφελλον occurs; both forms may appear without augment, ὄφελον, ὄφελλον. Other forms besides first person singular occur.

11.2.2.1. Wishes for the Present

Unfulfilled wishes for the present with ὤφελον use the Imperfect Infinitive.

ἀλλ' **ὤφελε** μὲν Κῦρος **ζῆν**· (X.*An.* 2.1.4.)
*Oh, **if only** Cyrus **were alive**.*

Lit. 'Oh, Cyrus ought to be alive'.

11.2.2.2. Wishes for the Past

Unfulfilled wishes for the past with ὤφελον generally use the Aorist Infinitive, rarely the Perfect Infinitive. If the reference is to past continuous or repeated action, the Imperfect Infinitive may be used.

ἔμπας τις αὐτὴν ἄλλος **ὤφελεν λαχεῖν**. (A.*Pr.* 48.)
*Nevertheless, **if only** someone else **had obtained** it.*

λαχεῖν (Aor. Infin.) is the usual construction. αὐτήν refers to Hephaestus's τέχνη.

Ἀτρεΐδη κύδιστε, ἄναξ ἀνδρῶν Ἀγάμεμνον,
μὴ **ὄφελες λίσσεσθαι** ἀμύμονα Πηλεΐωνα,
μυρία δῶρα διδούς· (Hom.*Il.* 9.697–699.)

Most honoured son of Atreus, lord of men Agamemnon,
***if only you had** not **entreated** the blameless son of Peleus,*
offering ten thousand gifts.

Lit. '…you ought not to have entreated…'; λίσσεσθαι (Imperf. Infin.) alludes to repeated or continuous action in the past.

11.2.2.3. Introductory Particles with ὤφελ(λ)ον

εἰ γάρ or εἴθε may introduce a wish expressed by ὤφελον with Infinitive. ὡς is also often used in Homer and rarely in Attic poetry.

Δύσπαρι, εἶδος ἄριστε, γυναιμανές, ἠπεροπευτά,
αἴθ' ὄφελες ἄγονός τ' **ἐμέναι** ἄγαμός τ' **ἀπολέσθαι**.
(Hom.*Il.* 3.39–40.)

Bad Paris, excellent in appearance, mad for women, deceiver,
***if only you were** unborn and **had perished** unmarried.*

αἴθ' ὄφελες (Past Aor. Indic.) with ἐμέναι (Infin. 'to be'), then with ἀπολέσθαι (Aor. Infin.), expresses an unfulfilled wish for the present, then for the past.

ὡς ὄφελον θανέειν καὶ πότμον **ἐπισπεῖν**
αὐτοῦ ἐν Αἰγύπτῳ· (Hom.*Od.* 14.274–275.)

*If only I had died and had met my fate
there in Egypt!*

ὡς ὄφελον (Past Aor. Indic) with θανέειν and ἐπισπεῖν (Aor. Infin.; Imperf. ἐφέπειν).

Lit. 'How I ought to have died…!'

…ὥς μ' **ὄφελ'** ἤματι τῷ ὅτε με πρῶτον τέκε μήτηρ
οἴχεσθαι προφέρουσα κακὴ ἀνέμοιο θύελλα
εἰς ὄρος ἢ εἰς κῦμα πολυφλοίσβοιο θαλάσσης …
(Hom.*Il.* 6.345–347.)

*…if only on that day, when first my mother bore me,
a bad squall of wind had carried me off and gone
into a mountain or into the swell of the loud-roaring sea …*

ὡς … ὄφελ(ε) (Past Aor. Indic.) with οἴχεσθαι (Imperf. Infin. with Perf. sense).

Lit. 'how a bad squall … ought to have gone …'

11.2.3. An Additional Homeric Construction

In Homer, although the constructions in §11.2.1 are not yet used, unfulfilled wishes for the Present are sometimes expressed by the Imperfect Optative. These wishes are usually introduced by εἰ γάρ or εἴθε.

εἴθ' ὣς **ἡβώοιμι** βίη δέ μοι ἔμπεδος **εἴη**,
ὡς ὁπότ' Ἠλείοισι καὶ ἡμῖν νεῖκος ἐτύχθη
ἀμφὶ βοηλασίῃ … (Hom.*Il.* 11.670–672.)

*If only I were thus young and my strength were firm,
as when a quarrel arose between the Eleans and us
over cattle-rustling …*

11.3. Reported Wishes

Wishes may be reported in an Infinitive phrase after verbs such as βούλεσθαι, (ἐ)θέλειν and ζητεῖν. When the Subject of the Infinitive is the same as the Subject of the verb of wishing, it is usually not expressed in Greek. If it is expressed, it is Nominative as in §11.4, second example (where κἀγώ = καὶ ἐγώ). When the Subject of the Infinitive is different to the Subject of the verb of wishing, it is expressed in the Accusative.

γράψαι δὲ **βουλόμεθα** καὶ ὡς δεῖ ὡπλίσθαι τὸν μέλλοντα ἐφ᾽ ἵππου κινδυνεύειν. (X.*Eq.* 12.1.)

*And **we want to describe** also how the man, who is going to face danger on horseback, needs to have been armed.*

βούλεσθαι + Infinitive only.

οὐ γάρ **σε βουλόμεθα** οὐδὲν ἄχαρι πρὸς Ἀθηναίων **παθεῖν** ἐόντα πρόξεινόν τε καὶ φίλον. (Hdt. 8.143.3.)

*For **we do** not **want you to suffer** anything unpleasant from the Athenians, since you are our patron and friend.*

βούλεσθαι + Accusative and Infinitive.

11.4. Reported Wishes Instead of Direct Wishes

An unfulfilled wish for the present or the past is occasionally expressed by the Past Imperfect Indicative ἐβουλόμην with Imperfect Infinitive (referring to the present) or Aorist Infinitive (referring to the past). This idiom expresses the wish less directly and therefore more gently.

ἐβουλόμην μὲν οὖν καὶ τὴν βουλὴν τοὺς πεντακοσίους καὶ τὰς ἐκκλησίας ὑπὸ τῶν ἐφεστηκότων ὀρθῶς **διοικεῖσθαι** καὶ τοὺς νόμους οὓς ἐνομοθέτησεν ὁ Σόλων περὶ τῆς τῶν ῥητόρων εὐκοσμίας **ἰσχύειν** ... (Aeschin. 3.2.)

*Well then, **I wish** that both the council of the five hundred and the assemblies **were** (now) **being** properly **organised** by those in charge, and that the laws which Solon framed concerning the proper behaviour of public speakers **were** (now) **in force** ...*

διοικεῖσθαι, ἰσχύειν: Imperfect Infinitive.

ἐβουλόμην, ὦ ἄνδρες, ὥσπερ Ξεναίνετος οὑτοσὶ δύναται ψευδῆ λέγειν θαρραλέως, οὕτω κἀγὼ τἀληθῆ πρὸς ὑμᾶς περὶ ὧν ἀμφισβητοῦμεν εἰπεῖν **δυνηθῆναι**· (Is. 10.1.)

***I wish**, O men, that, just as Xenaenetus here can confidently tell lies, so **I** too **could have** told you the truth about the points on which we disagree.*

δυνηθῆναι: Aorist Infinitive.

This idiom is made less direct by the use of ἄν with ἐβουλόμην.

ἐβουλόμην μέντ' **ἂν** αὐτοὺς οὕτω προθύμους **εἶναι** σῴζειν τὴν πόλιν, ὥσπερ οὗτοι ἀπολλύναι· (Lys. 12.86.)

*But **I wish** that they **were** (now) so eager to save the city, as these men <are eager > to destroy it.*

Lit. 'But I would (now) be wishing …'

11.5. Interrogative Wishes Combined with Deliberative Subjunctive

Classical Greek uses a particular idiom corresponding to the English question: 'Do you want me to do this?' The verb of wishing is regularly second person (sg. or pl.) and the verb of doing is regularly first person (sg. or pl.). In prose, βούλεσθαι is used as the verb of wishing; in verse, both βούλεσθαι and (ἐ)θέλειν are used. The structure of these questions is coordinate (paratactic)—'Do you wish it? Am I to do it?'

βούλῃ τὸ πρᾶγμα τοῖς θεαταῖσιν **φράσω**; (Ar.*Eq.* 36.)
***Do you want me to tell** the matter to the spectators?*

Lit. 'Do you want? Am I to tell …?'

                        ὦ σεμνὰς πλάκας
ναίοντες ὀρέων, **θέλετε θηρασώμεθα**
Πενθέως Ἀγαύην μητέρ' ἐκ βακχευμάτων
χάριν τ' ἄνακτι θώμεθα; (E.*Ba.* 718–721.)

> O <you>, inhabiting
> the holy plateaus of the mountains, **do you want us to hunt**
> Agaue mother of Pentheus from her Bacchic rites
> and do a favour to our master?

Lit. 'Do you want? Are we to hunt …?'

References

Denniston (1954), *The Greek particles*, pp. 89–95 (εἰ γάρ).

Goodwin (1889), *Syntax of the moods and tenses of the Greek verb*, §§246, 287–288, 720–739.

Smyth (1956), *Greek grammar*, §§1780–1782, 1789, 1806, 1814–1815, 1832, 2156.

EXERCISE 11

Translate the following passages. All expressions which may have the function of a wish should be translated as wishes.

1. μηδάμ' ὁ πάντα νέμων
   θεῖτ' ἐμᾷ γνώμᾳ κράτος ἀντίπαλον Ζεύς …

μηδαμά	*never* (accent affected by elision)
νέμειν	*to control, to manage*
γνώμη, -ης, ἡ	*will* (here with Doric spelling)
ἀντίπαλος, -ον	*in opposition to, against* (+ Dat.) (here predicative)

2. εἰ γὰρ γενοίμην, τέκνον, ἀντὶ σοῦ νεκρός.

3. Ζεῦ πάτερ, αἴθ' ὅσα εἶπε τελευτήσειεν ἅπαντα
   Ἀλκίνοος·

Ἀλκίνοος, -ου, ὁ	*Alcinous*

4. ὦ τέκνα τέκνα, πῶς ἄν, εἴ τις ἔντοπος,
   τὸν πάντ' ἄριστον δεῦρο Θησέα πόροι;

ἔντοπος, -ον	at hand
πάντ(α)	neut. pl. adj. as Acc. of Respect
Θησεύς, -έως, ὁ	*Theseus*
πορεῖν (Aor.)	*to bring* (usually, *to provide*)

5.   ὦ πάτερ πάτερ,
   τίς ἂν θεῶν σοι τόνδ' ἄριστον ἄνδρ' ἰδεῖν
   δοίη, τὸν ἡμᾶς δεῦρο προσπέμψαντά σοι;

διδόναι	*to grant, to allow* (+ Dat. and Infin.)
προσπέμπειν	*to conduct (to)* (+ Dat.)

6. εἴθ' ἦν ἐμαυτὸν προσβλέπειν ἐναντίον
   στάνθ', ὡς ἐδάκρυσ' οἷα πάσχομεν κακά.

εἶναι	*to be <possible>*
ἐναντίος, -α, -ον	*opposite*
στάνθ'	στάντα (Acc. sg. masc.)
ὡς ἐδάκρυσ(α)	*so that I might lament* (Unfulfilled Purpose clause with Indic., dependent on unfulfilled wish [Smyth, 1956, §2185.c; Goodwin, 1889, §333]).

7. εἴθ' ηὕρομεν σ', Ἄδμητε, μὴ λυπούμενον.

8.   ... αἴθ' ὤφελλες ἀεικελίου στρατοῦ ἄλλου
   σημαίνειν ...

ἀεικέλιος, -α, -ον	*inferior*
σημαίνειν	*to be in command (of)* (+ Gen.)

9. καὶ μηδὲ σαυτῆς γ' ἐκμαθεῖν ζήτει πόνους.

μηδέ	*not ... either*
πόνος, -ου, ὁ	*trouble*

LESSON 11. WISHES

10. Astyages, wishing the boy to dine as pleasantly as possible, was setting all sorts of foods before him.

Astyages	Ἀστυάγης, -ους, ὁ
to dine	δειπνεῖν
to set (Acc.) *before* (Dat.)	προσάγειν
all sorts of	παντοδαποί, -αί, -ά
food	βρῶμα, -ατος, τό

11. And I [would] wish, O council, that Simon had the same attitude as I …

I [would] wish	Use Past Imperf. Indic. of βούλεσθαι with ἄν.
Simon	Σίμων, -ωνος, ὁ
same … as	αὐτός, -ή, -όν (+ Dat.)
attitude	γνώμη, -ης, ἡ

12. Do you [pl.], therefore, want me … to converse with you to the accompaniment of the flute?

to converse (with)	διαλέγεσθαι (Mid.; also Aor. Pass.) (+ Dat.)
to the accompaniment of	ὑπό + Acc.
flute	αὐλός, -οῦ, ὁ

LESSON 12
Directly Reported Speech

All speaking or writing may be directly reported in the exact words of the original speaker or writer. The following sections quote examples from a range of genres and periods.

12.1. Homer

Normally, the speeches in the Homeric epics were formally introduced. And either their conclusion was marked, or the immediate response of the next speaker was introduced.

πολλὰ δ' ἔπειτ' ἀπάνευθε κιὼν **ἠρᾶθ' ὁ γεραιὸς Ἀπόλλωνι ἄνακτι**, τὸν ἠΰκομος τέκε Λητώ·
κλῦθί μευ, ἀργυρότοξ', ὃς Χρύσην ἀμφιβέβηκας
Κίλλαν τε ζαθέην Τενέδοιό τε ἶφι ἀνάσσεις,
Σμινθεῦ, εἴ ποτέ τοι χαρίεντ' ἐπὶ νηὸν ἔρεψα,
ἢ εἰ δή ποτέ τοι κατὰ πίονα μηρί' ἔκηα
ταύρων ἠδ' αἰγῶν, τόδε μοι κρήηνον ἐέλδωρ·
τίσειαν Δαναοὶ ἐμὰ δάκρυα σοῖσι βέλεσσιν.
ὣς ἔφατ' εὐχόμενος, τοῦ δ' ἔκλυε Φοῖβος Ἀπόλλων ...
(Hom.*Il.* 1.35–43.)

And then, going far away, **he, the old man,** *earnestly* **prayed to lord Apollo,** *whom lovely-haired Leto bore:*
'Hear me, you with the silver bow, who have taken your stand over Chryse
and sacred Cilla and rule with strength over Tenedos,
Smintheus, if ever I roofed over a shrine pleasing to you,
or if indeed ever I burned up for you fat thighs
of bulls and goats, fulfil this wish for me:
may the Danaans pay for my tears by your arrows'.
So he spoke as he prayed, *and Phoebus Apollo heard him ...*

12.2. Drama

All dramatic dialogue is, by its nature, direct speech; but it is not directly reported speech. However, in drama short passages of direct speech may be quoted within a longer speech. Most commonly, this may occur within a messenger's speech.

Πενθεὺς δ' ὁ τλήμων θῆλυν οὐχ ὁρῶν ὄχλον
ἔλεξε τοιάδ'· ὦ ξέν', οὗ μὲν ἕσταμεν,
οὐκ ἐξικνοῦμαι μαινάδων ὄσσοις νόθων·
ὄχθων δ' ἔπ', ἀμβὰς ἐς ἐλάτην ὑψαύχενα,
ἴδοιμ' ἂν ὀρθῶς μαινάδων αἰσχρουργίαν. (E.*Ba.* 1058–1062, within the speech 1043–1152.)

*But **Pentheus**, the poor man, not seeing the female crowd,*
***spoke in the following way**: 'O stranger, <from> where we are standing*
I do not reach with my eyes the spurious maenads;
but on a mound, getting up into a stately fir-tree,
I would see properly the disgraceful-behaviour of the maenads'.

12.3. Historiography

The first passage of directly reported speech in Thucydides's *History of the Peloponnesian War* is formally introduced, begins with an elaborate opening sentence, continues for five chapters and has its conclusion formally marked.

καταστάσης δὲ ἐκκλησίας ἐς ἀντιλογίαν ἦλθον· καὶ **οἱ μὲν Κερκυραῖοι ἔλεξαν τοιάδε**. δίκαιον, ὦ Ἀθηναῖοι, τοὺς μήτε εὐεργεσίας μεγάλης μήτε ξυμμαχίας προυφειλομένης ἥκοντας παρὰ τοὺς πέλας ἐπικουρίας, ὥσπερ καὶ ἡμεῖς νῦν, δεησομένους ἀναδιδάξαι πρῶτον, μάλιστα μὲν ὡς καὶ ξύμφορα δέονται, εἰ δὲ μή, ὅτι γε οὐκ ἐπιζήμια, ἔπειτα δὲ ὡς καὶ τὴν χάριν βέβαιον ἕξουσιν· ... **τοιαῦτα μὲν οἱ Κερκυραῖοι εἶπον**· (Th. 1.31.4–1.32.1; 1.36.4.)

*And when an assembly had been arranged, they came to put their arguments; and **the Corcyreans spoke in the following way**. '<It is> (only) fair, O Athenians, that those, who have come to their neighbours, when there is prior indebtedness neither for a great benefit nor for an alliance, to ask for aid, just as indeed we <have> now, should first explain, especially that they are actually making a request that is advantageous* [i.e. to those who are asked], *but* *otherwise, that at least <it is> one that is not disadvantageous <to them>, and secondly that they* [= providers] *will get gratitude that is sure; …'* **Such** *<were the words which>* **the Corcyreans spoke**.

12.4. Prose Quotation Formulae

In prose, short passages of reported speech are often marked by the insertion of a form of φάναι ('to say') after an opening word, phrase or clause.

ἢν μέντοι ἐγὼ γένωμαι στρατηγός, **ἔφη**, πολεμήσω σοι, ὦ Ἀγησίλαε, ὡς ἂν ἐγὼ δύνωμαι κράτιστα. (X.*Ages.* 3.5; biography.)

'But if I become general', **he said**, *'I shall make war on you, O Agesilaus, as forcefully as I possibly can'.*

ἔφην is listed in Liddell and Scott (1996) as (Past) second Aorist. In some grammars and in Montanari (2015), this form is treated as Past Imperfect. According to Smyth (1956, §788), ἔφην is both (Past) Imperfect and (Past) Aorist. Even those grammars which present the ἔφην forms as Past Imperfect may translate these forms as 'I said', etc. It is indeed usual to translate the ἔφην forms into English by a simple Past Tense, 'I said', etc.

Present and Past Imperfect forms of ἠμί ('I say') are used in the same way, but they occur only in first person singular and third person singular. These forms are regularly followed by δ(έ) (which serves no function) and then by the first and third person singular pronouns ἐγώ and ὅς, ἥ. The Past Imperfect forms function as a general Past Tense.

πρότερον δέ μοι, **ἦ δ' ὅς**, εἰπέ, σὺ αὐτὸς παρεγένου τῇ συνουσίᾳ ταύτῃ ἢ οὔ; (Pl.*Smp.* 172 B; philosophical dialogue.)

'But first tell me', **he said**, *'did you yourself attend this gathering or not?'*

12.5. ὅτι and ὡς as Quotation Markers

In prose, ὅτι (rarely ὡς) is sometimes used immediately before a passage of directly reported speech. In this usage, ὅτι has the function of quotation marks and should not be translated. This idiom is colloquial; it first occurs at Hdt. 2.115.4–6. The fact that the following example contains a directly reported statement, and not just a Vivid indirectly reported statement, is confirmed by the second person pronouns ὑμᾶς and ὑμῶν.

... ὁ τελευταῖος διαπλεύσας αὐτοῖς ἀπὸ τῶν ἐκ τῆς ἠπείρου Λακεδαιμονίων ἀνὴρ ἀπήγγειλεν **ὅτι** Λακεδαιμόνιοι κελεύουσιν ὑμᾶς αὐτοὺς περὶ ὑμῶν αὐτῶν βουλεύεσθαι μηδὲν αἰσχρὸν ποιοῦντας· (Th. 4.38.3.)

... the last man to sail across to them from the Spartans on the mainland reported: 'The Spartans order you yourselves to decide concerning yourselves, provided that you do nothing shameful'.

References

Goodwin (1889), *Syntax of the moods and tenses of the Greek verb*, §§662, 711.

Smyth (1956), *Greek grammar*, §§2589–2590.

EXERCISE 12

Translate the following passages.

1. καὶ τότε δή με ἔπεσσι προσηύδα πότνια Κίρκη·
   ταῦτα μὲν οὕτω πάντα πεπείρανται·

προσαυδᾶν	*to address*

2. ἐπεὶ δὲ μόχθων τέρματ' οὐκ ἐξήνυτον,
   ἔλεξ' Ἀγαύη· φέρε, περιστᾶσαι κύκλῳ
   πτόρθου λάβεσθε, μαινάδες, ...

μόχθος, -ου, ὁ	*labour*
ἐξανύ(τ)ειν	*to accomplish, to attain*
φέρε	*come on!* (sg. Impv. used also for pl.)
πτόρθος, -ου, ὁ	*sapling*
λαμβάνεσθαι (Mid.)	*to take hold (of)* (+ Partitive Gen.)

LESSON 12. DIRECTLY REPORTED SPEECH

3. παρελθὼν δὲ Σθενελαΐδας τελευταῖος, εἷς τῶν ἐφόρων τότε ὤν, ἔλεξεν τοῖς Λακεδαιμονίοις ὧδε. τοὺς μὲν λόγους τοὺς πολλοὺς τῶν Ἀθηναίων οὐ γιγνώσκω· ...

παρελθεῖν (Aor.)	to come forward
Σθενελαΐδας, -ου, ὁ	Sthenelaidas
ἔφορος, -ου, ὁ	ephor (one of five annual magistrates at Sparta)
Λακεδαιμόνιος, -α, -ον	Spartan

4. ταῦτα μὲν τοίνυν προθυμησόμεθα, ἔφη, οὕτω ποιεῖν· θάπτωμεν δέ σε τίνα τρόπον;
ὅπως ἄν, ἔφη, βούλησθε, ἐάνπερ γε λάβητέ με καὶ μὴ ἐκφύγω ὑμᾶς.

τοίνυν	well then
προθυμεῖσθαι (Mid.)	to be eager, to be keen (+ Infin.)
θάπτειν	to bury
τίνα (τρόπον)	delayed interrogative
The second speaker responds to the first.	

5. ἀλλὰ μὰ Δία, ἦν δ' ἐγώ, οὐκ οἶδα, ἀλλὰ τῷ ὄντι αὐτὸς εἰλιγγιῶ ὑπὸ τῆς τοῦ λόγου ἀπορίας ...

τῷ ὄντι	in reality
(ἐ)ἰλιγγιᾶν	to be(come) dizzy
ὑπό (+ Gen.)	under (the influence/effect of)
ἀπορία, -ας, ἡ	difficulty

6. προσελθόντες δέ μοι τῇ ὑστεραίᾳ Μέλητος καὶ Εὐφίλητος ἔλεγον ὅτι γεγένηται, ὦ Ἀνδοκίδη, καὶ πέπρακται ἡμῖν ταῦτα.

ὑστεραίᾳ	Understand ἡμέρᾳ (standard idiom)
γίγνεσθαι	to happen
ἡμῖν	Dat. of Agent with Perf. Pass. verb

7. '*I* know', he said, 'both that you had been born a private citizen, and that you are now a monarch'.

to have been born	γεγενῆσθαι (Perf. Pass.)
private citizen	ἰδιώτης, -ου, ὁ
monarch	τύραννος, -ου, ὁ

LESSON 13
Reported Statements with ὅτι or ὡς

13.1. Introduction

This Lesson deals with reported statements in the form of a Simple sentence and of the Main clause of a Complex sentence. The negative for these reported statements is regularly οὐ. (Subordinate clauses in reported discourse will be treated in Lesson 21.)

A statement may be reported indirectly after a verb of saying by means of a Subordinate clause introduced by ὅτι or ὡς. ὅτι is generally used after a positive leading verb. ὡς is likely to be used when the reported statement is open to doubt. ὅτι and ὡς are regularly used with λέγειν and εἰπεῖν, but rarely with φάναι (which normally takes an Infin. phrase; see Lesson 14).

13.2. Reported Statements in Primary Sequence

In Primary sequence, that is, after a verb of saying in Present or Future Time, the original Mood and Tense of direct speech are retained in the reported clause after ὅτι or ὡς. There may, however, be a change of person as in English idiom.

Directly reported statement: He says, '*I am* the king'.
Indirectly reported statement: He says that *he is* the king.

καὶ λέγουσιν ὅτι ἐπὶ τοῦτο ἔρχονται ... (X.*Cyr.* 1.2.6.)
And they say that they come for this purpose ...

Direct form: ἔρχονται, 'They come'; Present Indicative retained in reported form.

λέγει δ' ὡς ὑβριστής εἰμι καὶ βίαιος καὶ λίαν ἀσελγῶς διακείμενος ... (Lys. 24.15.)

And he says that I am insolent and violent and have a very outrageous attitude ...

Direct form: ὑβριστής ἐστι, 'He is insolent'; change of person in reported form. Here, the speechwriter uses ὡς rather than ὅτι, since he does not want his client to appear to admit the allegations against him.

ἴσως δ' Εὐθύνους ἐρεῖ..., ὅτι οὐκ ἄν ποτ' ἀδικεῖν ἐπιχειρῶν τὰ μὲν δύο μέρη τῆς παρακαταθήκης ἀπέδωκε ... (Isoc. 21.16.)

But perhaps Euthynus will say ..., that, if attempting to do wrong, he would not ever have paid back two-thirds of the deposit ...

Direct form: οὐκ ἄν ποτ' ... ἀπέδωκα, 'I would not ever ... have paid back'; Past Aorist Indicative with ἄν retained; change of person.

ἴσως οὖν εἴποιεν ἄν πολλοὶ τῶν φασκόντων φιλοσοφεῖν, ὅτι οὐκ ἄν ποτε ὁ δίκαιος ἄδικος γένοιτο ... (X.*Mem.* 1.2.19.)

Perhaps, therefore, many of those who claim to be philosophers would say, that the just <man> would not ever become unjust ...

Direct form: οὐκ ἄν ποτε ὁ δίκαιος ἄδικος γένοιτο, 'the just man would not ever become unjust'; Optative retained.

13.3. Reported Statements in Past Sequence

In Past sequence, that is, after a verb of saying in Past Time:

- Primary and Past Aorist Tenses of the Indicative are changed to the same Aspect of the Optative
- Past Aorist Indicative with ἄν denoting potentiality is retained
- Past Imperfect and Past Perfect Indicatives are usually retained
- all Optatives are retained.

εἶπον αὐτοῖς ὅτι νομίζοιμι μὲν διὰ τὸ πρᾶγμα Εὐφίλητον πονηρὸν εἶναι ... (And. 1.64.)

I told them that I thought that Euphiletus was wicked because of the action ...

Direct form: νομίζω, 'I think'; Imperfect Aspect is retained in reported form.

ἔλεξαν γὰρ ὡς ἐγὼ μηνύσαιμι περὶ τῶν μυστηρίων ... (And. 1.19.)
For they said that I had lodged information concerning the mysteries ...

LESSON 13. REPORTED STATEMENTS WITH ὅτι OR ὡς

Direct form: ἐμήνυσε, 'He lodged information'; Aorist Aspect is retained in reported form, with change of person. Here, Andocides uses ὡς, since he does not admit the allegation.

ἐπιλέγων δὲ τὸν λόγον τόνδε ταῦτα ἐνετέλλετο, ὡς, εἰ μὲν ἀπώλοντο οἱ κατάσκοποι, οὔτ' ἂν τὰ ἑωυτοῦ πρήγματα προεπύθοντο οἱ Ἕλληνες ἐόντα λόγου μέζω, οὔτ' ἄν τι τοὺς πολεμίους μέγα ἐσίναντο ἄνδρας τρεῖς ἀπολέσαντες· (Hdt. 7.147.1.)

And he was giving this command while explaining that, if the scouts had perished, neither would the Greeks have learnt in advance that his own importance was greater than common report, nor would they [= Persians] have done any great harm to their enemy by destroying three men.

Past Aorist Indicative with ἄν retained in reported form. The use of ὡς may be influenced by the potential nature of the expression.

ἐλθὼν δὲ ... ἐς τὴν Λακεδαίμονα, ἢν κατηγορήσωσιν οἱ περὶ τὸν Ἰσχαγόραν ὅτι οὐκ ἐπείθετο, ... ἐπειδὴ εὗρε κατειλημμένους, ... κατὰ τάχος ἐπορεύετο. (Th. 5.21.3.)

And coming ... to Sparta, in case the followers of Ischagoras made an accusation that he had not been obedient, ... when he found that they [= Spartans] had been bound <by the agreement>, ... he moved on with haste.

Direct form: οὐκ ἐπείθετο, 'He was not obedient'; Past Imperfect Indicative is retained in reported form.

Although the Past Imperfect Indicative of direct speech is usually retained in reported speech after ὅτι or ὡς, the Imperfect Optative does sometimes occur where the context is clear.

ἐπεὶ δὲ ἐψηφίσαντο αὐτῷ τὴν ἄδειαν, ἔλεγεν ὅτι ἐν τῇ οἰκίᾳ Πουλυτίωνος γίγνοιτο μυστήρια· (And. 1.12.)

And when they had voted immunity to him, he said that mysteries had been celebrated in the house of Poulytion.

In the context, it is clear that the speaker (in court) did not mean that mysteries were *currently* being celebrated, but that they had *previously* been (being) celebrated. Thus, the Imperfect Optative can be used without ambiguity.

κατέκλησαν δὲ τοῦ αὐτοῦ χειμῶνος καὶ Μακεδόνας Ἀθηναῖοι, Περδίκκᾳ ἐπικαλοῦντες … ὅτι … ἔψευστο τὴν ξυμμαχίαν … (Th. 5.83.4.)

And within the same winter the Athenians also blockaded the Macedonians, bringing an accusation against Perdiccas …, that … he had cheated the alliance …

Original Past Perfect Indicative is retained in the reported form.

Εὐρυβιάδης δὲ τὴν ἐναντίην ταύτῃ γνώμην ἐτίθετο, λέγων ὡς, εἰ λύσουσι τὰς σχεδίας, τοῦτ' ἂν μέγιστον πάντων σφεῖς κακὸν τὴν Ἑλλάδα ἐργασαίατο. (Hdt. 8.108.2.)

But Eurybiades put forward the opinion opposite to this one, saying that, if they disconnected the pontoons, they would thereby wreak the greatest trouble of all upon Greece.

Direct form: εἰ λύσομεν τὰς σχεδίας, τοῦτ' ἂν μέγιστον πάντων ἡμεῖς κακὸν Ἑλλάδα ἐργασαίμεθα, 'If we [shall] disconnect the pontoons, we would thereby wreak …' (Mixed Fut. Open, Fut. Unfulfilled Condition). Original potential Optative with ἄν is retained. τοῦτ(ο) is strictly direct Object, and μέγιστον … κακόν Predict Accusative ἐργασαίατο = ἐργάσαιντο (3rd pers. pl.).

13.4. Vivid Construction

The Optative Mood in Past sequence in reported statements is just beginning to be used in Aeschylus (earlier fifth century BCE). By the time of the late fifth to early fourth century BCE, usage still depends on the preference of the writer. Thus, Thucydides more often than not uses the Vivid construction, retaining the Mood and Tense of the direct form of speech. But the orators and Plato and Xenophon prefer the Optative. Both constructions may even occur within the same sentence written by the same author.

οὗτοι ἔλεγον ὅτι Κῦρος μὲν τέθνηκεν, Ἀριαῖος δὲ πεφευγὼς ἐν τῷ σταθμῷ εἴη μετὰ τῶν ἄλλων βαρβάρων ὅθεν τῇ προτεραίᾳ ὥρμηντο … (X.An. 2.1.3.)

These <men> said that Cyrus had died, but that Ariaeus having fled was with the rest of the natives at the stopping-point from where they had set out on the previous day …

Direct form: Κῦρος μὲν τέθνηκεν, Ἀριαῖος δὲ ... ἐν τῷ σταθμῷ ἐστὶ ... ὅθεν ὡρμήμεθα. 'Cyrus has died, but Ariaeus ... is at the stopping-point ... from where we had set out ...'. In Xenophon's actual form, the original Mood and Tense has been retained in τέθνηκεν (Vivid); Optative has been used in εἴη (normal Past sequence); and Past Perfect Indicative has been retained in ὡρμήμεθα (the usual Vivid construction for this Mood and Tense).

References

Goodwin (1889), *Syntax of the moods and tenses of the Greek verb*, §§662–676, 681.

Smyth (1956), *Greek grammar*, §§2574–2600, 2613–2615, 2623.

EXERCISE 13

Translate the following passages.

1. ὥσπερ δὲ καὶ προεῖπον ὑμῖν, ὦ ἄνδρες, ἐξ ἀρχῆς περὶ πάντων ποιήσομαι τὴν ἀπολογίαν, ... περὶ τῶν μυστηρίων ὡς οὔτ' ἐμοὶ ἠσέβηται οὐδὲν οὔτε μεμήνυται οὔθ' ὡμολόγηται ...

προειπεῖν (Aor.)	*to mention previously* (here 1st pers. sg.)
ἀσεβεῖν	*to commit impiety*
μηνύειν	*to lay information*
ὁμολογεῖν	*to make a confession*

The last three verbs are used impersonally in the Passive here.

2. διὰ ταῦτα εἶπον τῇ βουλῇ ὅτι εἰδείην τοὺς ποιήσαντας, καὶ ἐξέδειξα τὰ γενόμενα, ὅτι εἰσηγήσατο μὲν ... ταύτην τὴν βουλὴν Εὐφίλητος, ἀντεῖπον δὲ ἐγώ ...

βουλή, -ῆς, ἡ	*council* (1st instance); *plan* (2nd instance)
ἐκδεικνύναι	*to reveal*
εἰσηγεῖσθαι	*to introduce*

3. ἐπειδὴ δὲ ταῦτα ἐγένετο, Πείσανδρος καὶ Χαρικλῆς ... ἔλεγον ὡς εἴη τὰ ἔργα τὰ γεγενημένα οὐκ ὀλίγων ἀνδρῶν ἀλλ' ἐπὶ τῇ τοῦ δήμου καταλύσει ...

δῆμος, -ου, ὁ	*democracy*
κατάλυσις, -εως, ἡ	*dissolution, overthrow*

4. ... ὁ Κῦρος εἰσκομίσας τὰ θηρία ... ἔλεγεν ὅτι αὐτὸς ταῦτα θηράσειεν ...

εἰσκομίζειν	*to carry in*
θηρίον, -ου, τό	*(wild) animal*
θηρᾶν	*to hunt*

5. ἐν ᾧ δὲ ὡπλίζοντο, ἧκον λέγοντες οἱ προπεμφθέντες σκοποὶ ὅτι οὐχ ἱππεῖς εἶεν, ἀλλ' ὑποζύγια νέμοιτο.

ἐν ᾧ (χρόνῳ)	*in which (time)* (i.e. *while*)
ὑποζύγιον, -ου, τό	*pack-animal*
νέμειν	(Mid., of animals) *to feed, to graze* (Intr.)

6. And he went there and said, that he was a freeman and a Milesian by birth, and [that] Pasion had sent him there to explain about the money.

And he	ὅς (coordinating relative pronoun)
free(man)	ἐλεύθερος, -ου (masc. adj.)
Milesian	Μιλήσιος, -α, -ον
birth	γένος, -ους, τό (Use Acc. of Respect)
Pasion	Πασίων, -ωνος, ὁ
to send there	εἰσπέμπειν
to explain	διδάσκειν (Use Intentive/'Fut.' Partc.)
money	χρήματα, -ων, τά

LESSON 14
Reported Statements with Infinitive

14.1. Aspect of the Infinitive

In classical Greek, some verbs of saying (especially φάναι) report a statement by means of an Infinitive phrase. In this construction, the Infinitive preserves the Aspect of the direct form of the statement. Thus, an Imperfect Infinitive generally represents either a Present Imperfect or a Past Imperfect Indicative of the original statement. A Future (or 'Intentive') Infinitive represents an original Future Indicative. An Aorist Infinitive generally represents a Past Aorist Indicative. And a Perfect Infinitive generally represents either a Present Perfect or a Past Perfect Indicative. Where an original potential statement with ἄν and the Indicative is reported, ἄν is retained in the Infinitive phrase. In addition, an original potential statement with ἄν and the Optative may be reported in an Infinitive phrase with ἄν; the Infinitive preserves the Aspect of the original Optative.

14.2. Accusative and Infinitive Phrases

Where the Subject of the direct statement is different to the Subject of the verb of saying, it appears in the Accusative Case as the Subject of the Infinitive. The whole Accusative and Infinitive phrase is the Object of the verb of saying. In the following examples, the Subject of the Infinitive is in the Accusative Case. These examples also illustrate the Aspect of the Infinitive (as noted in §14.1).

φησὶ γὰρ ὁ κατήγορος οὐ δικαίως με λαμβάνειν τὸ παρὰ τῆς πόλεως ργύριον· (Lys. 24.4.)

For my accuser says that I am unjustly receiving the money from the state.

Direct form: οὐ δικαίως λαμβάνει, 'He is unjustly receiving' (Pres. Imperf.). There is a change from third person (λαμβάνει, 'he is receiving') of the direct form to first person (με, 'I') of the reported form.

... καὶ τὸν πατέρα ἔφη τὸν ἐμὸν παρεῖναι μέν, καθεύδειν δὲ ἐγκεκαλυμμένον. (And. 1.17.)

... and he said that my father had been present, but had been asleep covered up.

Direct form: ὁ πατὴρ ὁ τούτου παρῆν μέν, ἐκάθευδε δέ, 'The father of this <man> was present, but was sleeping' (Past Imperf.). There is a change from third person (τούτου, 'of this <man>') in the direct form to first person (ἐμόν, 'my') in the reported form.

... ἔφη ... τὸν ... πατέρα τὸν ἐμὸν τυχεῖν ἐξιόντα ... (And. 1.41.)
... he said that my father had happened to be going out ...

Direct form: ὁ πατὴρ ὁ τούτου ἔτυχεν ἐξιών, 'His father happened to be going out' (Past Aor.). There is a change of person as in the previous example.

οἱ δ' Ἀθηναῖοι ... οὐκ πεδίδοσαν, ἰσχυριζόμενοι ὅτι δὴ εἴρητο, ἐὰν ὁτιοῦν παραβαθῇ, λελύσθαι τὰς σπονδάς. (Th. 4.23.1.)

But the Athenians ... were not giving back <the ships>, affirming that it had indeed been stated, that, if any infringement at all had occurred, the treaty had been broken.

Direct form: λέλυνται αἱ σπονδαί, 'the treaty has been broken' (Pres. Perf.).

14.3. Nominative and Infinitive Phrases

The Subject of an Infinitive phrase is normally omitted when it is the same as the Subject of the verb of saying. An attribute or Complement of the Subject of the Infinitive appears in the Nominative Case.

ἥκειν ἔφη τῇ ὑστεραίᾳ καὶ δὴ κόπτειν τὴν θύραν· (And. 1.41.)

He said that he had come on the following day and actually had been knocking on the door.

Direct form: ἧκον ... καὶ δὴ ἔκοπτον, 'I had come and was actually knocking' (Past Imperf.). The Subject of the two Infinitives in the reported form is omitted because it is the same as the Subject of ἔφη.

οἱ δὲ Θηβαῖοι ... παρελθόντες ἔφασαν καὶ αὐτοὶ βούλεσθαι εἰπεῖν ... (Th. 3.60.)

And the Thebans ... coming forward said that they themselves also wanted to speak ...

Direct form: καὶ αὐτοὶ βουλόμεθα εἰπεῖν, 'we ourselves also want to speak' (Pres.). The attribute αὐτοί ('-selves') remains Nominative in the reported form, because it refers to the Subject of ἔφασαν. The change of person of the verb in the English reported form is not evident in Greek because of the change of construction from Indicative to Infinitive.

... ἔφασαν ... οὐδενὸς ὕστεροι γνώμῃ φανῆναι. (Th.1.91.5.)
... they said ... that they had appeared inferior to none in judgment.

Direct form: οὐδενὸς ὕστεροι γνώμῃ ἐφάνημεν, 'we appeared inferior to none in judgment' (Past Aor.). The Complement ὕστεροι remains Nominative in the reported form, because it refers to the Subject of ἔφασαν.

14.4. Exceptional Accusative and Infinitive Phrases

For emphasis, an Accusative and Infinitive phrase is sometimes used, even when the Subject of the Infinitive is the same as the Subject of the leading verb. This usually occurs where a contrast or comparison is expressed or implied. (The same phenomenon also appears with verbs of thinking and hoping, and with Acc. and Partc. after verbs of perception.)

τῶν δ' ἄλλων ἐμέ φημι πολὺ προφερέστερον εἶναι ...
(Hom.*Od.* 8.221.)

But I say that I am much more proficient than the rest ...

φημι (1st pers. sg.) with ἐμέ (Acc. 1st pers. sg.) and Infin. εἶναι.

14.5. Negative

The negative for statements reported by Infinitive phrases is regularly οὐ and its compounds. The negative is usually placed before forms of φάναι, unless it negates a particular word within the reported statement as in the first example in §14.2 above.

καὶ γιγνομένων λόγων Εὐφαμίδας ὁ Κορίνθιος οὐκ ἔφη τοὺς λόγους τοῖς ἔργοις ὁμολογεῖν· (Th. 5.55.1.)

And while discussions were taking place, Euphamidas the Corinthian said that their discussions did not correspond with their actions.

The sentence does not mean: 'he did not say that their discussions corresponded with their actions'.

14.6. Usage

Among the verbs which introduce reported statements, whereas λέγειν and εἰπεῖν are usually followed by ὅτι or ὡς, φάναι is usually followed by an Infinitive phrase (see Lesson 13.1). When λέγειν and verbs of saying other than φάναι are followed by an Infinitive, the meaning is usually 'to command', 'to tell someone to do something'. And in keeping with the reported command, the negative is μή.

τά τε ἔξω ἔλεγον αὐτοῖς μὴ δικεῖν. (Th. 2.5.5.)
and they told them not to maltreat those outside.

14.7. Passive of λέγειν

A statement may be reported by the Passive of λέγειν used either personally or impersonally with an Infinitive phrase. The personal construction is the more usual.

καί τις καὶ ἄνεμος λέγεται αὐτοὺς κωλῦσαι. (Th. 2.93.4.)
And a certain wind also is said to have hindered them.

Personal: Nominative and Infinitive.

γνώμῃ δὲ τοιᾷδε λέγεται τὸν Ἀρχίδαμον περί τε τὰς Ἀχαρνὰς ὡς ἐς μάχην ταξάμενον μεῖναι καὶ ἐς τὸ πεδίον ἐκείνῃ τῇ ἐσβολῇ οὐ καταβῆναι· (Th. 2.20.1.)

And it is said that with such an intention Archidamus formed his army as for battle and remained around Acharnae, and did not descend to the plain at the time of that invasion.

Impersonal: Accusative and Infinitive. Structurally, the whole Accusative and Infinitive phrase is Subject of λέγεται (cf. Lessons 3.4.1 and 6.2).

References

Goodwin (1889), *Syntax of the moods and tenses of the Greek verb*, §§683–685, 753–754.

Smyth (1956), *Greek grammar*, §§1866–1867, 1982, 2016–2017, 2616, 2722–2723.

EXERCISE 14

Translate the following passages.

1. φήσει τις δημοκρατίαν οὔτε ξυνετὸν οὔτ' ἴσον εἶναι, τοὺς δ' ἔχοντας τὰ χρήματα καὶ ἄρχειν ἄριστα βελτίστους.

ξυνετός, -ή, -όν	intelligent, wise
εἶναι	Understand again with τοὺς δ' ἔχοντας ... βελτίστους.
καί	also
ἄρχειν	Depends on βελτίστους; see Lesson 3.4.3.3.

2. Σωκράτη φησὶν ἀδικεῖν τούς τε νέους διαφθείροντα καὶ θεοὺς οὓς ἡ πόλις νομίζει οὐ νομίζοντα ...

Σωκράτης, -ους, ὁ	Socrates (here Acc.; see Smyth, 1956, §264.)
διαφθείρειν	to corrupt
νομίζειν	to believe in (+ Acc.)

3. ἔφασαν δὲ πολλοὺς προσχωρήσεσθαι μίσει τῶν Λακεδαιμονίων.

προσχωρεῖν	*to come over* (to another side) (Mid. in Fut.)
μῖσος, -ους, τό	*hatred* (felt by πολλούς)
τῶν Λακεδαιμονίων	Objective Gen.

4. Λακεδαιμόνιοι δὲ τὰ μὲν δυνατὰ ἔφασαν πεποιηκέναι· τοὺς γὰρ παρὰ σφίσι δεσμώτας ὄντας Ἀθηναίων ἀποδοῦναι καὶ τοὺς ἐπὶ Θρᾴκης στρατιώτας ἀπαγαγεῖν …

δυνατός, -ή, -όν	*possible*
δεσμώτης, -ου, ὁ	*prisoner*
ἀποδιδόναι	*to give over*
στρατιώτης, -ου, ὁ	*soldier*

5. προσελθόντες οὖν τοῖς Λακεδαιμονίοις ἔφασαν βούλεσθαι καὶ αὐτοὶ ἐς τὸ πλῆθος αὐτῶν εἰπεῖν …

ἐς	*to, before* (persons, with verbs of speaking)
πλῆθος, -ους, τό	*assembly*

6. οὔ φησ' ἐάσειν τόνδε τὸν νεκρὸν ταφῆς ἄμοιρον, ἀλλὰ πρὸς βίαν θάψειν ἐμοῦ.

φησ(ί)	The Subject is masc.
ταφή, -ῆς, ἡ	*burial*
ἄμοιρος, -ον	*without a share (in)* (+ Gen.)
πρὸς βίαν	*in spite (of), in defiance (of)* (+ Gen.)

7. … λέγομεν ὑμῖν, ἕως ἔτι αὐθαίρετος ἀμφοτέροις ἡ εὐβουλία, σπονδάς μὴ λύειν μηδέ παραβαίνειν τοὺς ὅρκους …

αὐθαίρετος, -ον	*available*
εὐβουλία, -ας, ἡ	*prudence*

LESSON 14. REPORTED STATEMENTS WITH INFINITIVE

8. ... he said that he desired to impose punishment on him ...

... *he... he ...*	Refer to same person.
to desire	χρῄζειν
to impose (Acc.) *on* (Dat.)	ἐπιτιθέναι
punishment	δίκη, -ης, ἡ

9. And the Locrians are said to have established only this law in more than two hundred years.

Locrians	Λοκροί, -ῶν, οἱ
are said	Use personal construction.
to establish	τίθεσθαι (Mid.; use Aor. Infin.)
law	νόμος, -ου, ὁ
in	ἐν (+ Dat.)
more (adv. Acc.)	πλεῖν (for πλεῖον)
two hundred	διακόσιοι, -αι, -α
year	ἔτος, -ους, τό

LESSON 15
Reported Knowledge and Perception

15.1. Introduction

Verbs of knowing and perceiving may take either ὅτι or ὡς with a Subordinate clause, or a Participial phrase (or occasionally an Infin. phrase). The negative for reported knowledge and perception, both after ὅτι or ὡς and with Participial and Infinitive phrases, is normally οὐ. For the occasional use of μή with Participial or Infinitive phrases, see the examples at the end of §15.3 below.

15.2. Reported Knowledge or Perception with ὅτι or ὡς

Reported knowledge or perception with ὅτι or ὡς is expressed in the same way as reported statements. For Primary sequence, see Lesson 13.2. For Past sequence, see Lesson 13.3; a Vivid construction may also be used for reported knowledge or perception.

πάντες γὰρ **ἐπίστασθε ὅτι** ἐν ἐκείνῳ τῷ χωρίῳ, ὅταν τὰς τοῦ φόνου δίκας δικάζωνται, **οὐ** διὰ τούτου τοῦ ὀνόματος τὰς διωμοσίας **ποιοῦνται** ... (Lys. 10.11.)

*For **you** all **know that** in that place, when they try cases of murder, **they do not make** sworn-statements by means of this term ...*

In Primary sequence, the verbs in the reported form have the same Mood and Tense as in the direct form. There is no change of person in this particular sentence. The negative is οὐ.

ἔνθα δὴ ὁ Ἀγεσίλαος, **γιγνώσκων ὅτι** τοῖς μὲν πολεμίοις **οὔπω παρείη** τὸ πεζόν, αὐτῷ δὲ **οὐδὲν ἀπείη** τῶν παρεσκευασμένων, καιρὸν **ἡγήσατο** μάχην συνάψαι, εἰ δύναιτο. (X.*Ages.* 1.31.)

*Then indeed Agesilaus, **realising that** the infantry **were not yet present** for the enemy, but for himself **nothing** of what had been prepared **was missing**, **thought** it the time to join battle, if he could.*

In Past sequence, the verbs in the reported form appear in the Optative Mood instead of the Indicative Mood of the direct form. The Past sequence is set by the Main verb ἡγήσατο ('thought'), to which the Participle γιγνώσκων ('realising') is subordinate. The negatives are οὐ compounds.

Direct form: οὔπω πάρεστι τὸ πέζον, … οὐδὲν ἄπεστι, 'the infantry are not yet present, … nothing is missing'.

καὶ **ᾔσθετο** μὲν **ὅτι νικῶσιν** οἱ μεθ' ἑαυτοῦ … (Th.5.11.10.)
*And **he perceived that** those with him **were victorious** …*

Vivid construction: in Past sequence the direct form νικῶσιν (Pres. Indic.) is retained, instead of being changed to Optative.

15.3. Reported Knowledge or Perception with a Participial Phrase

With verbs of knowing and (intellectually) perceiving, the content of knowledge or perception may be expressed by a Participial phrase, analogous to the Infinitive phrase with verbs of saying such as φάναι. Like the Infinitive, the Participle preserves the Aspect of the direct form of expression. (Cf. Lesson 14.1.) The regular constructions are as follows.

Where the Subject of reported knowledge or perception is different to the Subject of the verb of knowing, it appears in the Accusative Case with an Accusative Participle.

οἶσθα οὖν **μηνύσαντα Ἀνδρόμαχον** τὰ ἐν τῇ οἰκίᾳ τῇ Πουλυτίωνος γιγνόμενα; (And. 1.14.)

*So **do you know that Andromachus reported** what had been going on in Poulytion's house?*

Direct form: ἐμήνυσεν Ἀνδρόμαχος, 'Andromachus reported'. In the reported form, the Participle μηνύσαντα retains the Aspect of the direct form.

LESSON 15. REPORTED KNOWLEDGE AND PERCEPTION

Where the Subject of a Participial phrase is the same as the Subject of the verb of knowledge or perception, it is omitted, and the Participle itself and any attribute or Complement appears in the Nominative Case.

καὶ νῦν **ὁρῶ** μὲν **ἐξαμαρτάνων**, γύναι,
ὅμως δὲ τεύξῃ τοῦδε. (E.*Med.* 350–351.)

*And now **I see that I am making a mistake**, woman,
but nevertheless you will obtain this.*

Direct form: ἐξαμαρτάνω, 'I am making a mistake'. In the reported form, the Participle retains the Aspect of the direct form.

Besides the regular constructions, the following variations also occur.

καὶ ὡς **ᾔσθοντο παρόντα**, ἐσκομίζουσι παρ' αὐτοὺς ἐγχειρίδια ἔχοντας ἄνδρας ψιλοὺς ἑπτά ... (Th. 4.110.2.)

*and when **they realised that <he> was present**, they brought in* [Hist. Pres.] *to their presence seven light-armed men holding daggers ...*

The Accusative Subject of παρόντα is not expressed, since in the context the Participle clearly refers to 'him' (Brasidas). The pronoun to be understood as Subject of παρόντα must be in the same Case, Gender and Number as the Participle, thus αὐτόν.

ὁρῶ δέ **μ'** ἔργον δεινὸν **ἐξειργασμένην**. (S.*Tr.* 706.)
*But **I see that I have done** a terrible deed.*

Although the Subject of the Participle ἐξειργασμένην is the same as the Subject of ὁρῶ, it is expressed and is in the Accusative Case. The construction implies a greater degree of objectivity in the one who 'see(s)'.

οἶδ' ἐγώ σε **μή τινα**
ἐνθένδ' **ἀπάξοντ'** ἄνδρα πρὸς βίαν ἐμοῦ. (S.*OC* 656–657.)

*I **know that no man
will take** you **away** from here in defiance of me.*

Accusative and Participle with negative μή. Indefinite Subject (τινα) and reference to a future situation.

καίτοι τοσοῦτόν γ᾽ **οἶδα**, **μήτε** μ᾽ ἂν νόσον
μήτ᾽ ἄλλο **πέρσαι μηδέν**· (S.*OT* 1455–1456.)

*And yet so much **I know**, **that neither would** plague
nor anything else **destroy** me.*

Accusative and Infinitive with negative μή. Reference to a potential situation.

15.4. Physical Perception

A Participle may also be used with a verb expressing physical perception.

ὁρῶ δὲ καὶ **Κρέοντα**, τῆσδ᾽ ἄνακτα γῆς,
στείχοντα, καινῶν ἄγγελον βουλευμάτων. (E.*Med.* 269–270.)

*But **I see** Creon, lord of this land,
approaching, messenger of new intentions.*

ὁρῶ has a direct Object Κρέοντα followed by a supplementary Participle στείχοντα.

The difference in function between physical and intellectual perception is clear with verbs which normally take the Genitive Case.

ἐγὼ γὰρ ἐν τῷ χρόνῳ ᾧ **ὑμῶν ἀκούω ἀπορούντων** τί τὸ δίκαιον,
ἐν τούτῳ δικαιοτέρους τοὺς ἀνθρώπους ποιῶ. (X.*Smp.* 4.1.)

*For in the time in which **I hear you puzzling** as to what justice <is>,
meantime I am making people more just.*

Physical perception: Genitive and supplementary Participle after ἀκούειν.

... ἐπεὶ δὲ **ἤκουσεν** ἔργα ἀνδρὸς ἤδη **διαχειριζόμενον τὸν Κῦρον**, ἀπεκάλει δή, ὅπως τὰ ἐν Πέρσαις ἐπιχώρια ἐπιτελοίη. (X.*Cyr.* 1.4.25.)

*... and when **he heard that Cyrus was** already **managing** the actions of a man, he proceeded to recall <him>, so that he might complete the <training> customary among the Persians.*

Intellectual perception: Accusative and Participle after ἀκούειν.

15.5. Reported Knowledge or Perception with an Infinitive Phrase

A common view is that the Infinitive construction expresses perception of what is hypothetical or possible, whereas the Participial construction expresses perception of what is actual.

πυνθάνομαι ἐπιβουλεύειν σε πρήγμασι μεγάλοισι, καὶ χρήματά τοι οὐκ **εἶναι** κατὰ τὰ φρονήματα. (Hdt. 3.122.3.)

*I hear that you are planning for great projects, and that you **do** not **have** financial resources in accordance with your ideas.*

τοι (Ionic) = σοι (Attic), Possessive Dative with εἶναι.

Thus, Montanari (2015) introducing ἀκούειν 1.C states that the Participle usually expresses real indirect perception, the Infinitive generic perception. On the other hand Goodwin (1889, §914) states that many verbs which have the Participle in reported discourse may also take the Infinitive 'in nearly or quite the same sense'. Similarly, Smyth (1956, §2144) gives a list of verbs which take Participle or Infinitive in reported discourse 'with no (or only slight) difference in meaning'. The following phrases from the same paragraph of Herodotus would support this view.

πυθόμενοι δὲ Παίονες **τοὺς Πέρσας** ἐπὶ σφέας **ἰέναι**, ἁλισθέντες ἐξεστρατεύσαντο πρὸς θαλάσσης … οἱ δὲ Παίονες, ὡς ἐπύθοντο **ἐχομένας τὰς πόλιας**, αὐτίκα διασκεδασθέντες κατ' ἑωυτοὺς ἕκαστοι ἐτράποντο … (Hdt. 5.15.1, 3.)

*And the Paeonians, learning that **the Persians were coming** against them, gathered together and marched to the sea… And the Paeonians, when they learned that **their towns were occupied**, immediately scattered and each turned to his own way…*

There is also variation of usage between one author and another. The following statistics are limited to a sample of three words and to three authors. Only the Accusative plus Participle and Accusative plus Infinitive in reported discourse are considered. For Xenophon, only *Anabasis*, *Cyropaedia* and *Historia Graeca* are considered.

	αἰσθάνεσθαι		ἀκούειν		πυνθάνεσθαι	
	Acc. + Partc.	Acc. + Infin.	Acc. + Partc.	Acc. + Infin.	Acc. + Partc.	Acc. + Infin.
Hdt.	1	0	1	7	34	40
Th.	28	2	1	0	10	9
X.	10	0	0	23	2	1

References

Goodwin (1889), *Syntax of the moods and tenses of the Greek verb*, §§669, 687–688, 884, 914.

Smyth (1956), *Greek grammar*, §§1874, 2106–2114, 2123, 2144–2145, 2576, 2614–2616, 2727, 2729–2731.

EXERCISE 15

Translate the following passages.

1. ... γιγνώσκω ὅτι οἱ τὰ μὴ πιστὰ δοκοῦντα εἶναι ἢ λέγοντες ἢ ἀπαγγέλλοντες οὐ μόνον οὐ πείθουσιν, ἀλλὰ καὶ ἄφρονες δοκοῦσιν εἶναι·

2. οἱ δὲ πράσσοντες αὐτῷ εἰδότες ὅτι ἥξοι, ... ἐτήρουν τὴν πρόσοδον ...

πράσσειν	to deal with (+ Dat.)
ἥκειν	to (have) come
τηρεῖν	to watch for (+ Acc.)
πρόσοδος, -ου, ἡ	approach

3. ... ὡς ... ᾐσθάνοντο τὰ πυρὰ ἐξαίφνης πολλὰ ἐν τῇ πολεμίᾳ φανέντα, ἔγνωσαν ὅτι ἐσπλέουσιν οἱ Πελοποννήσιοι.

| ὡς | when |
| πυρά, -ῶν, τά | (watch-)fires |

LESSON 15. REPORTED KNOWLEDGE AND PERCEPTION

ἐξαίφνης (adv.)	*suddenly*
πολεμία, -ας, ἡ	*enemy <territory>* (fem. adj. as noun)
ἐσπλεῖν	*to sail in*

4. τίς γὰρ οὐκ οἶδεν ὑμῶν πολλοὺς τῶν ὑπὸ τοῖς σοφισταῖς γενομένων οὐ φενακισθέντας οὐδ' οὕτω διατεθέντας ὡς οὗτοι λέγουσιν ...;

ὑμῶν	Partitive Gen. with τίς
γίγνεσθαι ὑπό (+ Dat.)	*to come under (the influence of)*
φενακίζειν	*to cheat*
διατιθέναι	*to treat*

5. οἱ δ' Ἀθηναῖοι ἔγνωσαν οὐκ ἐπὶ τῷ βελτίονι λόγῳ ἀποπεμπόμενοι, ἀλλά τινος ὑπόπτου γενομένου ...

λόγος, -ου, ὁ	*reason*
ἀποπεμπόμενοι	Pass.
ὕποπτον, -ου, τό	*suspicion* (neut. adj. as noun; here in Gen. abs.)

6. ἀκούω δὲ καὶ ἄλλα ἔθνη πολλὰ τοιαῦτα εἶναι, ἃ οἶμαι ἂν παῦσαι ἐνοχλοῦντα ἀεὶ τῇ ὑμετέρᾳ εὐδαιμονίᾳ.

ἔθνος, -ους, τό	*tribe*
ἐνοχλεῖν	*to cause trouble (for)* (+ Dat.)

7. And immediately they all realised that [the Persian] king had been encamping somewhere nearby.

that	Use ὅτι.
to encamp	στρατοπεδεύεσθαι (Mid.)
somewhere	που (enclitic)
nearby	ἐγγύς

8. ... when they realised that the army had come in and that it was impossible to take the city by force, they withdrew ...

that	Use Acc. and Partc.
to take	αἱρεῖν, Aor. ἑλεῖν
force	βία, -ας, ἡ

LESSON 16
Reported Thoughts, Hopes, Promises and Oaths

16.1. Reported Thoughts

The usual construction with verbs of thinking is an Infinitive phrase. Where the Subject of the reported thought is different to the Subject of the verb of thinking, it appears in the Accusative Case. Where the Subject of the reported thought is the same as the Subject of the verb of thinking, it is usually omitted. In this construction, an attribute or Complement of the Subject of the reported thought appears in the Nominative Case. For comparison or contrast the Subject of the Infinitive is sometimes expressed in the Accusative, even when it is the same as the Subject of the leading verb. The Infinitive preserves the Aspect of the direct form of thought. An Infinitive with ἄν represents a direct form of thought with ἄν and potential Indicative or Optative. The usual negative is οὐ. The negative may precede the leading verb, rather than be attached to the Infinitive (cf. Lesson 14.5).

οἱ γὰρ βάρβαροι ... ἐς τὸ πλέον οὐκέτ' ἐπηκολούθουν, **νομίζοντες** καὶ ἐν μεθορίοις **εἶναι αὐτοὺς** ἤδη καὶ **διαπεφευγέναι**. (Th.4.128.2.)

For the foreigners ... for the most part no longer pursued, **thinking** *both* **that they were** *on the borders by now and* **that they had escaped**.

Direct form: ἐν μεθορίοις εἰσὶν ἤδη καὶ διαπεφεύγασι, 'They are on the borders by now and have escaped'. αὐτούς (Acc.) shows that 'they' are not the 'foreigners'. διαπεφευγέναι preserves the Aspect of διαπεφεύγασι.

οὐ γὰρ **ἱκανοὶ ἐνόμιζον εἶναι** ἔν τε τῷ ἰσθμῷ φρουρεῖν καὶ ἐς τὴν Παλλήνην διαβάντες τειχίζειν ... (Th. 1.64.1.)

For **they thought that they were not competent** *to keep watch on the isthmus and to cross over to Pallene and build a wall ...*

Direct form: οὐχ ἱκανοί ἐσμεν … φρουρεῖν καὶ … διαβάντες τειχίζειν, 'We are not competent to keep watch … and … to cross over and build a wall'. In the reported form, the Subject of the Infinitives is omitted, since it is the same as the Subject of ἐνόμιζον; and the Complement ἱκανοί and the circumstantial Participle διαβάντες remain in the Nominative Case. The negative οὐ precedes ἐνόμιζον (as does the Complement ἱκανοί in this instance).

καὶ σχεδόν τι **οἶμαι ἐμὲ** πλείω χρήματα **εἰργάσθαι** ἢ ἄλλους σύνδυο οὕστινας βούλῃ τῶν σοφιστῶν. (Pl.*Hp.Ma.* 282 E.)

*And **I** just about **think that I have made** more money than any other two together of the sophists whom you wish <to name>.*

Direct form: ἐγὼ πλείω χρήματα εἴργασμαι ἢ ἄλλοι σύνδυο, 'I have made more money than any other two together'. For comparison of 'I' with 'any other two', the Subject (ἐμέ) of the Infin. εἰργάσθαι is expressed in the Accusative Case, although it is the same as the Subject of the leading verb (οἶμαι).

… καὶ λαμπρότερόν τ' **ἂν φανῆναι** τὸ ἔργον τῆς θήρας καὶ ἱερείων **ἂν** πολλὴν ἀφθονίαν **ἐνόμιζε γενέσθαι**. (X.Cyr. 1.4.17.)

*… and **he thought that** the action of the hunt **would appear** more illustrious and **that there would** turn out to be a great abundance of animals for slaughter.*

Direct form: λαμπρότερόν τ' ἂν φανείη τὸ ἔργον … καὶ … ἂν πολλὴ ἀφθονία γένοιτο, 'The action … would appear more illustrious and there would turn out to be a great abundance'. ἄν used with the potential Optative in the direct form is retained with the Infinitive in the reported form.

ὡς ἐγὼ ἀκούων τινῶν ἐπαινουμένων, ὅτι νόμιμοι ἄνδρες εἰσίν, **οἶμαι μὴ ἂν** δικαίως τούτου **τυχεῖν** τοῦ ἐπαίνου **τὸν μὴ εἰδότα**, τί ἐστι νόμος. (X.Mem. 1.2.41.)

*For, when I hear some people assigning praise, because men are law-abiding, I **think that the** <man>, **who does not know** what a law is, **would not** justly **obtain** this praise.*

LESSON 16. REPORTED THOUGHTS, HOPES, PROMISES AND OATHS

In this sentence, μή with ἄν and the Infinitive may be influenced by the Subject of the Infinitive, τὸν μὴ εἰδότα, where μή is generic, referring to 'anyone who does not know'. (For the coordinating use of ὡς and ἐπεί, see Lesson 23.4.)

16.2. Reported Hopes and Promises

In most respects, expressions of hoping (or expecting) and promising follow the pattern of reported thoughts (§16.1). Because of their meaning, hopes and promises are most often used with an Intentive ('Fut.') Infinitive.

However, hopes and promises may also be reported with an Imperfect Infinitive expressing continuous action or with an Aorist Infinitive expressing momentary action. Occasionally, the Aorist Infinitive reports a hope that something had previously happened. And sometimes manuscripts are divided in reading an Aorist or an Intentive Infinitive.

Frequently, in reported hopes, and regularly in reported promises, the negative used with the Infinitive is μή; but οὐ does also occur.

καὶ **ἤλπιζον** πάσας τὰς ναῦς **ἀπολήψεσθαι**. (Th. 2.90.4.)
*and **they were hoping that they would cut off** all their ships.*

Direct form: ἀποληψόμεθα, 'We shall cut off'. The Intentive ('Fut.') Infinitive of the reported form corresponds to the Future Indicative of the direct form.

καὶ νῦν ἐθέλομεν **πίστιν δοῦναι**, ἥτις ἐστὶ μεγίστη τοῖς ἀνθρώποις, **μὴ ἔχειν** τῶν Ἀριστοφάνους χρημάτων … (Lys. 19.32.)

*and now we are willing **to give a pledge**, which is the most serious for human beings, **that we do not hold** <any parts> of the property of Aristophanes …*

Direct form: οὐκ ἔχομεν, 'We do not hold'. The Imperfect Infinitive and negative μή of the reported form correspond to the Present Indicative and negative οὐ of the direct form.

ὑπολείπεται τοίνυν αὐτῷ λέγειν ὡς … ἀδύνατος κατέστη βοηθῆσαι εἰς τὸν Πειραιᾶ, … **ἐπαγγειλάμενος** αὐτὸς ἢ χρήματ' **εἰσενεγκεῖν** εἰς τὸ πλῆθος τὸ ὑμέτερον ἢ **ὁπλίσαι** τινὰς τῶν ἑαυτοῦ δημοτῶν … (Lys. 31.15.)

> *It remains, therefore, for him to state that ... he became incapable of helping at the Piraeus ... although **promising** either **to contribute** money himself to your community or **to arm** some of his fellow-citizens ...*

Direct form: εἰσενέγκω ... ὁπλίσω, 'Let me contribute ... let me arm'. The hortatory Aorist Subjunctive could be postulated as the equivalent direct form. But at any rate the Aorist Infinitives εἰσενεγκεῖν ... ὁπλίσαι as verbal nouns are the direct Objects of ἐπαγγειλάμενος. (Some scholars classify such Infinitives as 'not in indirect discourse'.) And the promise relates to action subsequent to the time at which it was made.

ἦ θήν **μιν** μάλα **ἔλπετο** θυμὸς ἑκάστου
χερσὶν ὑπ' Αἴαντος **θανέειν** Τελαμωνιάδαο. (Hom.Il. 15.288–289.)

> *Certainly the heart of each firmly **hoped**
> that **he had died** under the hands of Ajax, son of Telamon.*

Direct form: εἰ γὰρ ἔθανε, 'If only he had died!' Such an unfulfilled wish for the past is perhaps the closest approximation to a direct form of this reported hope (cf. Lesson 11.2.1.2.). Unlike the previous example, the Aorist Infinitive here relates to action prior to the time at which the hope was reported.

ἤλπιζε γὰρ αὐτῶν **οὐ μενεῖν τὴν τάξιν** ... (Th. 2.84.2.)
*For **he hoped that** their **battle-line would not remain** <intact> ...*

Here, the negative οὐ is used with the Infinitive μενεῖν, rather than the more usual μή as in Lys. 19.32 above.

16.3. Reported Oaths

Like hopes and promises, oaths about an intended action are most commonly reported with an Intentive ('Fut.') Infinitive, and oaths about a continuing action may be reported with an Imperfect Infinitive or oaths about an action viewed as momentary may be reported with an Aorist Infinitive. Again, the Aorist Infinitive may report an oath about an intended action (swear to do something) or an oath about a prior action (swear that one did something). An oath about completed action may also be reported with a Perfect Infinitive. As with reported thoughts, hopes and promises, ἄν is sometimes used to express potentiality.

LESSON 16. REPORTED THOUGHTS, HOPES, PROMISES AND OATHS

ὀμωμόκατε ψηφιεῖσθαι κατὰ τοὺς νόμους καὶ τὰ ψηφίσματα τὰ τοῦ δήμου καὶ τῆς βουλῆς τῶν πεντακοσίων. (D. 19.179.)

***You have sworn that you will vote** according to the laws and the decrees of the people and of the council of the five hundred.*

The Subject of the Intentive Infinitive is not expressed since it is the same as the Subject of the leading verb.

ὅ τε πατὴρ ἡμῶν, ἐπειδὴ ἐγενόμεθα, εἰς τοὺς φράτορας ἡμᾶς εἰσήγαγεν, **ὀμόσας** κατὰ τοὺς νόμους τοὺς κειμένους ἦ μὴν ἐξ ἀστῆς καὶ ἐγγυητῆς γυναικὸς **εἰσάγειν**· (Is. 18.19.)

*And our father, when we had been born, introduced us to the clansmen, **swearing** in accordance with the established customs, **that** assuredly **he was introducing** <children> from a married [and] Athenian woman.*

The Imperfect Infinitive expresses a continuing action.

ὤμοσε δὲ πρὸς ἔμ' αὐτόν, ἀποσπένδων ἐνὶ οἴκῳ, **νῆα κατειρύσθαι** ... (Hom.Od. 14.331–332.)

*And **he swore** to me myself, as he poured a libation in his house, **that the ship had been drawn down** ...*

The Accusative and Perfect (Pass.) Infinitive expresses completed action.

ἀλλ' **ὄμοσον μὴ** μητρὶ φίλῃ τάδε **μυθήσασθαι** ... (Hom.Od. 2.372.)
*But **swear not to tell** this to my dear mother ...*

The Aorist Infinitive expresses intended action.

ἵππων ἁψάμενος γαιήοχον ἐννοσίγαιον
ὄμνυθι μὴ μὲν ἑκὼν τὸ ἐμὸν δόλῳ ἅρμα **πεδῆσαι**.
(Hom.Il. 23.584–585.)

*laying a hand on your horses, **swear** by the one who holds the earth <and> shakes the earth **that you** certainly **did not** intentionally **impede** my chariot by trickery.*

The Aorist Infinitive expresses prior action, with negative μή.

References

Goodwin (1889), *Syntax of the moods and tenses of the Greek verb*, §§204–212, 683–686, 751–752.

Smyth (1956), *Greek grammar*, §§1845–1849, 1868, 2018, 2022–2024, 2580, 2692, 2722–2723, 2725–2726.

EXERCISE 16

Translate the following passages.

1. ἴσως με οἴεσθε ... ἀπορίᾳ λόγων ἑαλωκέναι τοιούτων οἷς ἂν ὑμᾶς ἔπεισα ...

ἀπορία, -ας, ἡ	*lack*
οἴεσθαι	*to think* (Mid. with Aor. Pass.)
ἁλίσκεσθαι	*to be convicted* (Intr. Aor. and Perf. Act. forms have Pass. sense)

2. ὅπλα μὲν οὖν ἔχοντες οἰόμεθα ἂν καὶ τῇ ἀρετῇ χρῆσθαι, παραδόντες δ᾽ ἂν ταῦτα καὶ τῶν σωμάτων στερηθῆναι.

παραδιδόναι	*to hand over, to surrender*

3. εἴ τοι νομίζεις ἄνδρα συγγενῆ κακῶς δρῶν οὐχ ὑφέξειν τὴν δίκην, οὐκ εὖ φρονεῖς.

ὑπέχειν	*to suffer*

4. ἐξ ὧν ἐλπίζω, εἰ τὴν πρὸς ἐμὲ ὁδὸν τράποιο, σφόδρ᾽ ἄν σε τῶν καλῶν καὶ σεμνῶν ἐργάτην ἀγαθὸν γενέσθαι ...

ἐξ ὧν	*And as a result of this* (ὧν: coordinating relative pronoun)
τρέπειν	*to turn*
σφόδρ(α)	*certainly*
σεμνός, -ή, -όν	*noble* (here neut., as also καλῶν)
ἀγαθός, -ή, -όν	*beneficial*

LESSON 16. REPORTED THOUGHTS, HOPES, PROMISES AND OATHS

5. καὶ αὐτοὺς ἀπέπεμψαν ἐπαινέσαντες τοὺς λόγους ... καὶ πρέσβεις ὑποσχόμενοι ἀποστελεῖν περὶ τῆς ξυμμαχίας ἐς Ἄργος.

| πρέσβεις, -εων, οἱ | *ambassadors* (here Acc.) |
| ἀποστέλλειν | *to send out* |

6. ὀμόσας ἀπάξειν οἴκαδ', ἐς Τροίαν μ' ἄγει·

7. οἶμαι δὲ καὶ ἐμὲ τῶν ἔτι πόρρωθεν ἀφεστηκότων εἶναι.

| πόρρωθεν | *far off* (no emphasis on -θεν here) |

8. But I think that I shall quickly make clear that we would not even be able to establish this sovereignty.

to make clear	δηλοῦν
to establish	καθιστάσθαι (rarely Middle in this sense)
sovereignty	ἀρχή, -ῆς, ἡ

9. But when he had arrived in Nemea, he delayed there, hoping that he would catch the Athenians as they were going past ...

Nemea	Νεμέα, -ας, ἡ
to arrive in	γίγνεσθαι ἐν
to delay	διατρίβειν
to catch	λαμβάνειν
to go past	παριέναι

LESSON 17
Questions

17.1. Ordinary Questions

Ordinary questions may be expressed with or without an introductory interrogative particle. The particles are normally the first element in a sentence. Interrogative phrases, which include the negative οὐ, generally expect a positive answer. Interrogative phrases, which include μή, are more emotionally charged, but do not necessarily expect a negative answer.

καὶ νῦν φλογωπὸν πῦρ ἔχουσ' ἐφήμεροι; (A.Pr. 253.)
And now do ephemeral <mortals> have flaming fire?

No interrogative particle.

ἦ θεωρήσων τύχας
ἐμὰς ἀφῖξαι καὶ συνασχαλῶν κακοῖς; (A.Pr. 302–303.)

Have you come to see
my fortunes and to sympathise with my troubles?

Question with ἦ is neutral.

ἆρ' ἐγγὺς ἀνήρ; ἆρ' ἔτ' ἐμψύχου, τέκνα,
κιχήσεταί μου καὶ κατορθοῦντος φρένα; (S.OC 1486–1487.)

<Is> the man near? Will he find me, children,
still alive and in my right mind?

These questions with ἆρα are neutral.

ἆρ' ὑμῖν δοκεῖ
ὁ τῶν θεῶν τύραννος ἐς τὰ πάνθ' ὁμῶς
βίαιος εἶναι; (A.Pr. 735–737.)

Does it (not) seem to you
that the ruler of the gods in all respects alike
is violent?

This question with ἆρα expects a positive answer.

ἤδη δεῖ με δουλεύειν πάλιν
ἐν τοῖσιν ἐχθίστοισιν ἀνθρώπων ἐμοὶ
φονεῦσι πατρός. **ἆρά** μοι καλῶς ἔχει; (S.*El.* 814–816.)

*Now I must be a slave again
among the people most hateful to me,
the murderers of my father. Does it go well with me?*

This question with ἆρα expects a negative answer.

οὐ τοῦτο δειμαίνεις πλέον; (A.*Pr.* 41.)
Do you not fear this more?

Question with οὐ expects a positive answer.

ἆρ' οὐκ ἄμεινον ἢ σὺ τἀν Θήβαις φρονῶ; (S.*OC* 791.)
Do I not understand the <situation> in Thebes better than you?

Question with ἆρ' οὐκ expects a positive answer.

οὔκουν, Προμηθεῦ, τοῦτο γιγνώσκεις, ὅτι
ὀργῆς νοσούσης εἰσὶν ἰατροὶ λόγοι; (A.*Pr.* 377–378.)

*Do you not know this, Prometheus, that
words are healers of the disease of anger?*

οὔκουν with paroxytone accent emphasises the negative, and the question expects a positive answer.

οὐκοῦν, ἔφη ὁ Χρυσάντας, εὖ σοι δοκοῦσι βουλεύεσθαι;
(X.*Cyr.* 7.1.8.)

'Therefore do they not', said Chrysantas, 'seem to you to be laying their plans well?'

οὐκοῦν with perispomenon accent emphasises the inferential force of οὖν, while maintaining the negative value of οὐκ, and the question expects a positive answer.

οὐκοῦν ψυχὴ **οὐ** δέχεται θάνατον; – οὔ. (Pl.*Phd.* 105 E.)
Therefore the soul does not admit of death? – No.

The question with οὐκοῦν ... οὐ expects (and receives) a negative answer. For the accent on οὔ, see the comment preceding the second example in §17.2 below.

μή πού τι προύβης τῶνδε καὶ περαιτέρω; (A.*Pr.* 247.)
Did you perhaps go even somewhat further than this?

μή gives a worried tone to the question.

ἆρα μὴ δοκεῖς
λυτήρι᾽ αὐτῇ ταῦτα τοῦ φόνου φέρειν;
οὐκ ἔστιν. (S.*El.* 446–448.)

*Do you really think
that you are bringing these things as a deliverance for her from the murder?
It is not possible.*

Despite her own attitude, Electra does not expect her sister Chrysothemis to answer 'No'. ἆρα μή indicates Electra's emotion in opposing her sister's action.

τὴν δὲ τῆς μίξεως αἰτίαν καὶ γενέσεως τετάρτην λέγων **ἆρα μὴ** πλημμελοίην ἄν τι; (Pl.*Phlb.* 27 C.)

And I would not be making any mistake in calling the cause of mixing and generation the fourth <cause>, would I?

This question with ἆρα μή (delayed) expects a negative answer. ἆρα μή, used in this and the preceding example, is not common in classical Greek.

μῶν ἄλγος ἴσχεις τῆς παρεστώσης νόσου; (S.*Ph.* 734.)
Do you have pain from your current sickness?

μῶν (derived from μὴ οὖν) expresses Neoptolemus's concern at Philoctetes's pain.

17.2. Alternative Questions

Alternative questions are regularly introduced by πότερον (πότερα) ... ἤ ... ; Further alternatives may be added by repetition of ἤ. The initial πότερον (-α) is often omitted in Greek. And an initial 'whether' is no longer used in direct alternative questions in English.

πότερα δ' ἄν, εἰ νέμοι τις αἵρεσιν, λάβοις
φίλους ἀνιῶν αὐτὸς ἡδονὰς ἔχειν,
ἢ κοινὸς ἐν κοινοῖσι λυπεῖσθαι ξυνών; (S.Aj. 265–267.)

*And, if someone were to give <you> a choice, would you choose [lit. accept]
to have pleasure yourself while distressing your friends,
or to be grieved while being together as a partner among partners?*

The second alternative is sometimes a mere negative. If οὐ is immediately followed by punctuation at the end of a clause or sentence, it has an oxytone accent, οὔ.

... **πότερον** ταῦτα ποιῶν ἠδίκει καὶ παρεσπόνδει καὶ ἔλυε τὴν εἰρήνην, **ἢ** οὔ; (D. 18.71.)

*... in doing these things was he acting wrongly and was he violating the treaty
and was he breaking the peace, or not?*

In the following example, continuous with the preceding, the Infinitive construction with ἐχρῆν justifies μή as the negative for the second alternative. (Cf. Smyth, 1956, §2714.)

καὶ **πότερον** φανῆναί τινα τῶν Ἑλλήνων τὸν ταῦτα κωλύσοντα ποιεῖν αὐτὸν ἐχρῆν, **ἢ** μή; (D. 18.71.)

And was it right that one of the Greeks should appear as the one to prevent him doing this, or not?

17.3. Questions with Interrogative Adjectives or Adverbs

Questions may be introduced by interrogative adjectives or adverbs. The adjectives may be used with or without a noun. Without a noun, they function as pronouns.

τίς ἀχώ, **τίς** ὀδμὰ προσέπτα μ' ἀφεγγής; (A.Pr. 115.)
What sound, what smell came upon me, unseen?

τίς is used as an interrogative adjective.

τίς ὧδε τλησικάρδιος
θεῶν, ὅτῳ τάδ' ἐπιχαρῆ; (A.*Pr.* 160–161.)

*Who <is> so hard-hearted
among the gods, that this <is> a joy to him?*

τίς is used as an interrogative pronoun.

πῶς ἐτόλμησας, λιπὼν
ἐπώνυμόν τε ῥεῦμα καὶ πετρηρεφῆ
αὐτόκτιτ' ἄντρα, τὴν σιδηρομήτορα
ἐλθεῖν ἐς αἶαν; (A.*Pr.* 299–302.)

*How did you dare, leaving
the stream named after you and rock-vaulted
caverns formed by yourself, to come to this
iron-producing land?*

πῶς is an interrogative adverb.

17.4. Deliberative Questions

Deliberative questions normally occur in the first person singular or plural, and ask, for example: 'Am I to do this?' or 'What are we to do?' or 'Where are we to go?' They may be addressed to oneself, or to some other person. The Mood is Subjunctive, and the negative is μή.

οἴμοι, **τί δράσω**; **ποῖ φύγω** μητρὸς χέρας; (E.*Med.* 1271.)
Alas, what am I to do? Where am I to flee from my mother's hands?

Deliberation may also be expressed by the Future Indicative, by the modal expressions δεῖ or χρή, or by the verbal adjectives expressing necessity.

17.5. Rhetorical Questions

Rhetorical questions have the form of a question, but the function of a statement or a command. Thus, either they do not expect any answer or an answer is provided by the speaker. Rhetorical questions differ from other questions only in function, not in form.

τίς οὐ ξυνασχαλᾷ κακοῖς
τεοῖσι δίχα γε Διός; (A.Pr. 162–163.)

Who does not sympathise with your
troubles, apart from Zeus at least?

Function: *There is nobody who does not sympathise ...* (Statement).

εἶέν, **τί** μέλλεις καὶ κατοικτίζῃ μάτην; (A.Pr. 36.)
Enough! Why do you delay and pity <him> in vain?

Function: *Do not delay ...* (Command).

ἔνερθε δὲ χθονὸς
κεκρυμμέν᾽ ἀνθρώποισιν ὠφελήματα
χαλκὸν σίδηρον ἄργυρον χρυσόν τε, **τίς**
φήσειεν ἂν πάροιθεν ἐξευρεῖν ἐμοῦ;
οὐδείς, σάφ᾽ οἶδα, μὴ μάτην φλῦσαι θέλων. (A.Pr. 500–504.)

And <as for> aids
for mankind hidden beneath the earth,
bronze, iron, silver and gold, who
would say that he discovered <them> before me?
No one, I am sure, unless wishing to babble on in vain.

The question is answered by the speaker, who thereby shows that the question is equivalent to a statement: *No one would say that he discovered ... before me.*

References

Denniston (1954), *The Greek particles*, pp. 46–51 (ἆρα), 282–284 (ἦ), 430–436 (οὔκουν, οὐκοῦν).

Goodwin (1889), *Syntax of the moods and tenses of the Greek verb*, §§287–293.

Smyth (1956), *Greek grammar*, §§1805, 1807–1809, 2636–2662.

The present Lesson agrees with Denniston (1954) and Humbert (1954) on the use of μή, ἆρα μή and μῶν, contrary to Smyth (1956, §2651), Montanari (2015) and Liddell and Scott (1996). Smyth (1956) in §2657 has misquoted D. 18.71, which should be placed in §2656.

EXERCISE 17

Translate the following passages.

1. καὶ σὺ δὴ πόνων ἐμῶν ἥκεις ἐπόπτης;

ἐπόπτης, -ου, ὁ	observer

2. πῶς εἶπας; ἦ 'μὸς παῖς σ' ἀπαλλάξει κακῶν;

λέγειν, εἰπεῖν	to say; to mean
ἀπαλλάσσειν	to release

3. ἆρ' ἂν παρ' ὑμῶν, ὦ ξένοι, μάθοιμ' ὅπου τὰ τοῦ τυράννου δώματ' ἐστὶν Οἰδίπου;

4. ἆρ' οὐκ ἄν, εἰ μὲν ἐπιθυμῶν τοῦ δοκεῖν ἱκανὸς εἶναι ταῦτα πράττειν μὴ δύναιτο πείθειν, τοῦτ' εἴη λυπηρόν ...;

δοκεῖν	to seem
λυπηρός, -ά, -όν	distressing

5. μή τί σοι δοκῶ ταρβεῖν ὑποπτήσσειν τε τοὺς νέους θεούς;

ταρβεῖν	to be fearful
ὑποπτήσσειν	to cower before (+ Acc.)

6. τῆς δὲ κακῆς τε καὶ αἰσχρᾶς παιδείας ἐν πόλει ἆρα μή τι μεῖζον ἕξεις λαβεῖν τεκμήριον ...;

τεκμήριον, -ου, τό	evidence (here + Gen. τῆς ... παιδείας)

7. τίνες κατῆρξαν, πότερον Ἕλληνες, μάχης, ἢ παῖς ἐμός, πλήθει καταυχήσας νεῶν;

κατάρχειν	to begin (+ Gen.)
καταυχεῖν	to be overconfident

8. τί φῶ χέουσα τάσδε κηδείους χοάς;
   πῶς εὔφρον' εἴπω;

χεῖν	to pour
κήδειος, -ον	(*funereal, sepulchral;*) *for the dead*
χοή, -ῆς, ἡ	(*pouring out;*) *drink-offering*
εὔφρων, -ον	*gracious*

9. Therefore, the names of the men, against whom that [man] laid information, are these?

| *against* | κατά (+ Gen.) |
| *to lay information* | μηνύειν |

10. Does Aeschines seem to you, O men of Athens, to be an employee or a guest-friend of Alexander?

Does ... or	Use πότερον ... ἤ.
Aeschines	Αἰσχίνης, -ου, ὁ
employee	μισθωτός, -οῦ, ὁ
guest-friend	ξένος, -ου, ὁ
Alexander	Ἀλέξανδρος, -ου, ὁ

LESSON 18
Reported Questions

18.1. Reported Ordinary Questions

The verbs in reported questions have the same usage of Mood and Tense as in reported statements with ὅτι or ὡς. See Lessons 13.2 and 13.3. Reported ordinary questions are regularly introduced by the conjunction εἰ in the sense 'whether'. οὐ or μή may be retained from the presumed direct form of a reported question. The whole reported question is the direct Object of the leading verb.

ὅρα νυν **εἰ** σοι ταῦτ' ἀρωγὰ **φαίνεται**. (A.Pr. 997.)
*Come now, **see whether** this **seems** helpful to you.*

Direct form: (ἆρά) σοι ταῦτα ἀρωγὰ φαίνεται; 'Does this seem helpful to you?' In Primary sequence, the Mood and Tense of the verb in the reported form are the same as in the direct form.

ταῦτα εἰπὼν **ἐπήρετο** τὸν Μηδοσάδην **εἰ** ἀληθῆ ταῦτα **εἴη**. (X.An. 7.2.25.)

*After saying this **he asked** Medosades **in addition**, **whether** this **was** true.*

Direct form: (ἆρα) ἀληθῆ ταῦτά ἐστι; 'Is this true?' In Past sequence, the Indicative of the direct form becomes Optative in the reported form.

... καὶ **ἠρώτα εἰ οὐχ** ἱκανόν μοι **εἴη** αὐτῷ ἀπολυθῆναι τῆς ἐγγύης τῆς πρὸς τὴν τράπεζαν ... (D. 33.11.)

*... and **he asked whether** it was **not** enough for me to be released myself from the security-paid to the bank ...*

Direct form: (ἆρα) οὐχ ἱκανόν σοί ἐστιν αὐτῷ ἀπολυθῆναι ...; 'Is it not enough for you yourself to be released ...?' οὐχ of the direct form is retained in the reported form and implies the expectation of a positive answer.

ἔστι δ' ὁ **νῦν ἀγὼν καὶ ἡ διαδικασία** ... **εἰ μὴ** προσήκει ἐξελαθῆναι ἐκ τοῦ οἴκου τοῦ Ἁγνίου τοὺς οἰκείους τοὺς Ἁγνίου ... (D. 43.61.)

And the **present lawsuit and dispute** *are <about> ...* **whether** *it is* **really** *appropriate that the kinsmen of Hagnias should be driven out of the household of Hagnias ...*

Direct form: (ἆρα) μὴ προσήκει ...; 'Is it really appropriate ...?' μή of the direct form is retained in the reported form, and lends a more emotional tone to the question ('really'). μή does not in itself imply the expectation of a negative answer.

18.2. ἆρα in Reported Questions

Sometimes, ἆρα seems to be used to introduce a reported ordinary question. A noticeable proportion of the examples of this usage are exhortations to 'examine' whether something is the case, especially with forms of the verb σκέπτεσθαι. As in the following example, it is frequently ambiguous whether the question is reported or actually direct.

τοῦτο μὲν τοίνυν, εἶπον, ἐν ἡμῖν κείσθω· δεύτερον δὲ τὸ ἐχόμενον τούτου **σκεψώμεθα ἆρά** τι προσήκει ἡμῖν. (Pl.R. 526 C.)

Reported: '*Let this one point, therefore*', *I said*, '*be assumed for us; and* **let us consider** *a second, following from this one, (as to)* **whether** *it is of any concern to us*'.

Direct: '*and let us consider a second, following from this one. Is it of any concern to us?*'

18.3. Reported Alternative Questions

Reported alternative questions may be introduced by πότερον (-α)...ἤ, as with direct alternative questions, or by ὁπότερον (-α)...ἤ. Or they may be introduced by several other combinations of conjunctions, as in the following examples. Where the second alternative is negative, μή is sometimes used, rather than οὐ, without any obvious syntactical justification.

LESSON 18. REPORTED QUESTIONS

... ἢ που περί γε τοῦ μήθ' ἑαλωκότος μήτ' ἐγνωσμένου, **πότερον** δέδρακεν **ἢ** οὔ, καὶ **πότερ'** ἄκων **ἢ** ἑκών, πάνδεινον γράφειν ὡς ἐκδοτέον τοῖς ἐγκαλοῦσιν. (D. 23.79.)

*... surely in the case of a man who has been neither convicted nor judged as to **whether** he has done <something> **or** not, and **whether** accidentally **or** deliberately, <it is> outrageous to draft <a law>, that it is necessary to hand <him> over to his accusers.*

πότερον (-α) ... ἤ with two sets of alternatives. Negative οὐ with the second alternative of the first set.

εἰ μέντοι χρήμαθ' ἕξει τοσαῦτα ὅσα σὺ δίδως **ἢ** καὶ ἄλλα πολλαπλάσια τούτων, οὐκ ἂν ἔχοιμι εἰπεῖν· (X.Cyr. 5.2.12.)

*But **whether** he will have so much money as you are offering **or** actually other <funds> many times more than this, I would not be able to say.*

εἰ...ἤ gives preference to the second alternative, here reinforced by καί.

... καὶ δίδωμι ὑμῖν σὺν τοῖς ἄλλοις Χαλδαίοις βουλεύσασθαι **εἴτε** βούλεσθε πολεμεῖν ἡμῖν **εἴτε** φίλοι εἶναι. (X.Cyr. 3.2.13.)

*... and I am allowing you to consult with the rest of the Chaldaeans as to **whether** you want to go to war with us **or** to be friends.*

εἴτε...εἴτε gives equal value to each alternative.

δρᾶσαι γάρ, ὥσπερ ἔστιν, οὐκ ἀρνούμεθα·
ἀλλ' **εἰ** δικαίως **εἴτε** μὴ τῇ σῇ φρενὶ
δοκεῖ, τόδ' αἷμα κρῖνον ... (A.Eu. 611–613.)

*For, as it is, we do not deny that we did it.
But judge this murder, as to **whether** to your mind
it seems justly <done> **or** not ...*

εἰ...εἴτε also gives equal value to each alternative. Negative μή is used with the second alternative.

18.4. Reported Questions with Interrogative Adjectives or Adverbs

Reported questions may be introduced by the indirect form of interrogative adjectives or adverbs. Corresponding to the direct forms τίς ('Who?'), πῶς ('How?') and so on, are the indirect forms ὅστις, ὅπως and so on. However, quite often the direct forms are also used to introduce reported questions. And sometimes the relative forms ὅς, ὡς and so on are used.

φέρε γὰρ
σήμαιν' **ὅ τι** χρή σοι συμπράσσειν· (A.Pr. 294–295.)

*So come,
indicate **what** <I> should do to help you.*

Indirect interrogative pronoun ὅ τι.

σήμηνον **ὅποι**
γῆς ἡ μογερὰ πεπλάνημαι. (A.Pr. 564–565.)

*Indicate **to where**
on earth I poor girl have wandered.*

Indirect interrogative adverb ὅποι.

ὥστε οὐ ῥᾴδιον εὑρεῖν **τί** ἐν τῇ θήρᾳ ἄπεστι τῶν ἐν πολέμῳ παρόντων. (X.Cyr. 1.2.10.)

*And so <it is> not easy to find out **which** of the <elements> present in war is absent in hunting.*

Direct interrogative pronoun τί in reported question.

... κἄκρινα πρῶτος ἐξ ὀνειράτων **ἃ** χρὴ
ὕπαρ γενέσθαι ... (A.Pr. 485–486.)

*... and I first discerned among dreams, **which ones** should become reality ...*

Relative adjective ἅ in reported question.

... τὸ μέλλον **ᾗ κραίνοιτο** προυτεθεσπίκει,
ὡς οὐ κατ' ἰσχὺν οὐδὲ πρὸς τὸ καρτερὸν
χρείη, δόλῳ δὲ τοὺς ὑπερέχοντας κρατεῖν. (A.Pr. 211–213.)

... (she) had foretold **in what way** the future **was being brought to pass**,
how not by strength nor with force
should the winners **prevail**, but by cunning.

Direct form: πῆ τὸ μέλλον κραίνεται; πῶς χρὴ τοὺς ὑπερέχοντας κρατεῖν; 'In what way is the future being brought to pass? How should the winners prevail?' Relative adverbs ᾗ and ὡς in reported questions. κραίνοιτο and χρείη are Optative in Past sequence after προυτεθεσπίκει (Past Perf.).

18.5. Reported Deliberative Questions

Reported Deliberative questions follow a pattern of usage similar to that of other types of reported discourse.

οὐκ οἶδ' **ὅπως** σε **φῶ** βεβουλεῦσθαι καλῶς· (S.*OT* 1367.)
*I do not know **how I am to say** that you have made a good decision.*

Direct form: πῶς φῶ ...; 'How am I to say ...?' In Primary sequence, the Mood and Aspect of the verb in the reported form is the same as in the direct form.

φοιτᾷ γὰρ ἡμᾶς ἔγκος ἐξαιτῶν πορεῖν,
γυναῖκά τ' οὐ γυναῖκα, μητρῷαν δ' **ὅπου**
κίχοι διπλῆν ἄρουραν οὗ τε καὶ τέκνων. (S.*OT* 1255–1257.)

*For he was wandering around, asking us to provide a sword,
and **where he was to find** the wife that was no wife, and the double maternal field of himself and his children.*

Direct form: ποῦ κίχω ...; 'Where am I to find ...?' In Past sequence, the Subjunctive of the direct form becomes Optative in the same Aspect in the reported form.

ἐπειδὴ γὰρ ἔδει τῷ ὀρφανῷ τὰ χρήματα ἀποδιδόναι, ὁ δ' οὐκ εἶχεν **ὁπόθεν ἀποδῷ** ..., τὸ χωρίον ἐπώλει. (Is. 2.28.)

*For when it had become necessary to pay back the money to the orphan, and he did not know **from where he was to pay** <it> **back** ..., he was <in favour of> selling the property.*

Direct form: πόθεν ἀποδῶ; 'From where am I to pay <it> back?' In a Vivid construction in Past sequence, the Mood and Aspect of the direct form are retained in the reported form.

References

Goodwin (1889), *Syntax of the moods and tenses of the Greek verb*, §§665, 667, 669–672, 677–681.

Smyth (1956), *Greek grammar*, §§2663–2679.

EXERCISE 18

Translate the following passages. For the Exercise, εἰ should preferably be translated as 'whether'.

1. ἐκ δὲ τούτου ἐπυνθάνετο ἤδη αὐτῶν καὶ ὁπόσην ὁδὸν διήλασαν καὶ εἰ οἰκοῖτο ἡ χώρα.

ἐκ	*after*
πυνθάνεσθαι	*to inquire (of someone)* (+ Gen. and reported questions)
καί ... καί ...	*also ... and ...*
διελαύνειν	*to ride over*

2. πέμπει οὖν πρὸς αὐτὸν καὶ ἐρωτᾷ πότερον βούλεται εἰρήνην ἢ πόλεμον ἔχειν.

πέμπει...ἐρωτᾷ ...	Hist. Pres.
βούλεται	Vivid construction

3. ... ἀκούσαντες σκοπεῖτ' εἴτ' ὀρθῶς λογίζομαι ταῦτ' εἴτε μή.

σκοπεῖτ(ε)	Impv.
λογίζεσθαι (Mid.)	*to assess*

4. ὃς μέν νυν τῶν ὑπάρχων στρατὸν κάλλιστα ἐσταλμένον ἀγαγὼν τὰ προκείμενα παρὰ βασιλέος ἔλαβε δῶρα, οὐκ ἔχω φράσαι.

μέν νυν	*well now* (transitional phrase)
ὕπαρχος, -ου, ὁ	*commander*
στέλλειν	*to equip*
προκεῖσθαι	*to be proffered*
βασιλέος (Ionic Gen.)	βασιλέως (Attic)

LESSON 18. REPORTED QUESTIONS

5. οὐκ οἶδ' ὅπως ὑμῖν ἀπιστῆσαί με χρή ...

ἀπιστεῖν	*to disobey* (+ Dat.)

6. ὁ δ' ἔς τε Πυθὼ κἀπὶ Δωδώνης πυκνοὺς
   θεοπρόπους ἴαλλεν, ὡς μάθοι τί χρὴ
   δρῶντ' ἢ λέγοντα δαίμοσιν πράσσειν φίλα.

ὁ δ(έ)	*and he*
Πυθώ, -οῦς, ἡ	*Pytho* (region around Delphi)
ἐπί (+ Gen.)	*in the direction of, to*
πυκνός, -ή, -όν	*frequent*
θεοπρόπος, -ου, ὁ	*messenger* (adj. as noun)
ἰάλλειν	*to send*
φίλα (n. pl. Acc.)	*pleasing (to)* (+ Dat.)

7. And all the aliens who are residents will know whether unjustly they are excluding the thirty from the[ir] cities, or justly.

all ... who	ὅσοι (+ Indic.)
alien	ξένος, -ου, ὁ
to be a resident	ἐπιδημεῖν
to exclude (by proclamation)	ἐκκηρύττειν
thirty (tyrants)	τριάκοντα (indeclinable), οἱ (installed in 404 BCE)

8. And on hearing this, Clearchus asked the messenger approximately how big the country between the Tigris and the canal was.

Clearchus	Κλέαρχος, -ου, ὁ
approximately how big	Use τις (enclitic) in agreement with (and after) the appropriate gender of (ὁ)πόσος.
between	ἐν μέσῳ (+ Gen.)
Tigris	Τίγρης, -ητος, ὁ
canal	διῶρυξ, -υχος, ἡ

LESSON 19
Conditions

19.1. Introduction

In the study of Greek syntax, various schemes of classification have been used for Conditions. The following scheme is intended to be as simple and clear as possible. It classifies the usual practice of the classical period, according to type of Condition, with subdivisions according to time reference. (Homeric Conditions show some differences; see Lesson 20.) The negative in all types of Conditional clause is regularly μή.

Conditional clauses are adverbial clauses, which modify the verb in the clause on which they depend. Most commonly, the leading clause is the Main clause of a sentence. But a Conditional clause may depend on another Subordinate clause, as in §19.4.1 below.

19.2. Open Conditions

Open Conditions leave it 'open' whether the Condition is, or is likely to be, fulfilled.

19.2.1. Particular

Open Particular Conditions refer to 'particular' circumstances and, therefore, use εἰ with Indicative in the if-clause, and Indicative in the Main clause (if the Main clause is a statement).

Present

εἰ τοῦτο ποιοῦσιν, ἁμαρτάνουσιν.
If they are doing this, they are making a mistake.

Past

εἰ τοῦτο ἐποίουν, ἡμάρτανον.
If they were doing this, they were making a mistake.

Past Imperfect Indicative denotes continuous or repeated action.

εἰ τοῦτο ἐποίησαν, ἥμαρτον.
If they did this, they made a mistake.

Past Aorist Indicative denotes momentary action.

Future

εἰ τοῦτο ποιήσουσιν, ἁμαρτήσονται.
If they do this, they will make a mistake.

In English idiom, a Present form is regularly used in the if-clause of a Future Open Condition (so also in §19.2.2 below). Future Open Particular Conditions, with Indicative in the if-clause, are less common but more emphatic than Future Open General Conditions. They are used especially in threats or warnings.

εἰ σ' ἡ 'πιοῦσα λάμπας ὄψεται θεοῦ
καὶ παῖδας ἐντὸς τῆσδε τερμόνων χθονὸς,
θανῇ· (E. *Med.* 352–354.)

If the coming light of god sees you
and your children within the limits of this land,
you will die.

19.2.2. General

Open General Conditions all refer to the circumstances of the Condition in a 'general' or 'indefinite' way. Parallel to other indefinite constructions, they therefore use ἐάν with Subjunctive in Primary sequence in if-clauses, and εἰ with Optative in Past sequence. Alternative forms for ἐάν also occur: ἤν, ἄν (with long α).

Present

ἐὰν τοῦτο ποιῶσιν, ἁμαρτάνουσιν.
If (ever) they do this, they are making a mistake.

ἐάν + Subjunctive in if-clause; Indicative in Main clause.

Past

εἰ τοῦτο ποιοῖεν, ἡμάρτανον.
If (ever) they were doing this, they were making a mistake.

Imperfect Optative and Past Imperfect Indicative denote continuous or repeated action.

εἰ τοῦτο ποιήσειαν, ἥμαρτον.
If (ever) they did this, they made a mistake.

Aorist Optative and Past Aorist Indicative denote momentary action.

In both Past examples, εἰ + Optative in if-clause; Indicative in Main clause.

Future

ἐὰν τοῦτο ποιῶσιν, ἁμαρτήσονται.
If (ever) they do this, they will make a mistake.

ἐάν + Subjunctive in if-clause; Indicative in Main clause.

19.3. Unfulfilled Conditions

Unfulfilled Conditions imply that the circumstances of the if-clause are contrary to fact or 'unfulfilled'. From a chronological point of view, any Future Condition is necessarily unfulfilled. But the term 'unfulfilled' is not applied to other Future Conditions. Future Unfulfilled Conditions are unlikely to be fulfilled. They belong to the same category of Condition as Present and Past Unfulfilled Conditions.

Especially in the scheme of Unfulfilled Conditions, it should be noted that the headings 'Present', 'Past' and 'Future' indicate the time reference of the Conditions, not necessarily the Tense of the Indicative verbs, and certainly not the Aspect of the Optative verbs. The form of the Past *continuous* Unfulfilled Condition is the same as the form of the Present Unfulfilled Condition. In the if-clause of English Present and Future Unfulfilled Conditions, 'were' is a Subjunctive form, not a Past Indicative form.

Present

εἰ τοῦτο ἐποίουν, ἡμάρτανον ἄν.
If they were (now) doing this, they would be making a mistake.

εἰ + Past Imperfect Indicative in if-clause; Past Imperfect Indicative with ἄν in Main clause.

Past

εἰ τοῦτο ἐποίουν, ἡμάρτανον ἄν.
If they had been doing this, they would have been making a mistake.

εἰ + Past Imperfect Indicative in if-clause; Past Imperfect Indicative with ἄν in Main clause; continuous.

εἰ τοῦτο ἐποίησαν, ἥμαρτον ἄν.
If they had done this, they would have made a mistake.

εἰ + Past Aorist Indicative in if-clause; Past Aorist Indicative with ἄν in Main clause; momentary.

Future

εἰ τοῦτο ποιοῖεν, ἁμαρτάνοιεν ἄν.
If they were to (be) do(ing) this, they would be making a mistake. Imperfect Aspect; continuous.

εἰ τοῦτο ποιήσειαν, ἁμάρτοιεν ἄν.
If they were to do this, they would make a mistake. Aorist Aspect; momentary.

(Often expressed as: *If they did this, …*)

In both Future examples, εἰ + Optative in if-clause; Optative with ἄν in Main clause.

19.4. Mixed Conditions

19.4.1. Mixed Times and Types

In some Conditional sentences, there may be a difference of time reference or of type of Condition (or both) between the Main clause and the if-clause, as in the following sentence.

καὶ δῆλον ὅτι, εἰ τοῖς πλέοσιν ἀρέσκοντές ἐσμεν, τοῖσδ᾽ ἂν μόνοις οὐκ ὀρθῶς ἀπαρέσκοιμεν … (Th. 1.38.4.)

And <it is> clear that, if we are acceptable to the greater number, we would not rightly be unacceptable to these <people> alone …

Present Open Particular if-clause, Future Unfulfilled Main clause.

19.4.2. General Principles (with Primary Time Reference)

Open General Conditions, expressing a general principle, may sometimes have Optative (rather than Subjunctive) in the if-clause, and Indicative in the Main clause. The Indicative of the Main clause is usually Present (sometimes with Future implications), sometimes Future, or rarely Present Perfect. And sometimes, in the Main clause the verb 'to be' is unexpressed.

καὶ οὐκ ἄδικος αὕτη ἡ ἀξίωσίς ἐστιν, εἰ τύχοιεν πρὸς ἀλλήλους οἵ τε ἀφιστάμενοι καὶ ἀφ' ὧν διακρίνοιντο ἴσοι μὲν τῇ γνώμῃ ὄντες καὶ εὐνοίᾳ ... (Th. 3.9.2.)

And this assessment is not unfair, if those who secede <from an alliance> and <those> from whom they are separated [were to] happen to be on an equal footing towards each other in attitude and good will ...

In English style, it would be natural to omit the words '[were to]'. But then the distinctive form of the Greek construction is lost in translation.

λυπουμένοις ὀχληρός, εἰ μόλοι, ξένος. (E.*Alc.* 540.)
A visitor, if he were to come, <is> annoying to people who are grieving.

The verb 'to be' is unexpressed in the Main clause in Greek. Again, in English style it would be natural to say 'comes' rather than 'were to come'.

19.4.3. Iterative Past Conditions

There is also an iterative form of Past Open General Condition, using εἰ + Optative in the if-clause, and ἄν with either Past Imperfect Indicative or Past Aorist Indicative in the Main clause. The term 'iterative' indicates repeated action.

... εἰ πολιορκουμένῃ τινὶ τῶν πόλεων τῶν συμμαχίδων εἷς μόνος Λακεδαιμονίων βοηθήσειεν, ὑπὸ πάντων ἂν ὡμολογεῖτο παρὰ τοῦτον γενέσθαι τὴν σωτηρίαν αὐτοῖς. (Isoc. 6.52.)

... if a single one of the Spartans came to help one of our allied cities when it was under siege, it used to be agreed by all that due to this man safety had come to them.

Past Imperfect Indicative in Main clause denotes continuous action.

εἰ δέ τις ὑμᾶς ὑποθωπεύσας λιπαρὰς καλέσειεν Ἀθήνας,
εὕρετο πᾶν διὰ τὰς λιπαράς, ἀφύων τιμὴν περιάψας.
(Ar.*Ach.* 639–640.)

And if anyone, using flattery, called you 'shining Athens',
he obtained everything on account of that 'shining', by surrounding small fry
with honour.

Past Aorist Indicative in Main clause denotes momentary action.

19.5. The Negative in If-Clauses

The negative in if-clauses is regularly μή (as noted in §19.1 above). In particular circumstances, οὐ may occur:

- οὐ negates an individual word, for example, οὐκ ἐθέλειν, 'to be un-willing'
- the factuality of a condition is emphasised
- οὐ negates one of two contrasted clauses, which are introduced by a single εἰ with Indicative
- with expressions of emotion, οὐ may occur in a clause where 'if' is equivalent to 'that' (Lesson 34.4)
- οὐ may negate a clause, in which 'if' is virtually Causal, meaning 'since', 'because' (Lessons 23.1 and 1.1).

References

Goodwin (1889), *Syntax of the moods and tenses of the Greek verb*, §§162, 378–513.

Smyth (1956), *Greek grammar*, §§2280–2368, 2696–2698, 2701.

The analyses of Goodwin (1889) and Smyth (1956) are more complex than that which has been attempted here, and their terminology is different in part.

EXERCISE 19

Translate the following passages.

1. εἰ δ' ἔστιν ὅστις δαιμόνων ὑπερφρονεῖ,
   ἐς τοῦδ' ἀθρήσας θάνατον ἡγείσθω θεούς.

ὑπερφρονεῖν	to look down on, to despise (+ Gen.)
ἀθρεῖν ἐς (+ Acc.)	to look at, to observe
ἡγεῖσθαι	to believe in (+ Acc.)

2. εἰ δ' ἐργάσῃ
   μὴ ταῦτα, λύπην πᾶσιν Ἀργείοις βαλεῖς.

3. εἰ γὰρ τὰ τοῦδε τόξα μὴ ληφθήσεται,
   οὐκ ἔστι πέρσαι σοι τὸ Δαρδάνου πέδον.

τόξα, -ων, τά	bow
πέρθειν	to ravage, to sack
Δάρδανος, -ου, ὁ	Dardanus (mythical ancestor of kings of Troy)
πέδον, -ου, τό	land

4. εἰ δ' αὖ τι πράξαιτ' ἀγαθὸν ἀττικωνικοί
   κἄλθοιεν οἱ Λάκωνες εἰρήνης πέρι,
   ἐλέγετ' ἂν ὑμεῖς εὐθύς· ἐξαπατώμεθα …

δ' αὖ	and/but again (often enumerating)
ἀττικωνικοί	οἱ Ἀττικωνικοί, 'the Atticononians' (coined to rhyme with Λακωνικοί, Laconians)
κἄλθοιεν	καὶ ἔλθοιεν
Λάκωνες, -ων, οἱ	Laconians
ἐξαπατᾶν	to deceive (here Pass., and beginning direct speech)

5. ἢν δ' αὖ γένηται ξυμφορά τις ἐς λέχος,
   τὰ λῷστα καὶ κάλλιστα πολεμιώτατα
   τίθεσθε.

λέχος, -ους, τό	(*bed*, often referring to) *marriage*
λῷστος, -η, -ον	*best*
τίθεσθαι (Mid.)	*to regard (as)* (here Indic.)

6. εἰ παρῆσθα, τὸν θεὸν τὸν νῦν ψέγεις
   εὐχαῖσιν ἂν μετῆλθες …

τόν (2nd instance)	ὅν
ψέγειν	*to criticise*
εὐχή, -ῆς, ἡ	*prayer*
μετελθεῖν (Aor.)	*to approach (someone:* Acc.) *with (something:* Dat.)

7. ἐγὼ μὲν ἄν, ἔφη ὁ Κῦρος, εἰ σὺ εἴην, ὡς τάχιστα ὅπλα ποιοίμην πᾶσι Πέρσαις τοῖς προσιοῦσιν …

προσιέναι	*to approach, to come (here)* (in friendly sense)

8. And perhaps I would have been put to death because of this, if the government had not been quickly dissolved.

perhaps	ἴσως
to be put to death = to die	ἀποθνῄσκειν
government	ἀρχή, -ῆς, ἡ
to dissolve	καταλύειν

9. For I would not be speaking, if I did not care greatly for the whole of Greece.

to care (for)	κήδεσθαι (Mid.; + Gen.)

LESSON 20
Homeric Conditions

20.1. Introduction

In the Homeric poems, Conditional sentences have not yet attained the regularity of the classical period. Some Homeric Conditions have the same form as those of the classical period. Some may be explained as mixed types. But some Homeric constructions no longer appear in the classical period. On the other hand, some classical constructions have not yet developed at the stage of the Homeric poems. The Doric and Aeolic form αἰ may be used instead of εἰ in Homer. And the enclitic κε may be used instead of ἄν. When κε occurs before a word beginning with a vowel, either movable ν may be added, or ε may be elided.

The following sections of this Lesson contain some representative examples of Homeric constructions which differ from the classical standard. At the risk of anachronism, but for the sake of comparison, the same categories are used as in Lesson 19. However, scholars do not always agree in the classification or translation of Homeric Conditions.

20.2. Open Conditions

20.2.1. Open Particular Conditions

Open Particular Conditions normally have the same form in Homer as in the classical period. However, in addition to the usual form of Future Open Particular Condition (εἰ + Indic. in if-clause, Indic. in Main clause), κε may appear with the Indicative in the if-clause in Homer.

σοὶ μὲν δή, Μενέλαε, κατηφείη καὶ ὄνειδος
ἔσσεται, **εἴ κ'** Ἀχιλῆος ἀγαυοῦ πιστὸν ἑταῖρον
τείχει ὕπο Τρώων ταχέες κύνες **ἑλκήσουσιν·** (Hom. *Il.* 17.556–558.)

*For you indeed, Menelaus, there will be dejection
and reproach, **if** swift hounds **tear apart** the trusted companion
of noble Achilles under the wall of the Trojans.*

20.2.2. Open General Conditions

20.2.2.1. Present

In Present Open General Conditions, Homer regularly uses εἰ (αἰ) alone and the Subjunctive without ἄν or κε.

εἰ δ' ἄρα τις καὶ μοῦνος ἰὼν **ξύμβληται** ὁδίτης,
οὔ τι κατακρύπτουσιν, ἐπεί σφισιν ἐγγύθεν εἰμέν,
ὥς περ Κύκλωπές τε καὶ ἄγρια φῦλα Γιγάντων.
(Hom.*Od.* 7.204–206.)

*And **if**, then, any one going alone as a wayfarer **meets up with** <them>,
they do not conceal at all, since we are near to them,
just as the Cyclopes and the wild tribes of the Giants.*

ξύμβληται is third person singular Aorist Subjunctive Middle of συμβάλλειν.

A classical equivalent of the Homeric construction occurs in the following example.

τέλει γάρ, **εἴ** τι νὺξ **ἀφῇ**,
τοῦτ' ἐπ' ἦμαρ ἔρχεται· (S.*OT* 198–199.)

*For, **if** night **leaves** anything **out**,
this day comes on for completion.*

(Most editors emend τέλει to τελεῖν, and take τοῦτ(ο) as Acc.: *day comes on to complete this*. On either reading ἐπ(ί) is an adv. not a preposition.)

20.2.2.2. Future

a. Future Open General Conditions are far more common in Homer than Future Open Particular Conditions. (This tendency continues into the classical period.) Homer most often uses εἰ (αἰ) and the Subjunctive with κε (or occasionally ἄν), equivalent to classical ἐάν and the Subjunctive, in the if-clause, and Future Indicative in the Main clause. For the if-clause, ἤν is also frequent; but the forms ἐάν and ἄν (with long α) do not occur in Homer.

τούτῳ μὲν γὰρ κῦδος ἅμ' ἕψεται, **εἴ κεν** Ἀχαιοὶ
Τρῶας δῃώσωσιν ἕλωσί τε Ἴλιον ἱρήν ... (Hom.*Il.* 4.415–416.)

*For renown will follow after this <man>, **if** the Achaeans
cut down the Trojans and **capture** sacred Ilios ...*

Future Indicative in Main clause, εἴ κεν with Subjunctive in if-clause.

b. Instead of the usual Future Indicative of the Main clause of a Future Open General Conditional sentence, the Subjunctive (with κε or ἄν) may occur in Homer. However, this usage is equivalent in function to the Future Indicative, and is to be translated as a Future Indicative.

καὶ δέ κέ τοι **εἴπῃσι**, διοτρεφές, **αἴ κ' ἐθέλῃσθα**,
ὅττι τοι ἐν μεγάροισι κακόν τ' ἀγαθόν τε τέτυκται ...
(Hom.*Od.* 4.391–392.)

*And **he will** also **tell** you, <O man> favoured by Zeus, **if you are willing**,
what evil and what good has been done in your halls ...*

εἴπῃσι (3rd pers. sg. Aor. Subj. Act.) instead of ἐρεῖ (Fut. Indic.) in Main clause. τοι = σοι.

c. A variation of this form is a mixed Condition, which uses εἰ with Optative for the if-clause and κε or ἄν with Subjunctive in the Main clause. The if-clause has the form of a Future Unfulfilled Condition, but is to be translated as a Future Open General Condition (Pres. Indic. in English). And the Main clause, again, is to be translated by a Future Indicative in English. This form occurs especially in threats or warnings; and the negative with the Subjunctive in the Main clause is οὐ, not μή.

... **εἰ** μὲν δὴ ἀντίβιον σὺν τεύχεσι **πειρηθείης**,
οὐκ ἄν τοι χραίσμῃσι βιὸς καὶ ταρφέες ἰοί·
(Hom.*Il.* 11.386–387.)

*... **if** indeed in opposition **you [were to] make an attempt** with weapons,
your bow and dense <shower of> arrows will not protect you.*

Negative οὐ with χραίσμῃσι (3rd pers. sg. Aor. Subj. Act.) in Main clause.

d. εἰ alone without ἄν or κε is occasionally used with the Subjunctive in Future Open General Conditions in Homer.

σχέτλιος· **εἴ** περ γάρ σε **κατακτάνῃ**, οὔ σ᾽ ἔτ᾽ ἐγώ γε
κλαύσομαι ἐν λεχέεσσι, φίλον θάλος, ὃν τέκον αὐτή,
οὐδ᾽ ἄλοχος πολύδωρος· (Hom.*Il.* 22.86–88.)

<He is> cruel. For **if** indeed **he kills** you, I for my part shall no longer lament for you on your deathbed, dear child, whom I myself bore, nor will your gifted wife.

A classical equivalent of the Homeric construction occurs in the following example.

οὔ τοι μὰ τὴν Δήμητρά γ᾽, **εἰ** μὴ σ᾽ **ἐκφάγω**
ἐκ τῆσδε τῆς γῆς, οὐδέποτε βιώσομαι. (Ar.*Eq.* 698–699.)

No indeed by Demeter, **if I do** not **eat you up**
out of this land, I shall not even ever live.

(The reading of the earliest manuscript is given for line 698. Some other manuscripts read ἐάν for εἰ and adjust the metre. But it is unlikely that an original classical construction would have been altered to a Homeric one.)

20.3. Unfulfilled Conditions

20.3.1. Present

There seem to be no Unfulfilled Conditional sentences in Homer, where both the if-clause and the Main clause refer to the present. However, there are mixed Conditions, in which the if-clause is Past Unfulfilled with εἰ and Past Aorist Indicative, whereas the Main clause is Present Unfulfilled with Optative and κε(ν) (not Past Imperf. Indic. with ἄν).

... **εἰ** μέν τις τὸν ὄνειρον Ἀχαιῶν ἄλλος **ἔνισπεν**,
ψεῦδός **κεν φαῖμεν** καὶ **νοσφιζοίμεθα** μᾶλλον. (Hom.*Il.* 2.80–81.)

... *if any other of the Achaeans* **had reported** *this dream,*
we would be calling *<it> a falsehood and* **would** *rather* **be turning away**
from *<it>*.

20.3.2. Past

Past Aorist Indicative is used in Past Unfulfilled Conditions in Homer as in classical Attic. But Past Imperfect Indicative in Unfulfilled Conditions in Homer *always* refers to *past continuous* action, and does not express a Present Unfulfilled Condition.

Occasionally, Homer uses Indicative in the if-clause, but Optative with κε(ν) in the Main clause of a Past Unfulfilled Condition. (There are further examples of Main clauses of this type, without any if-clause.)

ἔνθα **κε** ῥεῖα **φέροι** κλυτὰ τεύχεα Πανθοΐδαο
Ἀτρεΐδης, **εἰ** μή οἱ **ἀγάσσατο** Φοῖβος Ἀπόλλων ...
(Hom.*Il.* 17.70–71.)

*Then easily **would** the son of Atreus **have been carrying off** the splendid armour*
*of the son of Panthoüs, **if** Phoebus Apollo **had** not **envied** him.*

20.3.3. Future

For Future Unfulfilled Conditions, Homer does use the same construction as writers of the classical period: εἰ with Optative in the if-clause and Optative with ἄν (κε) in the Main clause. But he also uses εἰ (αἰ) with κε(ν) and Optative in the if-clause.

εἴ κ' ἐθέλοις μοι, ξεῖνε, παρήμενος ἐν μεγάροισι
τέρπειν, οὔ **κέ** μοι ὕπνος ἐπὶ βλεφάροισι **χυθείη**.
(Hom.*Od.* 19.589–590.)

If you were to be willing, stranger, to sit by me in my halls
*and cheer me up, sleep **would** not **be poured** over my eyelids.*

References

Goodwin (1889), *Syntax of the moods and tenses of the Greek verb*, §§434–443, 450–454, 460–461, 468–471, 474, 488.

Smyth (1956), *Greek grammar*, §§2311, 2327, 2334.

EXERCISE 20

Translate the following passages.

1. εἰ δέ τίς ἐσσι βροτῶν, οἳ ἀρούρης καρπὸν ἔδουσιν,
ἆσσον ἴθ'…

ἐσσι (enclitic)	εἶ (Attic)
ἄρουρα, -ας, ἡ	earth, land
καρπός, -οῦ, ὁ	roduce, harvest
ἔδειν	to eat (Attic: ἐσθίειν)
ἆσσον (adv.)	earer (comparative of ἄγχι)
ἴθ'	ἴθι

2. εἰ δ' αὖ τις ῥαίῃσι θεῶν ἐνὶ οἴνοπι πόντῳ,
τλήσομαι, ἐν στήθεσσιν ἔχων ταλαπενθέα θυμόν·

ῥαίειν	to cause a shipwreck
ῥαίη-σι	3rd pers. sg. Imperf. Subj. Act. with suffix
ἐνί	ἐν
ταλαπενθής, -ές	long-suffering

3. εἰ δέ κε μὴ δώωσιν, ἐγὼ δέ κεν αὐτὸς ἕλωμαι
ἢ τεὸν ἢ Αἴαντος ἰὼν γέρας, ἢ Ὀδυσῆος
ἄξω ἑλών·

δώωσιν	Attic: δῶσι(ν)
δέ (2nd instance)	then (apodotic after preceding Conditional clause)
τεός, -ά, -όν	Attic: σός, σή, σόν
Αἴας, -αντος, ὁ	Ajax

LESSON 20. HOMERIC CONDITIONS

4.   οὐδὲ πόλινδε
ἔρχομαι, εἰ μή πού τι περίφρων Πηνελόπεια
ἐλθέμεν ὀτρύνῃσιν, ὅτ' ἀγγελίη ποθὲν ἔλθῃ.

πόλιν-δε	-δε, adv. suffix: motion towards
πού τι	*perhaps*
ἐλθέμεν	ἐλθεῖν (Attic)
ὀτρύνειν	*to urge*
ὀτρύνῃ-σι	3rd pers. sg. Aor. Subj. Act. with suffix
ὅτ'	ὅτε

5. καί νύ κεν ἔνθ' ἀπόλοιτο Ἄρης ἆτος πολέμοιο,
εἰ μὴ μητρυιὴ περικαλλὴς Ἠερίβοια
Ἑρμέᾳ ἐξήγγειλεν·

νυ (enclitic)	*indeed*
ἄατος, (ἆτος) -ον	*insatiable (in)* (+ Gen.)
μητρυιά, -ᾶς, ἡ	*stepmother* (of the sons of Aloeus, just mentioned)
περικαλλής, -ές	*very beautiful*
Ἑρμῆς, -οῦ, ὁ	*Hermes* (here Dat. uncontracted)

6. εἰ χ' ἕτερον ἄξαις, ἕτερον κ' ἐπὶ βουσὶ βάλοιο.

ἀγνύναι	*to break*
ἕτερον	Refers to one of two ploughs (τὰ ἄροτρα)

7. ἀλλά μοι αἰνὸν ἄχος σέθεν ἔσσεται, ὦ Μενέλαε,
αἴ κε θάνῃς καὶ πότμον ἀναπλήσῃς βιότοιο.

αἰνός, -ά, -όν	*terrible*
ἄχος, -ους, τό	*distress*
σέθεν	σοῦ (as Objective Gen.)
ἔσσεται	ἔσται (Attic)
βίοτος, -ου (-οιο), ὁ	*life*

8. τόν γ' εἴ πως σὺ δύναιο λοχησάμενος λελαβέσθαι,
   ὅς κέν τοι εἴπῃσιν ὁδὸν καὶ μέτρα κελεύθου
   νόστον θ', ὡς ἐπὶ πόντον ἐλεύσεαι ἰχθυόεντα.

τόν	*him*
λοχᾶν	*to ambush*
(λε)λαβέσθαι	reduplicated Aor. Mid. Infin.
ὅς	*he*
τοι (Epic)	σοι (Attic)
εἴπῃ-σιν	3rd pers. sg. Aor. Subj. Act. with suffix
ὡς	*how*
ἐπί	*over*
ἐλεύσεαι	ἐλεύσῃ (Attic)
ἰχθυόεις, -εσσα, -εν	*fish-filled*

LESSON 21
Subordinate Clauses in Reported Discourse

21.1. Reported Complex Sentences

A Complex sentence has a Main clause and one or more Subordinate clauses. When a Complex sentence is reported, the Main clause has the construction of a reported Simple sentence; any Subordinate clauses have one of the following constructions in Primary (Pres. or Fut.) and Past sequence respectively (§§21.2 and 21.3 below). The possible constructions are the same, whether the Subordinate clauses depend on original statements, questions, commands, knowledge, thoughts, hopes, promises or oaths. And in reported statements, these constructions are the same, whether the original Main clause is reported after ὅτι or ὡς, or in an Infinitive phrase or a Participial phrase.

21.2. Reported Subordinate Clauses in Primary Sequence

In reported Subordinate clauses in Primary sequence, the verb has the same Mood and Tense (for Indic. verbs) or the same Aspect (for non-Indic. verbs) as in the direct form of expression.

πιστεύω γὰρ δίκαια εἶναι **ἃ λέγω** ... (Pl.*Ap.* 17 C.)
*For I believe that **what I am saying** is just ...*

Direct form: δίκαιά ἐστιν ἃ λέγω, 'What I am saying is just'.

21.3. Reported Subordinate Clauses in Past Sequence

Reported Subordinate clauses in Past sequence are treated as follows.

Primary Tenses of the Indicative and all Subjunctives are regularly changed to the same Aspect of the Optative.

All Past Tenses of the Indicative are retained.

All Optatives are retained.

ἄν with a subordinate Subjunctive in direct expression is omitted, when the Subjunctive is changed to Optative in Past sequence. Thus, ἐάν, ἐπειδάν, ὅταν, etc. become εἰ, ἐπειδή, ὅτε, etc.

Θηραμένης δέ, ὦ ἄνδρες δικασταί, … εἶπεν ὅτι οὐδὲν αὐτῷ μέλοι τοῦ ὑμετέρου θορύβου, **ἐπειδὴ** πολλοὺς μὲν Ἀθηναίων **εἰδείη** τοὺς τὰ ὅμοια πράττοντας αὐτῷ… (Lys. 12.74.)

*And Theramenes, O men of the jury, … said that he had no concern about your uproar, **since he knew** many of the Athenians who were doing the same thing as himself …*

Direct form: οὐδὲν ἐμοὶ μέλει …, ἐπειδὴ … οἶδα …, 'I have no concern …, since I know …'

Indicative οἶδα becomes Optative εἰδείη (with change of person) in the reported form.

… ἤλπιζον ἀποτρέψειν αὐτοὺς μάλιστα, **εἰ ἀντιπαραλυποῖεν** πέμψαντες ἐπὶ τοὺς ξυμμάχους αὐτῶν στρατιάν … (Th. 4.80.1.)

*… they [Spartans] hoped that they would best deter them [Athenians], **if they annoyed** them **in turn** by sending an army against their allies …*

Direct form: ἀποτρέψομεν …, ἐὰν ἀντιπαραλυπῶμεν …, 'We shall deter …, if we annoy them in turn …'

ἐάν with Subjunctive becomes εἰ with Optative (with change of person) in the reported form.

... τούς τε φεύγοντας ἐκέλευον κατ' ἐπήρειαν δέχεσθαι αὐτούς ... τούς τε φρουρούς, **οὓς** Κορίνθιοι **ἔπεμψαν**, καὶ τοὺς οἰκήτορας ἀποπέμπειν. (Th. 1.26.3.)

*... they peremptorily ordered them to receive the exiles ... and to send away the garrison members, **whom** the Corinthians **had sent**, and the colonists.*

Direct form: τοὺς φρουρούς, οὓς Κορίνθιοι ἔπεμψαν ... ἀποπέμπετε, 'Send away the garrison members whom the Corinthians sent ...'

Past (Aor.) Indicative ἔπεμψαν is retained in the reported form. (The first τε anticipates the second.)

καὶ γὰρ ἔργῳ ἐπεδείκνυτο καὶ ἔλεγεν ὅτι οὐκ ἄν ποτε προοῖτο, **ἐπεὶ** ἅπαξ φίλος αὐτοῖς **ἐγένετο**, οὐδ' **εἰ** ἔτι μὲν μείους **γένοιντο**, ἔτι δὲ κάκιον **πράξειαν**. (X.An. 1.9.10.)

*For he showed in action and stated that he would not ever abandon <them>, **when** once **he had become** a friend to them, not even **if they became** even fewer and **fared** even worse.*

προοῖτο: third person singular second Aorist Middle Optative of προιέναι.

Direct form: οὐκ ἄν ποτε προοῖμι, ἐπεὶ ἅπαξ φίλος ὑμῖν ἐγενόμην, οὐδ' εἰ ... γένοισθε ... πράξαισθε, 'I would not ever abandon <you>, when once I had become a friend to you, not even if ... you became [OR: were to become] ... and fared [OR: were to fare] ...'

Past Indicative ἐγενόμην (as in previous example) and Optative γένοισθε and πράξαισθε are retained (all with appropriate change of person).

21.4. Assimilation of Construction

Normally, all Subordinate clauses, in both direct and reported discourse, have a finite verb. However, in reported discourse, where an original Main clause is reported in an Infinitive phrase, the Subject and verb of a Subordinate clause are sometimes assimilated to the Accusative and Infinitive construction of the reported Main clause.

καὶ τῇ πόλει ὠφελιμώτερον ἔφη εἶναι πρὸς τοὺς ἐν τῇ χώρᾳ σφῶν ἐπιτειχίζοντας τὸν πόλεμον ποιεῖσθαι ἢ Συρακοσίους, **οὓς** οὐκέτι ῥᾴδιον **εἶναι** χειρώσασθαι· (Th. 7.47.4).

And he said that it was more helpful for the city to carry on the war against those who were building fortifications in their own country than against the Syracusans, ***whom it was*** *no longer easy to defeat.*

Direct form: ὠφελιμώτερόν ἐστι πρὸς τοὺς ... ἐπιτειχίζοντας τὸν πόλεμον ποιεῖσθαι ἢ Συρακοσίους, οὓς οὐκέτι ῥᾴδιόν ἐστι χειρώσασθαι, 'it is more helpful to carry on the war against those who are building fortifications ... than <against> the Syracusans, whom it is no longer easy to defeat'.

21.5. Vivid Construction

The Optative is not always used to represent Primary Indicatives and any Subjunctives in Subordinate clauses in Past sequence. Sometimes a Vivid construction, retaining the Mood of direct expression, is used.

τῶν τε παρόντων στρατιωτῶν πολλοὺς καὶ τοὺς πλείους **ἔφη**, οἳ νῦν **βοῶσιν** ὡς ἐν δεινοῖς ὄντες, ἐκεῖσε ἀφικομένους τἀναντία βοήσεσθαι, ὡς ὑπὸ χρημάτων καταπροδόντες οἱ στρατηγοὶ ἀπῆλθον. (Th. 7.48.4).

And ***he said*** *that many, indeed the majority, of the soldiers present* [in Sicily], *who now* ***were crying out*** *on the grounds that they were in dire straits, on arriving there* [at Athens] *would cry out the opposite, that under the influence of money the generals had left them in the lurch and had gone away.*

Indicative βοῶσιν is retained, instead of being converted to Optative.

References

Goodwin (1889), *Syntax of the moods and tenses of the Greek verb*, §§689–693, 755.

Smyth (1956), *Greek grammar*, §§2617–2620, 2623, 2625, 2631–2632.

LESSON 21. SUBORDINATE CLAUSES IN REPORTED DISCOURSE

EXERCISE 21

Translate the following passages.

1. ... συλλέγεσθαί φησιν ἀνθρώπους ὡς ἐμὲ πονηροὺς καὶ πολλούς, οἳ τὰ μὲν ἑαυτῶν ἀνηλώκασι, τοῖς δὲ τὰ σφέτερα σῴζειν βουλομένοις ἐπιβουλεύουσιν.

συλλέγειν	*to gather together* (Mid.: Intr.)
ὡς (+ Acc. of motion)	*to* (a person)
ἀναλίσκειν	*to use up, to spend*

2. ... ἔλεγεν ὁ Θηραμένης, ὅτι, εἰ μή τις κοινωνοὺς ἱκανοὺς λήψοιτο τῶν πραγμάτων, ἀδύνατον ἔσοιτο τὴν ὀλιγαρχίαν διαμένειν.

κοινωνός, -οῦ, ὁ	*participant, partner (in)* (+ Gen.)
πράγματα, -ων, τά	*public affairs; the government*

3. Τισσαφέρνης μὲν ὤμοσεν Ἀγησιλάῳ, εἰ σπείσαιτο, ἕως ἔλθοιεν, οὓς πέμψειε πρὸς βασιλέα ἀγγέλους, διαπράξεσθαι αὐτῷ ἀφεθῆναι αὐτονόμους τὰς ἐν τῇ Ἀσίᾳ πόλεις Ἑλληνίδας ...

σπένδεσθαι (Mid.)	*to keep a truce*
διαπράσσεσθαι	*to bring about, to accomplish* (here + Acc. and Infin.)
ἀφιέναι	*to set free*

4. ... καὶ νομίσαντες, εἰ αὐτὸν ἐξελάσειαν, πρῶτοι ἂν εἶναι, ἐμεγάλυνον καὶ ἐβόων ὡς ἐπὶ δήμου καταλύσει τά τε μυστικὰ καὶ ἡ τῶν Ἑρμῶν περικοπὴ γένοιτο καὶ οὐδὲν εἴη αὐτῷ ὅ τι οὐ μετ' ἐκείνου ἐπράχθη ...

αὐτόν, ἐκείνου	Both terms refer to Alcibiades.
ἐξελαύνειν	*to drive out, to expel*
μεγαλύνειν	*to exaggerate*
δῆμος, -ου, ὁ	*democracy*
κατάλυσις, -εως, ἡ	*overthrow*
μυστικός, -ή, -όν	*connected with the mysteries*

τὰ μυστικά	*the matter of the mysteries* (alluding to an illegitimate private celebration)
Ἑρμῆς, -οῦ, ὁ	*(statue of) Hermes*
αὐτῶν	neut.

5. For I know that, wherever I go, the young [men] will listen to me [masc.] talking as I do here.

6. ... they thought that within a few years they would demolish the power of the Athenians, if they kept ravaging their land.

to demolish	καθαιρεῖν
to keep ravaging	τέμνειν (Use Imperf. Aspect.)

LESSON 22
Result Constructions

22.1. Natural Result

Natural Result is regularly expressed by ὥστε with Infinitive (normally Imperf. or Aor.). The construction indicates what is *likely* to happen as a result of the clause on which the ὥστε phrase depends. The result may or may not *actually* happen. If the Subject of the Infinitive is the same as the Subject of the leading verb, it is usually not expressed. If the Subject of the Infinitive is different to that of the leading verb, it is usually expressed in the Accusative Case. The negative is regularly μή. This construction has hardly yet developed in Homer. (To preserve the open nature of the result, it may sometimes be necessary to use a paraphrase in English translation.)

οὐκ εὐθὺς ἐπειδὰν λάβωσι τὰς δυναστείας, ἐν τοσούτοις ἐμπεπλεγμένοι κακοῖς εἰσιν, **ὥστ' ἀναγκάζεσθαι** πολεμεῖν μὲν ἅπασι τοῖς πολίταις, μισεῖν δ' ὑφ' ὧν οὐδὲν κακὸν πεπόνθασιν …; (Isoc. 8.111–112.)

*Immediately after they have acquired supreme powers, have they not become involved in troubles so serious, **as to be compelled** to make war on all their fellow-citizens, and to hate those from whom they have experienced no trouble… ?*

Result Infinitive only, where the Subject of the Infinitive is the same as the Subject of the leading verb εἰσιν.

τί οὖν; εἴποι τις ἄν, σὺ τοσοῦθ' ὑπερῆρας ῥώμῃ καὶ τόλμῃ **ὥστε** πάντα **ποιεῖν αὐτός**; (D. 18.220.)

*'What, then?' someone might say, 'Were you so superior in strength and daring **as to do** everything **yourself**?'*

Result Infinitive with Nominative attribute of Subject of leading verb ὑπερῆρας.

οὐδὲ σθένειν τοσοῦτον ᾠόμην τὰ σὰ
κηρύγμαθ', **ὥστ'** ἄγραπτα κἀσφαλῆ θεῶν
νόμιμα **δύνασθαι θνητὸν ὄνθ'** ὑπερδραμεῖν. (S.Ant. 453–455.)

*And I did not think that your pronouncements had so much
strength,* ***that a mortal being could***
outrun the unwritten and secure laws of the gods.

Result Infinitive with Accusative Subject, which is different to the Subject of the leading verb ᾠόμην.

ἐγὼ δέ, ὦ Ἀθηναῖοι, οὐκ ἀξιῶ τοὺς θεοὺς τοιαύτην γνώμην ἔχειν,
ὥστ' εἰ ἐνόμιζον ὑπ' ἐμοῦ ἀδικεῖσθαι, λαμβάνοντάς με ἐν τοῖς
μεγίστοις κινδύνοις **μὴ τιμωρεῖσθαι**. (And. 1.137.)

But I, O men of Athens, do not expect the gods to have such an attitude,
as not to punish *me, when they caught me in the greatest danger, if they
thought that they were being wronged by me.*

Negative μή with Result Infinitive.

ἄν with the Infinitive after ὥστε represents a potential construction, corresponding to ἄν with Indicative or (as in the following example) Optative.

εἴργασαι δέ μ' ἄσκοπα,
ὥστ' εἰ πατήρ μοι ζῶν ἵκοιτο, **μηκέτ' ἂν**
τέρας **νομίζειν** αὐτό, **πιστεύειν** δ' ὁρᾶν. (S.El. 1315–1317.)

And you have had a strange effect on me,
so that*, if my father were to come here alive,* ***I would no longer
think*** *it a miracle, but* ***would believe*** *that I were seeing him.*

Here, the Subject of the Infinitives νομίζειν and πιστεύειν is not expressed, but is the same as the Object of the leading verb (εἴργασαι ... μ(ε)), and is identical with the speaker.

22.2. Comparative Result

After a Comparative adjective or adverb, ἢ ὥστε with Infinitive is used in the Result construction.

εἰ ... ὑπ' ἀναγκαίης **μέζονος** κατάζευχθε **ἢ ὥστε ἀπίστασθαι**, ὑμεῖς δὲ ἐν τῷ ἔργῳ, ἐπεὰν συμμίσγωμεν, ἐθελοκακέετε ... (Hdt. 8.22.1.)

*If ... you have been tied down under compulsion **too great to revolt from**, then you are to be deliberate losers in the action, when we join together in battle ...*

... μέζονος ... ἢ ὥστε ἀπίστασθαι: lit. 'greater than so as to revolt from'.

22.3. Actual Result

Actual Result is regularly expressed by ὥστε with finite Moods, usually Indicative. The Indicative emphasises that the result actually happens. This construction first appears in Sophocles. The negative is οὐ.

σὺ δ' εἰς τοσοῦτον τῶν μανιῶν ἐλήλυθας,
ὥστ' ἀνδράσιν **πείθῃ** χολῶσιν; (Ar.*Nu.* 832–833.)

*Have you come to so great <a degree> of madness, **that you trust** provocative men?*

οὕτω δὴ ἰόντες ἅμα τοὺς λόγους περὶ αὐτῶν ἐποιούμεθα, **ὥστε**, ὅπερ ἀρχόμενος εἶπον, **οὐκ** ἀμελετήτως **ἔχω**. (Pl.*Smp.* 173 B–C.)

*As we were going along at the same time we were conducting the discussion about it in just such a way, **that**, as I said when I was beginning, **I am not unprepared**.*

Negative οὐκ in ὥστε clause.

Potential Indicative with ἄν or potential Optative with ἄν may also appear in a finite Result clause.

ἥ τε γὰρ ἀγορὰ μεστὴ ἦν παντοδαπῶν καὶ ὅπλων καὶ ἵππων ὠνίων, οἵ τε χαλκοτύποι καὶ οἱ τέκτονες καὶ οἱ σιδηρεῖς καὶ οἱ σκυτεῖς καὶ οἱ γραφεῖς πάντες πολεμικὰ ὅπλα κατεσκεύαζον, **ὥστε** τὴν πόλιν ὄντως **ἂν ἡγήσω** πολέμου ἐργαστήριον εἶναι. (X.*Ages.* 1.26.)

*For the market was full of all sorts of weapons and horses for sale, and the coppersmiths, carpenters, ironworkers, cobblers and painters were all manufacturing weapons of war, **so that you would have thought** that the city was really a factory of war.*

ἂν ἡγήσω is potential Indicative.

καὶ ὁ μὲν Θεόδοτος τετέλευκεν, **ὥστε** οὐκ **ἂν** ἐκεῖνός γε αὐτοῦ **καταδεηθείη**. (Pl.*Ap.* 33 E.)

*And Theodotus has died, **so that he** at least **would not entreat** him.*

ἂν ... καταδεηθείη is potential Optative.

22.4. Adjectival Clauses of Result

Adjectival clauses of Result use the Indicative Mood, or potential Optative with ἄν, parallel to ὥστε clauses with the Indicative. The antecedent of these clauses is mostly negative or interrogative (implying a negative). The indefinite form of the relative pronoun (ὅστις) is more common than ὅς in this construction. The negative is οὐ.

καὶ τίς οὕτως ἐστὶν ἀναίσθητος **ὅστις οὐκ ἂν ἀλγήσειε** τοιαύτης διαβολῆς περὶ αὐτὸν γιγνομένης; (Isoc. 15.218.)

*And who is so insensitive **that he would not feel pained** if such a slander were being made about himself?*

22.5. Provisos

ἐφ' ᾧ and ἐφ' ᾧτε with the Infinitive (or Accusative and Infinitive) are used in the sense 'on the condition that'. The negative is μή.

... συνεχώρησαν αὐτοῖς καὶ Φλεασίοις καὶ τοῖς ἐλθοῦσι μετ' αὐτῶν εἰς Θήβας τὴν εἰρήνην, **ἐφ' ᾧτε ἔχειν** τὴν ἑαυτῶν ἑκάστους. (X.*HG* 7.4.10.)

*... they granted peace to them and to the Phleasians and to those who had come with them to Thebes, **on the condition that** each group **should keep** their own <territory>.*

ἐφ' ᾧ and ἐφ' ᾧτε are also used with the Future Indicative, at least in the historians Herodotus, Thucydides and Xenophon. Both οὐ and μή occur as negatives.

... ὁ Κλεομένης συντίθεται Λευτυχίδῃ ..., **ἐπ' ᾧ τε**, ἢν αὐτὸν καταστήσῃ βασιλέα ἀντὶ Δημαρήτου, **ἕψεταί** οἱ ἐπ' Αἰγινήτας. (Hdt 6.65.1.)

... *Cleomenes made an agreement with Leutychides ...* **on condition that**, *if he* [Cleomenes] *made him* [Leutychides] *king instead of Demaretus*, **he would follow** *him against the Aeginetans*.

ἐφ' ᾧ or ἐφ' ᾧτε sometimes follows a demonstrative antecedent phrase: ἐπὶ τούτῳ or ἐπὶ τούτοις or ἐπὶ τοῖσδε. In English idiom, the phrases need to be abbreviated to: 'on this/these condition(s), that ...'. In Greek, the plural antecedents τούτοις and τοῖσδε are followed by the singular form ᾧ. Both Infinitive and Indicative constructions occur after these antecedent phrases.

οἳ δὲ **ἐπὶ τοισίδε** δώσειν ἔφασαν, **ἐπ' ᾧ ἀπάξουσι** ἔτεος ἑκάστου τῇ Ἀθηναίῃ τε τῇ πολιάδι ἱρὰ καὶ τῷ Ἐρεχθέϊ. (Hdt. 5.82.3.)

And they [= Athenians] *said that they would give <the olive trees>* **on these conditions, that they** [= Epidaurians] **would pay** *each year sacred <offerings> to Athena Polias and to Erechtheus.*

ἐφ' ᾧ and ἐφ' ᾧτε may also express 'for the purpose of'. This usage is not treated in this Lesson and Exercise.

22.6. Antecedents for Result Constructions

Result clauses and phrases are frequently preceded by a demonstrative adjective or adverb. The following examples have occurred in the preceding sections.

τοσοῦτος ... ὥστε
τοιοῦτος ... ὥστε
οὕτω(ς) ... ὥστε
οὕτως ... ὅστις

22.7. ὥστε = 'And so'

ὥστε may introduce a new sentence and have the meaning 'And so'. In this usage, it functions as a coordinating conjunction.

ἔπειτα καὶ ταῦθ' ὑμῶν δέομαι, εὖ ποιῶν ὑμᾶς ὑφ' ὑμῶν τιμᾶσθαι. **ὥστ'** ἐμοὶ μὲν πειθόμενοι οὐκ ἀποστερεῖσθε εἴ τι ἐγὼ δυνήσομαι ὑμᾶς εὖ ποιεῖν· (And. 1.149.)

*Secondly I ask this also of you, that, since I am your benefactor, I be held in honour by you. **And so** by obeying me you are not <going to be> deprived if I can bestow any benefit on you* [OR: *deprived of any benefit which I shall be able to bestow on you*].

References

Denniston (1954), *The Greek particles*, p. 528 (Provisos).

Goodwin (1889), *Syntax of the moods and tenses of the Greek verb*, §§575–610.

Smyth (1956), *Greek grammar*, §§2249–2279, 2556–2559.

EXERCISE 22

Translate the following passages.

1. ἐνδεὴς μέν γε χρημάτων καταλειφθεὶς οὕτω δίκαιον ἐμαυτὸν παρέσχον, ὥστε μηδένα λυπῆσαι τῶν πολιτῶν·

2. ... ἀλλ' εἰς τοσοῦτον ἀνοίας ἐληλύθασιν, ὥστ' οἴονται καὶ παρ' ὑμῖν καὶ παρὰ τοῖς ἄλλοις εὐδοκιμήσειν ...

   εὐδοκιμεῖν   *to be* (Fut. and Aor.: *to become*) *highly regarded*

3. ... ἀλλ' ὅμως οὐδὲ τῶν τοιούτων οὐδείς ἐστιν οὕτως ἀκρατὴς ὅστις ἂν δέξαιτο καὶ τοὺς μαθητὰς εἶναι τοιούτους·

   ἀκρατής, -ές   *uncontrolled*
   καί   *also*

LESSON 22. RESULT CONSTRUCTIONS

4. ... τά τε ἄλλα καταφανέστερον ἢ ὥστε λανθάνειν οὐ προθύμως ξυνεπολέμει.

| τά ... ἄλλα | Acc. of Respect |
| τε | Joins this clause to the preceding. |

5. ὥστ' ἐξ ἁπάντων τούτων εἰκὸς αὐτοὺς βελτίους γίγνεσθαι.

| ἁπάντων τούτων | neut. |
| εἰκός, -ότος | neut. Perf. Partc. of ἐοικέναι; understand ἐστί; + Acc. and Infin. |

6. ... διελύθησαν, ἐφ' ᾧτε ... τὸν Λεωκράτην ... μήτε κακόνουν εἶναι Πολυεύκτῳ τῶν τε πρὸς ἀλλήλους ἐγκλημάτων ἀπηλλάχθαι πάντων.

διαλύειν	*to reconcile*
ἔκλημα, -ατος, τό	*charge*
τὸν Λεωκράτην is the Subject of εἶναι, but both men (unspecified) are the Subject of ἀπηλλάχθαι.	

7. ... no one among men would suppose *me* so completely senseless, as to bear false witness for this [man] ...

| *to suppose* | ὑπολαμβάνειν |
| *senseless* | ἄφρων, -ον |

8. And I so *strongly* dissent from the others who are giving advice, O men of Athens, that it does not even seem right to me to take thought now concerning the Chersonese nor Byzantium ...

so strongly	τοσοῦτον (emphasised by enclitic γε)
to dissent	ἀφεστηκέναι (Perf.; lit. 'to have stood away from') (+ Gen.)
to seem right	δοκεῖν
to give advice	συμβουλεύειν
Chersonese	Χερρόνησος, -ου, ἡ (Note spelling and gender.)
Byzantium	Βυζάντιον, -ου, τό

LESSON 23
Causal Constructions

23.1. Adverbial Clauses of Cause

Adverbial clauses of Cause are introduced by several subordinating conjunctions: ὅτι, διότι, ἐπεί, ἐπειδή, ὡς and in poetry οὕνεκα (= οὗ ἕνεκα) and ὁθούνεκα (= ὅτου ἕνεκα). ἐπεί is more frequent than ἐπειδή in a Causal sense in early prose. The Indicative Mood is normally used. The negative is οὐ, which is also used in virtual Causal clauses introduced by εἰ (with Indic.) or by ἐάν or ἤν (with Subj.).

23.1.1. Indicative

ἆρα τὸ ὅσιον, **ὅτι** ὅσιόν ἐστι, φιλεῖται ὑπὸ τῶν θεῶν, ἤ, **ὅτι** φιλεῖται, ὅσιόν ἐστι; (Pl.*Euthphr.* 10 A.)

*Is holiness loved by the gods **because** it is holy, or is it holy **because** it is loved <by the gods>?*

τίθημι γάρ σε ὁμολογοῦντα, **ἐπειδὴ** οὐκ ἀποκρίνῃ. (Pl.*Ap.* 27 C.)
*For I regard you as agreeing, **since** you do not reply.*

Negative οὐ.

ἂν δὲ σιωπᾶν [sc. φῇ], πῶς οὐκ ἀδικεῖ, **εἰ**, παρὸν ἐξαμαρτάνειν μέλλοντας ἀποτρέπειν, τοῦτο μὲν **οὐκ** ἐποίει … (D. 22.41.)

*But if <he says> that he kept quiet, how is he not acting unjustly, **since** [lit. 'if'], although it was possible to turn <them> aside when they were intending to do wrong, he was **not** doing this…?*

Virtual Causal clause introduced by εἰ with negative οὐ.
(Cf. Lesson 19.5, last dot point)

23.1.2. Potential Indicative or Optative

Potential Indicative or potential Optative with ἄν may also appear in a Causal clause.

κακῶς ὄλοισθ'· ὀλεῖσθε δ' ἠδικηκότες
τὸν ἄνδρα τόνδε, θεοῖσιν εἰ δίκης μέλει.
ἔξοιδα δ' ὡς μέλει γ' **ἐπεὶ** οὔποτ' **ἂν** στόλον
ἐπλεύσατ' ἂν τόνδ' οὕνεκ' ἀνδρὸς ἀθλίου,
εἰ μή τι κέντρον θεῖον ἦγ' ὑμᾶς ἐμοῦ. (S.Ph. 1035–1039.)

*May you perish miserably; and you will perish for having wronged this man, if the gods are concerned about justice.
And I am sure that they are concerned, **since** never **would you have sailed** on this voyage on account of a wretched man, if some divine incentive to get me had not been driving you on.*

ἐπεί with potential Indicative ἐπλεύσατ(ε) and ἄν (repeated).

οὐ γὰρ ἡλικίαν ἔχει
παρὰ σοὶ καθεύδειν τηλικοῦτος ὤν, **ἐπεὶ**
μήτηρ **ἂν** αὐτῷ μᾶλλον **εἴης** ἢ γυνή. (Ar.Ec. 1038–1040.)

*For he is not of an age
to sleep with you, being of such a <young> age, **since
you would be** a mother for him rather than a wife!*

ἐπεί with potential Optative and ἄν.

23.1.3. Optative of Alleged Reason

In Past sequence, the Optative (without ἄν) is used in a Causal clause to denote an alleged reason. In the following sentence, ὡς with Optative ἀποχωρήσειαν expresses the reason of the Athenians in the city, not that of the writer Thucydides.

ἐλθόντας δὲ τοὺς στρατηγοὺς οἱ ἐν τῇ πόλει Ἀθηναῖοι τοὺς μὲν φυγῇ ἐζημίωσαν, Πυθόδωρον καὶ Σοφοκλέα, τὸν δὲ τρίτον Εὐρυμέδοντα χρήματα ἐπράξαντο, **ὡς** ἐξὸν αὐτοῖς τὰ ἐν Σικελίᾳ καταστρέψασθαι δώροις πεισθέντες **ἀποχωρήσειαν**. (Th. 4.65.3.)

*But when the commanders came, the Athenians in the city punished the <first two>, Pythodorus and Sophocles, with exile and exacted money from the third, Eurymedon, **on the grounds that**, although it had been possible for them to gain control of affairs in Sicily, **they** had been bribed by gifts and **had departed**.*

23.1.4. ὅτε with a Causal Meaning

ὅτε sometimes has a virtual Causal force, already in Homer, and extending to the classical period. (The practice of distinguishing ὅτε [Temporal] from ὅ τε [Causal] in print dates only from the nineteenth century.)

Ζεῦ πάτερ, οὐκέτ' ἐγώ γε μετ' ἀθανάτοισι θεοῖσι
τιμήεις ἔσομαι, **ὅτε** με βροτοὶ οὔ τι τίουσι …
(Hom.*Od.* 13.128–129.)

*Father Zeus, no longer shall I for my part be honoured among
the immortal gods, **since** mortals do not honour me at all …*

Here, ὅτε does not denote a particular time (or particular times) 'when' mortals do not honour Poseidon. Rather, it gives the reason why gods will not honour him, 'since' mortals do not honour him 'at all'. The argument proceeds *a minore ad maius* (from the lesser to the greater).

ὅτε δὴ τοῦτο οὕτως ἔχει, τόδε μοι ἀποκρίνασθε, φήσω.
(Pl.*Prt.* 356 C.)

'***Since*** *indeed this is so, answer this for me', I shall say.*

Both ὅτι and ὅτε seem to be derived from the neuter singular relative pronoun ὅ. ὅτι is the indefinite form of this pronoun. ὅτε is simple ὅ followed by generalising enclitic τε, primarily an Epic usage (Liddell & Scott, 1996: τε B.). The basic early meaning of either form could be expressed as: 'with respect to which', or 'with regard to the fact that'.

Many examples, from Homer and Hesiod onwards, are ambiguous because of elision: ὅτ(ι) or ὅτ(ε). The usual view is that only ὅτ(ε) allows elision. But two notable Hesiod scholars doubt this.

τῆς ὅτε δὴ Περσεὺς κεφαλὴν ἀπεδειροτόμησεν,
ἐξέθορε Χρυσάωρ τε μέγας καὶ Πήγασος ἵππος·
τῷ μὲν ἐπώνυμον ἦν **ὅτ'** ἄρ' Ὠκεανοῦ παρὰ πηγὰς
γένθ'… (Hes.*Th.* 280–283.)

*Just when Perseus cut off her head,
there leapt out great Chrysaor and Pegasus the horse;
the latter had a significant name, **because** of course he was born beside
the waters of Ocean …*

γένθ' = ἐγένετο

Acknowledging the usual view, West (1966, p. 247) has commented on this passage: 'But if we ask which word we should see if it were not before a vowel, the answer is certainly that we should see ὅτι …'. More succinctly, Paley (1883, p. 204) has commented on the same passage: 'ὅτ' for ὅτι, not ὅτε'. If elision of the final iota of ὅτι is allowed in general, there will be far fewer instances of ὅτ(ε) with a Causal meaning.

23.2. Adjectival Clauses of Cause

Cause may be expressed in adjectival clauses. The definite relative adjective ὅς is more common than the indefinite ὅστις. The Mood is generally Indicative and the negative is οὐ. (Similar clauses with μή are probably better classified as Conditional adjectival clauses.)

ταῦτα λέγων τῷ Κροίσῳ οὔ κως οὔτε ἐχαρίζετο, οὔτε λόγου μιν ποιησάμενος οὐδενὸς ἀποπέμπεται, κάρτα δόξας ἀμαθέα εἶναι, **ὃς** τὰ παρεόντα ἀγαθὰ μετεὶς τὴν τελευτὴν παντὸς χρήματος ὁρᾶν **ἐκέλευε**. (Hdt. 1.33.)

*In saying this he was not at all pleasing to Croesus, and <the latter> considering him of no importance sent him away, thinking him to be very ignorant, **since**, setting aside present benefits, **he was telling** him to look at the outcome of every matter.*

ἀποπέμπεται is Historic Present.

23.3. Causal Participles

Participles may express Cause. See Lesson 4 on Participles, Lesson 5 on Genitive absolute and Lesson 6 on Accusative absolute. Such Participles may be reinforced by certain adverbs. ὡς before a Causal Participle indicates that the Cause is expressed on the authority of the main Subject or of another person prominent in the sentence. ἅτε, οἷα and οἷον indicate that the Cause is expressed on the authority of the writer (or of the person delivering a speech). Herodotus also uses ὥστε in a similar way.

... καὶ τὸν μὲν Περικλέα ἐν αἰτίᾳ εἶχον **ὡς πείσαντα** σφᾶς πολεμεῖν ... (Th. 2.59.2.)

*... and they held Pericles to blame **on the grounds that he had persuaded** them to go to war ...*

The reason introduced by ὡς is attributed to the Athenians, who are the Subject of εἶχον.

... **ἅτε** τὸν χρυσὸν **ἔχων** πάντα τὸν ἐκ τῶν Σαρδίων, ἐπικούρους τε ἐμισθοῦτο καὶ τοὺς ἐπιθαλασσίους ἀνθρώπους ἔπειθε σὺν ἑωυτῷ στρατεύεσθαι. (Hdt. 1.154.)

*... **inasmuch as he held** all the gold from Sardis, he was hiring mercenaries and was persuading the men of the coast to go on campaign with him.*

The reason introduced by ἅτε is that of the author Herodotus.

ὥστε δὲ περὶ πολλοῦ **ποιεόμενος** αὐτούς, παῖδάς σφι παρέδωκε τὴν γλῶσσάν τε ἐκμαθεῖν καὶ τὴν τέχνην τῶν τόξων. (Hdt. 1.73.3.)

*And **inasmuch as he regarded** them highly, he committed boys to them to learn their language and the technique of the bow.*

23.4. Coordinating Use of ἐπεί and ὡς

Editors sometimes treat ἐπεί and ὡς as introducing a Main clause at the beginning of a sentence, and thus as being equivalent to γάρ. It might be argued that this is a subordinating use in some long sentences. But that argument is less convincing where the clause introduced by ἐπεί or ὡς constitutes a question, wish or command rather than a statement.

ἐγὼ μὲν γὰρ πολλάκις θέλω τεθνάναι, εἰ ταῦτ' ἔστιν ἀληθῆ· **ἐπεὶ** ἔμοιγε καὶ αὐτῷ θαυμαστὴ ἂν εἴη ἡ διατριβὴ αὐτόθι, ὁπότε ἐντύχοιμι Παλαμήδει καὶ Αἴαντι τῷ Τελαμῶνος καὶ εἴ τις ἄλλος τῶν παλαιῶν διὰ κρίσιν ἄδικον τέθνηκεν ... (Pl. *Ap.* 41 A–B.)

***For** I am willing to die many times, if this is true. **For** to me myself at least the lifestyle would be wonderful there, when I met up with Palamedes and Ajax son of Telamon and anyone else among early figures who has died because of an unjust judgment ...*

References

Goodwin (1889), *Syntax of the moods and tenses of the Greek verb*, §§580–581, 712–719, 862–865.

Smyth (1956), *Greek grammar*, §§2085–2086, 2240–2248, 2555.

Paley (Ed.) (1883), *The Epics of Hesiod*, p. 204.

West (Ed.) (1966), *Hesiod: Theogony*, p. 247.

EXERCISE 23

Translate the following passages.

1. ἐπεί σε μανθάνω
    θνητὴν φρονοῦσαν θνητὰ κοὐκ ἀγνώμονα,
    πᾶν σοι φράσω τἀληθές, οὐδὲ κρύψομαι.

ἀγνώμων, -ον	*senseless* (here Acc. neut. pl., as is θνητά)

2. ἐπεὶ σὺ φέγγος, Τειρεσία, τόδ' οὐχ ὁρᾷς,
    ἐγὼ προφήτης σοι λόγων γενήσομαι.

φέγγος, -εος, τό	*light (of day)*
Τειρεσίας, -ου, ὁ	*Tiresias*
λόγων	*(with)in my words* (Gen. of Limits)

3. ἀλλά νιν περιπτυχεῖ
    φάρει καλύψω τῷδε παμπήδην, ἐπεὶ
    οὐδεὶς ἄν, ὅστις καὶ φίλος, τλαίη βλέπειν ...

νιν (enclitic)	*him*
περιπτυχής, -ές	*enfolding, wrapped around*
φᾶρος, -εος, τό	*cloak*
παμπήδην (adv.)	*completely*
τλῆναι (2nd Aor.)	*to endure, to bear*

LESSON 23. CAUSAL CONSTRUCTIONS

4. ... Κῦρος ... τῷ Κλεάρχῳ ἐβόα ἄγειν τὸ στράτευμα κατὰ μέσον τὸ τῶν πολεμίων, ὅτι ἐκεῖ βασιλεὺς εἴη·

κατά	at

5. ... ἐβουλεύοντο ἰθυμαχίην μὲν μηδεμίαν ποιέεσθαι ἐκ τοῦ ἐμφανέος, ὅτε δή σφι οὗτοί γε σύμμαχοι οὐ προσεγίνοντο ...

ἰθυμαχία, -ας, ἡ (Attic)	direct attack
ἐμφανής, ές (Attic)	open (ground) (neut. adj. as noun)
προσγίγνεσθαι (Attic)	to be added (to) (+ Dat.)

6. τί γὰρ ἂν καὶ βουλόμενος Ἀνδοκίδης ἀγῶνα τοσοῦτον ὑπομείνειεν, ᾧ ἔξεστι μὲν ἀπελθόντι ἐντεῦθεν ἔχειν πάντα τὰ ἐπιτήδεια ...;

ἀγών, -ῶνος, ὁ	trial
ὑπομένειν	to submit to (+ Acc.)
ἐντεῦθεν (adv.)	from here
ἐπιτήδειος, -α, -ον	necessary, requisite

7. ... the Sicilian Greeks themselves provided a greater number [of troops] in all categories, inasmuch as they inhabited large cities.

Sicilian Greek	Σικελιώτης, -ου, ὁ
number	πλῆθος, -ους, τό
in all categories	κατὰ πάντα
inasmuch as	ἅτε (+ Partc.)

8. And you [pl.] think that the affairs of the Thebans are in a bad state because they are mistreating their neighbours ...

to be in a (certain) state	ἔχειν (+ adv.)
to mistreat	ἀδικεῖν (+ Acc.)
neighbour	περίοικος, -ου, ὁ (adj. as noun)

LESSON 24
Constructions with Verbs of Effort and Caution

24.1. Introduction

The most common construction with verbs of effort and caution is ὅπως with Future Indicative in both Primary and Past sequence. The ὅπως clause is a noun clause, Object of the verb of effort or caution. Besides the construction with Future Indicative, there are other constructions in Greek. These vary from one verb to another, and from one author to another. Moreover, manuscripts may vary between Future Indicative and Aorist Subjunctive in their reading of the same word. And editors have been inclined to prefer a Future Indicative reading or to emend Aorist Subjunctive to Future Indicative. The negative for all constructions is μή.

24.2. Primary Sequence

24.2.1. ὅπως with Future Indicative

εἰ δὲ Φοινίκων μᾶλλον βούλεσθε διαπειρᾶσθαι, **ποιέειν** χρεόν ἐστι ὑμέας, ὁκότερα ἂν δὴ τούτων ἕλησθε, **ὅκως** τὸ κατ' ὑμέας **ἔσται** ἥ τε Ἰωνίη καὶ ἡ Κύπρος ἐλευθέρη. (Hdt. 5.109.2.)

But if you wish rather to try out the Phoenicians, it is right that you **should ensure**, *whichever of these <options> you choose,* **that** *so far as depends on you, Ionia and Cyprus* **will be** *free.*

ὅρα δ' **ὅπως ὠθήσομεν** τούσδε τοὺς ἐξ ἄστεως
    ἥκοντας ... (Ar.*Ec.* 300–301.)

And **see to it that we push aside** *these people who have come
    from town ...*

... **ὁρᾶτε ὅπως μὴ** αἴσχιον καὶ ἀπορώτερον τῇ Πελοποννήσῳ **πράξομεν**. (Th. 1.82.5.)

... **take care that we do not create** <a situation> *more shameful and more difficult for the Peloponnese.*

Negative μή.

24.2.2. ὅπως with Subjunctive

... **ἐπιμελητέον** μὲν **ὅπως τρέφωνται** οἱ ἵπποι, ὡς ἂν δύνωνται πόνους ὑποφέρειν· (X.*Eq.Mag.* 1.3.)

... *<it is>* **necessary to take care that** *the horses* **are nourished**, *so that they can endure hard work.*

καὶ **ὅρα**, ὦ Κρίτων, ταῦτα καθομολογῶν, **ὅπως μὴ** παρὰ δόξαν **ὁμολογῇς**. (Pl.*Cri.* 49 D.)

And **see to it**, *Crito, in agreeing to this,* **that you do not agree** *contrary to <your real> opinion.*

Negative μή.

24.2.3. μή with Subjunctive

ἀλλὰ πρῶτον **εὐλαβηθῶμέν** τι πάθος **μὴ πάθωμεν**.
τὸ ποῖον; ἦν δ' ἐγώ.
μὴ γενώμεθα, ἦ δ' ὅς, μισόλογοι, ὥσπερ οἱ μισάνθρωποι γιγνόμενοι. (Pl.*Phd.* 89 C.)

'But first **let us take care that we do not suffer** *any calamity'.*
'What sort <of calamity>?' said I.
'That we do not become', *said he, 'haters of argument, just as those who become haters of mankind'.*

24.2.4. εἰ with Indicative

Some verbs of effort and caution occasionally have an εἰ clause as Subject or Object. In the examples, in Primary and Past sequence the Indicative Mood is used. And the leading verb either is negated or is a negative compound.

καὶ **οὐ** τοσοῦτόν μοι **μέλει, εἰ** με **δεῖ** τὰ ὄντα ἀπολέσαι· (Lys. 21.12.)

*And **it is not** so great **a concern** to me, **whether** I **must** lose my possessions.*

εἰ clause with Present Indicative is Subject of μέλει; lit. 'Whether I must lose ... is not so great a concern ...'.

ὥστε μηκέτι **ἀπόρει**, ὦ Σώκρατες, **εἴ** τι τοὐμὸν κάλλος ἀνθρώπους **ὠφελήσει**. (X.Smp. 4.16.)

*And so no longer **be at a loss**, O Socrates, <about> **whether** my beauty **will bring** any **benefit to** people.*

εἰ clause with Future Indicative is Object of ἀπόρει.

24.3. Past Sequence

24.3.1. ὅπως with Future Indicative

... καὶ **παρεσκευάζοντο ὅπως** κατὰ κορυφὴν **ἐσβαλοῦσιν** ἐς τὴν κάτω Μακεδονίαν, ἧς ὁ Περδίκκας ἦρχε. (Th. 2.99.1.)

*... and **they were preparing to** <go> over the ridge <and> **invade** lower Macedonia, of which Perdiccas was ruler.*

ἐγὼ δέ, ἐπείτε παρέλαβον τὸν θρόνον τοῦτον, **ἐφρόντιζον ὅκως μὴ λείψομαι** τῶν πρότερον γενομένων ἐν τιμῇ τῇδε **μηδὲ** ἐλάσσω **προσκτήσομαι** δύναμιν Πέρσῃσι· (Hdt. 7.8.α.2.)

*And I, after I had succeeded to this throne, **was wondering how I should not be left behind** those who had come before in this office, **nor gain** for the Persians less power* [i.e. than they did].

Here, ὅκως with Future Indicative is represented by 'how I should...' in English. Negative μή and compound.

24.3.2. ὅπως with Subjunctive

δεδιώς τε **ἔπρασσεν** ἔς τε τὴν Λακεδαίμονα πέμπων **ὅπως** πόλεμος **γένηται** αὐτοῖς πρὸς Πελοποννησίους ... (Th. 1.57.4.)

*And in trepidation **he** [= Perdiccas] **was trying to bring it about**, by sending <agents> to Sparta, **that** war **would break out** between them [= Athenians] and the Peloponnesians ...*

(The second τε anticipates a following καί.)

ἐπεμελήθη δέ τις ἄλλως πώποτε πλὴν Ἀγεσίλαος, ἢ ὅπως φῦλόν τι ἀποστήσεται τοῦ Πέρσου ἢ **ὅπως** τὸ ἀποστὰν **μὴ ἀπόληται** ... (X.Ages.7.7.)

*But **did** anyone except Agesilaus ever otherwise **take care**, either that some tribe should revolt from the Persian or **that** the <tribe> which rebelled **should not perish** ...?*

Negative μή. (The first ὅπως clause uses Fut. Indic.)

24.3.3. ὅπως with Optative

In accordance with the more usual practice of sequence of Moods in subordinate constructions, ὅπως with Imperfect or Aorist Optative in Past sequence corresponds to Subjunctive of the same Aspects in Primary sequence. Likewise, ὅπως with Intentive ('Fut.') Optative corresponds to the Future Indicative of Primary sequence.

ἐπεμέλετο γὰρ καὶ τούτου ὁ Κῦρος, **ὅπως ἁλίσκοιντο** παρ' ὧν ἔμελλε πεύσεσθαί τι· (X.Cyr. 6.2.9.)

*For Cyrus **used to be concerned** for this also, **that** <prisoners> **should be captured**, from whom he was likely to learn something.*

Imperfect Optative. The ὅπως clause is in apposition with τούτου.

πῶς οὖν, ἐὰν μὴ βοηθῆτε οὕτω περιφανῶς ἡμῖν ἀδικουμένοις, οὐ παρὰ τοὺς ὅρκους ποιήσετε; καὶ ταῦτα ὧν αὐτοὶ **ἐπεμελήθητε** ὅρκων **ὅπως** πᾶσιν ὑμῖν πάντες ἡμεῖς **ὀμόσαιμεν**; (X.HG 6.5.37.)

*How, then, if you do not help us when we are so obviously being wronged, will you not act contrary to your oaths? And these, oaths which **you** yourselves **took care that** we all **should swear** to you all?*

LESSON 24. CONSTRUCTIONS WITH VERBS OF EFFORT AND CAUTION

Aorist Optative.

ἐπεμελήθη δ', **ὅπως** οἱ στρατιῶται τοὺς πόνους **δυνήσοιντο** ὑποφέρειν· (X.*Ages.* 2.8.)

And **he took care that** the soldiers **would be able** to endure their labours.

Intentive ('Fut.') Optative.

ἐπεμέλετο δὲ καὶ τούτου ὁ Κῦρος **ὅπως μήποτε** ἀνίδρωτοι γενόμενοι ἐπὶ τὸ ἄριστον καὶ τὸ δεῖπνον **εἰσίοιεν**. (X.*Cyr.* 2.1.29.)

And Cyrus **took care** of this too, <namely> **that they should never go in** to lunch and dinner without having raised a sweat.

Negative μήποτε.

24.3.4. μή with Optative

οὐ μέντοι οὐδὲ ἀπέκλινε, **φυλαττόμενος μὴ δοκοίη** φεύγειν ... (X.*An.* 2.2.16.)

However, he was not turning aside either, **being careful that he should not seem** to be retreating ...

24.3.5. εἰ with Indicative

Corresponding to the examples in Primary sequence (§24.2.4), the following examples have the same structure in Past sequence.

οὐ γὰρ ἂν αὐτοῖς **ἔμελεν, εἴ** τις ἐν Πελοποννήσῳ τινὰς **ὠνεῖται** καὶ **διαφθείρει**, μὴ τοῦθ' ὑπολαμβάνουσιν· (D. 9.45.)

For it would **not have been a concern** to them, **whether** any one in the Peloponnese **was bribing** and **corrupting** any <persons>, if they had not been making this assumption.

εἰ clause with Present Indicative (Vivid) is Subject of ἔμελεν (in a Past potential Main clause); lit. 'Whether any one ... was bribing ... would not have been a concern ...'. ὑπολαμβάνουσιν is a Dative plural Participle with Conditional force, agreeing with αὐτοῖς.

οὕτω δ' **ἠμέλησας, εἰ μηδὲν** ὁμολογούμενον **ἐρεῖς**, ὥστε φῂς μὲν αὐτὸν τὴν Αἰόλου καὶ τὴν Ὀρφέως ζηλῶσαι δόξαν, ἀποφαίνεις δ' οὐδὲν τῶν αὐτῶν ἐκείνοις ἐπιτηδεύσαντα. (Isoc. 11.7.)

*And **you were so careless**, <about> **whether you were going to say nothing** consistent, that you say that he emulated the reputation of Aeolus and Orpheus, but you show that he accomplished none of the same <achievements> as they <did>.*

εἰ clause with Future Indicative is Object of ἠμέλησας, which is Past Aorist Indicative of negative compound ἀμελεῖν.

24.4. Variations of the Constructions in §§24.2 and 24.3

In some Attic authors (especially Aristophanes, Xenophon and Plato), ἄν may be added to ὅπως with Subjunctive.

Xenophon mostly uses the common constructions. But in addition, he sometimes uses ὡς (instead of ὅπως) with Future Indicative, Subjunctive and Optative, and ἄν may be added to ὡς with Subjunctive.

With verbs of planning and trying (especially φράζεσθαι, βουλεύειν, μερμηρίζειν and πειρᾶν), Homer uses ὅπως or ὡς with Subjunctive in Primary sequence and Optative (but sometimes Subj.) in Past sequence. κε(ν) (enclitic), equivalent to ἄν, is generally used with ὡς and Subjunctive, less often with ὅπως and Subjunctive.

24.5. Infinitive Constructions

Besides the constructions with Subordinate clauses, Infinitive phrases are sometimes used with verbs of effort and caution.

ἃ γάρ, ὅτε ἐσπένδοντο, **διεπράττοντο, μὴ καίειν** τὴν βασιλέως χώραν, νῦν αὐτοὶ καίουσιν ὡς ἀλλοτρίαν. (X.*An.* 3.5.5.)

*For as to what **they were arranging** when they were making the truce, <namely> **not to burn** the king's territory, now they themselves are burning <it>, as <if it were> someone else's.*

The use of μή with the Infinitive after a verb of caution may reinforce the idea of caution rather than contradicting it. Compare the following two uses of εὐλαβεῖσθαι with Infinitive.

καλῶς ἔλεξεν, **εὐλαβουμένῳ πεσεῖν** ... (S.*OT* 616.)
*He spoke well, in the judgment of anyone **wary of falling** ...*

... ὀρχησάμενοι θεοῖσιν **εὐλαβώμεθα**
τὸ λοιπὸν αὖθις **μὴ 'ἐξαμαρτάνειν** ἔτι. (Ar.*Lys.* 1276–1277.)

*... leading the dance in honour of the gods **let us take care not to offend** ever again in future.*

24.6. Omission of Main Clause

Expressions of effort or caution may be made by means of a ὅπως clause without any Main clause. However, an imperatival or hortatory verb is always implied as introducing the ὅπως clause: '<See to it> that ...', '<Take care> that ... (not) ...'. Consequently, such ὅπως clauses are always in Primary sequence. Positive clauses use ὅπως with Future Indicative. Negative clauses use ὅπως μή with Future Indicative or with Subjunctive.

ἀλλὰ μᾶλλον **ὅκως** λόγον **δώσεις** τῶν μετεχείρισας χρημάτων. (Hdt. 3.142.5.)

*But rather <make sure> **that you give** an account of the money which you managed.*

ὅκως (for Attic ὅπως) with Future Indicative τῶν (Ionic) = ὧν (Attic).

ὅπως τοίνυν ταῦτα **μηδεὶς** ἀνθρώπων **πεύσεται**· (Lys. 1.21.)
*So <make sure> **that no one** among men **learns about** this.*

ὅπως ... μηδείς with Future Indicative.

καὶ **ὅπως** γε **μηδὲ** τὸ χωρίον ἡδέως **ὁρῶσιν** ἔνθα κατέκανον ἡμῶν τοὺς συμμάχους· (X.*Cyr.* 5.4.21.)

*And <let us make> quite <sure> **that they will not even see** with pleasure the place where they killed our allies.*

ὅπως μηδέ with Imperfect Subjunctive.

References

Goodwin (1889), *Syntax of the moods and tenses of the Greek verb*, §§130, 271–278, 339–354, 361.

Smyth (1956), *Greek grammar*, §§2209–2217, 2220.

EXERCISE 24

Translate the following passages.

1. … χρημάτων μὲν οὐκ αἰσχύνῃ ἐπιμελούμενος ὅπως σοι ἔσται ὡς πλεῖστα, καὶ δόξης καὶ τιμῆς, φρονήσεως δὲ καὶ ἀληθείας καὶ τῆς ψυχῆς ὅπως ὡς βελτίστη ἔσται οὐκ ἐπιμελῇ οὐδὲ φροντίζεις;

χρήματα, -ων, τά	*money*
αἰσχύνεσθαι (Mid. and Pass.)	*to be ashamed (of)* (+ Partc.)
ἐπιμελούμενος	+ Gen. χρημάτων, δόξης, τιμῆς.
πλεῖστα (neut. pl.)	Refers to χρημάτων.
ἐπιμελῇ	+ Gen. φρονήσεως, ἀληθείας, τῆς ψυχῆς.

2. … ἀλλὰ τοῦτ' ἐφιλοσοφεῖ καὶ τοῦτ' ἔπραττεν, ὅπως μηδεμία τῶν πόλεων αὐτὸν φοβήσεται τῶν Ἑλληνίδων, ἀλλὰ πᾶσαι θαρρήσουσι πλὴν τῶν ἀδικουσῶν.

φιλοσοφεῖν	*to pursue* (an aim or activity)
πράττειν	*to strive for* (+ Acc.)
θαρρεῖν	*to be confident*

3. περὶ μέντοι ἡγεμονίας αὐτόθεν διεπράττοντο ὅπως ἐν τῇ ἑαυτῶν ἕκαστοι ἡγήσοιντο.

μέντοι	*moreover* (less common than the adversative meaning)
αὐτόθεν	*immediately*
τῇ	Understand γῇ.

LESSON 24. CONSTRUCTIONS WITH VERBS OF EFFORT AND CAUTION

4. εὐλαβοῦ δὲ μὴ 'κφύγῃ σε·

(ἐ)κφύγῃ	The Subject is masc.

5. φυλάξομαι δὲ τάσδε μεμνῆσθαι σέθεν
κεδνὰς ἐφετμάς·

κεδνός, -ή, -όν	wise
ἐφετμή, -ῆς, ἡ	command

6. οὐδ' ὄμμ' ἔδειξεν, ἀλλ' ἐπὶ σκήπτροις ἔχων
τὴν ἐλπίδ' ηὐλαβεῖτο μὴ σῴζειν φίλους.

ὄμμα, -ατος, τό	face
σκῆπτρον, -ου, τό	staff; sceptre; (often in pl., as here) royal power
φίλος, -ου, ὁ	family member

Orestes speaks ironically to Electra about Menelaus.

7. Πενθεὺς δ' ὅπως μὴ πένθος εἰσοίσει δόμοις
τοῖς σοῖσι, Κάδμε·

Πενθεύς	Belongs within ὅπως clause.

8. ... those who are going to be capable of this ... must see to it that they have a more sensible attitude than the others.

to be capable of	δύνασθαι (+ Acc.)
to see to it	σκοπεῖν
to have an attitude	διακεῖσθαι (Mid.; + adv.)
sensible	φρόνιμος, (-η,) -ον

9. And these [men], by canvassing each of the citizens, were trying to ensure that they would make the city revolt from the Athenians.

to canvass	μετιέναι
to try to ensure	πράσσειν (Use Past Imperf. Indic.)
to make ... revolt	ἀφιστάναι

LESSON 25
Adjectival Clauses

25.1. Introduction

An adjectival clause performs the same function as an adjective in qualifying a noun or pronoun. In form, adjectival clauses are introduced by a relative adjective or pronoun and normally contain a finite verb (although this is sometimes only implied in the context). The construction of the adjectival clause may be any of the constructions possible in a Simple sentence or in the Main clause of a Complex sentence—Indicative, Imperative, Jussive (Subjunctive) or potential (ἄν with Indicative or Optative). In Greek (as in English), the antecedent noun or pronoun is not always expressed. Thus, οἵ, for example, may stand for '<those> who'.

The present Lesson is concerned primarily with the distinction in form and function between definite and indefinite adjectival clauses. From this point of view, three main categories of adjectival clause will be considered:

1. Definite clauses introduced by ὅς
2. Indefinite clauses introduced by ὅς
3. Indefinite clauses introduced by ὅστις.

25.2. Definite Clauses Introduced by ὅς

Definite clauses refer to a particular person or thing as antecedent. Provided that the adjectival clause represents a statement, its verb is in the Indicative Mood. The negative within such a clause is οὐ.

Ἥφαιστε, σοὶ δὲ χρὴ μέλειν ἐπιστολὰς
ἅς σοι πάτηρ **ἐφεῖτο** ... (A.Pr. 3–4.)

*And the commands, **which** the father **laid upon** you, should be your concern, Hephaestus ...*

... νόμον δὲ ἔθεντο ἐν τῷ παρόντι, **ὃς οὔπω** πρότερον **ἐγένετο** αὐτοῖς· (Th. 5.63.4.)

*... but in the present situation they made a law, **which did not yet** previously **exist** for them.*

Negative οὐ compound.

However, if the adjectival clause represents a command, its verb is Imperative or Subjunctive. And the negative within such a clause is μή.

κάτισον τῶν δορυφόρων ἐπὶ πάσῃσι τῇσι πύλῃσι φυλάκους, **οἳ λεγόντων** πρὸς τοὺς ἐκφέροντας τὰ χρήματα ἀπαιρεόμενοι ὡς σφεα ἀναγκαίως ἔχει δεκατευθῆναι τῷ Διί. (Hdt. 1.89.3.)

*Set at all the gates guards from among the spearmen, **who are to say** to those carrying out the goods, as they take <them> away, that it is necessary that they be paid as a tithe to Zeus.*

Third person plural Imperfect Imperative Active.

ἥξεις δ' Ὑβριστὴν ποταμὸν οὐ ψευδώνυμον, **ὃν μὴ περάσῃς** ... (A.Pr. 717–718.)

*And you will come to the Raging River, not falsely named, **which you are not to cross** ...*

A potential Optative may also be used in a definite adjectival clause.

οὓς γὰρ **ὁμολογήσαιμεν ἂν** πονηροτάτους εἶναι τῶν πολιτῶν, τούτους πιστοτάτους φύλακας ἡγούμεθα τῆς πολιτείας εἶναι· (Isoc. 8.53.)

*For we think that these, **whom we would agree** to be the most wicked of the citizens, are the most reliable guards of the community.*

25.3. Indefinite Clauses Introduced by ὅς

Indefinite clauses do not normally refer to a particular person or thing but to 'anyone who' or 'whoever'. Two types of construction occur:

1. ὅς ἄν with Subjunctive in Primary sequence, and ὅς with Optative in Past sequence
2. ὅς with Indicative.

The negative for both these types of construction is μή.

25.3.1. Subjunctive and Optative

πρῶτον δὴ ἡμῖν, ὡς ἔοικεν, ἐπιστατητέον τοῖς μυθοποιοῖς, καὶ **ὃν** μὲν **ἂν** καλὸν **ποιήσωσιν**, ἐγκριτέον, **ὃν** δ᾽ **ἂν μή**, ἀποκριτέον. (Pl.*R.* 377 B–C.)

<It is> first *necessary for us, as it seems, to take charge of the makers of myths, and to accept the one **which they make** good, but to reject the one **which they do not**.*

ὅς ἄν with Subj. in Primary sequence; negative μή. As antecedent of ὅν, μῦθον is to be understood from μυθοποιοῖς.

ὁ δὲ Σάκας ... ἐτύγχανε ... τιμὴν ἔχων προσάγειν τοὺς δεομένους Ἀστυάγους καὶ ἀποκωλύειν **οὓς μὴ** καιρὸς αὐτῷ **δοκοίη** εἶναι προσάγειν. (X.*Cyr.* 1.3.8.)

*And Sacas ... happened ... to have the duty to introduce those requesting <an audience with> Astyages and to exclude those **whom it did not seem** to him to be appropriate to introduce.*

οὕς with Optative in Past sequence; negative μή.

25.3.2. Indicative

Positive indefinite clauses with Indicative have the same form as positive definite clauses. Their indefinite reference must be deduced from their context and content. However, negative indefinite clauses with Indicative use μή, whereas negative definite clauses with Indicative use οὐ.

ὃς δ᾽ ἐπ᾽ ἐόντι **φέρει**, ὃ δ᾽ ἀλέξεται αἴθοπα λιμόν. (Hes.*Op.* 363.)

*And he, **who adds** to what is <in store>, [he] then will ward off raging hunger.*

Indicative in positive indefinite clause.

ὅ is masculine; the second δέ is apodotic ('then'), as if the ὅς clause were Conditional.

ὃ δὲ **μὴ βλάπτει** κακόν τι ποιεῖ; (Pl.*R.* 379 B.)
'*And does <that>, **which does not cause harm**, produce any evil?*'

μή with Indicative in negative indefinite clause.

25.4. Indefinite Clauses Introduced by ὅστις

ὅστις, when used as an indefinite relative adjective or pronoun, shows a mixture of the constructions in §§25.2 and 25.3 above. Its antecedent is generally indefinite or negative or interrogative, and it may be unexpressed.

25.4.1. ὅστις with Indicative and Negative οὐ

In one usage, ὅστις is treated as containing the notion of indefiniteness within itself. And in texts of Homer it is conventionally written as two words, ὅς τις. The negative within the ὅστις clause is οὐ.

ὅστις ποθ' ὑμῶν Λάϊον τὸν Λαβδάκου
κάτοιδεν ἀνδρὸς ἐκ τίνος διώλετο,
τοῦτον κελεύω πάντα σημαίνειν ἐμοί· (S. *OT* 224–226.)

*I command this <man>, who ever among you
knows by what man Laius son of Labdacus
perished, to reveal all to me.*

The grammatical antecedent (τοῦτον) of the ὅστις clause is indefinite.

πέμψει δέ τοι οὖρον ὄπισθεν
ἀθανάτων **ὅς τίς** σε **φυλάσσει** τε **ῥύεταί** τε. (Hom. *Od.* 15.34–35.)

*And indeed **whichever one** of the immortals
guards and **protects** you, will send a fair wind behind <you>.*

The antecedent is indefinite and unexpressed.

οὐ γὰρ **γυναικὶ** τοὺς λόγους ἐρεῖς **κακῇ**,
οὐδ' ἥτις οὐ κάτοιδε τἀνθρώπων … (S. *Tr.* 438–439.)

*For you will **not** be addressing your words **to an incompetent woman**,
nor (to one) **who** does **not** understand the <ways> of mankind …*

In this sentence, the antecedent clause is negative (οὐ … οὐδ(έ)), the negative within the ὅστις clause is οὐ and, although the antecedent is definite (the speaker refers to herself), the ὅστις clause is used in a characterising way. (Deianeira claims not to be an incompetent *sort* of person.)

οὐ is used as a negative within a ὅστις clause especially in the stereotyped phrase οὐδεὶς ὅστις οὐ, '<There is> no one who does not ...'. (οὐδείς is often attracted to the Case of ὅστις in Acc., Gen. and Dat.)

τοῦτο μὲν γὰρ ἡμέων ἐόντων τοιῶνδε **οὐδεὶς ὅστις οὐ** παρήσει ... (Hdt. 3.72.3.)

*For on the one hand, since we are such as we are, <there is> **no one who** will **not** let <us> pass ...*

25.4.2. ὅστις with Indicative and Negative μή

ὅστις with Indicative sometimes has μή as its negative, parallel to the use of ὅς with the Indicative and μή in negative indefinite clauses.

τοὺς μὲν Ἀθηναίους **ὅστις μὴ βούλεται** οὕτω κακῶς φρονῆσαι καὶ ὑποχειρίους ἡμῖν γενέσθαι ἐνθάδε ἐλθόντας, ἢ δειλός ἐστιν ἢ τῇ πόλει οὐκ εὔνους· (Th. 6.36.1.)

***Whoever does not want** the Athenians to think so wrongly and to become subject to us when they come here, is either cowardly or not well disposed to the city.*

25.4.3. ὅστις with Subjunctive and Optative

ὅστις may also have a construction with ἄν and Subjunctive in Primary sequence and Optative in Past sequence.

... ἅπας δὲ τραχὺς **ὅστις ἂν** νέον **κρατῇ**. (A.Pr. 35.)
*... and everyone, **who is** new **to power**, <is> harsh.*

ὅστις ἄν with Subjunctive in Primary sequence.

... Ἀντιφῶν ἦν ... πλεῖστα εἷς ἀνήρ, **ὅστις ξυμβουλεύσαιτό** τι, δυνάμενος ὠφελεῖν. (Th. 8.68.1.)

*... Antiphon was ... the one man most able to help anyone **who asked for** some **advice**.*

ὅστις with Optative in Past sequence. ὅστις presumes an indefinite Accusative antecedent, Object of ὠφελεῖν.

25.5. Coordinating Use of the Relative Adjective or Pronoun

The relative adjective or pronoun may be used to begin a new sentence. In this situation, ὅς needs to be translated not as 'Who', but by such phrases as 'And he', 'But he' or 'For he'. To some extent it is a matter of editorial choice whether such occurrences are to be treated as coordinating or subordinating. But certainly some Greek sentences would be artificially long, if this rationale were not adopted.

θεὸς θεῶν γὰρ οὐχ ὑποπτήσσων χόλον
βροτοῖσι τιμὰς ὤπασας πέρα δίκης·
ἀνθ' **ὧν** ἀτερπῆ τήνδε φρουρήσεις πέτραν
ὀρθοστάδην ἄυπνος, οὐ κάμπτων γόνυ· (A.*Pr.* 29–32.)

For you, a god, not cowering before the anger of the gods,
bestowed honours on mortals beyond due measure.
And *in return for* ***this*** *you will guard this joyless rock,*
standing upright, unsleeping, not bending the knee.

25.6. Parenthetic ὅστις Clause

A clause introduced by ὅστις may be used parenthetically in Greek, more often with the Indicative ('whoever he is'), but sometimes with Subjunctive and ἄν ('whatever it may be'). The idiom occurs both with and without an antecedent.

... κλύω δὲ νεοχμὰ τήνδ' ἀνὰ πτόλιν κακά,
γυναῖκας ἡμῖν δώματ' ἐκλελοιπέναι
πλασταῖσι βακχείαισιν, ἐν δὲ δασκίοις
ὄρεσι θοάζειν, τὸν νεωστὶ δαίμονα
Διόνυσον, **ὅστις ἔστι**, τιμῶσας χοροῖς· (E.*Ba.* 216–220.)

... and I hear of new troubles throughout this city,
that our women have abandoned their homes
in feigned Bacchic rites, and on shadowy
mountains are running around, honouring with dances
this newfound deity, Dionysus, ***whoever he is***.

ὅστις with Indicative and antecedent Διόνυσον.

ὅ τι δ' ἂν τούτων πρᾶξαι **δυνηθῇς** ἢ καὶ μόνον **ἐπιχειρήσῃς**, οὐκ ἔσθ' ὅπως οὐ μᾶλλον τῶν ἄλλων εὐδοκιμήσεις ... (Isoc. 5.123.)

But **whatever** <part> of this **you may be able** to accomplish or even **may only attempt**, it is not possible that you will not become more distinguished than the rest ...

ὅ τι with ἄν and Subjunctive but no antecedent.

ὅ τι γὰρ **μὴ** τοιοῦτον **ἀποβήσεται** παρ' ὑμῶν, εἰς ἐμὲ τὸ ἐλλεῖπον ἥξει. (X. Cyr. 1.5.13.)

For **whatever does not turn out** from you <to be> such, the deficiency will fall upon me.

ὅ τι with Indicative and negative μή (cf. §25.4.2 above), but no antecedent.

25.7. Special Uses of ὅστις and ὅς ἄν

In some sentences, ὅστις and ὅς ἄν clauses are not properly related to the Main clause grammatically, but in function they usually serve as Subject for the Main clause. ὅστις and ὅς may appear in any Gender and may be singular or plural, but they are regularly used in the Nominative Case. ὅστις clauses of this type regularly have an Indicative verb. (But, for example, the oldest manuscript of Sophocles's *Ajax* at line 761 has a Subj. φρονῇ [without ἄν], which a later scribe has altered to Indic. φρονεῖ.) ὅς ἄν clauses have Subjunctive verbs.

ὅστις μὲν οὖν ἐς μίαν ἀποβλέπων τύχην
πρὸς θεῶν **κακοῦται**, βαρὺ μέν, οἰστέον δ' ὅμως. (E. *Hel.* 267–268.)

Well then, **when any one**, focusing on one fortune,
is maltreated by the gods, <that is> burdensome, but still able to be borne.

Structurally: 'Maltreatment by the gods <is> burdensome'. (Subject)

οὐκ αἰνῶ φόβον,
ὅστις φοβεῖται μὴ διεξελθὼν λόγῳ. (E. *Tr.* 1165–1166.)

I do not approve fear,
when someone has fear without examining it with reason.

Structurally: 'I do not approve irrational fear'. (In this passage, the ὅστις clause serves as Object in apposition with φόβον, the grammatical Object of the Main clause.)

τὸ δ' εὐτυχές, **οἳ ἂν** τῆς εὐπρεπεστάτης **λάχωσιν**, ὥσπερ οἵδε μὲν νῦν, τελευτῆς ... (Th. 2.44.1.)

And <it is> good fortune, **when** <men> **obtain** a most decent end, just as these <do> now ...

Structurally: 'Obtaining a most decent end <is> fortunate'. (Subject)

References

Goodwin (1889), *Syntax of the moods and tenses of the Greek verb*, §§514–564.

Smyth (1956), *Greek grammar*, §§2488–2552(–2573).

Lesson 25 does not cover all issues in the Sections of Goodwin (1889) and Smyth (1956), and it is not always in agreement with them.

EXERCISE 25

Translate the following passages.

1. σπορᾶς γε μὴν ἐκ τῆσδε φύσεται θρασύς,
   τόξοισι κλεινός, ὃς πόνων ἐκ τῶνδ' ἐμὲ
   λύσει.

σπορά, -ᾶς, ἡ	*origin*
γε μήν	*but at any rate* (Denniston, 1954, p. 348)
θρασύς, (-εῖα, -ύ)	*(a) courageous (figure)* (Subject)
κλεινός, -ή, -όν	*famous* (+ Causal Dat.; in apposition with Subject)

2. ὃς πρῶτον μὲν τῆς προτέρας ὀλιγαρχίας αἰτιώτατος ἐγένετο, πείσας ὑμᾶς τὴν ἐπὶ τῶν τετρακοσίων πολιτείαν ἑλέσθαι.

αἴτιος, -α, -ον	*responsible (for)* (+ Gen.)
ἐπί (+ Gen.)	*in the time of*
πολιτεία, -ας, ἡ	*administration, government*

LESSON 25. ADJECTIVAL CLAUSES

3. ... καὶ τοὺς αὐτοὺς τούτους κυρίους ἁπάντων τῶν κοινῶν καθίσταμεν, οἷς οὐδεὶς ἂν οὐδὲν τῶν ἰδίων ἐπιτρέψειεν.

κοινῶν (Gen. neut. pl.)	*public affairs*
καθίσταμεν	Pres. Indic.
ἰδίων	neut.

4. τοιαῦτα φῆμαι μαντικαὶ διώρισαν,
   ὧν ἐντρέπου σὺ μηδέν·

ἐντρέπειν	*to pay attention (to)* (+ Gen.)

5. οἳ δὲ δίκας ξείνοισι καὶ ἐνδήμοισι διδοῦσιν
   ἰθείας καὶ μή τι παρεκβαίνουσι δικαίου,
   τοῖσι τέθηλε πόλις, λαοὶ δ' ἀνθεῦσιν ἐν αὐτῇ·

δίκη, -ης, ἡ	*judgment*
ξεῖνος	ξένος
διδοῦσιν	διδόασι(ν)
ἰθύς, -εῖα, -ύ	*straight* (lit. and metaphorical)
τοῖσι	demonstrative pronoun, antecedent of οἵ
θάλλειν	*to sprout;* (Perf. in Imperf. sense) *to flourish*
ἀνθεῖν	*to bloom* (here Ionic 3rd pers. pl.)

6. ταῦτ' οὐχὶ δεινῆς ἀγχόνης ἔστ' ἄξια,
   ὕβρεις ὑβρίζειν, ὅστις ἔστιν ὁ ξένος;

ἀγχόνη, -ης, ἡ	*hanging*
ὕβρις, -εως, ἡ	*(act of) insolence* (here internal Acc. with cognate verb)

7. ... *I became reconciled on account of this danger with none of my enemies, who more gladly speak ill of me than commend themselves.*

to reconcile (with)	διαλλάσσειν, Aor. Pass. διαλλαγῆναι (also διαλλαχθῆναι) (+ Dat.)
to commend	ἐπαινεῖν

8. … but they are sending against me such [men], whom *you* [pl.] would not rightly trust.

| *to send* (Acc.) *against* (Dat.) | ἐπιπέμπειν |
| *to trust* | πιστεύειν (+ Dat.) |

LESSON 26
Concessive Constructions

26.1. Introduction

Concession may be expressed by a Participial phrase or by a Subordinate clause. In both constructions ὅμως ('nevertheless') often appears in the leading clause (that is, the clause on which the Concessive clause or phrase depends).

26.2. Concessive Participial Phrases

When a Participial phrase expresses Concession, the Participle itself may carry the Concessive force; or the Participle may be reinforced by καίπερ or occasionally by καί or (mainly in Homer and tragedy) by περ alone. After καίπερ, the Participle of the verb 'to be' may be omitted with an adjective or noun. In Homer, καί and περ are almost always separated by the Participle or by another significant word. A Genitive absolute or an Accusative absolute may have Concessive force. See Lessons 4, 5 and 6 on Participles.

A negated Concessive Participial phrase ('not even if', 'not even though') has οὐδέ (regularly reinforced by περ) in place of καίπερ, when the phrase is subordinate to a verb which is (or could be) negated by οὐ, as with Indicative or potential Optative. In Homer, περ is regularly separated from οὐδέ.

εἶπον δὲ καὶ πρίν, οὐκ ἄνευ δήμου τάδε
πράξαιμ' ἄν, **οὐδέ περ κρατῶν** ... (A.*Suppl.* 398–399.)

*And I said also previously: 'I would not do this
without <the consent of> the people, **not even though I am ruling** ...'*

οὐκ with potential Optative is followed by οὐδέ περ.

INTERMEDIATE ANCIENT GREEK LANGUAGE

... οὐκ ἄρ' ἔμελλες,
οὐδ' ἐν σῇ **περ ἐὼν** γαίῃ, λήξειν ἀπατάων ...
(Hom.*Od.* 13.293–294.)

... so you were not likely,
***not even when you were** in your own land, to cease from deceits ...*

οὐκ with Indicative is followed by οὐδ' ... περ.

μηδέ is used with a Participle subordinate to a verb which is (or could be) negated by μή, as with Imperative or Subjunctive.

μὴ γὰρ ἐγχάνῃ ποτὲ
μηδέ περ γέροντας **ὄντας** ἐκφυγὼν Ἀχαρνέας. (Ar.*Ach.* 221–222.)

*For he is not ever to taunt us
with his having escaped the Acharnians, **not even if we are** old.*

μή with Jussive Subjunctive is followed by μηδέ περ.

26.3. Concessive Clauses

26.3.1. The Usual Constructions

Greek Concessive clauses are, in form, a variety of Conditional clause. They are introduced by καὶ εἰ or καὶ ἐάν and by εἰ καί or ἐὰν καί. A broad distinction can be made between καὶ εἰ (ἐάν) meaning 'even if' and εἰ (ἐὰν) καί meaning 'although', 'even though'. The range of constructions corresponds to that of other Conditional sentences. The negative *within* a Concessive clause ('even if ... not', 'although ... not') is μή, as in a Conditional clause. (Contrast §26.3.5 below.)

κερδαλέος κ' εἴη καὶ ἐπίκλοπος, ὅς σε παρέλθοι
ἐν πάντεσσι δόλοισι, **καὶ εἰ** θεὸς **ἀντιάσειε**. (Hom.*Od.* 13.291–292.)

*Crafty would he be and wily, who surpassed you
in all tricks, **even if** a god **were to encounter** <you>.*

καὶ εἰ with Optative.

φήσουσι γὰρ δή με σοφὸν εἶναι, **εἰ καὶ μή εἰμι**, οἱ βουλόμενοι ὑμῖν ὀνειδίζειν. (Pl.*Ap.* 38 C.)

*For indeed those, who want to censure you, will say that I am wise, **although I am not**.*

εἰ καί with Indicative and negative μή.

26.3.2. Variations from the Usual Constructions

The senses 'even if' (καὶ εἰ) and 'although' (εἰ καί) not only overlap, but appear to be reversed in some Greek sentences. This is especially true in verse.

Moreover, not every sentence with καὶ εἰ or εἰ καί will have the Concessive meanings 'even if' or 'although'. καί and εἰ, in either order, may function separately at the beginning of a Conditional clause. Thus, καὶ εἰ may mean 'and if'. And εἰ καί may mean:

a. 'if indeed', referring to the whole clause
b. 'if also/even/actually', referring to a particular item following in the clause.

26.3.3. εἴπερ (εἴ περ, ἐάν περ)

εἴπερ may have the meaning 'even if'. It is sometimes followed (immediately or later) by other particles such as καί, τε, γε.

καὶ μὴν οὐδὲ τοῦτο εἰκὸς αὐτῷ πιστεύειν, **εἴπερ** ἀληθῆ λέγει φάσκων ἀντειπεῖν, ὡς αὐτῷ προσετάχθη. (Lys. 12.27.)

*Moreover, **even if** he is telling the truth in saying that he spoke in opposition, <it is> not reasonable to believe him in this claim either, that instructions were given to him.*

οὐδέ = 'not ... either'; τοῦτο anticipates the ὡς clause.

26.3.4. εἰ or ἐάν Alone

εἰ or ἐάν alone may have Concessive force.

εἰ γὰρ εἴρηται ἐν ταῖς σπονδαῖς ἐξεῖναι παρ' ὁποτέρους τις βούλεται τῶν ἀγράφων πόλεων ἐλθεῖν, οὐ τοῖς ἐπὶ βλάβῃ ἑτέρων ἰοῦσιν ἡ ξυνθήκη ἐστίν … (Th. 1.40.2.)

*For <even> **if** it has been stated in the treaty that it is permissible for any one of the unregistered city-states to go to whichever of the two sides it wishes, the clause is not <intended> for those going to harm the others …*

26.3.5. Negated Concessive Clauses

For negated Concessive clauses ('not even if'), οὐδέ or μηδέ precedes the Conditional conjunctions εἰ or ἐάν. οὐδέ is used where the leading clause requires οὐ, as with Indicative or potential Optative. μηδέ is used where the leading clause requires μή, as with Imperative, Subjunctive, or Optative in Past sequence representing a Primary Subjunctive. (Cf. §26.2 above.) The negative is often repeated within the leading clause.

σέθεν δ' ἐγὼ **οὐκ** ἀλεγίζω
χωομένης, **οὐδ' εἴ** κε τὰ νείατα πείραθ' ἵκηαι
γαίης καὶ πόντοιο … (Hom.*Il.* 8.477–479.)

*But I am **not** worried about you
in your anger, **not even if** you go so far as the furthest limits
of earth and sea …*

ἵκηαι is second person singular Aorist Middle Subjunctive.

οἱ δὲ Συρακόσιοι τόν τε λιμένα εὐθὺς παρέπλεον ἀδεῶς καὶ τὸ στόμα αὐτοῦ διενοοῦντο κλῄσειν, ὅπως **μηκέτι μηδ' εἰ** βούλοιντο λάθοιεν αὐτοὺς οἱ Ἀθηναῖοι ἐκπλεύσαντες. (Th. 7.56.1.)

*And the Syracusans immediately began to sail along the harbour without fear and were intending to block its mouth, so that the Athenians might **no longer** escape their notice in sailing out, **not even if** they wanted to.*

References

Denniston (1954), *The Greek particles*, pp. 299–305, 486–487.

Goodwin (1889), *Syntax of the moods and tenses of the Greek verb*, §§842, 859–861 (Participles only).

Smyth (1956), *Greek grammar*, §§2066, 2070.c, 2082–2083 (Participles); 2369–2382 (clauses).

EXERCISE 26

Translate the following passages.

1. ὁρῶ, Προμηθεῦ, καὶ παραινέσαι γέ σοι
   θέλω τὰ λῷστα καίπερ ὄντι ποικίλῳ.

παραινεῖν	to give advice (Acc.) to (Dat.)
λῷστος, -η, -ον	best
ποικίλος, -η, -ον	subtle, ingenious

2. τὸ γὰρ ἐμόν ποτ' εὐγενὲς
   οὐκ ἂν προδοίην, οὐδέ περ πράσσων κακῶς.

εὐγενής, -ές	of noble birth (here neut. of adj. for abstract noun)
προδιδόναι	to betray
πράσσειν	to fare, to get on

3. ... αὐτὴ ξίφος λαβοῦσα, κεἰ μέλλω θανεῖν,
   κτενῶ σφε ...

σφε	them (Acc.)

4. καὶ ταῦτ' Ἰάσων παῖδας ἐξανέξεται
   πάσχοντας, εἰ καὶ μητρὶ διαφορὰν ἔχει;

ἐξανέχεσθαι (Mid.)	to endure, to put up with (+ Acc.)
διαφορά, -ᾶς, ἡ	difference, disagreement

5. φίλους δὲ λέγεις εἶναι πότερον τοὺς δοκοῦντας ἑκάστῳ χρηστοὺς εἶναι, ἢ τοὺς ὄντας κἂν μὴ δοκῶσι;

δοκεῖν	to seem
χρηστός, -ή, -όν	good
This sentence is a direct Alternative Question.	

6. ἐγὼ γὰρ δή σοι λέγω ..., ὅτι οὐ πείθομαι οὐδ᾽ οἶμαι ἀδικίαν δικαιοσύνης κερδαλεώτερον εἶναι, οὐδ᾽ ἐὰν ἐᾷ τις αὐτὴν ... πράττειν ἃ βούλεται·

κερδαλέος, -α, -ον	profitable

7. For this city must realise fully, even if it is not willing [to], that it is uninitiated in my Bacchic rites ...

to realise fully	ἐκμανθάνειν (+ Acc. and Partc.)
even if	Use a clause.
uninitiated (in)	ἀτέλεστος, -ον (+ Gen.)

8. But I think that, although concerning the other [matters] it is appropriate that the [men] of such an age should keep silent, at least concerning going to war or not, it is fitting that these especially should give advice ...

to think	ἡγεῖσθαι (Mid.; + Infin.)
to be appropriate	πρέπειν (+ Acc. and Infin.)
of such an age	τηλικοῦτος, -αύτη, -οῦτον
concerning going to war	preposition + articular Infin. πολεμεῖν
to be fitting	προσήκειν (+ Acc. and Infin.)
especially	μάλιστα
to give advice	συμβουλεύειν

LESSON 27
Purpose Constructions

27.1. Prepositions

Purpose may be expressed by the prepositions εἰς, ἐπί and πρός with the Accusative, ἐπί with the Dative, and ὑπέρ with the Genitive of the articular Infinitive.

τὸν οὖν παρόντα πέμψον **ἐς** κατασκοπήν ... (S.Ph. 45.)
*So send the man, who is present, **to** reconnoitre ...*

ἦλθον οἱ Ἰνδοὶ ἐκ τῶν πολεμίων, οὓς ἐπεπόμφει Κῦρος **ἐπὶ** κατασκοπήν ... (X.Cyr. 6.2.9.)

*the Indians, whom Cyrus had sent **to** reconnoitre, came from the enemy ...*

τὰ μὲν γὰρ ἑστίας μεσομφάλου
ἕστηκεν ἤδη μῆλα **πρὸς** σφαγὰς πάρος. (A.Ag. 1056–1057.)

*For now the animals
stand <ready> **for** slaughter before the central hearth.*

Ἀχιλλέως παῖ, δεῖ σ' **ἐφ'** οἷς ἐλήλυθας
γενναῖον εἶναι. (S.Ph. 50–51.)

*Son of Achilles, you must be noble <for the purposes>
for which you have come.*

πολῖται γὰρ δορυφοροῦσι ... ἀλλήλους ἄνευ μισθοῦ ... ἐπὶ τοὺς κακούργους **ὑπὲρ τοῦ** μηδένα τῶν πολιτῶν βιαίῳ θανάτῳ **ἀποθνῄσκειν**. (X.Hier. 4.3.)

*For the citizens guard ... one another without pay ... against evil-doers,
so that no one of the citizens **may die** by a violent death.*

27.2. Infinitive

For the Infinitive expressing Purpose with certain verbs, see Lessons 3.4.3.1 and 3.5.3.

27.3. Participles

Participles may express Purpose, occasionally in the Imperfect Aspect, but mainly in the Intentive Aspect. ὡς is frequently used with the Intentive ('Fut.') Participle expressing Purpose. A Participle is used to express Purpose especially with such verbs as 'come', 'go', 'send' and 'summon'.

τούτους θανόντας ἦλθον **ἐξαιτῶν** πόλιν. (E.*Supp.* 120.)
*I went to the city **to request** these dead <men>.*

Imperf. Partc.

... καὶ ὡς **διαβαλὼν** δὴ ἔρχεται εἰς τὸ δικαστήριον ... (Pl.*Euthphr.* 3 B.)
*... and he is going to court precisely **to slander** <you> ...*

Intentive ('Fut.') Participle.

27.4. Adjectival Clauses of Purpose

Adjectival clauses with the Future Indicative may be used to express Purpose. (Goodwin [1889, §565], Smyth [1956, §§2554, 2705.f.] and other elementary and advanced grammars state that the negative for this construction is μή. However, they cite no negative examples. Negative examples can be cited for adverbial clauses of Place.)

ἀλλὰ νῦν οἱ μὲν πολιτευόμενοι ἐν ταῖς πατρίσι καὶ νόμους τίθενται, ἵνα μὴ ἀδικῶνται, ... καὶ ὅπλα κτῶνται, **οἷς ἀμυνοῦνται** τοὺς ἀδικοῦντας ... (X.*Mem.* 2.1.14.)

*But now those who participate in the government in their fatherlands not only frame laws, so that they may not be wronged, ... but also obtain weapons, **with which to ward off** wrongdoers ...*

LESSON 27. PURPOSE CONSTRUCTIONS

In adjectival clauses of Purpose, Homer normally uses the Subjunctive, generally with κε(ν), in Primary sequence, and Optative, without κε(ν), in Past sequence. The Optative in Past sequence also occurs in Attic literature sometimes.

ἀλλ' ἄγετε, κλητοὺς ὀτρύνομεν, **οἵ κε** τάχιστα
ἔλθωσ' ἐς κλισίην Πηληϊάδεω Ἀχιλῆος. (Hom.*Il.* 9.165–166.)

*Well come on, let us urge on recruited men, **that they may** very quickly **go** to the hut of Peleus's son, Achilles.*

Subjunctive with κε in Primary sequence. ὀτρύνομεν is an Epic Aorist Subjunctive form with short vowel, equivalent to Attic ὀτρύνωμεν.

οὐδένα γὰρ εἶχον **ὅστις ἀγγεῖλαι** μολὼν
ἐς Ἄργος αὖθις, τάς ‹τ'› ἐμὰς ἐπιστολὰς
πέμψειε σωθεὶς τῶν ἐμῶν φίλων τινί. (E.*IT* 588–590.)

*For I had no one **to go back** to Argos and **report**, and, having been saved, **to convey** my letter to one of my dear ones.*

Optative ἀγγεῖλαι and πέμψειε in Past sequence.

27.5. Adverbial Clauses of Purpose

Adverbial clauses of Purpose are introduced by a variety of conjunctions, but mainly ἵνα and ὅπως. They regularly have Subjunctive in Primary sequence and Optative in Past sequence. In early Greek, negative Purpose clauses could be introduced by μή alone. But μή increasingly came to be used only as a negative within a Purpose clause introduced by one of the other (positive) conjunctions.

ἠῶθεν δ' ἀγορήνδε καθεζώμεσθα κιόντες
πάντες, **ἵν'** ὑμῖν μῦθον ἀπηλεγέως **ἀποείπω**,
ἐξιέναι μεγάρων· (Hom.*Od.* 1.372–374.)

*And from dawn let us all go to the place of assembly and sit down, **so that I may declare** to you my word unrestrainedly, to go out from the halls.*

ἵνα with Subjunctive in Primary sequence.

... ἐγὼ δ' ἄπειμι, **μὴ κατοπτευθῶ** παρών ... (S.*Ph.* 124.)
... *but I shall go away,* **so that I may not be observed** *being present* ...

μή alone with Subjunctive in Primary sequence.

ἐπὶ δ' αὐτῷ εἴκοσι ἔταξαν τὰς ἄριστα πλεούσας, **ὅπως** ... **μὴ διαφύγοιεν** πλέοντα τὸν ἐπίπλουν σφῶν οἱ Ἀθηναῖοι ... (Th. 2.90.2.)

And on it [= the right wing] *they stationed the twenty <ships> which sailed best,* **in order that** ... *the Athenians* **might not escape through** *their line-of-attack as it sailed* ...

ὅπως μή with Optative in Past sequence.

ἵνα is the main Purpose conjunction in Herodotus, Aristophanes, Plato and the orators. ὅπως is the main conjunction in Thucydides. ὅπως is slightly more common than ἵνα in Xenophon. ὅπως with Subjunctive sometimes has ἄν in positive clauses.

ὡς with κε(ν) or ἄν and the Subjunctive occurs in Homer, Attic poetry and Herodotus (Ionic). ὄφρα is the most common Purpose conjunction in Homer; occasionally κε(ν) or ἄν is used with ὄφρα and the Subjunctive.

The Vivid construction, with Subjunctive instead of Optative in Past sequence, is used more often than not by the historians Herodotus and Thucydides.

The Future Indicative may be used instead of the Subjunctive especially in poetry, mainly with ὅπως, rarely with ὄφρα, ὡς and μή, but never with ἵνα.

ἐπειδὴ δὲ ἤλθομεν ὡς αὐτὸν ἡμεῖς οἱ πρέσβεις, ἐμισθώσατο μὲν τοῦτον εὐθέως, **ὅπως συνερεῖ** καὶ **συναγωνιεῖται** τῷ μιαρῷ Φιλοκράτει καὶ τῶν τὰ δίκαια βουλομένων ἡμῶν πράττειν **περιέσται** ... (D. 19.316.)

But when we, the ambassadors, had come to him, he immediately hired this <fellow>, **so that he might speak with** *and* **assist** *the abominable Philocrates and* **overtake** *us who wanted to do the right thing* ...

ὅπως with Future Indicative.

References

Goodwin (1889), *Syntax of the moods and tenses of the Greek verb*, §§302–338; 802; 840.

Smyth (1956), *Greek grammar*, §§1686.1.d, 1689.2.c, 3.d, 1695.3.c, 1697.1.b (Prepositions); 2065, 2086 (Participles); 2554 (adjectival clauses); 2193–2206 (adverbial clauses).

EXERCISE 27

Translate the following passages.

1. ὅταν τι δρᾷς ἐς κέρδος, οὐκ ὀκνεῖν πρέπει.

2. ὣς ἄρα οἱ φρονέοντι δοάσσατο κέρδιον εἶναι,
λίσσεσθαι ἐπέεσσιν ἀποσταδὰ μειλιχίοισι,
μή οἱ γοῦνα λαβόντι χολώσαιτο φρένα κούρη.

οἱ	Dat. masc. sg.
δοάσσατο	*it seemed*
ἀποσταδά (adv.)	*standing apart*
μειλίχιος, -α, -ον	*gentle, soothing*
γόνυ, γόνατος, τό	*knee* (here Acc. pl. with alternative spelling)

3. προεῖπε δὲ καὶ τοῦτο τοῖς στρατιώταις, ὡς εὐθὺς ἡγήσοιτο τὴν συντομωτάτην ἐπὶ τὰ κράτιστα τῆς χώρας, ὅπως αὐτόθεν αὐτῷ τὰ σώματα καὶ τὴν γνώμην παρασκευάζοιντο ὡς ἀγωνιούμενοι.

προειπεῖν (Aor.)	*to say in advance*
σύντομος, -ον	*short* (Here understand ὁδόν, Acc. of Extent.)
αὐτόθεν	*at once*
ἀγωνίζεσθαι (Mid.)	*to take part in the struggle*

4. φίλος ἐβούλετο εἶναι τοῖς μέγιστα δυναμένοις, ἵνα ἀδικῶν μὴ διδοίη δίκην.

φίλος	Complement of εἶναι
διδόναι δίκην	to pay the penalty

5. μὴ πρόσλευσσε, γενναῖός περ ὤν, ἡμῶν ὅπως μὴ τὴν τύχην διαφθερεῖς.

προσλεύσσειν	to look at (Understand αὐτόν as Object.)

6. For not in order that I may criticise the city of the Spartans in the presence of the rest have I spoken in this way about them, but in order that I may stop those [men] themselves … [from] having such an attitude.

in order that	ἵνα (both instances)
to criticise	διαβάλλειν
Spartan	Λακεδαιμόνιος, -α, -ον
in the presence of	πρός (+ Acc.)
attitude	γνώμη, -ης, ἡ

7. … and he was no longer willing to accept payment from me, pushing [me] aside, so that that [man], but not I, might seem to be burying my grandfather.

to accept payment	ἀπολαμβάνειν (no Object necessary)
to push aside	ὑποπαρωθεῖν
so that	ὅπως
grandfather	πάππος, -ου, ὁ

LESSON 28
Clauses of Comparison

28.1. Introduction

Clauses of Comparison are introduced by relative adjectives and by relative adverbs of manner, quality, quantity or degree. The relative adjective or adverb is frequently balanced by the corresponding demonstrative adjective or adverb in the leading clause (on which the clause of Comparison depends). For example: ὡς … οὕτω(ς) … 'As … so …' Either or both of these adverbs may be reinforced by καί: ὡς καί … οὕτω καί …: 'Just as …, even so …' [OR: 'so too …']. In Homer, ὥς (accented) frequently stands for οὕτως.

28.2. Definite Comparison

The simplest form of comparison presents the circumstances of the comparison as factual and uses the Indicative Mood in the clause of Comparison.

καὶ οἱ μὲν Δήλιοι Ἀτραμύττειον Φαρνάκου δόντος αὐτοῖς ἐν τῇ Ἀσίᾳ ᾤκησαν **οὕτως ὡς** ἕκαστος ὥρμητο. (Th. 5.1.)

And the Delians settled Atramyttium in Asia, when Pharnaces had granted it to them, **in such a way as** *each <man> had set out.*

(There was no organised colony, but settlement was individual and piecemeal.)

As adverbs, οὕτως modifies the verb ᾤκησαν, and ὡς modifies the verb ὥρμητο.

28.3. Indefinite Comparison

An indefinite form of comparison uses the Subjunctive Mood with ἄν in Primary sequence. Compare the difference between Open Particular and Open General Conditions, Lesson 19.2.1 and Lesson 19.2.2. In the following sentence, the ὅπως clause refers to any occasion on which Nicocles influences the attitude of his citizens.

ὅπως γὰρ **ἂν** τοὺς ἄλλους πρὸς σαυτὸν **διαθῇς, οὕτω καὶ** σὺ πρὸς ἐκείνους ἕξεις. (Isoc. 2.23.)

*For **as you dispose** the rest <of the community> towards yourself, **so too** will you be inclined towards those <people>.*

The equivalent of this construction in Past sequence has the Optative without ἄν. (A Vivid construction, using Subj. with ἄν, may also occur in Past sequence.)

ἐπιπόνως δὲ ηὑρίσκετο, διότι οἱ παρόντες τοῖς ἔργοις ἑκάστοις οὐ ταὐτὰ περὶ τῶν αὐτῶν ἔλεγον, ἀλλ' **ὡς** ἑκατέρων τις εὐνοίας ἢ μνήμης **ἔχοι**. (Th. 1.22.3.)

*And the discoveries were painstakingly made, because those who had been present at particular actions did not say the same things about the same <events>, but <spoke> **as any one had** some goodwill towards either side or some memory <of what had happened>.*

(The Partitive Genitives singular εὐνοίας and μνήμης function as direct Objects of ἔχοι. Cf. Lesson 37.3.4.)

28.4. Potential, Conditional and Temporal Constructions

Potential, Conditional and Temporal constructions may occur within a comparison.

28.4.1. Potential

... ἐγὼ δὲ οὐδὲν ἄρα τούτων ποιήσω, καὶ ταῦτα κινδυνεύων, **ὡς ἂν δόξαιμι**, τὸν ἔσχατον κίνδυνον. (Pl.*Ap.* 34 C.)

... *but* I *shall actually do none of these things—and this, when I am running,* **as I would seem** *<to be>, the extreme risk.*

ὡς with ἄν and potential Optative in Primary sequence.

28.4.2. Conditional

αὐτὰρ ἔπειτα
λαοὶ ἕπονθ', **ὡς εἴ** τε μετὰ κτίλον **ἕσπετο** μῆλα
πιόμεν' ἐκ βοτάνης· (Hom.*Il.* 13.491–493.)

*And then
the men were following,* **as if** *sheep <had>* **followed** *after a ram
from pasture, going to drink.*

ὡς εἰ with Past Aorist Indicative in Past sequence.

οὗτος γὰρ ἐμοὶ φαίνεται τὰ ἐναντία λέγειν αὐτὸς ἑαυτῷ ἐν τῇ
γραφῇ, **ὥσπερ ἂν εἰ εἴποι**· ἀδικεῖ Σωκράτης θεοὺς οὐ νομίζων,
ἀλλὰ θεοὺς νομίζων. (Pl.*Ap.* 27 A.)

*For this <man> appears to me to say the opposite [himself] to himself in his
indictment,* **as** *(he would)* **if he were to say**: *'Socrates does wrong in not
believing in gods but in believing in gods'.*

ὥσπερ ἂν εἰ with Optative in Primary sequence.

28.4.3. Temporal

ὡς ὅτε (or ὡς ὁπότε) is especially common in Homeric similes. The Mood is sometimes Indicative. But in Homer, an initial Subjunctive without ἄν is often continued by Indicatives. The construction with Subjunctive is indefinite.

αὐτὰρ ὁ θυμὸν ἄϊσθε καὶ ἤρυγεν, **ὡς ὅτε** ταῦρος
ἤρυγεν ἑλκόμενος ... (Hom.*Il.* 20.403–404.)

Then he was breathing out his spirit and bellowed, **as when** *a bull*
bellows *(lit. bellowed; Indic.) while being dragged along ...*

ὡς ὅτε with Past Aorist Indicative (definite).

ὡς δ' **ὅτ'** ἀνὴρ ἀπάλαμνος, ἰὼν πόλεος πεδίοιο,
στήῃ ἐπ' ὠκυρόῳ ποταμῷ ἅλαδε προρέοντι,
ἀφρῷ μορμύροντα ἰδών, ἀνά τ' **ἔδραμ'** ὀπίσσω,
ὣς τότε Τυδεΐδης ἀνεχάζετο ... (Hom.*Il.* 5.597–600.)

*And **as when** a helpless man, going over a large plain,*
***stops** (Subj.) at a swift-flowing river flowing on to the sea,*
*seeing it seething with foam, and **runs** (lit. ran; Indic.) backwards,*
***so** at that time the son of Tydeus was recoiling ...*

ὡς ὅτε with Aorist Subjunctive (indefinite) continued by Past Aorist Indicative (definite).

28.5. Other Correlative Adjectives and Adverbs

Other correlative adjectives and adverbs also express comparison.

Λοκρῶν δ' ἡγεμόνευεν Ὀϊλῆος ταχὺς Αἴας,
μείων, οὔ τι **τόσος** γε **ὅσος** Τελαμώνιος Αἴας,
ἀλλὰ πολὺ μείων. (Hom.*Il.* 2.527–529.)

And of the Locrians the leader was Oeleus's <son>, swift Ajax,
*smaller, not at all **so big as** Telamon's son Ajax,*
but much smaller.

References

Goodwin (1889), *Syntax of the moods and tenses of the Greek verb*, §§484–485, 543–549.

Smyth (1956), *Greek grammar*, §§2462–2487.

EXERCISE 28

Translate the following passages.

1. ... καὶ τὸ τελευταῖον, ὅπως ἐβούλοντο, οὕτω τὸν πόλεμον κατέθεντο.

τὸ τελευταῖον	adverbial
κατατίθεσθαι (Mid.)	to put an end to (+ Acc.)

2. ἦν μὲν γὰρ σελήνη λαμπρά, ἑώρων δὲ οὕτως ἀλλήλους ὡς ἐν σελήνῃ εἰκὸς τὴν μὲν ὄψιν τοῦ σώματος προορᾶν, τὴν δὲ γνῶσιν τοῦ οἰκείου ἀπιστεῖσθαι.

σελήνη, -ης, ἡ	moonlight
τὴν ... γνῶσιν	Subject of ἀπιστεῖσθαι (Pass.)
τοῦ οἰκείου	acquaintance (either masc. or collective neut.)

3. ὅμοιον γὰρ ὥσπερ ἂν εἰ φαίη εἰδέναι, καὶ μὴ παραγενόμενος, ὅσα ὑμεῖς πάντες πράττετε.

ὅμοιον (neut.)	Understand ἐστί.

4. ὡς δ' ἀπὸ σώματος οὔ τι λέοντ' αἴθωνα δύνανται
ποιμένες ἄγραυλοι μέγα πεινάοντα δίεσθαι,
ὥς ῥα τὸν οὐκ ἐδύναντο δύω Αἴαντε κορυστὰ
Ἕκτορα Πριαμίδην ἀπὸ νεκροῦ δειδίξασθαι.

αἴθων, -ωνος, ὁ, ἡ	tawny
ἄγραυλος, -ον	(living) in the field(s)
πεινᾶν	to be hungry
δίεσθαι (Mid.)	to put to flight, to drive away
ῥα (enclitic adv.)	just (modifying ὥς)
κορυστής, -οῦ, ὁ	(a) helmeted (man) (here dual)
δειδίσσεσθαι (Mid.)	to frighten, to alarm, to scare away

5. ὡς δ' ὅτ' ἂν ἐκ νεφέων πτῆται νιφὰς ἠὲ χάλαζα
ψυχρὴ ὑπὸ ῥιπῆς αἰθρηγενέος Βορέαο,
ὣς κραιπνῶς μεμαυῖα διέπτατο ὠκέα Ἶρις,
ἀγχοῦ δ' ἱσταμένη προσέφη κλυτὸν ἐννοσίγαιον·

πέτεσθαι	*to fly*
χάλαζα, -ης, ἡ	*hail*
αἰθρηγενής, -ές	*born in the (bright) sky*
κραιπνῶς	*quickly*
μεμονέναι	*to be eager* (Perf. with Imperf. meaning)
μεμαώς, -υῖα, -ός	short form of Partc. of μεμονέναι
ὠκύς, -εῖα, -ύ	*swift* (Epic fem. ὠκέα)
ἀγχοῦ (adv.)	*near*

6. And concerning the mutilation of the statues and the laying of information, just as I promised you (pl.), so too I shall do.

mutilation	περικοπή, -ῆς, ἡ
statue	ἀνάθημα, -ατος, τό
laying of information	μήνυσις, -εως, ἡ
to promise (to someone)	ὑπισχνεῖσθαι (+ Dat.)

LESSON 29
Expressions of Hindering, Forbidding, Denying and Failing

29.1. Introduction

Verbs (and other expressions) of hindering take a direct Object in the Accusative Case. The Object may be a person or a thing. Occasionally, both person and thing occur in the same expression with a double Accusative construction: 'to hinder someone <from> something'. More often the thing, from which someone is hindered, is expressed by a Genitive of Separation with or without a preposition (ἀπό, ἐκ). When a thing is the direct Object of such a verb, it is most often expressed by an Infinitive without, or less often with, the definite article. And the most common construction for expressing 'to hinder someone from doing something' is technically a double Accusative of person and thing (Infin.): lit. 'to hinder someone to do something'.

In positive and negative expressions of hindering, a redundant negative μή may occur with the Infinitive. And in negative (or interrogative) expressions of hindering, a double redundant negative μὴ οὐ may occur with the Infinitive.

Occasionally, an Accusative and Participle (instead of Infinitive) construction is used (cf. Lesson 4.3.3, Supplementary Participle). More rarely, constructions of Result, Effort and Condition are used with the function of a hindering expression; cf. Lessons 22, 24 and 19 respectively. In Passive expressions, the personal Object of the usual construction becomes the Subject and the Infinitive is retained: 'they are hindered from doing something' (lit. 'they are hindered to do something'). In the Passive form of an Accusative and Participle construction, both the Accusative noun or pronoun and the Participle become Nominative.

29.2. Direct Object

29.2.1. Person

ταῦτα δὲ βουλομένους ποιεῖν ἄνεμος καὶ χειμὼν **διεκώλυσεν αὐτοὺς** μέγας γενόμενος· (X.*HG* 1.6.35.)

*But although they were wanting to do this, a great wind and storm arose and **prevented them**.*

29.2.2. Thing

ἀλλὰ μὴ ἀστρολόγος, ἔφη, βούλῃ γενέσθαι; ὡς δὲ καὶ **τοῦτο ἠρνεῖτο**, ἀλλὰ μὴ ῥαψῳδός; ἔφη· (X.*Mem.* 4.2.10.)

*'Well, do you want', he said, 'to become an astronomer?' And since **he was denying this** also, 'Well', he said, 'a reciter?'*

29.2.3. Person and Thing

τί φῄς; τίς ἔσται **μ' οὑπικωλύσων τάδε**; (S.*Ph.* 1242.)
*What do you mean? Who will there be who **will debar me from this**?*

29.3. Genitive of Separation

29.3.1. Simple Genitive

... οὗτοι ἄν σοι, εἴ τινι ἐντυγχάνοιεν τῶν Ἀρμενίων, τοὺς μὲν ἂν συλλαμβάνοντες αὐτῶν **κωλύοιεν τῶν ἐξαγγελιῶν** ...
(X.*Cyr.* 2.4.23.)

*... these men, if they encountered any one of the Armenians, would seize some of them for you and **would prevent** <them> **from** <making> **reports** ...*

29.3.2. Preposition with Genitive

... ὁ δῆμος ... τούτῳ προσεῖχεν ... ὅπως ... τούς τε τοιούτους ἅπαντας **ἀπείργειν ἀπὸ τοῦ συμβουλεύειν** ἕκαστος οἰήσεται δεῖν ... (Isoc. 12.139–141.)

… *the people … attended to this … that each should think that it was necessary* **to debar** *all such <men>* ***from giving advice*** …

(τε anticipates a following τε.)

29.4. Infinitive after a Positive Expression

29.4.1. Infinitive Only

… τάδε καὶ θρηνῶ κἀπιθεάζω,
μαρτυρόμενος δαίμονας ὥς μοι
τέκνα κτείνασ' **ἀποκωλύεις**
ψαῦσαί τε χεροῖν **θάψαι** τε νεκρούς … (E.*Med.* 1409–1412.)

… I both make this lament and invoke the gods,
calling the deities to witness that, having
killed my children, ***you are preventing***
both ***the touching*** *with one's hands and* ***the burying*** *of their bodies …*

29.4.2. Accusative and Infinitive

εἰ δ' ὑμῖν γνώμη ἐστὶ **κωλύειν** τε **ἡμᾶς** ἐπὶ Κέρκυραν ἢ ἄλλοσε εἴ ποι βουλόμεθα **πλεῖν** καὶ τὰς σπονδὰς λύετε, ἡμᾶς τούσδε πρώτους λαβόντας χρήσασθε ὡς πολεμίοις. (Th. 1.53.2.)

But if you have the intention ***of preventing us from sailing*** *to Corcyra or to anywhere else that we want to, and (if) you are breaking the treaty, seize us here first and treat <us> as enemies.*

29.4.3. Infinitive with Redundant μή

κομίζετ' αὐτόν, ὡς ἰδὼν ἐν ὄμμασιν
τὸν τἄμ' **ἀπαρνηθέντα μὴ χρᾶναι** λέχη
λόγοις τ' ἐλέγξω δαιμόνων τε συμφοραῖς. (E.*Hipp.* 1265–1267.)

Bring him, so that I may see with my eyes
the one who ***denied that he polluted*** *my bed*
and (so that I) may make a refutation with words and with the disaster from the gods.

29.4.4. Accusative and Articular Infinitive

ἔστιν τις ἔστιν ὅς **σε κωλύσει τὸ δρᾶν**. (S.*Ph.* 1241.)
*There is, there is someone who **will prevent you from acting**.*

29.4.5. Accusative and Articular Infinitive with Redundant μή

τὸ δὲ **μὴ λεηλατῆσαι** ἑλόντας **σφέας** τὴν πόλιν **ἔσχε** τόδε. (Hdt. 5.101.1.)

*And this **kept them from plundering** the city when they captured it.*

29.4.6. Accusative and Genitive Articular Infinitive

τούτους αὖ τοιαῦτα λέγων **ἔσχε τοῦ ἐκπεπλῆχθαι**. (X.*HG* 4.8.5.)

*Moreover, by making such statements **he kept these men from being** [OR: having become] **panic-stricken**.*

29.4.7. Accusative and Genitive Articular Infinitive with Redundant μή

ὁ δὲ συννήσας πυρὴν μεγάλην ἀνεβίβασε ἐπ' αὐτὴν τὸν Κροῖσον..., βουλόμενος εἰδέναι εἴ τίς **μιν** δαιμόνων **ῥύσεται τοῦ μὴ** ζῶντα **κατακαυθῆναι**. (Hdt. 1.86.2.)

*And he, having built a big pyre, made Croesus go up on to it ... wanting to know whether any one of the deities **would rescue him from being burned alive**.*

29.5. ἐμποδών

The adverb ἐμποδών introduces a variety of constructions which express hindering. The basic idea is 'getting in the way', 'blocking'. The grammatical constructions include Infinitive with or without definite article. The definite article may be in the Accusative or the Genitive Case. The Infinitive may have an explicit or implicit Accusative Subject; the implicit Subject may be indicated by an Accusative Participle. Redundant negatives may be used with the Infinitive, with or without the definite article.

ὧν τίς ἄλλος φανήσεται προνοηθείς, ἢ τίς **ἐμποδὼν** καταστὰς **τοῦ μηδὲν** ἔτι **γενέσθαι τοιοῦτον** ... (Isoc. 12.80.)

*For who else among them will appear as taking precautions, or who as getting **in the way of any such thing happening** again ...?*

Genitive articular Infinitive with Accusative Subject.

ὥστε τὸ αὐτὸ πάντες **ἐμποδὼν** εἰσιν, **ἐάν** τι δι' ἄλλων ἀγαθὸν ὑμῖν **φαίνηται**. (Lys. 25.33.)

*And so all together they are **in the way for** any good **to appear** for you through other <people>.*

ἐάν + Subjunctive: 'in the way if any good should appear'. Conditional construction as in §29.8 below.

29.6. Infinitive after a Negative Expression

29.6.1. Infinitive Only

ἀκοῦσαι μέντοι γε **οὐδὲν κωλύει**. (X.*Cyr.* 5.5.24.)
*But at any rate **nothing prevents listening**.*

29.6.2. Accusative and Infinitive

... **οὐ** μέντοι ἱκανόν γε ἔσται **ἐπιτειχίζειν** τε **κωλύειν ἡμᾶς** πλεύσαντας ἐς τὴν ἐκείνων καί, ἧπερ ἰσχύομεν, ταῖς ναυσὶν **ἀμύνεσθαι**· (Th. 1.142.4.)

*... however, it will **not** be sufficient **to prevent us from building-a-fort** after sailing to their <territory> and, where our strength lies, **defending ourselves** with our ships.*

29.6.3. Infinitive with Redundant μή

... καὶ **μόλις φθάνει**
θρόνοισιν ἐμπεσοῦσα **μὴ** χαμαὶ **πεσεῖν**. (E.*Med.* 1169–1170.)

... and, by falling on to her chair,
***she scarcely avoided falling** to the ground.*

μόλις ('scarcely') is a virtual negative. φθάνει is Historic Present.

29.6.4. Articular Infinitive Only

μαθὼν γὰρ **οὐκ** ἂν **ἀρνοίμην τὸ δρᾶν**. (S.*Ph.* 118.)
For, if I learned <this>, ***I would not refuse to act****.*

29.6.5. Articular Infinitive with Redundant μή

... **οὐκ** ἂν **ἐσχόμην**
τὸ μὴ ἀποκλῇσαι τοὐμὸν ἄθλιον δέμας,
ἵν' ἦ τυφλός τε καὶ κλύων μηδέν· (S.*OT* 1387–1389.)

... ***I would not have kept myself
from shutting up*** *my wretched body,
so that I might be blind and hearing nothing.*

ἦ is Past Indicative in a Purpose clause dependent on the Main clause of an Unfulfilled Conditional sentence (Smyth, 1956, §2185.c.).

29.6.6. Accusative and Infinitive with Redundant μὴ οὐ

τοὺς οὔτε νιφετός, **οὐκ** ὄμβρος, **οὐ** καῦμα, **οὐ** νὺξ **ἔργει μὴ οὐ κατανῦσαι** τὸν προκείμενον αὐτῷ δρόμον τὴν ταχίστην. (Hdt. 8.98.1.)

Neither *snow* ***nor*** *rain* ***nor*** *heat* ***nor*** *night* ***hinder them from covering*** *in the quickest way the course appointed by him.*

29.6.7. Accusative and Articular Infinitive with Redundant μὴ οὐ

... καὶ τοσόνδ' ἐκόμπασεν,
μηδ' ἂν τὸ σεμνὸν πῦρ **νιν εἰργάθειν** Διὸς
τὸ μὴ οὐ κατ' ἄκρων περγάμων **ἑλεῖν** πόλιν. (E.*Ph.* 1174–1176.)

... *and he made his great boast,
that* ***not even*** *the sacred fire of Zeus* ***would prevent him
from capturing*** *the city down from its highest citadel.*

LESSON 29. EXPRESSIONS OF HINDERING, FORBIDDING, DENYING AND FAILING

29.6.8. Genitive Articular Infinitive

... Εὐθύδημος οὑτοσὶ ἐν ἡλικίᾳ γενόμενος, τῆς πόλεως λόγον περί τινος προτιθείσης, **οὐκ ἀφέξεται τοῦ συμβουλεύειν** ... (X.Mem. 4.2.3.)

... *Euthydemus here, when he comes of age, <and>when the city is proposing a discussion about something,* **will not restrain himself from giving advice**.

29.6.9. Genitive Articular Infinitive with Redundant μή

... ἐνούσης δ' **οὐδεμίας** ἔτ' ἀποστροφῆς **τοῦ μὴ** τὰ χρήματ' **ἔχειν** ὑμᾶς, Τιμοκράτης οὑτοσὶ τοσοῦθ' ὑπερεῖδεν ἅπαντα τὰ πράγματα ὥστε τίθησι τουτονὶ τὸν νόμον ... (D. 24.9.)

... *and when there was* **no** *longer* **any means-of-preventing** *your* **having** *the money, Timocrates here overlooked all the issues to so great an extent that he is proposing this law* ...

29.7. Result Construction

29.7.1. ὥστε with Simple Infinitive

ὥστε γὰρ τὴν σύντομον πρὸς τοὺς Πελληνέας **ἀφικέσθαι** ἡ πρὸ τοῦ τείχους φάραγξ **εἶργε**. (X.HG 7.2.13.)

For the ravine in front of the wall **was preventing** *<them>* **from reaching** *the Pellenians along the short <route>.*

29.7.2. ὥστε and Infinitive with Redundant μή

ἡμεῖς οὖν εἰ μέλλοιμεν **τούτους εἴργειν ὥστε μὴ δύνασθαι** βλάπτειν ἡμᾶς πορευομένους, σφενδονῶν τὴν ταχίστην δεῖ καὶ ἱππέων. (X.An. 3.3.16.)

Therefore, if we were going **to prevent these <men> from being able** *to harm us as we proceeded, there would be need of slingers very quickly and horsemen.*

δεῖ, as a modal verb ('need', 'must', 'ought', etc.), is used in the Indicative in Greek, where English uses a potential idiom.

29.8. Effort Construction

... **κωλυόντων** κοινῇ βασιλεὺς καὶ Λακεδαιμόνιοι καὶ οἱ ξύμμαχοι, **ὅπως μήτε** χρήματα **λαμβάνωσιν** Ἀθηναῖοι **μήτ'** ἄλλο **μηδέν**. (Th. 8.18.1.)

... **let** the king and the Spartans and their allies in common **prevent** the Athenians **from receiving** either the money or anything else.

κωλυόντων (3rd pers. pl. Imperf. Impv.) with ὅπως + Subjunctive and negative μή compounds.

29.9. Conditional Construction

οἶμαι τοίνυν ἐγὼ ταῦτα λέγειν ἔχειν, μὴ **κωλύων εἴ** τις ἄλλος **ἐπαγγέλλεταί** τι. (D. 4.15.)

So I think that I can say this without **preventing** anyone else **from making any promise**.

κωλύων with εἰ + Present Indicative: 'not preventing that anyone else should be making any promise'. εἰ introduces a noun clause (cf. Lesson 34).

29.10. Participial Construction

καὶ οὐκ ἔστιν ὅστις ... **πλέοντας ὑμᾶς** ... **κωλύσει**. (Th. 2.62.2.)
And there is no one who ... **will prevent** ... **you from sailing**.

This construction is parallel to the Accusative and Participle with παύειν: 'to stop someone from doing something'.

29.11. Passive Constructions

29.11.1. Passive Verb Only

μέγιστον δέ, τῇ τῶν χρημάτων σπάνει **κωλύσονται**, ὅταν σχολῇ αὐτὰ ποριζόμενοι διαμέλλωσιν· (Th.1.142.1.)

And most important, **they will be hindered** by lack of funds, when by procrastinating they delay in acquiring them.

29.11.2. Passive Verb with Infinitive

ἐδεήθησαν δὲ καὶ τῶν Μεγαρέων ναυσὶ σφᾶς ξυμπροπέμψαι, εἰ ἄρα **κωλύοιντο** ὑπὸ Κερκυραίων **πλεῖν**· (Th. 1.27.2.)

*And they asked the Megarians also to join in escorting them with ships, in case **they were prevented** by the Corcyreans **from sailing**.*

29.11.3. Passive Verb with Participle

ἐπορεύθησαν δὲ πεζῇ ἐς Ἀπολλωνίαν, Κορινθίων οὖσαν ἀποικίαν, δέει τῶν Κερκυραίων μὴ **κωλύωνται** ὑπ' αὐτῶν κατὰ θάλασσαν **περαιούμενοι**. (Th. 1.26.2.)

*And they travelled by land to Apollonia, since it was a colony of the Corinthians, out of fear of the Corcyreans, in case they **were prevented** by them **from crossing** by sea.*

References

Goodwin (1889), *Syntax of the moods and tenses of the Greek verb*, §§807–820.

Smyth (1956), *Greek grammar*, §§2739–2749.

EXERCISE 29

Translate the following passages.

1. πεφύκασί τε ἅπαντες καὶ ἰδίᾳ καὶ δημοσίᾳ ἁμαρτάνειν, καὶ οὐκ ἔστι νόμος ὅστις ἀπείξει τούτου …

πεφυκέναι	*to be inclined(to)* (+ Infin.; Perf. with Imperf. meaning)
τε	*and* (Joins whole sentence to preceding.)
τούτου	Refers to ἁμαρτάνειν.

2. βεβοηθηκότες γὰρ ἦσαν τοῖς Βιθυνοῖς, βουλόμενοι σὺν τοῖς Βιθυνοῖς, εἰ δύναιντο, ἀποκωλῦσαι τοὺς Ἕλληνας μὴ ἐλθεῖν εἰς τὴν Φρυγίαν·

3. τῶν γὰρ ἄλλων μόνους ἂν ὑμᾶς οἴονται ἐμποδὼν γενέσθαι τοῦ ἄρξαι αὐτοὺς τῶν Ἑλλήνων.

ἄρχειν	*to rule*

4. οὐ μὴν κωλύει γ' οὐδὲν κἀμὲ διὰ βραχέων ἐπιμνησθῆναι τῶν πεπραγμένων αὐτῷ.

μήν	*however*
οὐδέν	Nom.

5. λείπει μὲν οὐδ' ἃ πρόσθεν ᾔδεμεν τὸ μὴ οὐ βαρύστον' εἶναι·

λείπειν	*to fall short of* (+ Infin., here articular)
ᾔδεμεν	More often ᾖσμεν (Infin. εἰδέναι).

6. κἀκείνου τὸ μὲν παρ' ἐμοῦ κομισθὲν ἀργύριον οὐκ ἐθελήσαντος ἀπολαβεῖν, ... οὐκ ἐκωλυόμην συνθάπτειν ἀλλὰ πάντα συνεποίουν·

παρά (+ Gen.)	*by*
συνθάπτειν	*to join in the burial*

7. And these [men] were staying behind and preventing the Athenians from carrying stones and from dispersing further away.

to stay behind	ὑπομένειν
to carry stones	λιθοφορεῖν
to disperse (Intr.)	ἀποσκίδνασθαι (Pass.; α stem)
further away	μακροτέραν (adverbial Acc.)

8. For if I had not been caught off my guard with oaths to the gods, I would not ever have kept from declaring this to my father.

to catch	αἱρεῖν
off guard	ἄφαρκτος, -ον
oath (to)	ὅρκος, -ου, ὁ (+ Gen.)
to keep (Intr.) (*from*)	ἔχειν, (Aor.) σχεῖν (+ Infin. with redundant negatives μὴ οὐ)

LESSON 30
Temporal Constructions 1: Clauses in Primary Sequence

30.1. Introduction

Three Lessons will deal with Subordinate Temporal clauses and with the Temporal phrases which use πρίν and the Infinitive. For convenience, all πρίν constructions (clauses and phrases) will be treated together after the other Temporal constructions. Lesson 30 deals with Temporal clauses in Primary sequence—the verbs in the leading clause refer to the present or the future, as do the Temporal clauses themselves.

Some prepositions may have a Temporal force: ἀπό *from, since*; εἰς *until*; ἐκ *after*. Such prepositions will be considered here, only when they introduce an adjectival clause with Temporal force, for example, ἀφ' οὗ *from what <time>, ever since*.

Only the more common Temporal conjunctions and conjunctive phrases will be used in the Lessons and Exercises.

When a Temporal clause refers to a definite time, the Indicative Mood is used; the negative is οὐ. When a Temporal clause refers to an indefinite time, the Subjunctive Mood with ἄν is used in Primary sequence; the negative is μή. In Epic, κε(ν) (enclitic) is equivalent to ἄν. For the most part, Temporal clauses referring to the future use the indefinite construction, since what is in the future has not yet happened. In indefinite Temporal clauses in Primary sequence, some conjunctions, which end with a vowel, coalesce with ἄν.

ὅτε ἄν	=	ὅταν
ὁπότε ἄν	=	ὁπόταν
ἐπεὶ ἄν	=	ἐπήν, also ἐπάν (Aristotle +), ἐπεάν (Ionic)
ἐπειδὴ ἄν	=	ἐπειδάν

30.2. Contemporaneous Action in Temporal Clause

The main conjunctions are: ὅτε *when*; ὁπότε *when(ever)* (slightly less definite); ἡνίκα *(at the time) when*; ἔστε, ἕως, μέχρι *so long as, while*. The limits or duration of time may be emphasised in clauses introduced by ἐν ᾧ *during the time that, while*; ὅσον χρόνον *all through the time that, so long as*.

30.2.1. Definite

καὶ ... ἄν, ὦ Κυαξάρη, μᾶλλόν σε ἐκόσμουν ... ἢ νῦν, **ὅτε** σὺν τοιαύτῃ καὶ τοσαύτῃ δυνάμει οὕτω σοι ὀξέως ὑπακούω ... (X.*Cyr.* 2.4.6.)

*And would I be showing you, O Cyaxares, more respect ... than now, **when** I am obeying you so quickly with a force of such character and size ...?*

ὅτε with Present Indicative in the Temporal clause, contemporaneous with the Present potential Main clause (expressed by Past Imperf. Indic. with ἄν).

νὺξ δ᾽ ἔσται, **ὅτε** δὴ στυγερὸς γάμος ἀντιβολήσει
οὐλομένης ἐμέθεν, τῆς τε Ζεὺς ὄλβον ἀπηύρα.
(Hom.*Od.* 18.272–273.)

*And there will be a night, **when** indeed a hateful marriage will come upon poor me, <the one> whose happiness Zeus took away.*

ὅτε with Future Indicative in the Temporal clause (rare), contemporaneous with the Future Indicative of the Main clause. (τῆς τε: For this 'untranslatable τε' see Smyth, 1956, §2970; Hom.*Od.* 13.31, 60).

30.2.2. Indefinite

ἀλλ᾽ **ὅταν** σπεύδῃ τις αὐτός, χὠ θεὸς συνάπτεται. (A.*Pers.* 742.)
*But **when** someone himself hastens on <to his doom>, the god also cooperates.*

ὅταν with Subjunctive in the Temporal clause, contemporaneous with the Present Indicative of the Main clause (referring to repeated action).

καὶ **ἐν ᾧ ἂν** ζῶμεν, οὕτως, ὡς ἔοικεν, ἐγγυτάτω ἐσόμεθα τοῦ εἰδέναι, ἐὰν ὅτι μάλιστα μηδὲν ὁμιλῶμεν τῷ σώματι ... (Pl.*Phd.* 67 A.)

*And **while** we are alive, we shall on this condition, as it seems, be nearest to knowledge, if as much as possible we have no association with the body ...*

ἐν ᾧ with ἄν and Subjunctive (slightly emphasising the duration of time) in the Temporal clause, contemporaneous with the Future Indicative of the Main clause.

30.3. Prior Action in Temporal Clause

The conjunctions ἐπεί, ἐπειδή and ὡς all have the meaning: *when, since, after*. In prose, ἐπειδή is more frequent than ἐπεί in a Temporal sense.

ἐπεί, ἐπειδή and ὡς may be used with the Superlative adverb τάχιστα to emphasise immediate priority: *as soon as*. The adverb τάχιστα is sometimes separated from the conjunction by one or more words. The separation occurs especially with ὡς, to avoid confusion with the idiom ὡς τάχιστα meaning 'as soon as possible'.

In addition, the phrases ἐξ οὗ, ἐξ οὗτε, ἀφ' οὗ and ἀφ' οὗπερ all mean: *from what <time>, ever since*. These phrases introduce an adjectival-Temporal clause which emphasises a time limit, while the clause on which they depend expresses subsequent duration or repeated action.

30.3.1. Definite

ἐξ οὗ δ' οἱ διερωτῶντες ὑμᾶς οὗτοι πεφήνασι ῥήτορες, τί βούλεσθε; τί γράψω; τί ὑμῖν χαρίσωμαι; προπέποται τῆς παραυτίκα χάριτος τὰ τῆς πόλεως πράγματα ... (D. 3.22.)

*But **ever since** these orators have appeared, who constantly ask you, 'What do you want? What <law> am I to propose? In what <way> am I to oblige you?', the interests of the city have been squandered for <the price of> momentary gratification.*

ἐξ οὗ with Present Perfect Indicative emphasises a limit (which has been reached), while the Main clause expresses subsequent repeated action.

30.3.2. Indefinite

ἄνδρες γὰρ **ἐπειδάν**, ᾧ ἀξιοῦσι προύχειν, κολουσθῶσι, τό γ' ὑπόλοιπον αὐτῶν τῆς δόξης ἀσθενέστερον αὐτὸ ἑαυτοῦ ἐστιν … (Th. 7.66.3.)

For, ***when*** *men are thwarted in that in which they claim to excel, what is left of their reputation is weaker than its former self* [lit. 'is itself weaker than itself'] …

ἐπειδάν with Subjunctive in the Temporal clause denotes action prior to the ongoing state expressed by the verb 'to be' in the Main clause.

ὡς γὰρ ἡμεῖς εἰκάζομεν, οὐκ ἑκὰς πάρεσται ὁ βάρβαρος ἐσβαλὼν ἐς τὴν ἡμετέρην, ἀλλ' **ἐπειδὰν τάχιστα** πύθηται τὴν ἀγγελίην ὅτι οὐδὲν ποιήσομεν τῶν ἐκεῖνος ἡμέων προσεδέετο. (Hdt. 8.144.5.)

For as we surmise, the foreigner will invade our <country> and will be upon us not in any long time, but ***as soon as*** *he has heard the message, that we shall do nothing of what that man was asking of us.*

ἐπειδὰν τάχιστα with Subjunctive in the Temporal clause emphasises immediate priority in relation to the Future Indicative of the Main clause. τῶν (Ionic) = ὧν (Attic).

30.4. Subsequent Action in Temporal Clause: Indefinite

The conjunctions ἔστε, ἕως and μέχρι all have the meaning: *until.* (As noted in §30.2, these conjunctions may also express contemporaneous action: *while.*) Temporal clauses expressing subsequent action in Primary sequence are always indefinite, since it is not known exactly when the time limit ('until') will be reached. Temporal clauses expressing subsequent action may be anticipated by Temporal adverbs such as πρίν (Epic) or πρότερον (Attic), or by adverbial phrases such as μέχρι τούτον. These expressions are redundant but emphatic.

καὶ μέχρι γε τούτου πλανῶνται, **ἕως ἂν** τῇ τοῦ ξυνεπακολουθοῦντος τοῦ σωματοειδοῦς ἐπιθυμίᾳ ἐνδεθῶσιν εἰς σῶμα. (Pl.*Phd.* 81 D–E.)

*And right up to this <time> they wander around, **until**, by reason of the desire for the bodily-nature which follows along with <them>, they are bound to a body.*

ἕως ἄν with Subjunctive in the Temporal clause denotes action at any time prior to that of the Main clause. As here, the Subjunctive is most often Aorist.

References

Goodwin (1889), *Syntax of the moods and tenses of the Greek verb*, §§514–522, 529, 532–533, 539–540, 556, 558 (Temporal clauses awkwardly treated as 'Relative' clauses together with adjectival clauses and adverbial clauses of place and manner); 611–612, 613.3–613.5 and 615–620 (Temporal constructions referring to subsequent action, except πρίν).

Smyth (1956), *Greek grammar*, §§2383–2403, 2409–2413.

EXERCISE 30

Translate the following passages.

1. ἕως οὖν ἔτι ἀπαράσκευοι θαρσοῦσι ..., ἐγὼ μὲν ἔχων τοὺς μετ' ἐμαυτοῦ καὶ φθάσας, ἢν δύνωμαι, προσπεσοῦμαι δρόμῳ κατὰ μέσον τὸ στράτευμα·

δρόμῳ	*at a run*

2. τῶν μὲν γὰρ ὀργιζομένων ἐστὶν ὀξέως τι κακὸν τὸν λελυπηκότ' ἐργάσασθαι, τῶν δ' ἀδικουμένων, ὅταν ποθ' ὑφ' αὑτοῖς λάβωσι τὸν ἠδικηκότα, τότε τιμωρήσασθαι.

ἐστίν	*it is <characteristic of> (+ Gen.)*
ὑπό (+ Dat.)	*under <the control of>*
τιμωρεῖν (Act. and Mid.)	*to punish*

3. ἐπὴν διαλλαγῆτε, ταῦτα δράσετε.

4. εἰ δ' ἂν ἐμοὶ τιμὴν Πρίαμος Πριάμοιό τε παῖδες
   τίνειν οὐκ ἐθέλωσιν Ἀλεξάνδροιο πεσόντος,
   αὐτὰρ ἐγὼ καὶ ἔπειτα μαχήσομαι εἵνεκα ποινῆς
   αὖθι μένων, ἧός κε τέλος πολέμοιο κιχείω.

τιμή, -ῆς, ἡ	price
Πριάμοιο (Epic)	Πριάμου (Attic)
Ἀλεξάνδροιο πεσόντος	Gen. abs. (Temporal)
αὐτάρ (adv.)	then (drawing consequence of a condition)
ποινή, -ῆς, ἡ	recompense
αὖθι (adv.)	here
ἧός κε (Epic)	ἕως ἄν (Attic)
κι(γ)χάνειν	to reach (here 1st pers. sg. Aor. Subj.)

5. τοῖς δὲ τυράννοις οὐδὲν ὑπάρχει τοιοῦτον, ἀλλ' ..., ἐπειδὰν εἰς τὴν ἀρχὴν καταστῶσιν, ἀνουθέτητοι διατελοῦσιν·

οὐδὲν ... τοιοῦτο(ν)	Nom. neut. sg.; understand *help, advantage*.
διατελεῖν	to continue

6. Wait until you [sg.] learn *the rest* in addition.

to learn in addition	προσμανθάνειν

7. And when I have accomplished what I want, I shall come fully prepared, in order to lead you [pl.] away to Greece and to go away myself to my own command.

to accomplish	διαπράσσεσθαι (Mid.)
fully prepared	Aor. or Perf. Mid. Partc. of συσκευάζειν
command	ἀρχή, -ῆς, ἡ

LESSON 31
Temporal Constructions 2: Clauses in Past Sequence

31.1. Introduction

In Past sequence, when a Temporal clause refers to a definite time, the Indicative Mood is used; the negative is οὐ. When a Temporal clause refers to an indefinite time, the Optative Mood without ἄν is used; the negative is μή. But sometimes the Primary construction is used even in Past sequence ('Vivid' construction). The common conjunctions and conjunctive phrases are the same as in Lesson 30.

31.2. Contemporaneous Action in Temporal Clause

31.2.1. Definite

ὅσον δὲ **χρόνον** ἐκαθέζετο ὁ Κῦρος ἀμφὶ τὴν περὶ τὸ φρούριον οἰκονομίαν, τῶν Ἀσσυρίων τῶν κατὰ ταῦτα τὰ χωρία πολλοὶ μὲν ἀπῆγον ἵππους, πολλοὶ δὲ ἀπέφερον ὅπλα, φοβούμενοι ἤδη πάντας τοὺς προσχώρους. (X.*Cyr.* 5.3.25.)

*And **all through the time that** Cyrus remained inactive concerning arrangements about the fort, many of the Assyrians in these parts were withdrawing their horses, and many were handing in weapons, since by now they were in fear of all their neighbours.*

ὅσον χρόνον with Past Imperfect Indicative emphasises the duration of time.

31.2.2. Indefinite

... ἀλλ' ἐπὶ τελευτῆς, **ὅτ'** ἤδη μέλλοιεν ἀποπλεῖν ὡς τοὺς γονέας καὶ τοὺς φίλους τοὺς ἑαυτῶν, οὕτως ἠγάπων τὴν διατριβὴν ὥστε μετὰ πόθου καὶ δακρύων ποιεῖσθαι τὴν ἀπαλλαγήν. (Isoc. 15.88.)

... *but at the end, **when** they were now about to sail away to their parents and their own family members, they were so content with their way of life as to make their departure with regret and tears.*

ὅτ(ε) and Optative without ἄν denotes any (rather than every) time contemporaneous with the repeated action of the Main clause.

31.3. Prior Action in Temporal Clause

With the Past Aorist Indicative, the conjunctions ἐπεί, ἐπειδή and ὡς usually imply action prior to that of the clause on which they depend. The Past Perfect Indicative is much less common in a Temporal clause, and often implies a past state resulting from completed action.

31.3.1. Definite

ἐπεὶ θεράπνας τῆσδε Θηβαίας χθονὸς
λιπόντες ἐξέβημεν Ἀσωποῦ ῥοάς,
λέπας Κιθαιρώνειον εἰσεβάλλομεν ... (E.*Ba*. 1043–1045.)

***When** we had left the dwellings of this Theban
land and had crossed the streams of Asopus,
we began to head into the broken-country of Cithaeron ...*

ἐπεί with Past Aorist Indicative denotes action prior to that of the Main clause.

ὡς γὰρ ἐπετρόπευσε **τάχιστα**, μετέστησε τὰ νόμιμα πάντα, καὶ ἐφύλαξε ταῦτα μὴ παραβαίνειν· (Hdt. 1.65.5.)

*For **as soon as** he had become guardian, he changed all the customs, and ensured that <people> should not transgress these.*

ὡς ... τάχιστα with Past Aorist Indicative emphasises immediate priority.

ὃς **ἐπειδὴ** ἐπολιορκέετο ὑπὸ Ἀθηναίων καὶ Κίμωνος τοῦ Μιλτιάδεω, παρεὸν αὐτῷ ὑπόσπονδον ἐξελθεῖν καὶ νοστῆσαι ἐς τὴν Ἀσίην, οὐκ ἐθέλησε … (Hdt. 7.107.1.)

*And **when** he was being besieged by the Athenians and Cimon son of Miltiades, although it was possible for him to go out under truce and to return to Asia, he refused …*

ἐπειδή with Past Imperfect Indicative denotes an action that has begun but not been completed. Thus, ἐπειδὴ ἐπολιορκέετο could be translated: 'after he began [OR: had begun] to be besieged'.

31.3.2. Indefinite

ἐπειδὴ γὰρ προσβάλοιεν ἀλλήλοις, οὐ ῥᾳδίως ἀπελύοντο ὑπό τε τοῦ πλήθους καὶ ὄχλου τῶν νεῶν … (Th. 1.49.3.)

*For **when**(ever) they (had) made an attack on each other, they did not easily extricate themselves due to the number and density of the ships …*

ἐπειδή and Optative without ἄν denotes any action in this battle prior to that of the clause. (τε anticipates a second καί in the next phrase.)

31.4. Subsequent Action in Temporal Clause

31.4.1. Definite

καὶ οἱ μὲν Ἕλληνες τεταγμένοι τε προσῇσαν καὶ διὰ φυλακῆς ἔχοντες, **ἕως** ἐστρατοπεδεύσαντο ἐν ἐπιτηδείῳ· (Th. 2.81.4.)

*And the Greeks kept advancing, drawn up in ranks and remaining on guard, **until** they pitched camp in a suitable <place>.*

ἕως with Past Aorist Indicative denotes instantaneous action subsequent to the continuous action expressed by the Past Imperfect Indicative of the Main clause.

31.4.2. Indefinite

... τά τε ἄλλα χωρία εἶχον, μένοντες **ἕως** σφισι κἀκεῖνοι ποιήσειαν τὰ εἰρημένα. (Th. 5.35.4.)

... *and they* [= Athenians] *kept control of the other places, waiting **until** those <troops> [= Spartans] should have done for them what had been stated.* (OR: *waiting for those <troops> to do for them what had been stated.*)

ἕως and Optative without ἄν denotes the anticipated but indefinite limit for which the Athenians (Subject of the Main clause) were waiting.

References

Goodwin (1889), *Syntax of the moods and tenses of the Greek verb*, §§514–522, 532, 535, 553, 613.1–613.2, 613.5, 614.2, 615–619.

Smyth (1956), *Greek grammar*, §§2388, 2395–2396, 2414–2417.

EXERCISE 31

Translate the following passages.

1. καὶ ὑπέσχετο μὲν δεομένου ουυ τὸ ναῦλον τῶν ξύλων παρασχήσειν, ὅτε ἀνήγου ὡς βασιλέα·

δεῖσθαι (Mid. + Aor. Pass.)	*to request*
ναῦλον, -ου, τό	*freight-payment*
ἀνάγεσθαι (Mid.)	*to set sail*

2. ἔτι δὲ ὁπότε αὐτόμολοι, ὡς εἰκός, πρὸς βασιλέα ἰόντες χρήματα ἐθέλοιεν ὑφηγεῖσθαι, καὶ ταῦτα ἐπεμέλετο ὡς διὰ τῶν φίλων ἁλίσκοιτο ...

αὐτόμολος, -ου, ὁ	*deserter* (adj. as noun)
χρήματα, -ων, τά	*merchandise*
ὑφηγεῖσθαι (Mid.)	*to show the way to* (+ Acc.)
καί	*also*, modifying ταῦτα
ταῦτα	direct Object of ἐπεμέλετο, anticipating ὡς clause

3. ἐπειδὴ δὲ εἰρήνης ἐπιθυμήσαντες οἱ πολέμιοι ἐπρεσβεύοντο, Ἀγησίλαος ἀντεῖπε τῇ εἰρήνῃ, ἕως τοὺς διὰ Λακεδαιμονίους φυγόντας Κορινθίων καὶ Θηβαίων ἠνάγκασε τὰς πόλεις οἴκαδε καταδέξασθαι.

πρεσβεύεσθαι (Mid.)	to send embassies
τοὺς ... φυγόντας	Object of καταδέξασθαι
Κορινθίων καὶ Θηβαίων	Possessive Gen. qualifying τὰς πόλεις

4. ἀναδιδάσκοντες αὐτὸν τῶν Αἰτωλῶν ὡς εἴη ῥᾳδία ἡ αἵρεσις, ἰέναι ἐκέλευον ὅτι τάχιστα ἐπὶ τὰς κώμας καὶ μὴ μένειν ἕως ἂν ξύμπαντες ἀθροισθέντες ἀντιτάξωνται ...

ἀναδιδάσκειν	to explain
Αἰτωλοί, -ῶν, οἱ	Aetolians (The Gen. pl. qualifies ἡ αἵρεσις.)
αἵρεσις, -εως, ἡ	capture
ὅτι τάχιστα	ὡς τάχιστα

5. ... διὰ παντὸς ἐπολέμουν ἀνθρώποις νεοκαταστάτοις, ἕως ἐξετρύχωσαν ...

διὰ παντός	constantly
νεοκατάστατος, -ον	newly established
ἐκτρυχοῦν	to wear (someone) out, to exhaust

6. ἐπειδὴ δέ τι ἐμφάγοιεν, ἀνίσταντο καὶ ἐπορεύοντο.

| ἐμφαγεῖν (Aor.) | to eat hastily |

7. ... and the rest of the foreigners, when they had seen them giving way, no longer held their ground, but took to flight.

| to give way | ἐνδιδόναι |
| to hold one's ground | ὑπομένειν |

8. Up to this [point] Lasthenes used to be named a friend, until he betrayed Olynthus.

up to	μέχρι (+ Gen.)
Lasthenes	Λασθένης, -ους, ὁ
Olynthus	Ὄλυνθος, -ου, ἡ (place)

LESSON 32
Temporal Constructions with πρίν

32.1. Introduction

In classical Attic Greek, πρίν introduces two basically different constructions, which express action subsequent to that of the leading clause.

When πρίν functions like a preposition and introduces an Infinitive phrase, it usually means 'before', and usually occurs in a positive sentence.

When πρίν functions as a conjunction and introduces a clause with a finite verb, it usually means 'until', and usually occurs in a negative sentence. πρίν may be preceded by a redundant πρίν (Homer) or by a redundant πρότερον or πρόσθεν (Attic) in the leading clause.

πρὶν(...)ἤ ('earlier than') is used with the same function as πρίν, mainly in Herodotus, and mostly with Infinitive; but Herodotus also uses πρὶν(...)ἤ with Indicative and with Subjunctive (without ἄν). Similarly, especially in Herodotus and Thucydides, πρότερον(...)ἤ may be used with Infinitive, or with Subjunctive without ἄν (mainly in Herodotus), or sometimes with Indicative.

32.2. πρίν with an Infinitive Phrase

The Subject of the Infinitive, if it is the same as the Subject of the leading verb, is normally not expressed; and if the Subject of the Infinitive has an adjective agreeing with it, or a Complement referring to it, the adjective or Complement is in the Nominative Case. However, sometimes an unexpressed Subject for the Infinitive is not the same as the Subject of the leading verb, but must be understood from the context. The Subject of the Infinitive, if it is different to the Subject of the leading verb, is normally expressed and is in the Accusative Case. Because πρίν denotes a chronological limit, it frequently introduces an *Aorist* Infinitive indicating a point of time.

... ἃ **πρὶν μολεῖν** δεῦρ' ἐκμεμόχθηκεν φράσω ... (A.*Pr.* 825.)
... *I shall tell what she has struggled through **before she came** here ...*

πρίν with Aorist Infinitive occurs in a positive sentence. The Subject of μολεῖν is not expressed, since it is the same as the Subject of the leading verb ἐκμεμόχθηκεν.

... **πρὶν ἔκπυστος γενέσθαι** προσῆλθε τῇ τῶν Μεγαρέων πόλει, λαθὼν τοὺς Ἀθηναίους ὄντας περὶ τὴν θάλασσαν ... (Th. 4.70.2.)

... ***before he was detected***, *he approached the city of the Megarians, escaping the notice of the Athenians since they were near the sea ...*

πρίν with Aorist Infinitive and Nominative Complement occurs in a positive sentence.

ὁ δὲ πεισθεὶς πορευομένους αὐτοὺς διὰ τῆς Θρᾴκης ἐπὶ τὸ πλοῖον ᾧ ἔμελλον τὸν Ἑλλήσποντον περαιώσειν, **πρὶν ἐσβαίνειν** ξυλλαμβάνει ... (Th. 2.67.3.)

*And he was persuaded and, as they were travelling through Thrace to the boat on which they were intending to cross the Hellespont, he seized them **before they (could) embark** ...*

πρίν with Imperfect Infinitive, whose unexpressed Subject is not the same as the Subject of the leading verb ξυλλαμβάνει (Hist. Pres.).

οὐδ' εἴ μοι τόσα δοίη ὅσα ψάμαθός τε κόνις τε,
οὐδέ κεν ὥς ἔτι θυμὸν ἐμὸν πείσει' Ἀγαμέμνων,
πρίν γ' **ἀπὸ** πᾶσαν ἐμοὶ **δόμεναι** θυμαλγέα λώβην.
(Hom.*Il.* 9.385–387.)

***Not even** if he were to give me so much as the sand and the dust,*
***not even** so would Agamemnon yet persuade my spirit,*
***before** at least **he repaid** me (for) all the heart-rending dishonour.*

πρίν with Aorist Infinitive occurs in a negative sentence.

... πολὺ πλείων ἐλπίς ἐστιν ἕτερον ἀποστῆναι **πρὶν ἐκεῖνον ἐκπολιορκηθῆναι**· (Isoc. 4.141.)

... *there is much greater expectation that another <may> revolt **before that <man> is forced-to-surrender-under-siege**.*

πρίν with Accusative and Aorist (Pass.) Infinitive occurs in a positive sentence.

32.3. πρίν with a Finite Verb

32.3.1. Definite

When πρίν with a finite verb refers to a definite time, the verb is in the Indicative Mood and is usually in the Past Aorist Tense.

... **οὐδ'** ἀπῆλθε, **πρὶν** ... τοὺς βαρβάρους **ἔπαυσεν** ὑβρίζοντας. (Isoc. 15.83.)

... ***nor** did he go away, **until** ... **he stopped** the foreigners (from) acting insolently.*

πρίν with Past Aorist Indicative occurs in a negative sentence.

παραπλήσια δὲ καὶ οἱ ἐπὶ τῶν νεῶν αὐτοῖς ἔπασχον, **πρίν** γε δὴ οἱ Συρακόσιοι καὶ οἱ σύμμαχοι ἐπὶ πολὺ ἀντισχούσης τῆς ναυμαχίας **ἔτρεψάν** τε τοὺς Ἀθηναίους καὶ ... **κατεδίωκον** ἐς τὴν γῆν. (Th. 7.71.5.)

*And those on the ships also were experiencing much the same as they <were>, **until** finally the Syracusans and their allies, after the naval battle had lasted for a long time, **put** the Athenians **to flight** and ... **vigorously pursued** them to land.*

πρίν with Past Aorist Indicative occurs in a positive sentence. This construction is much less common than Indicative in a negative sentence. γε δή ('finally') is literally 'at least indeed'.

32.3.2. Indefinite

32.3.2.1. Primary Sequence

When πρίν with a finite verb refers to an indefinite time in Primary sequence, the verb is regularly in the Subjunctive Mood, and in Attic (especially in prose) normally has ἄν.

στερεάς τ'
οὔποτ' ἀπειλὰς πτήξας τόδ' ἐγὼ
καταμηνύσω, **πρὶν ἄν** ἐξ ἀγρίων
δεσμῶν **χαλάσῃ** ποινάς τε τίνειν
τῆσδ' αἰκείας **ἐθελήσῃ**. (A.Pr. 173–177.)

and *never*,
cowering before his harsh threats, shall I
make this known, ***until he releases*** *<me>*
*from savage bonds and **becomes willing***
to make recompense for this maltreatment.

πρὶν ἄν with Aorist Subjunctive occurs in a negative sentence.

ὥστε χρὴ σκοπεῖν τινα αὐτὰ καὶ **μὴ** μετεώρῳ τῇ πόλει ἀξιοῦν κινδυνεύειν καὶ ἀρχῆς ἄλλης ὀρέγεσθαι, **πρὶν** ἣν ἔχομεν **βεβαιωσώμεθα** ... (Th. 6.10.5.)

And so one should examine them [= the points just mentioned] and ***not*** *think it right to put the city at risk when it is at sea and to reach for another empire,* ***until we make secure*** *the one which we have ...*

πρίν and Aorist Subjunctive (without ἄν) occurs in a negative sentence (μή). Homer does not yet use ἄν or κε in this construction. The Subjunctive without ἄν occurs occasionally in Herodotus, Thucydides and Attic drama.

τῇ πόλει ... κινδυνεύειν: lit. 'to run a risk to (the disadvantage of) the city'. μετεώρῳ is metaphorical.

ὄλοιο **μή** πω, **πρὶν μάθοιμ'** εἰ καὶ πάλιν
γνώμην μετοίσεις· (S.Ph. 961–962.)

*May you perish—**not yet**, **until I learn** whether you will actually change your mind again.*

In this negative sentence (μή), πρίν and Optative (without ἄν) depends on an Optative of Wish in the Main clause ('assimilation of Mood').

32.3.2.2. Past Sequence

In Past sequence, πρίν and Optative (without ἄν) occurs only in suboblique constructions—that is, where the Temporal clause is included in reported discourse (whether in a clause introduced by ὅτι or ὡς, or in a phrase with Infinitive or Participle), or depends on another Optative clause (cf. §32.3.2.1. Primary Sequence, last example). Vivid constructions with πρίν or πρὶν ἄν and Subjunctive also occur in Past sequence, but again only in suboblique constructions. All the following passages contain negative expressions antecedent to the πρίν clauses: 'not ... until'.

... **οὐχ** ἡγοῦντ' **οὐδὲν** οἱοί τ' εἶναι κινεῖν τῶν καθεστώτων, **πρὶν** ἐκποδὼν ἐκεῖνος αὐτοῖς **γένοιτο**. (Isoc. 16.5.)

*... they did **not** think that they were able to make **any** change in the constitution, **until** that <man> **got** out of their way.*

πρίν and Optative (without ἄν) depends on the Nominative and Infinitive construction of reported thought after a negated Main verb.

παρανῖσχον δὲ καὶ οἱ ἐκ τῆς πόλεως Πλαταιῆς ἀπὸ τοῦ τείχους φρυκτοὺς πολλοὺς ... ὅπως ἀσαφῆ τὰ σημεῖα τῆς φρυκτωρίας τοῖς πολεμίοις ἦ καὶ **μὴ** βοηθοῖεν, ... **πρὶν** σφῶν οἱ ἄνδρες οἱ ἐξιόντες **διαφύγοιεν** καὶ τοῦ ἀσφαλοῦς **ἀντιλάβοιντο**. (Th. 3.22.8.)

*But the Plataeans in [lit. 'out of'] the city also raised-in-answer from the wall many beacons ... in order that the enemy's beacon-signals might be unclear, and that ... they [= Thebans] might **not** come to help, **until** their own [= Plataeans'] men who were going out **escaped** and **reached** safety.*

πρίν and Optative (without ἄν) depends on a negative Purpose clause with Optative.

εἶπον **μηδένα** τῶν ὄπισθεν κινεῖσθαι, **πρὶν ἂν** ὁ πρόσθεν **ἡγῆται** ... (X.Cyr. 2.2.8.)

*I said that **none** of those at the rear was to move, **until** the one in front <of him> **led the way** ...*

πρὶν ἄν and Subjunctive in a Vivid construction depends on a negative reported command.

... ἐποιήσαντο νόμον τε καὶ κατάρην **μὴ πρότερον** θρέψειν κόμην Ἀργείων **μηδένα, μηδὲ** τὰς γυναῖκάς σφι χρυσοφορήσειν, **πρὶν** Θυρέας **ἀνασώσωνται**. (Hdt. 1.82.7.)

... they made a law and a curse that **no one** of the Argives would grow his hair, **nor** their women wear gold **any earlier**, **until** they recovered Thyreae.

πρίν and Subjunctive (without ἄν) in a Vivid construction depends on a negative reported command with anticipatory πρότερον.

References

Goodwin (1889), *Syntax of the moods and tenses of the Greek verb*, §§621–661.

Smyth (1956), *Greek grammar*, §§2430–2461.

EXERCISE 32

Translate the following passages.

1. βασιλεὺς δὲ Δαρεῖος, πρὶν μὲν αἰχμαλώτους γενέσθαι τοὺς Ἐρετριέας, ἐνεῖχέ σφι δεινὸν χόλον, οἷα ἀρξάντων ἀδικίης προτέρων τῶν Ἐρετριέων·

Ἐρετριεύς, -έως, ὁ	*Eretrian*
ἐνέχειν χόλον	*to harbour a grudge (against)* (+ Dat.)
σφι (enclitic)	*them* (Dat. pl.)
οἷα (adverbial)	*inasmuch as* (+ Partc. phrase)

2. ὦ σχέτλι', ἦ 'τολμήσατ' ἀντ' ἐμοῦ τινι
δοῦναι τὰ τεύχη τἀμά, πρὶν μαθεῖν ἐμοῦ;

σχέτλι(ε)	*scoundrel* (Voc.)
'τολμήσατ'	ἐτολμήσατε (pl. despite Voc. sg.)
τεῦχος, -ους, τό	(mostly pl.) *weapon(s)*

LESSON 32. TEMPORAL CONSTRUCTIONS WITH πρίν

3. οὗτοι γὰρ πρὶν ἢ Σκύθας ἀπικέσθαι ἦρχον τῆς Ἀσίης.

Σκύθης, -ου, ὁ	Scythian
ἀπικνεῖσθαι	to arrive (Ionic π for Attic φ)

4. καὶ Μεσσηνίους μὲν πολιορκοῦντες οὐ πρότερον ἐπαύσαντο, πρὶν ἐξέλαβον ἐκ τῆς χώρας …

πολιορκεῖν	to besiege

5. οἱ δὲ Ἕλληνες τήν τε ἱππασίαν ἐθαύμαζον ἐκ τοῦ στρατοπέδου ὁρῶντες καὶ ὅ τι ἐποίουν, πρὶν Νίκαρχος Ἀρκὰς ἧκε …

ἱππασία, -ας, ἡ	cavalry manoeuvre
ἀμφιγνοεῖν	to be doubtful about (+ Acc.; here with double augment)
Ἀρκάς, -άδος, ὁ, (ἡ)	Arcadian (proper adj.)

6. οὐκ ἔστιν αἴκισμ' οὐδὲ μηχάνημ', ὅτῳ
προτρέψεταί με Ζεὺς γεγωνῆσαι τάδε,
πρὶν ἂν χαλασθῇ δεσμὰ λυμαντήρια.

αἴκισμα, -ατος, τό	torture
προτρέπειν	to impel (Act. and Mid.)
γεγωνῆσαι	to declare (Aor. Infin. ending on Perf. stem with Imperf. meaning)
λυμαντήριος, -α, -ον	torturous, excruciating

7. Well then, *I* shall go out of the way of this disaster, before Agaue comes to the house.

out of the way	ἐκποδών (adv. + Dat.)
Agaue	Ἀγαύη, -ης, ἡ

8. Do not groan until you [sg.] learn [this].

to groan	στενάζειν

9. ... I decided not to make the voyage secretly, until I (had) told you [sg.] ...

to make	ποιεῖσθαι (Mid.)
voyage	πλοῦς, πλοῦ, ὁ (contracted from πλόος)
secretly	σῖγα (lit. 'in silence')
to tell	φράζειν, Aor. φράσαι

LESSON 33
Adverbial Clauses of Place and Manner

33.1. Adverbial Clauses of Place

33.1.1. Introduction

Adverbial clauses of Place (or Local clauses) are introduced by relative adverbs which have the function of subordinating conjunctions. These adverbs cover the meanings 'where', 'to where' ('whither') and 'from where' ('whence'). Some of these adverbs may be used in either a definite or an indefinite form. And all forms may be used with either the Indicative Mood or the Subjunctive in Primary sequence, and with either the Indicative Mood or the Optative in Past sequence. There is no established convention for expressing the full range of definiteness in English translation. For convenience, it is suggested that, for example, both οὗ and ὅπου when used with the Indicative should be translated as 'where', and that when used with the Subjunctive or Optative they should be translated as 'wherever'. Even so, the '-ever' suffix should be avoided in English translation, if the Greek implies 'any time' something happens, when the English implies 'every time' something happens. In Primary sequence, ἄν is normally used with the Subjunctive in prose, but may be omitted in verse.

οὗ, ὅπου; ᾗ, ὅπῃ	*where*
οἷ, ὅποι	*to where*
ὅθεν, ὁπόθεν	*from where*

There is also a pair of adverbs which may have a demonstrative meaning as well as their relative meaning.

ἔνθα	*where* (also 'there'), *to where, from where*
ἔνθεν	*from where* (also 'from there')

In addition, ἵνα appears to have been originally a relative adverb of place meaning 'where'. This usage continues into the classical period, but fades out in the Hellenistic period. (However, already in Homer the use of ἵνα as a Purpose conjunction outweighs its Local meaning.)

The negative is usually οὐ for the Indicative and μή for the Subjunctive and Optative. However, μή may also be used when the Indicative expresses a general situation, or when the Future Indicative expresses Purpose (see §33.3 below).

The relative adverbs may be emphasised by the enclitic particle περ. Editorial practice varies in treating this particle as part of the preceding word or as a separate word (e.g. ἵναπερ or ἵνα περ).

Quite often, a Genitive of Limits of Space (a subcategory of the Partitive Genitive) modifies a relative adverb. As the following two examples show, the relative adverbs may be used either in a literal sense, or in a figurative sense.

χωρήσομαί τἄρ' **οἷπερ** ἐστάλην **ὁδοῦ**. (S.*El.* 404.)
I shall go, then, **to that point of my path where** *I was sent.*

Literal reference to place; strictly: 'to where indeed within my path …'.

ὅμως δ', **ἵν'** ἕσταμεν **χρείας**, ἄμεινον ἐκμαθεῖν τί δραστέον. (S.*OT* 1442–1443.)

Nevertheless, **where (with)in our present need** *we stand, <it is> better to learn fully what <it is> necessary to do.*

Figurative reference to place.

33.1.2. Primary Sequence

33.1.2.1. Definite

… καὶ ἢν σφαλῶμεν, τὰ τῶν ξυμμάχων, **ὅθεν ἰσχύομεν**, προσαπόλλυται· (Th. 1.143.5.)

… and if we fail, the <resources> of our allies, **from where we draw our strength***, are lost as well.*

ὅθεν + Present Indicative.

ἐνθαῦτα λειμών ἐστι, **ἵνα** σφι ἀγορή τε **ἐγίνετο** καὶ πρητήριον· (Hdt. 7.23.4.)

*A meadow is there, **where** an assembly-area and market-place **was made** by them.*

ἵνα + Past Imperfect Indicative in the context of Present narrative.

33.1.2.2. Indefinite
καὶ ταῦτα οὖν κηρύττετε πάντα ἀποφέρειν πρὸς ὑμᾶς, **ὅπου ἂν καθέζησθε**· (X.Cyr. 4.5.41.)

*Tell <them>, therefore, to deliver all this also to you, **wherever you are situated**.*

ὅπου + ἄν with Subjunctive in prose.

ἀλλ' εἶμι κἀγὼ κεῖσ', **ὅποιπερ ἂν σθένω**. (S.Aj. 810.)
*But I too shall go there, **to wherever indeed I have the strength**.*

ὅποιπερ + ἄν with Subjunctive in verse.

φεῦ φεῦ, φρονεῖν ὡς δεινὸν **ἔνθα μὴ τέλη λύῃ** φρονοῦντι. (S.OT 316–317.)

*Oh oh, how terrible <it is> to be wise **where there is no profit** for the wise man.*

ἔνθα + negative μή and Subjunctive without ἄν in verse. (τέλη λύῃ is equivalent to λυσιτελῇ.)

οὗ μή 'στι καιρός, μὴ μακρὰν βούλου λέγειν. (S.El. 1259.)
***Where it is not** the right time, do not wish to speak at length.*

οὗ + negative μή and Indicative. Compare Lesson 25.3.2: indefinite adjectival clauses with negative μή and Indicative.

33.1.3. Past Sequence

33.1.3.1. Definite
παραπλέων δὲ πάλιν ἔσχε καὶ ἐς Νότιον τὸ Κολοφωνίων, **οὗ κατῴκηντο** Κολοφώνιοι ... (Th. 3.34.1.)

*And as he sailed back along the coast he also put in at Notium the <port> of the Colophonians, **where** the Colophonians **had settled** ...*

οὗ + Past Perfect Indicative.

οἱ δὲ Πελοποννήσιοι, ἐπειδὴ ἔτεμον τὸ πεδίον, παρῆλθον ἐς τὴν Πάραλον γῆν καλούμενον μέχρι Λαυρίου, **οὗ** τὰ ἀργύρεια μέταλλά **ἐστιν** Ἀθηναίοις. (Th. 2.55.1.)

*And the Peloponnesians, when they had ravaged the plain, passed on to the region called Paralus, **where** the Athenians **have** their silver mines.*

οὗ + Present Indicative in the context of past narrative.

33.1.3.2. Indefinite

καὶ προσβολαί, ὥσπερ εἰώθεσαν, ἐγίγνοντο τῶν Ἀθηναίων ἱππέων **ὅπῃ παρείκοι** … (Th. 3.1.2.)

*And attacks by the Athenian horsemen, as indeed had been customary, were being made, **wherever it was practicable** …*

ὅπῃ + Optative.

… οἱ Λακεδαιμόνιοι ἐψηφίσαντο τοὺς μὲν μετὰ Βρασίδου Εἵλωτας μαχεσαμένους ἐλευθέρους εἶναι καὶ οἰκεῖν **ὅπου ἂν βούλωνται**· (Th. 5.34.1.)

*… the Spartans voted that the Helots who had fought with Brasidas should be free and live **wherever they wished**.*

ὅπου + ἄν with Subjunctive in a Vivid construction.

33.2. Adverbial Clauses of Manner

In so far as the conjunctions introducing adverbial clauses of Comparison are 'properly conjunctive relative adverbs of manner' (Smyth, 1956, §2463), adverbial clauses of Manner have already been treated in Lesson 28. However, that Lesson included adjectival as well as adverbial clauses; and it covered the categories of quality, quantity and degree as well as Manner. On the other hand, the conjunctive relative adverbs ᾗ and ὅπῃ may express Manner ('in what way') as well as location ('in what place', 'to what place', 'by which route'). This section thus provides a link both to Lesson 28 and to the earlier part of the present Lesson. The following examples illustrate the same pattern as with clauses of Place.

ταῦτα μὲν οὖν, **ὅπως ἂν** ἡμῖν **συμπίπτῃ**, ποιήσομεν. (Isoc. 15.74.)
*Well then, we shall do this, **in whatever way it comes to pass** for us.*

ὅπως + ἄν with Subjunctive in Primary sequence (indefinite).

... ὁ μὲν δὴ Φεραύλας, οὕτω διαδοὺς **ᾗ ἐτάχθη**, εὐθὺς ἐπεμέλετο τῶν εἰς τὴν ἐξέλασιν ... (X.*Cyr.* 8.3.8.)

*... Pheraulas indeed, having thus made the distribution **as he had been instructed**, immediately took care of matters relating to the procession ...*

ᾗ with Indicative in Past sequence (definite).

ἐπεὶ δὲ ἤρξαντο βουλεύεσθαι ὅπως ἂν ἐξείη αὐτοῖς τῇ πόλει χρῆσθαι **ὅπως βούλοιντο**, ... ἔπεισαν Λύσανδρον φρουροὺς σφίσι συμπρᾶξαι ἐλθεῖν ... (X.*HG* 2.3.13.)

*But when they began to consider how it would be possible for them to treat the city **however they wished** ... they persuaded Lysander to cooperate in getting a garrison to come to them ...*

ὅπως + Optative in Past sequence (indefinite).

33.3. Adverbial Clauses of Place Expressing Purpose

Sometimes adverbial clauses of Place simultaneously express Purpose. The relative adverb of Place is expressed in translation as a Purpose conjunction + demonstrative adverb: '**where** you may ...' becomes '**in order that there** you may ...'. In Primary sequence, the Mood of the verb in these clauses is either Subjunctive with ἄν or Future Indicative; in Past sequence the Mood is Optative. The negative is μή.

μολών τε χῶρον **ἔνθ᾽ ἂν** ἀστιβῆ **κίχω**
κρύψω τόδ᾽ ἔγχος τοὐμόν ... (S.*Aj.* 657–658.)

*And going **where I may find** an untrodden place
I shall hide this sword of mine ...*

(i.e. '**in order that somewhere I may find ...**')

ἔνθα + ἄν with Subjunctive in Primary sequence.

μέλλουσι γάρ σ', εἰ τῶνδε μὴ λήξεις γόων,
ἐνταῦθα πέμψειν **ἔνθα μή** ποθ' ἡλίου
φέγγος **προσόψει** ... (S.*El.* 379–381.)

For they intend, if you do not cease from these laments,
*to send you there **where you may not** ever **look upon***
the light of the sun ...

(i.e. '**in order that there you may not** ever **look upon** the light of the sun ...')

ἔνθα + negative μή with Future Indicative in Primary sequence.

... κρύψασ' ἑαυτὴν **ἔνθα μή** τις **εἰσίδοι**,
βρυχᾶτο μὲν βωμοῖσι προσπίπτους' ὅτι
γένοιτ' ἐρήμη ... (S.*Tr.* 903–905.)

*... hiding herself **where no** one **might see**,*
falling before the altars she screamed that
she had become desolate ...

(i.e. 'hiding herself **that there no** one **might see** ...')

ἔνθα + negative μή with Optative in Past sequence.

33.4. Adverbial Clauses Distinguished from Noun Clauses

The same conjunctive relative adverbs as introduce *adverbial* clauses of Place or Manner may also introduce certain types of *noun* clause. Such noun clauses occur especially as reported questions, where the whole clause is the Object of a verb of saying, asking, knowing or seeing. Such a clause may also be the Subject of the verb 'to be', or the Object of a verb of effort or caution.

ὦ τλῆμον, οὐκ οἶσθ' **οἶ** κακῶν ἐλήλυθας,
Ἰᾶσον· (E.*Med.* 1306–1307.)

*O poor <man>, you do not know **to what point** of troubles you have come, Jason.*

The reported question, οἶ ... ἐλήλυθας, is the Object of οἶσθ(α).

οὐ γάρ τις ὅρμος ἔστιν, οὐδ' **ὅποι** πλέων
ἐξεμπολήσει κέρδος ἢ ξενώσεται. (S.Ph. 302–303.)

*For there does not exist any harbour, nor **anywhere** one will sail **to** and make a gainful trade or be welcomed as a guest.*

The noun clause, ὅποι ... ξενώσεται, is the Subject of ἔστιν. More literally: '(the place,) to where (by) sailing one will make a gainful trade ... does not exist'.

... τῶν δὲ ἀπείρων καὶ ἀνεπιστημόνων **ὅπῃ** τράπωνται, ἐσπίπτοντες ἔς τε χαράδρας καὶ τὰς προλελοχισμένας ἐνέδρας διεφθείροντο. (Th. 3.112.6.)

*... but since they were inexperienced and ignorant of **where** they were to turn, falling into ravines and ambushes set beforehand they were being destroyed.*

The reported question, ὅπῃ τράπωνται, is Object of the adjective ἀνεπιστημόνων (with ὄντων understood in an improper Gen. abs.).

References

Goodwin (1889), *Syntax of the moods and tenses of the Greek verb*, §§529, 540, 556.

Smyth (1956), *Greek grammar*, §§2498–2499. Cf. 346, 2463 (list of relative adverbs).

EXERCISE 33

Translate the following passages. (The Exercise does not include any reported questions or clauses of effort or caution.)

1. τὰ δ' ἐπιτήδεια, ὅπου μὲν ἡμεῖς ἐληλύθαμεν, ὑφ' ἡμῶν ἀνήλωται·

   ἐπιτήδεια, -ων, τά   *provisions* (neut. pl. adj. as noun)

2. ... ἐξέστω ἀπιέναι ὅποι ἂν βούλωνται ...

3. ἐκκλῄομαι γὰρ δωμάτων ὅποι μόλω.

   ἐκκλῄειν   *to shut out* (here Pass.)

4. ἔφευγον, ἔνθα μήποτ' ὀψοίμην κακῶν
   χρησμῶν ὀνείδη τῶν ἐμῶν τελούμενα.

φεύγειν	to be in exile
χρησμός, -οῦ, ὁ	oracle (i.e. oracular utterance)
ἐμός, -ή, -όν	my (i.e. about me)

5. ὅκου γὰρ ἰθύσειε στρατεύεσθαι, πάντα οἱ ἐχώρεε εὐτυχέως.

ὅκου (Ionic)	ὅπου (Attic)
ἰθύειν	to strive (+ Infin.)
οἱ	Dat. masc. sg.
χωρεῖν	to turn out (Intr.; uncontracted in Ionic)

6. καὶ ἐψηφίσαντο πλεύσαντα τὸν Πείσανδρον καὶ δέκα ἄνδρας μετ' αὐτοῦ πράσσειν, ὅπῃ αὐτοῖς δοκοίη ἄριστα ἕξειν, τά τε πρὸς τὸν Τισσαφέρνη καὶ τὸν Ἀλκιβιάδην.

πράσσειν	to negotiate (+ Acc.)

7. ... ἐλθόντες εἰς τὴν οἰκίαν ἵν' ἦν κεκρυμμένη, βίᾳ λαβόντες αὐτὴν καὶ ἀγαγόντες ἐπὶ τὸ δικαστήριον ζῶσαν ἅπασι τοῖς παροῦσιν ἐπέδειξαν.

   This passage concerns the concealment of a female slave, in order to gain a legal advantage by falsely claiming that she had died.

8. ... πρᾶσσε θαρσῶν καὶ τὰ ἐμὰ καὶ τὰ σὰ ὅπῃ κάλλιστα καὶ ἄριστα ἕξει ἀμφοτέροις.

9. And if they were to become subject, all matters would be accomplished as *we* wish.

subject (to authority)	ὑποχείριος, (-α,) -ον
as	ᾗ (+ Indic.)

   The Conditional clause may be translated by a Gen. abs.

10. ... they held out for a short time, but then they turned to Panormus, from where indeed they had set sail.

to hold out	ὑπομένειν (here referring to a naval battle)
to turn (Intr.)	τρέπεσθαι (Mid.)
Panormus	Πάνορμος, -ου, ὁ

LESSON 34
Noun Clauses with Expressions of Emotion

34.1. Introduction

Noun clauses introduced by ὅτι or εἰ meaning 'that' are used as the Object of various verbs of emotion, or as the Subject of the verb 'to be' with an adjective of emotion as Complement. Typical emotions are surprise, shame, blame, anger, love, hate, pleasure and pain. Since already in Homer ὅτι may mean either 'that' or 'because', it is necessary to distinguish noun clauses from adverbial clauses of Cause. And likewise, it is necessary to distinguish noun clauses introduced by εἰ from the common adverbial clauses of Condition introduced by the same conjunction. Other noun clauses, which are introduced by εἰ, are reported questions (Lesson 18), clauses of effort and caution (Lesson 24) and clauses of fearing (Lesson 35).

In order to demonstrate the construction of verbs of emotion with a direct Object, the following sections will contain examples of such verbs with a noun as direct Object, then with a pronoun, and then with a pronoun anticipating a noun clause introduced by ὅτι or εἰ. After that, examples of verbs of emotion with a plain ὅτι or εἰ clause as direct Object will be given.

Further sections will provide examples of εἰ introducing a noun clause as Subject of the verb 'to be' with an adjective of emotion as Complement. Such noun clauses are also sometimes the Subject of certain other verbs.

Finally, the use of negatives in noun clauses introduced by ὅτι or εἰ will be considered.

34.2. Verbs of Emotion

34.2.1. Noun as Direct Object

Verbs of emotion may have as direct Object a noun which is abstract or concrete and which refers to a person or thing.

νῦν δ' εἰς τοῦτο τὰ πράγματα περιέστηκεν, ὥσθ' οἱ μὲν **μισοῦσι τὴν πόλιν**, οἱ δὲ καταφρονοῦσιν ἡμῶν. (Isoc. 7.81.)

But now circumstances have come around to this <point>, that they [= Greeks] ***hate the city*** [= Athens], *and they* [= foreigners] *despise us.*

The Object is concrete and personal (collective).

Κλεόμενες, **σπουδὴν** μὲν **τὴν ἐμὴν** μὴ **θαυμάσῃς** τῆς ἐνθαῦτα ἀπίξιος· (Hdt. 5.49.2.)

*Cleomenes, **do** not **be surprised at my eagerness** for coming here.*

The Object is abstract and denotes a thing.

34.2.2. Pronoun as Direct Object

The pronoun is regularly neuter singular or plural.

καὶ **τοῦθ' ἥδομαι**. (Ar.*Ra.* 748.)
I enjoy this too.

The pronoun is neuter singular.

καίτοι τὸν τῶν νόμων καὶ τῆς πολιτείας φάσκοντα φροντίζειν ... τοῦτο γ' ἔχειν δεῖ, **ταὐτὰ λυπεῖσθαι** καὶ **ταὐτὰ χαίρειν** τοῖς πολλοῖς ... (D. 18.292.)

And yet the one who claims to be concerned for the laws and the constitution ... must be capable of this, ***to feel grief at the same things** and **to rejoice at the same things** as the general public ...*

The pronouns are neuter plural.

34.2.3. Pronoun Anticipating a ὅτι Clause

In the following example, ταῦτα refers to the content of the ὅτι clause: 'my father' is annoyed at 'this', namely, 'that I am proceeding'. ὅτι does not mean 'because': the ὅτι clause expresses *what* 'my father' is annoyed at, not *why* he is annoyed. Thus, the ὅτι clause is the direct Object of ἀγανακτεῖ and in apposition with ταῦτα. In other words, the ὅτι clause is an Objective predicate of the pronoun ταῦτα.

ταῦτα δὴ οὖν καὶ **ἀγανακτεῖ** ὅ τε πατὴρ καὶ οἱ ἄλλοι οἰκεῖοι, **ὅτι** ἐγὼ ὑπὲρ τοῦ ἀνδροφόνου τῷ πατρὶ φόνου ἐπέρχομαι ... (Pl.*Euthphr.* 4 D.)

So indeed my father and the rest of the family members **are annoyed at this, that** *I, on behalf of the murderer, am proceeding against my father for murder ...*

34.2.4. Pronoun Anticipating an εἰ Clause

Similarly in this next example αὐτὸ τοῦτο refers to the content of the εἰ clause. This clause expresses *what* the Subject of the leading clause is surprised at, rather than *why* he is surprised. In function the εἰ clause is not an adverbial Conditional clause, but a noun clause as direct Object of θαυμάζω and in apposition with αὐτὸ τοῦτο. In other words, the εἰ clause is an Objective predicate of the pronominal phrase αὐτὸ τοῦτο.

ἐγὼ δὲ πρῶτον μὲν **αὐτὸ τοῦτο θαυμάζω, εἰ** στεφανοῦν ἐπὶ τοῖς ἠτυχημένοις ἠξίου τὴν βουλήν· (D. 22.17.)

But **I** *in the first place* **am surprised at this very <point>, that** *he thought it appropriate to reward the council for the unfortunate <events>.*

34.2.5. ὅτι Clause Alone as Direct Object

A ὅτι clause may be the direct Object of a verb of emotion even without an anticipatory pronoun. But again, the ὅτι clause is a noun clause, not an adverbial Causal clause.

θαυμάζω δ' **ὅτι** τοὺς αὐτοὺς ὁρῶ ὑπὲρ Αἰγυπτίων τἀναντία πράττειν βασιλεῖ τὴν πόλιν πείθοντας, ὑπὲρ δὲ τοῦ Ῥοδίων δήμου φοβουμένους τὸν ἄνδρα τοῦτον. (D. 15.5.)

But **I am surprised that** I see the same <men> trying-to-persuade the city to act in opposition to the (Persian) king where the Egyptians are concerned, but being afraid of this man where the democracy of the Rhodians is concerned.

34.2.6. εἰ Clause Alone as Direct Object

Similarly, an εἰ clause may be the direct Object of a verb of emotion without an anticipatory pronoun. And the εἰ clause also is a noun clause, not an adverbial Conditional clause.

θυμοῦμαι μὲν τῇ ξυντυχίᾳ, καί μου τὰ σπλάγχν' **ἀγανακτεῖ**,

εἰ πρὸς τοῦτον δεῖ μ' ἀντιλέγειν· (Ar.*Ra.* 1006–1007.)

*I am angry at the turn of events, and my emotions **are annoyed**,*

***that** it is necessary that I should speak against this <fellow>.*

34.2.7. εἰ Clause as Direct Object with an Adjective of Emotion

An εἰ clause may be a direct Object in apposition with an adjective of emotion. In the following example, it is appropriate to understand the adjective as an Objective predicate.

ἦ **θαυμαστὸν** νομίζεις **εἰ** καὶ τῷ θεῷ δοκεῖ ἐμὲ βέλτιον εἶναι ἤδη τελευτᾶν; (X.*Ap.* 5.)

*Do you think <it> **surprising that** even to (the) god it seems to be better that I should die now?*

English idiom regularly uses the pronoun 'it' anticipating the 'that' clause; compare the Greek anticipatory pronouns in §§34.2.3 and 34.2.4 above.

34.3. εἰ Clause as Subject

34.3.1. εἰ Clause as Subject of εἶναι

When an εἰ clause is the Subject of a sentence, it is most commonly the Subject of the verb 'to be' εἶναι and has an adjectival Complement. Sometimes, the Complement is a full adjectival clause. And sometimes, the negative pronoun οὐδέν or the interrogative pronoun τί is combined with the adjectival Complement.

ἐμοὶ μὲν **θαυμαστὸν** δοκεῖ εἶναι, **εἴ** τις ἐλεύθερος ἄνθρωπος ἢ κτῆμά τι τούτου ἥδιον κέκτηται ἢ ἐπιμέλειαν ἡδίω τινὰ ταύτης εὕρηκεν ἢ ὠφελιμωτέραν εἰς τὸν βίον. (X.*Oec.* 5.11.)

*To me <it> seems to be **amazing, that** any free man has obtained any possession more pleasant than this or has found any occupation more pleasant than this or more helpful for his livelihood.*

As in the previous example, English idiom uses the anticipatory pronoun 'it'. More literally: '**That** any free man has obtained ... seems to me to be **amazing**'.

Indicative forms of εἶναι are regularly omitted, as in the following four examples.

καίτοι **δεινόν**, **εἰ** ἐπὶ μὲν τοῖς ὑμετέροις αὐτῶν πράγμασιν ἐμμένετε τοῖς ὅρκοις, ἐπὶ δὲ τῇ τούτου συκοφαντίᾳ παραβαίνειν ἐπιχειρήσετε ... (Isoc. 17.24.)

*And yet <it is> **terrible, that** in the matter of your own affairs you abide by your oaths, but in the case of the vexatious prosecution by this <man> you are going to attempt to transgress them ...*

More literally: '**That** in the matter of your own affairs you abide ... **<is> terrible**'.

ὃ δὲ πάντων **σχετλιώτατον**, **εἰ** φιλοπονώτατοι δοκοῦντες εἶναι τῶν Ἑλλήνων ῥᾳθυμότερον τῶν ἄλλων βουλευσόμεθα περὶ τούτων. (Isoc. 6.56.)

*And what **<is> most shocking** of all **<is> that** we, although seeming to be the most energetic of the Greeks, are going to deliberate more lightly than the rest about this.*

In this example, the Complement is a full adjectival clause, ὃ ... σχετλιώτατον, and the Indicative of the verb 'to be' is omitted both as the Main verb and as the verb of the ὅ clause. Both Greek and English allow a reversal of word order for the sake of emphasis. The order Subject, <verb>, Complement would run: 'And **that** we are going to deliberate more lightly than the rest about this **<is> what <is>** most shocking of all'.

τὸν μὲν οὖν πρόσθεν χρόνον ὑμεῖς τε τοξόται καὶ ἀκοντισταὶ ἦτε καὶ ἡμεῖς, καὶ **εἴ** τι χείρους ἡμῶν ταῦτα ποιεῖν ἦτε, **οὐδὲν θαυμαστόν**· (X.*Cyr.* 2.1.16.)

Well then, during the previous time you *were archers and lancers and <so were> we, and **that** you were somewhat inferior to us at doing this, <is>* **nothing surprising**.

[OR: '<it is> **nothing surprising that...**'.] The negative pronoun οὐδέν is combined with the adjectival Complement θαυμαστόν.

... **τί θαυμαστὸν εἰ** καὶ τὰ νῦν καθεστῶτα λήψεταί τινα μετάστασιν; (Isoc. 6.40.)

... ***what*** *<is>* ***surprising*** *<about the idea>* ***that*** *also our present circumstances are going to undergo* [lit. 'receive'] *some change?*

The interrogative pronoun τί is combined with the adjectival Complement θαυμαστόν.

34.3.2. εἰ Clause as Subject of Other Verbs

An εἰ clause may also be the Subject of a limited number of other verbs of emotion. ἐξαρκεῖν and μεταμελεῖν belong to this group.

ἆρ' οὖν **ἂν ἐξαρκέσειεν** ἡμῖν, **εἰ** τήν τε πόλιν ἀσφαλῶς **οἰκοῖμεν** καὶ τὰ περὶ τὸν βίον εὐπορώτεροι **γιγνόμεθα** ... (Isoc. 8.19.)

Would <it> ***satisfy*** *us, then,* ***that we should inhabit*** *the city in safety and* ***should become*** *well provided regarding what concerns our livelihood ...?*

Grammatical structure: 'Would <the possibility>, that we should inhabit ... satisfy us?' The Optative οἰκοῖμεν in the εἰ clause corresponds to the potential Optative ἐξαρκέσειεν of the Main verb. The construction of the whole sentence is analogous to a Future Unfulfilled Conditional sentence. However, the εἰ clause is a noun clause, expressing *what* 'would satisfy us', not an adverbial Conditional clause.

Similarly, an adjective of emotion is sometimes used in apposition with the εἰ clause as Subject of a non-emotional verb.

ὥστε πάντων **ἄν** μοι **συμβαίη δεινότατον, εἰ** τοιαύτην πολιτείαν εἰσηγούμενος νεωτέρων δόξαιμι πραγμάτων ἐπιθυμεῖν. (Isoc. 7.59.)

*And so **the strangest** of all things **would happen** to me, **that** in introducing such a form of government I should seem to desire revolution.*

Here, συμβαίνειν corresponds to εἶναι as used in §34.3.1 above, but δεινότατον is part of the Subject not the Complement.

34.4. Negatives with ὅτι and εἰ Clauses

ὅτι clauses regularly use οὐ and its compounds. εἰ clauses sometimes use οὐ, but often use μή and its compounds. οὐ and μή may even occur in the same εἰ clause, when it is divided by μέν and δέ.

καὶ σέ γε ἐζήτουν κατ' ἀγορὰν καὶ **ἐθαύμαζον ὅτι οὐχ** οἷός τ' ἦ εὑρεῖν. (Pl. *Tht.* 142 A.)

*And I was looking for you (all) over the market-place and **I was surprised that** I was **not** able to find <you>.*

ὅτι with negative οὐ and Indicative.

... ἔφη τοὺς ξυμπρέσβεις ἀναμένειν ... καὶ **θαυμάζειν ὡς οὔπω** πάρεισιν. (Th. 1.90.5.)

*... he said that he was waiting for his fellow-ambassadors ... and that **he was surprised that** they were **not yet** present.*

ὡς with negative οὔπω and Indicative. (ὡς is an unusual alternative for ὅτι. Here it is sometimes regarded as meaning 'how' not 'that'.)

δεινὸν δέ μοι δοκεῖ εἶναι, **εἰ**, ὅταν εἰσφορὰν εἰσενεγκεῖν δέῃ, ἣν πάντες εἴσεσθαι μέλλουσιν, **οὐκ** ἐθέλουσιν ... (Lys. 30.32.)

*And it seems to me to be **terrible, that**, when it is necessary to pay a contribution, which all are going to know about, they are **not** willing ...*

εἰ with οὐ and Indicative, which would not normally occur in a genuine Condition (cf. Lesson 19.5).

θαυμάζω δ' **εἰ μὴ** δύνασθε συνιδεῖν ὅτι γένος οὐδέν ἐστι κακονούστερον τῷ πλήθει πονηρῶν ῥητόρων καὶ δημαγωγῶν· (Isoc. 8.129.)

But *I am surprised that* you are *not* able to see that no group is more ill-disposed to the general public than incompetent orators and politicians.

εἰ with μή and Indicative.

σχέτλιον δ' ἂν εἴη, **εἰ** οὗτος μὲν ἅπαντας τοὺς πολίτας περὶ **οὐδενὸς** ἡγήσατο, ὑμεῖς δὲ τοῦτον ἕνα ὄντα **μὴ** ἀποδοκιμάσαιτε. (Lys. 31.31.)

It would be shocking, that this <man> considered all the citizens worth nothing, but <that> you should not disqualify this <man> when he is <just> one <person>.

εἰ with οὐδενός and Indicative denoting a past fact, then with μή and Optative denoting an imminent possibility from which the speaker is dissuading his audience. The εἰ clause is divided by μέν and δέ.

34.5. General Comments

34.5.1. ἐάν

Sometimes, ἐάν with Subjunctive is mentioned as having the same function as εἰ or ὅτι with expressions of emotion. However, there are few examples. And, it may be that ἐάν should be regarded as introducing a genuine Conditional clause, even with an expression of emotion. Moreover, the classical prose author Isocrates frequently uses εἰ to introduce noun clauses with expressions of emotion; but all (18) ἐάν clauses are genuine Conditional clauses, and are not used with expressions of emotion.

34.5.2. Scholarly Views

Standard treatments of Ancient Greek grammar in English, French and German differ somewhat in their view of expressions of emotion with clauses introduced by ὅτι and εἰ. In German, Kühner (1890–1904) regards such clauses as noun clauses (*Substantivsätze*). Schwyzer (1950) appears to agree for ὅτι and ὡς clauses; for εἰ (ἐάν), he merely refers

LESSON 34. NOUN CLAUSES WITH EXPRESSIONS OF EMOTION

to Kühner. In French, Humbert (1954) first discusses Causal clauses introduced by ὅτι or ὡς, then adds Object (*completive*) clauses with verbs of emotion. 'The content of these emotions *is expressed* by the Causal clause, introduced by εἰ, "if it is true that, since…"' (§337). This formulation seems deliberately to blur the distinction between adverbial Conditional and Causal clauses on the one hand and noun clauses on the other hand.

In English, Goodwin (1889) treats clauses with expressions of emotion in a separate section in the midst of Conditional clauses. He acknowledges that, with many expressions of emotion, 'a protasis with εἰ may be used to express the object of the emotion', although 'a causal sentence would generally seem more natural' (§494). And he maintains, 'These expressions may also be followed by ὅτι and a causal sentence' (§496). After treating the usual Causal constructions including ὅτι and ὡς clauses, Smyth (1956, §2247) continues by writing that, 'Many verbs of emotion state the cause more delicately with εἰ (ἐάν) *if* as a mere supposition than by ὅτι'. He acknowledges that ὅτι clauses are also used with these verbs (§2248). But he ends with the comment, 'ὅτι after verbs of emotion really means *that*, not *because*' (§2248.a.).

This Lesson follows the view that, with expressions of emotion, clauses introduced by ὅτι, ὡς and εἰ are noun clauses, and that the subordinating conjunctions are appropriately translated as 'that', not 'because' nor 'if'.

References

Goodwin (1889), *Syntax of the moods and tenses of the Greek verb*, §§494–496.

Humbert (1954), *Syntaxe Grecque*, §337.

Kühner (1904), *Ausführliche Grammatik der Griechischen Sprache* (Vol. 2.2), pp. 369–370.

Liddell & Scott (1996), *A Greek–English lexicon*, εἰ B. V.

Schwyzer (1950), *Syntax und Syntaktische Stilistik* (Griechische Grammatik, vol. 2), pp. 645–646, 688.

Smyth (1956), *Greek grammar*, §§2247–2248.

EXERCISE 34A

Translate the following passages. Both ὅτι and εἰ, when introducing noun clauses of the type treated in Lesson 34, should consistently be translated as 'that'.

1. ... τίς οὐκ οἶδε τῶν πρεσβυτέρων τοὺς μὲν δημοτικοὺς καλουμένους ... δεινὸν ἡγουμένους, εἴ τις ὄψεται τὴν πόλιν τὴν τῶν Ἑλλήνων ἄρξασαν ταύτην ὑφ' ἑτέροις οὖσαν ...;

πρεσβύτερος, -α, -ον	older
ἡγουμένους	Reflects Past Imperf. of direct knowledge: ἡγοῦντο.

2. θαυμαστὸν δ', εἰ τοὺς μὲν ἐπὶ τῆς ὀλιγαρχίας ὑβρίσαντας ἀξίους θανάτου νομίζετε, τοὺς δ' ἐν δημοκρατίᾳ ταῦτ' ἐκείνοις ἐπιτηδεύοντας ἀζημίους ἀφήσετε.

ὑβρίζειν	to act violently
ἐπιτηδεύειν	to commit
ἀζήμιος, -ον	unpunished

3. ὥστ' οὐδὲν θαυμαστόν, εἰ πάνυ ἐν τάχει πάλιν ἡμῖν πράγματα παρέχειν δυνήσονται.

πράγματα παρέχειν	to cause trouble

4. ἤν τε γὰρ αὐτὸν μετρίως θωμάζῃς, ἄχθεται, ὅτι οὐ κάρτα θεραπεύεται, ἤν τε θεραπεύῃ τις κάρτα, ἄχθεται ἅτε θωπί.

θωμάζειν (Ionic)	to admire
ἄχθεσθαι	to be annoyed
θεραπεύειν	to pay attention to (1st instance Pass.)
θώψ, θωπός, ὁ	flatterer

5. ... προειλόμην πορρωτέρωθεν ποιήσασθαι τὴν ἀρχήν, ... αἰσχυνόμενος, εἰ ... περὶ τῶν προγόνων τῶν τὴν πόλιν κάλλιστα διοικησάντων μηδὲ μικρὰν ποιήσομαι μνείαν ...

LESSON 34. NOUN CLAUSES WITH EXPRESSIONS OF EMOTION

The speaker is referring to the composition of his speech.

διοικεῖν	to administer

6. And let no one of you be surprised, that we know [this] accurately.

accurately	ἀκριβῶς

7. For we are able to make also this criticism against them, that for their own city they compel their neighbours to be serfs ...

to make a criticism against	ἐπιτιμᾶν (+ Acc. 'this' and Dat. 'them')
neighbour	ὅμορος, -ου, ὁ
to be a serf	εἰλωτεύειν

EXERCISE 34B

Translate the following passages. Both ὅτι and εἰ, when introducing noun clauses of the type treated in Lesson 34, should consistently be translated as 'that'.

1. αἰσχύνομαι γάρ, εἴ τισι δόξω δεδιὼς ὑπὲρ γήρως καὶ μικροῦ βίου προδιδόναι τὴν ἀλήθειαν.

αἰσχύνεσθαι	to be ashamed
γῆρας, -ως (-αος), τό	old age
μικροῦ	Refers to speaker's remaining, not total, life.

2. πάντων δ' ἂν εἴη δεινότατον, εἰ ... ἐγὼ διὰ τὴν ἐκείνου φυγὴν ζημιωθείην.

φυγή, -ῆς, ἡ	exile
ζημιοῦν	to punish

3. ὃ δὲ πάντων δεινότατον, εἰ τοῖς μὲν συνεχῶς μετὰ Λακεδαιμονίων γεγενημένοις δεδογμένον ὑμῖν ἐστι βοηθεῖν ...

4. ... τί θαυμαστόν, εἰ περὶ τῆς ἀρχῆς τῆς κατὰ θάλατταν ἀγνοοῦσι ...;

5. ὥστε πάντων ἂν συμβαίη δεινότατον, εἰ τοὺς βουλομένους τοῖς αὐτοῖς τούτοις διενεγκεῖν τῶν ἡλικιωτῶν ... διαφθείρεσθαι ψηφίσαισθε ...

τοῖς αὐτοῖς τούτοις	neut.
διαφέρειν	*to outclass* (+ Gen. of Comparison)
ἡλικιώτης, -ου, ὁ	*comrade*
διαφθείρειν	*to corrupt*

6. δεινὸν δέ μοι δοκεῖ εἶναι, ὦ ἄνδρες δικασταί, εἰ τούτου ... οὐκ ἐπεχείρησαν δεῖσθαι, ὡς χρή, παύσασθαι εἰς ὑμᾶς ἐξαμαρτάνοντα ...

δεῖσθαι	*to request (of)* (+ Gen.)
ἐξαμαρτάνοντα	Acc. masc. sg.; refers to τούτου despite change of Case.

7. For I am ashamed, that, having said so much in advance about the excellence of Agamemnon, I am going to mention nothing of what has been achieved by that [man]...

to have said in advance	προειρηκέναι (Perf.)
Agamemnon	Ἀγαμέμνων, -ονος, ὁ
to mention	μιμνήσκεσθαι

8. But it seems to me that I would reasonably be annoyed, ... that they were willing to make the mattter equal to the most serious grounds of complaint.

to make equal with	ἐξισοῦν (+ Acc. 'matter' and Dat. 'ground')
ground of complaint	ἔγκλημα, -ατος, τό

LESSON 35
Expressions of Fearing

35.1. Introduction

Fears are most commonly expressed by a verb of fearing with a direct Object. The Object may be a noun or a pronoun referring to a person or a thing. But the Object may also be an Infinitive phrase, with or without the neuter singular definite article. A verb of fearing may also have as its direct Object a noun clause, which is most commonly introduced by μή.

The following verbs are those which are most often used in expressions of fearing. φοβεῖσθαι is Passive in form, but Active in function, since it has a direct Object. (Coincidentally, 'to be afraid' in English was originally a Pass. form of the Act. verb 'to affray'.) δεδοικέναι (or δεδιέναι) is a Perfect form with Imperfect meaning: 'to have become afraid' and hence 'to be afraid' or 'to fear'. δειμαίνειν has the same meaning. ταρβεῖν, also synonymous, is mainly restricted to verse. In addition to expressions of fear with verbs, there are various idioms which use nouns such as ὁ φόβος, τὸ δέος, τὸ δεῖμα and τὸ τάρβος.

35.2. Verbs of Fearing with Noun or Pronoun as Object

πολὺ δὲ κἀκεῖνοι μᾶλλον **ἡμᾶς φοβήσονται**, ὅταν ἀκούσωσιν ὅτι οὐ **φοβούμενοι πτήσσομεν αὐτοὺς** οἴκοι καθήμενοι ... (X. *Cyr.* 3.3.18.)

*And those <men> also **will** much more **be afraid of us**, when they hear that we **are** not cowering **in fear before them**...*

Acc. pronouns (persons) as Object.

... ἀλλὰ **δείσας τό** τε **μῆκος** τοῦ πλόου καὶ **τὴν ἐρημίην** ἀπῆλθε ὀπίσω ... (Hdt. 4.43.1.)

... but **fearing the length** of the voyage and **the isolation** he went back again ...

Acc. nouns (abstract things) as Object.

35.3. Verbs of Fearing with Infinitive Phrase as Object

... καὶ οὐκ αἰσχύνονται τοιαύτῃ παρρησίᾳ χρώμενοι περὶ τοῦ τεθνεῶτος, ἣν **ἔδεισαν ἂν ποιήσασθαι** περὶ ζῶντος, ... (Isoc. 16.22.)

... and they are not ashamed to employ such outspokenness about him now that he is dead, as [lit. 'which'] **they would have feared to use** concerning <him when he was> living ...

Plain Infin. as Object.

αὐτὸ μὲν γὰρ **τὸ ἀποθνῄσκειν** οὐδεὶς **φοβεῖται**, ὅστις μὴ παντάπασιν ἀλόγιστός τε καὶ ἄνανδρός ἐστι, **τὸ** δ' **ἀδικεῖν φοβεῖται**· (Pl. *Grg.* 522 E.)

For no one, who is not altogether irrational and unmanly, **fears** actual **dying**, but **he fears acting unjustly**.

Articular Infin. as Object.

[The sentence is slightly illogical. The intended meaning is as follows.

'For any one, who is not altogether irrational and unmanly, does not fear actual dying, but he fears acting unjustly'.

ὅστις γὰρ μὴ παντάπασιν ἀλόγιστός τε καὶ ἄνανδρός ἐστι, αὐτὸ τὸ ἀποθνῄσκειν οὐ φοβεῖται, τὸ δ' ἀδικεῖν φοβεῖται.]

35.4. Verbs of Fearing with a μή Clause as Object

35.4.1. Fears that Something May Happen

In Primary sequence, fears that something may happen are generally expressed by μή with the Subjunctive Mood. In Past sequence, the Optative Mood may replace the Subjunctive; but a Vivid construction, retaining the Subjunctive, is also common.

δέδοικα δέ, **μὴ** λίαν ὁμολογούμενα λέγων ἐνοχλεῖν ὑμῖν **δόξω**. (Is. 8.34.)

But *I fear, that I may seem* to you to be annoying you by saying what is generally agreed.

Primary sequence with μή and Subj.

... ἠπόρουν καὶ **ἐδεδοίκεσαν, μὴ** σφῶν χειμὼν τὴν φυλακὴν **ἐπιλάβοι** ... (Th. 4.27.1.)

... *they were puzzled and **were afraid**, that winter **might overtake*** their blockade ...

Past sequence with μή and Optative.

... καὶ **ἐδέδισαν, μὴ** ποτε αὖθις ξυμφορά τις αὐτοῖς **περιτύχῃ**, οἵα καὶ ἐν τῇ νήσῳ ... (Th. 4.55.3.)

... *and **they were afraid**, that one day some disaster **might** again **befall** them, such as <had happened> also on the island* ...

Vivid construction with μή and Subj.

... καὶ ἅμα **δεδιὼς τὸν Φίλιππον, μὴ καταμαρτυροίη** αὐτοῦ ἐν τῷ ἀγῶνι, προσελθὼν τῷ πατρὶ τῷ ἐμῷ **ἐδεήθη** ἀπαλλάξαι τὸν Φίλιππον ... (D. 49.17.)

... *and at the same time **fearing, that Philip might testify against** him at the trial, he approached my father and **begged** <him> to pay off Philip* ...

Past sequence with μή and Opt. τὸν Φίλιππον is Acc. Object of δεδιώς instead of Nom. Subject of καταμαρτυροίη. 'He' does not fear 'Philip', but fears 'that' Philip may testify.

... **ἐκεῖνο φοβοῦμαι, μὴ** τῶν εἰργασμένων αὐτῷ κακῶν **ὑποληφθῇ** οὗτος ἐλάττων· (D. 18.142.)

*... **I am afraid of that**, **that** this <man> **may be supposed** incapable of the evils perpetrated by him.*

Primary sequence with μή and Subj. ἐκεῖνο is neut. Acc. pronoun as Object of φοβοῦμαι and in apposition with the whole μή clause.

35.4.2. Fears that Something May Not Happen

When a fear is expressed that something may *not* happen, οὐ and its compounds are used within the μή clause. In Primary sequence, the Subjunctive Mood is used. But it is doubtful whether the Optative Mood is ever used in Past sequence. A Vivid construction is used instead, whether the leading verb is Past or Historic Present.

ὃ καὶ **δέδοικα, μή** με δικτύων ἔσω
λαβόντες **οὐκ ἐκφρῶσ'** ἀναίμακτον χρόα. (E.*Ph.* 263–264.)

*And in regard to this **I am also afraid, that** having caught me inside the nets **they may not let** me **out** with my flesh unstained by blood.*

Primary sequence with Subj. and negative οὐκ. ἐκφρῶσ(ι) from ἐκφρεῖν. ἀναίμακτον Accusative agreeing with με; χρόα Accusative of Respect referring to ἀναίμακτον: lit. 'not (ἀν-) bloodstained as to my flesh'.

δεδιότες δέ, **μὴ οὐδ'** οὕτω **δύνωνται** ὀλίγοι πρὸς πολλοὺς ἀντέχειν, προσεπεξηῦρον τόδε· (Th. 2.76.3.)

*But **fearing, that not even so might they be able** to hold out, <being> few against many, they contrived this <plan> in addition.*

Vivid construction with Subj. and negative οὐδ(έ).

ἀλλὰ **ἀρρωδέομεν, μὴ** ὑμῖν **οὐκ** ἡδέες **γένωνται** οἱ λόγοι. (Hdt. 9.46.3.)

*But **we were afraid, that** our words **might not turn out to be** pleasing to you.*

Vivid construction with Subj. and negative οὐκ after Historic Pres. leading verb.

35.5. Fears that Something is (etc.) Actually Happening

In order to emphasise a fear that something is actually happening, the Indicative Mood is used in some μή clauses in Primary sequence. Within the μή clauses there are examples of Present, Future, Past Aorist and Present Perfect Indicative verbs. In Past sequence, an Optative in the μή clause represents an Indicative of the Primary form of the expression of fear. The negative within the μή clause is again οὐ, as in §35.4.2.

εἰ δ᾽ οἱ μὲν κακοὶ μηδὲν ποιήσουσιν, οἱ δ᾽ ἀγαθοὶ καὶ δυνατοὶ ἀθυμῶς ἕξουσι, **δέδοικα**, ἔφη, **μὴ** ἄλλου τινὸς μᾶλλον ἢ τοῦ ἀγαθοῦ **μεθέξω** πλεῖον μέρος ἢ ἐγὼ βούλομαι. (X.*Cyr.* 2.3.6.)

'But if the bad do nothing, and the good and powerful become fainthearted, **I fear**', he said, '**that I shall have a** rather larger **share** than I wish of something other than good'.

Primary sequence with μή and Fut. Indic.

ἣν **δέδοικα** μέν, ὦ ἄνδρες Ἀθηναῖοι, **δέδοικα**, **μὴ λελήθαμεν** ὥσπερ οἱ δανειζόμενοι ἐπὶ πολλῷ ἄγοντες· (D. 19.99.)

And **I fear**, O men of Athens, **I do fear**, **that we have missed seeing** that we are enjoying it just as those who are borrowing at a high interest rate.

Primary sequence with μή and Pres. Perf. Indic. ἥν is coordinating relative pronoun: 'And ... it', referring to 'peace' (εἰρήνη) in the previous sentence.

Δημοκήδης δὲ **δείσας, μή** εὖ **ἐκπειρῷτο** Δαρεῖος, οὔτι ἐπιδραμὼν πάντα τὰ διδόμενα **ἐδέκετο** ... (Hdt. 3.135.3.)

But Democedes **fearing**, **that** Darius **was testing** him, **was** in no hurry to accept all that was being offered ... [lit. 'not at all rushing was accepting']

Past sequence with μή and Imperfect Optative, representing Present Indicative of Primary sequence: δείδω μή μου ἐκπειρᾶται Δαρεῖος, 'I am afraid that Darius is testing me'. (A Subj. in Primary sequence would mean: 'I am afraid that Darius *may test* me'. This would not make sense in the context, despite the ambiguity of the Indic. and Subj. form ἐκπειρᾶται.) εὖ is Ionic Genitive third person singular masculine pronoun (enclitic).

... κατέβαλε τὸ Ἡρακλεωτῶν τεῖχος, δῆλον ὅτι οὐ **φοβούμενος**, **μή** τινες ἀναπεπταμένης ταύτης τῆς παρόδου **πορεύσοιντο** ἐπὶ τὴν ἐκείνου δύναμιν ... (X.*HG* 6.4.27.)

... *he overthrew the fortress of the Heracleots, clearly not **fearing**, **that**, since this passage had been laid open, certain people **would proceed** against that <man's> power ...*

Past sequence with μή and Intentive ('Fut.') Opt., representing Fut. Indic. of Primary sequence: οὐ φοβεῖται μή τινες πορεύσονται, 'he does not fear that certain people will proceed ...'.

35.6. Fears Expressed with Other Conjunctions

35.6.1. ὅπως μή

In this construction, ὅπως should be translated as 'that'. μή may be regarded as redundant and should not be translated.

δέδοιχ', **ὅπως** μοι **μὴ** λίαν **φανῇς** σοφή. (E.*Hipp.* 518.)
I am afraid, that you may appear too clever for my good.

Primary sequence with ὅπως μή and second Aor. Subj.

ἐκ δὲ τούτων περιγίγνεται ὑμῖν μὲν ἡ σχολὴ καὶ τὸ μηδὲν ἤδη ποιεῖν, ἃ **δέδοιχ' ὅπως μὴ** ποθ' **ἡγήσεσθ'** ἐπὶ πολλῷ γεγενῆσθαι ... (D. 8.53.)

*But from this there results for you leisure and doing nothing now, which **I am afraid that** one day **you will think** has been achieved at a high price ...*

Primary sequence with ὅπως μή and Fut. Indic.

καὶ γὰρ ... **ἐδεδοίκει** ... περὶ τοῦ γραμματείου, **ὅπως μὴ** ὑπὸ τοῦ Μενεξένου **συλληφθήσοιτο**. (Isoc. 17.22.)

*For indeed ... **he was afraid** ... concerning the document, **that it would be seized** by Menexenus.*

Past sequence with ὅπως μή and Intentive ('Fut.') Opt., representing Fut. Indic. of Primary sequence: δέδοικα, ὅπως μὴ ... συλληφθήσεται, 'I am afraid, that it will be seized ...'.

35.6.2. ὅτι

When a ὅτι clause occurs in relation to an expression of fear, the ὅτι clause is usually an adverbial clause of Cause and not part of a fearing construction as such. Moreover, in a construction of the form διὰ τοῦτο φοβεῖσθαι, ὅτι ... 'to fear on account of this, (namely) that ...', the ὅτι clause is indeed a noun clause, but is in apposition with the pronoun τοῦτο. Cause is here expressed by the preposition διά in the adverbial phrase διὰ τοῦτο; so Isoc. 6.60 and X.*HG* 3.5.10, cited by Goodwin (1889, §377). However, in the following example, the ὅτι clause is a genuine noun clause of fearing. And ὅτι should be translated as 'that', not 'because'.

ἐπεὶ καὶ τῷ πλήθει τῶν νεῶν οὐκ ὠφελήσονται, εἴ τις καὶ **τόδε** ὑμῶν, **ὅτι** οὐκ ἴσαις **ναυμαχήσει, πεφόβηται**. (Th. 7.67.3.)

*For indeed they will not be helped by the number of their ships, if any one of you **has become afraid of this**, **that he will fight at sea** with an unequal number.*

In Primary sequence, the ὅτι clause with Fut. Indic. is in apposition with the neut. pronoun τόδε as Object of πεφόβηται.

35.6.3. ὡς

ὡς may be used in the same way as ὅτι, and should also be translated 'that'.

μηδὲν μέντοι **τοῦτο φοβεῖσθε**, **ὡς** ἢ τὸ δημόσιον οὕτω κατασκευαζόμενον **παραλυπήσει** τοὺς ἰδιώτας ἢ οἱ ἰδιῶται τὸ δημόσιον· (X. *Vect.* 4.32.)

*However, **do** not at all **fear this**, **that** either the public company being set up in this way **will bother** private citizens or private citizens <bother> the company.*

In Primary sequence the ὡς clause with Fut. Indic. is in apposition with the neut. pronoun τοῦτο as Object of φοβεῖσθε. (παραλυπήσει is an emendation for the impossible readings of the manuscripts, παραλυπηση or παραλυπησειν.)

... κατέστησεν ἐπὶ γηλόφων τινῶν ἐναντίους αὐτοῖς καὶ ἱππέας καὶ ὁπλίτας, **φόβον** βουλόμενος καὶ τούτοις **παρέχειν, ὡς**, εἰ βοηθήσαιεν, ὄπισθεν οὗτοι **ἐπικείσοιντο** αὐτοῖς. (X.*HG* 7.5.24.)

*... he set up on some hills both horsemen and infantrymen opposite them, wishing **to create fear** in these also, **that**, if they came to help, these **would press upon** them from behind.*

In Past sequence, the ὡς clause with Intentive ('Fut.') Opt. represents a Fut. Indic. of Primary sequence: βούλομαι φόβον παρέχειν, ὡς ἐπικείσονται, 'I wish to create fear, that they will press upon …'. (For the introductory noun phrase, cf. §35.7 below.)

35.6.4. εἰ

In both Primary and Past sequence, a fear is sometimes expressed by an εἰ clause with Present or Future Indicative. The construction is similar to that of reported questions with εἰ (= 'whether'). However, in the following example the negative within the εἰ clause is μή, used as in Conditions, not as in reported questions. (Cf. Lessons 18.1, 19.1 and 19.5.)

... εἷς ἕκαστος ὑμῶν ... οἴκαδ' ἄπεισιν οὐδὲν φροντίζων οὐδὲ μεταστρεφόμενος οὐδὲ **φοβούμενος**, οὔτ' **εἰ** φίλος οὔτ' **εἰ μὴ** φίλος αὐτῷ **συντεύξεταί** τις, οὐδέ γε **εἰ** μέγας ἢ μικρός, οὐδ' **εἰ** ἰσχυρὸς ἢ ἀσθενής, οὐδὲ τῶν τοιούτων οὐδέν. (D. 21.221.)

*... each one of you ... will go off home not worrying about anything nor looking behind nor **fearing**, neither **whether** any friend nor **whether** any one **not** a friend **is going to encounter** him, nor yet **whether** <he is> big or little, nor **whether** strong or weak, nor any of such <issues>.*

Primary sequence with εἰ μή and Fut. Indic. (A Pres. or Fut. verb 'to be' may be understood with the subsequent two occurrences of εἰ.)

35.7. Introductory Noun Phrases

Various noun phrases may be used instead of a verb to introduce a clause of fearing. A selection of examples follows.

ὡς **ἔστι** μάλιστα τοῦτο **δέος, μὴ** πανοῦργος ὢν καὶ δεινὸς ἄνθρωπος πράγμασι χρῆσθαι ... **τρέψηται** καὶ **παρασπάσηταί** τι τῶν ὅλων πραγμάτων. (D. 1.3.)

*For **there exists** especially this **fear**, **that** being unscrupulous and a person clever at exploiting circumstances ... **he may turn to his own advantage** and **wrest aside** something of the whole set of circumstances.*

δέος (Nom.) with verb ἔστι and μή with Subj. in Primary sequence.

ἀτειχίστου γὰρ οὔσης τῆς Ἰωνίας μέγα **τὸ δέος ἐγένετο, μὴ** παραπλέοντες οἱ Πελοποννήσιοι ... **πορθῶσιν** ἅμα προσπίπτοντες τὰς πόλεις. (Th. 3.33.2.)

*For, since Ionia was unfortified, great <was> **the fear** <which> **arose, that** the Peloponnesians ... as they were sailing past **might** fall upon their cities and **ravage** <them>.*

τὸ δέος (Nom.) with verb ἐγένετο and μή with Subj. in Vivid construction.

... **φόβον** δὲ οὐκ ἂν **ἔχοις**, ἀλλ᾽ ἄλλοις **παρέχοις, μή** τι **πάθῃς** ... (X.*Hier.* 11.11.)

*... and **you would** not **have fear**, but **you would create** for others <fear>, **that you might suffer** something ...*

Verbs ἔχοις and παρέχοις with φόβον (Acc.) and μή with Subj. in Primary sequence.

... σοὶ δ᾽ οὐ **δέος ἔστ᾽ ἀπολέσθαι**· (Hom.*Il.* 12.246.)

*... yet **there is** no **fear that** you **should perish**.* [lit. 'there is not fear for you to perish']

δέος (Nom.) with verb ἔστ(ι) and Infin.

... ἀλλ' αἰεὶ **διὰ φόβου εἰσί, μή** ποτε Ἀθηναῖοι αὐτοῖς ἐπὶ τὴν πόλιν **ἔλθωσιν** ... (Th. 6.34.2.)

... *but* **they are** *constantly* **in fear,** **that** *at some time the Athenians* **may come against** *them <and attack> their city* ...

Prepositional phrase διὰ φόβου with verb εἰσί and μή with Subj. in Primary sequence.

35.8. Note

English translations of fearing clauses in the Greek passages in the Lesson observe the following conventions of Tense and Mood, especially where English auxiliary verbs are required:

- 'may' is used in Primary sequence for the Greek Subj.
- 'might' is used in Past sequence for Imperf. or Aorist Opt. or for Vivid Subj.
- 'would' is used in Past sequence for Intentive ('Fut.') Opt.
- Indic. is used for Greek Indic. and for Opt. in Past sequence when it represents a Pres. or Past Indic. of Primary sequence.

It is recommended that these conventions be observed in the Exercise.

References

Goodwin (1889), *Syntax of the moods and tenses of the Greek verb*, §§131, 365–373, 376–377.

Smyth (1956), *Greek grammar*, §§2221–2238.

EXERCISE 35A

Translate the following passages.

1. καὶ δέδοικα μέντοι, μή ποτε πολλὰ πειρῶντες καὶ κατορθώσωσιν.

μέντοι	*moreover*
κατορθοῦν	*to succeed*

2. ... δεδιώς, μὴ ἀντιχειροτονῶν κακόνους δόξειεν εἶναι τῇ πόλει, ἡσυχίαν ἦγεν.

ἀντιχειροτονεῖν	*to vote in opposition*

3. ... ἔδεισαν, μὴ μονωθῶσι καὶ ἐς Λακεδαιμονίους πᾶσα ἡ ξυμμαχία χωρήσῃ·

μονοῦν	*to isolate*
χωρεῖν	*to go over*

4. ...ἐγὼ δ' αὐτὸ τοῦτο φοβοῦμαι, μὴ διὰ τὴν ἀπειρίαν οὐ δυνηθῶ δηλῶσαι περὶ τῶν πραγμάτων ὑμῖν·

δηλοῦν	*to explain*

5. φοβοῦμαι ... μή, ὥσπερ ἀνθρώποις ἀλαζόσι, λόγοις τισὶ τοιούτοις ἐντετυχήκαμεν περὶ τοῦ φίλου.

ὥσπερ	*(just) as if*
ἀλαζών, -όνος, ὁ, ἡ	*deceptive*
λόγος, -ου, ὁ	*argument*
ἐντυγχάνειν	*to meet up with* (+ Dat., both ἀνθρώποις and λόγοις)
τοῦ φίλου	neut. Adj. for abstract noun

6. μηκέτ' ἐκφοβοῦ,
   μητρῷον ὥς σε λῆμ' ἀτιμάσει ποτέ.

λῆμα, -ατος, τό	*spirit*

7. τοὺς δὲ θεατὰς,
    εἰ καινοτομεῖν ἐθελήσουσιν καὶ μὴ τοῖς ἤθάσι λίαν
    τοῖς τ' ἀρχαίοις ἐνδιατρίβειν, τοῦτ' ἔσθ' ὃ μάλιστα δέδοικα.

θεατής, -οῦ, ὁ	spectator
καινοτομεῖν	to try something new
ἠθάς, -άδος, τό	usual <practice> [more often a masc. or fem. adj.]
λίαν (adv.)	too long
ἐνδιατρίβειν	to continue in (+ Dat.)

8. δέος δ' ἐγένετο τῇ πανηγύρει μέγα, μὴ ξὺν ὅπλοις ἔλθωσιν οἱ Λακεδαιμόνιοι ...

| πανήγυρις, -εως, ἡ | assembly |

9. ... they are afraid of him, but perhaps they would become willing actually to bear witness for me.

10. For only so many of the twenty men at first appointed did not become afraid to enter.

| twenty | εἴκοσι(ν) (indeclinable) |
| to appoint | τάσσειν |

EXERCISE 35B

Translate the following passages.

1. ... φοβοῦμαι δέ, μὴ λίαν ἐγγὺς ᾖ τοῦτ' ἤδη.

2. ... ἔδεισαν, μὴ ὁμολογήσωσι τῷ Πέρσῃ Ἀθηναῖοι, αὐτίκα τέ σφι ἔδοξε πέμπειν ἀγγέλους.

| σφι | Dat. 3rd pers. pl. masc. pronoun |

3. καὶ τοὺς ξυμμάχους ἅμα ἐδέδισαν σφῶν, μὴ διὰ τὰ σφάλματα ἐπαιρόμενοι ἐπὶ πλέον ἀποστῶσι ...

| ἐδέδισαν | 3rd pers. pl. Past Perf. Indic. Act. δεδιέναι |

LESSON 35. EXPRESSIONS OF FEARING

4. ... δείσαντες δέ, μὴ οὐ σφίσι πιστοὶ ὦσι, πέμπουσι ἐς Λακεδαίμονα ἑλόμενοι πρεσβευτὴν Τεισαμενόν.

| πέμπουσι | Hist. Pres. |
| πρεσβευτής, -οῦ, ὁ | *ambassador* |

5. ξύμφημι δή σοι καὶ δέδοικα, μὴ 'κ θεοῦ πληγή τις ἥκει.

| πληγή, -ῆς, ἡ | *blow* (lit. and metaphorical) |

6. τὸ δὲ θατέρου σχῆμα διὰ τὴν ἐν τοῖς λόγοις κυλίνδησιν ἔχει πολλὴν ὑποψίαν καὶ φόβον, ὡς ἀγνοεῖ ταῦτα ...

θατέρου	τοῦ ἑτέρου
σχῆμα, -ατος, τό	*character*
κυλίνδησις, -εως, ἡ	*involvement*
ὑποψία, -ας, ἡ	*suspicion*

7. φόβος γάρ, εἴ μοι ζῶσιν, οὓς ἐγὼ θέλω.

8. So then, are *we* to fear this [man], whom fortune and the divine demonstrate [to be] an unprofitable friend and an appropriate foe?

So then, ...;	εἶτα ...;
divine	δαιμόνιος, -α, -ον
to demonstrate	ἐμφανίζειν
unprofitable	λυσιτελής, -ές
appropriate	συμφέρων, -ουσα, -ον (Partc. as ordinary adj.)

9. ... and I would be afraid to follow the guide whom he gave, in case he led us [to a place] from where it will not be possible to go out.

guide	ἡγεμών, -όνος, ὁ
gave, led	Both terms refer to a future possibility.
in case	μή + Subj.

LESSON 36
Nominative and Vocative Cases

36.1. Nominative as Subject

The primary function of the Nominative Case is to express the Subject of a finite verb.

ἰδίᾳ γὰρ ταῦτα **οἱ Κορίνθιοι** ἔπραξαν. (Th. 1.66.)
For **the Corinthians** did this independently.

36.2. Nominative as Complement

The Nominative also expresses the Complement of verbs such as 'to be', 'to become', or 'to seem (to be)'. The Complement refers back to the Subject.

οὐκ ἦσθ' ἄρ' ὀρθῶς τοῦδε σώματος **πατήρ**; (E.Alc. 636.)
Were you, then, not genuinely **father** of this person?

The noun Complement refers back to the Subject contained within the verb ἦσθα.

εἰ γὰρ δόξει **δίκαιος** εἶναι, ἔσονται αὐτῷ τιμαὶ καὶ δωρεαὶ δοκοῦντι τοιούτῳ εἶναι· (Pl.R. 361 B–C.)

For if he is going to seem to be **just**, there will be honours and gifts for him as seeming to be such.

The adjectival Complement refers back to the Subject contained within the verb δόξει.

36.3. Predicate Nominative with Passive Verb

Some verbs in the Active Voice may take a double direct Object, where the second Accusative term is a predicate of the first.

ποῦ χρὴ τίθεσθαι ταῦτα, ποῦ δ' αἰνεῖν, ὅταν
τὰ θεῖ' ἐπαινῶν **τοὺς θεοὺς** εὕρω **κακούς**; (S.*Ph.* 451–452.)

*How should I regard this, and how approve, when
while I praise the <actions> of the gods I find **the gods nasty**?*

κακούς (without article) refers back to τοὺς θεούς (with article).

If such Active constructions are transposed to the Passive Voice, the first Accusative becomes the Subject and the predicate Accusative becomes a predicate Nominative.

κεῖνος δ' ἀπ' οἴκων εὐθὺς ἐξορμώμενος
ἄνους καλῶς λέγοντος ηὑρέθη πατρός. (S.*Aj.* 762–763.)

*But that <man>, as soon as he was setting out from home,
was found <to be> **senseless**, although his father spoke well.*

The Active equivalent of this expression would be: 'they found that <man> <to be> senseless'. In the actual Passive expression, the first Accusative ('that <man>') becomes the Subject; and the predicate Accusative ('senseless') becomes a predicate Nominative (ἄνους).

36.4. Quoted Nominative

A term may be quoted in the Nominative, even if the syntax of its clause requires another Case (usually Acc., in practice). Sometimes, the quoted term appears without introduction, or preceded only by the neuter singular definite article τό (regardless of the Number and Gender of the quoted term itself). Sometimes, a word such as ὄνομα ('term') or σύνθημα ('watchword') introduces the quoted term.

ταῦτ' εἰπὼν καὶ σύνθημα παρεγγυήσας **Ζεὺς σωτὴρ καὶ ἡγεμὼν** ἐπορεύετο. (X.*Cyr.* 7.1.10.)

*After saying this and passing along the watchword **'Zeus saviour and leader'**, he moved on.*

36.5. Nominative Address

Nominative forms are sometimes used with a Vocative function. (In poetry there may be metrical reasons for this usage.) In the following sentence, στυγνός is unambiguously Nominative: the Vocative form is στυγνέ. The form αἰών in itself may be either Nominative or Vocative; but, following στυγνός, it is to be understood as Nominative. The Main verbs of the sentence (ἔχεις, ἀφῆκας) address the 'life' (αἰών) in the second person singular. The opening phrase ὦ στυγνὸς αἰών is, thus, a Nominative address, not an exclamation.

ὦ στυγνὸς αἰών, τί με, τί δῆτ' ἔχεις ἄνω
βλέποντα, κοὐκ ἀφῆκας εἰς Ἅιδου μολεῖν; (S.Ph. 1348–1349.)

O hateful life, *why, why indeed do you keep me up here
seeing <the light of day>, and <why> did you not allow me to go to <the house> of Hades?*

36.6. Nominative Exclamation

In the following quotation, there is no Main verb. In the long opening phrase, all nouns and adjectives, except one, are unambiguously Nominative. The form νυμφεῖον, therefore, which could in itself be either Nominative or Vocative, should be understood as Nominative. The opening phrase is thus a Nominative exclamation.

**ὦ τύμβος, ὦ νυμφεῖον, ὦ κατασκαφὴς
οἴκησις ἀείφρουρος**, οἷ πορεύομαι
πρὸς τοὺς ἐμαυτῆς, ὧν ἀριθμὸν ἐν νεκροῖς
πλεῖστον δέδεκται Φερσέφασσ' ὀλωλότων· (S.Ant. 891–894.)

*O tomb, O bridal chamber, O deep-hollowed
dwelling ever-guarding*, *to where I am going
to my own <relatives>, the largest number of whom,
having perished, Persephone has received among the dead.*

36.7. Vocative

The Vocative Case is used to address someone or something. It is isolated from the syntax of the sentence in which it occurs. Hence, it has sometimes been regarded as 'not really a case'. However, the forms of the Vocative are just as much a part of the inflexion of nouns and adjectives as the other Cases. But again, the Vocative uses the shortest form of the stem of nouns and adjectives. And, although some subtypes of the three main declensions have separate forms for the Vocative, other subtypes use the same form as the Nominative. For example, ἄνθρωπε (2nd declension masc. sg. Voc.) is distinguished from ἄνθρωπος (Nom.); but τέκνον (2nd declension neut. sg.) serves both as Nominative and as Vocative.

Vocative forms are frequently preceded by ὦ. (Conventionally, ὦ is used with Vocatives, and ὤ with exclamations. But this convention is not consistently observed in manuscripts and printed texts.) Especially where there are not separate forms for Nominative and Vocative, a preceding ὦ helps to indicate the function of a Vocative phrase.

Typically, a Vocative is placed after the opening phrase of a sentence in order to catch the addressee's attention. However, since the positions of primary and secondary emphasis in a sentence are the beginning and the end, a Vocative may occur first or even last. When a Vocative phrase is placed first in a sentence, a connective particle may be delayed until after the Vocative.

In addition to its basic function, a Vocative phrase may mark the beginning of a new paragraph in speeches. For example, ὦ ἄνδρες is used after the opening phrase at Andocides 1.1, 3, 5, 6, 8, 10, etc.

παῦσαι δέ, **πρέσβυ**, παῖδα σὸν κακορροθῶν. (E.*Alc.* 707.)
*And stop, **old man**, abusing your son.*

Simple Voc. after opening phrase.

**ὦ τόνδε μὲν σώσασ', ἀναστήσασα δὲ
ἡμᾶς πίτνοντας**, χαῖρε, κἀν Ἅιδου δόμοις
εὖ σοι γένοιτο. (E.*Alc.* 625–627.)

*O you who saved this <man>, and raised us up
when we were falling, farewell, and may it go well for you
in the house of Hades.*

Elaborate Voc. with ὦ and Participial phrases at beginning of sentence.

γυνὴ μὲν οὖν ὄλωλεν Ἀδμήτου, **ξένε**. (E.*Alc.* 821.)
No, *<it is> the wife of Admetus <who> has perished,* ***friend***.

Simple Voc. at end of sentence (in stichomythia).

ὦ παῖ, σὺ δ' ἡμᾶς ἄπαγε πρὸς δόμους, ἵνα
τὸν θυμὸν οὗτος ἐς νεωτέρους ἀφῇ… (S.*Ant.* 1087–1088.)

But *you,* ***O <my> boy****, lead us away to our home, so that
this man may vent his anger on younger people* …

Connective particle δέ delayed until after opening Voc.

36.8. Hanging Vocative

Some Vocative phrases are left 'hanging' without a proper Main clause. This may happen when an opening Vocative phrase is immediately followed either by an explanatory clause with γάρ, or by an adjectival or adverbial clause.

**Ἀχελῴου θύγατερ,
πότνι' εὐπάρθενε Δίρκα,**
σὺ **γὰρ** ἐν σαῖς ποτε παγαῖς
τὸ Διὸς βρέφος ἔλαβες,
ὅτε μηρῷ πυρὸς ἐξ ἀθανάτου Ζεὺς
ὁ τεκὼν ἥρπασέ νιν, τάδ' ἀναβοάσας·
ἴθι, Διθύραμβ', ἐμὰν ἄρ-
σενα τάνδε βᾶθι νηδύν·
ἀναφαίνω σε τόδ', ὦ Βάκ-
χιε, Θήβαις ὀνομάζειν.
σὺ δέ μ', **ὦ μάκαιρα Δίρκα**,
στεφανηφόρους ἀπωθῇ
θιάσους ἔχουσαν ἐν σοί. (E.*Ba.* 519–532.)

***Achelous's daughter,
virgin queen Dirce****, <I invoke you>;
for you once received in your waters
the infant-child of Zeus,
when Zeus who begot him snatched him
from the immortal fire <and put him> in his thigh, letting out this cry:
'Come, Dithyrambos, enter this*

> *male womb of mine;*
> *I proclaim to Thebes, O Bacchius,*
>   *that I call you by this name'.*
> *But you thrust me away from yourself,*
> ***O blessed Dirce****, when I hold*
> *my garlanded celebrations on you<r banks>.*

In this passage, the Chorus of Bacchants address the river Dirce and then immediately explain why they are invoking the addressee. The construction drifts away from the Vocative by way of the explanatory clause with γάρ, a Temporal clause with ὅτε and direct quotation of the cry of Zeus. At this point, the Chorus state their complaint against Dirce ('But you thrust me away …') and renew the Vocative in briefer form ('O blessed Dirce').

> ἰὼ **δαῖμον**,
> μόνον **ὅς** με κασίγνητον συλᾷς
> Ἅιδᾳ πέμψας, ᾧ τάσδε χοὰς
> μέλλω κρατῆρά τε τὸν φθιμένων
> ὑδραίνειν γαίας ἐν νώτοις
> πηγάς τ' οὐρείων ἐκ μόσχων
> Βάκχου τ' οἰνηρὰς λιβὰς
> ξουθᾶν τε πόνημα μελισσᾶν,
> ἃ νεκροῖς θελκτήρια κεῖται. (E.*IT* 157–166.)

> *Ah,* ***deity****,*
> ***who****, by sending <him> to Hades, rob<bed> me*
> *of my only brother, for whom I am going to sprinkle*
> *on the surface of the earth this*
> *bowl of liquid-offerings for the departed:*
> *streams from the mountain heifers*
> *and libations of the wine of Bacchus*
> *and produce of the busy bees,*
> *which are appointed as charms for the dead.*

Hanging Vocative with adjectival clause.

LESSON 36. NOMINATIVE AND VOCATIVE CASES

Ἀσιάτιδος γῆς **σχῆμα, Θηβαία πόλι**,
ὅθεν ποθ' ἕδνων σὺν πολυχρύσῳ χλιδῇ
Πριάμου τύραννον ἑστίαν ἀφικόμην
δάμαρ δοθεῖσα παιδοποιὸς Ἕκτορι,
ζηλωτὸς ἔν γε τῷ πρὶν Ἀνδρομάχη χρόνῳ,
νῦν δ', εἴ τις ἄλλη, δυστυχεστάτη γυνή· (E.Andr. 1–6.)

Form *of the Asian land,* ***city of Thebe****,*
from where *once with the glory of my dowry rich-in-gold*
I came to the royal hearth of Priam
given as wife to produce children for Hector,
Andromache, to be envied at least in that early time,
but now, if anyone else <is>, a most unfortunate woman.

Hanging Vocative with adverbial clause.

References

Denniston (1954), *The Greek particles*, pp. lx, 189 (on postponement of connective particles in sentences beginning with a Vocative, exclamation or oath); 60 (γάρ clauses explaining what has just been said, including hanging Vocatives).

Smyth (1956), *Greek grammar*, §§907, 917–918, 927, 938–945, 973–974 (Nominative); 949–972 (variations of agreement in Number between Subject and Predicate); 1283–1288 (Vocative).

EXERCISE 36

1. Translate the following passages.
2. Indicate for each term or phrase printed in **bold type**:
   - whether it is Nominative or Vocative in function
   - whether, if Nominative (except Nom. Address), it is Subject, Complement, predicative Nominative or quoted Nominative, and with which verb (citing the form in the text) it is constructed
   - whether, if Vocative, it is a particular usage (hanging Voc., initial Voc. with delayed connective particle, etc.)
   - whether there are contextual grounds for deciding the *function* of any examples which are ambiguous in *form*.

Example

ἀφικόμενος προπέρυσιν εἰς τὴν πόλιν, οὔπω δύο μῆνας ἐπιδεδημηκὼς κατελέγην **στρατιώτης**. (Lys. 9.4.)

*Having arrived the year before last in the city, when I had not yet been in residence for two months I was enlisted <as> **a soldier**.*

Predicate Nominative with Passive verb κατελέγην.

1. ὁ δὲ **πρεσβύτης** ἀκούσας ἔδεισέ τε καὶ ἀπῄει σιγῇ...

πρεσβύτης, -ου, ὁ	*old man*
δεῖσαι (Aor.)	*to become afraid*

2. ἐδόκει γὰρ αὐτοῖς ... **πολὺς** ὁ παράλογος εἶναι ...

παράλογος, -ου, ὁ	*uncertain element* (adj. as noun)

3. αὐτὸς δὲ δοκῶν εὐνούστατος εἶναι ... **στρατηγὸς** ὑπ' αὐτῶν ᾑρέθη.

4. ἕως δ' ἔτι ἔξω βελῶν ἦσαν, παρηγγύα ὁ Κῦρος σύνθημα **Ζεὺς σύμμαχος καὶ ἡγεμών**.

ἔξω	*outside <the range of>*

5. ψυχὴ γὰρ ηὔδα πολλά μοι μυθουμένη· **τάλας**, τί χωρεῖς οἷ μολὼν δώσεις δίκην;

αὐδᾶν	*to speak out* (here Intr.)
μυθεῖσθαι (Mid.)	*to converse* (+ internal Acc. and Dat.)

6. φέρε δή, **ὦ ἄνδρες**, μετὰ ταῦτα τί ἐγένετο;

φέρε δή	*well now* (+ rhetorical question)

7. **ὦ γῆς μέγιστα τῆσδ' ἀεὶ τιμώμενοι**, οἷ' ἔργ' ἀκούσεσθ', οἷα δ' εἰσόψεσθ', ὅσον δ' ἀρεῖσθε πένθος ...

αἴρεσθαι (Mid.)	*to take upon oneself*

8. ἥκω κακοῖσι σοῖσι συγκάμνων, **τέκνον**·

9. **ἰήϊε Φοῖβε**, σοὶ **δὲ**
   ταῦτ' ἀρέστ' εἴη.

ἰήϊος, (-α,) -ον	*healing*
ἀρεστός, -ά, -όν	*pleasing* (accent affected by elision)

10. **ὦ παγκάκιστε**, τοῦτο **γάρ** σ' εἰπεῖν ἔχω
    γλώσσῃ μέγιστον εἰς ἀνανδρίαν κακόν·

LESSON 37
Accusative Case

37.1. Accusative as Direct Object

37.1.1. Simple Direct Object

The most basic function of the Accusative Case is to express the direct Object of a verb.

καί μοι ἐπίλαβε **τὸ ὕδωρ.** (Lys. 23.4.)
And please stop **the water(-clock).**

37.1.2. Predicate Accusative

A second Accusative term may be added to the simple direct Object after factitive verbs such as 'to make', 'to appoint', 'to think', 'to call' (somebody something). (Cf. Lesson 36.3.)

... οἱ βουλεύοντες γεραίτεροι αἱροῦνται αὐτὸν **ἄρχοντα** τῆς εἰς Μήδους στρατιᾶς. (X.*Cyr.* 1.5.5.)

... *the elders sitting in council chose* [Hist. Pres.] *him **commander** of the expedition to the Medes.*

37.1.3. Double Object

Some verbs may have a double Object, where the second Accusative is not predicative. Frequently, the first Object is a person, the second a thing, for example, 'to teach' somebody something, 'to ask' somebody something and (in Greek) 'to deprive' somebody (of) something or 'to conceal' something (from) somebody.

πᾶσι γὰρ ἀνθρώποισιν ἐπιχθονίοισιν ἀοιδοὶ
τιμῆς ἔμμοροί εἰσι καὶ αἰδοῦς, οὕνεκ' ἄρα **σφέας**
οἴμας μοῦσ' ἐδίδαξε, φίλησε δὲ φῦλον ἀοιδῶν.
(Hom.*Od.* 8.479–481.)

For among all people on the earth singers
are participants in honour and respect, just because the muse
*taught **them the ways** <of singing>, and loved the race of singers.*

The second Object is an ordinary noun.

Τηλέμαχ', ἦ μάλα δή **σε** διδάσκουσιν θεοὶ αὐτοὶ
ὑψαγόρην τ' **ἔμεναι** καὶ θαρσαλέως **ἀγορεύειν**.
(Hom.*Od.* 1.384–385.)

*Telemachus, assuredly the gods themselves are teaching **you***
***to be** a boaster and **to speak** boldly.*

The second Object is a pair of Infinitive phrases (i.e. verbal noun phrases).

37.1.4. Retained Accusative

When a verb, which may take a double Object of person and thing, is used in the Passive Voice, the person becomes the Subject and the thing is 'retained' in the Accusative.

ἐν γὰρ τῇ πόλει τῇ ἡμετέρᾳ αὐτῶν ... σεσυλήμεθα **τὰ ἡμέτερ'**
αὐτῶν ὑπὸ Φασηλιτῶν ... (D. 35.26.)

*For in our own city ... we have been robbed of **our own <possessions>** by the people of Phaselis ...*

Active equivalent: 'The people of Phaselis have robbed us of our own <possessions>' (double Acc.).

An equivalent Passive construction may be used with verbs, which in the Active take a direct Object of the thing in the Accusative and an indirect Object of the person in the Dative. For example, ἐπιστέλλειν in the Active Voice may mean 'to give instructions (Acc.) to someone (Dat.)'.

καὶ οἱ μὲν Βοιωτοὶ καὶ Κορίνθιοι **ταῦτα** ἐπεσταλμένοι ... ἑκάτεροι ἀνεχώρουν. (Th. 5.37.1.)

*And the Boeotians and the Corinthians, having been given **these** instructions ... both withdrew.*

Active equivalent: 'having given these instructions to the Boeotians and Corinthians' (Acc. and Dat.).

37.1.5. Accusative with a Phrase Equivalent to a Verb

An Accusative term sometimes provides a virtual direct Object for a phrase, in which a verb with Object is equivalent to a simple verb.

ὑμεῖς δ' ἐπευφημήσατ᾽, ὦ νεανίδες,
παιᾶνα τἠμῇ συμφορᾷ Διὸς **κόρην**
Ἄρτεμιν· (E.*IA* 1467–1469.)

But you, O young women, sing
praise *<to>* ***the daughter*** *of Zeus,* ***Artemis****, for my situation.*

The phrase ἐπευφημήσατ(ε) ... παιᾶνα is equivalent to παιωνίσατε ('praise') with direct Object κόρην Ἄρτεμιν. Some scholars prefer to explain this construction in terms of a noun directly dependent on another noun (of action), without reference to a verb.

37.1.6. Accusative of Whole and Part

Sometimes a direct Object is more narrowly defined by a second Accusative in apposition with it. The usage is mainly poetic.

μέθες **με**, πρὸς θεῶν, **χεῖρα**, φίλτατον τέκνον. (S.*Ph.* 1301.)

Let ***me*** *go, by the gods, <let go my>* ***hand****, dearest boy.*

37.1.7. Cognate Accusative

So far in this Lesson, all examples in §§37.1.1–3 and 37.5–6 have contained 'external' or 'affected' Objects. The action of the verb is exercised upon an already existing person or thing. An 'internal' or 'effected' Object denotes the content or result of the action of the verb: the grammatical Object does not exist until the action of the verb takes place. Usually such an internal or effected Object is a noun either etymologically or conceptually related to (or 'cognate' with) the verb whose Object it is. Otherwise, the cognate Accusative may be a demonstrative or relative adjective used as a pronoun.

πλεῖς δ' ὡς πρὸς οἶκον, ἐκλιπὼν τὸ ναυτικὸν
στράτευμ' Ἀχαιῶν, **ἔχθος** ἐχθήρας **μέγα** ... (S.*Ph.* 58–59.)

*And you are sailing as for home, leaving the naval
expedition of the Achaeans, having developed **a great hatred** ...*

The Accusative ἔχθος is etymologically cognate with ἐχθήρας.

... ἀλλ' αὐτός, ὦ παῖ, **τοῦτο** κήδευσον **λέχος**. (S.*Tr.* 1227.)
... *but you yourself, my boy, undertake **this marriage**.*

The Accusative λέχος is conceptually cognate with κήδευσον.

Λάμαχος μὲν **ταῦτα** εἰπὼν ὅμως προσέθετο καὶ αὐτὸς τῇ Ἀλκιβιάδου γνώμῃ. (Th. 6.50.1.)

*Although having made **these** statements, Lamachus himself nevertheless sided with the opinion of Alcibiades.*

The internal Accusative of the demonstrative adjective ταῦτα refers to the content of the verb. (In the second example in §37.1.4 above, ταῦτα is a retained internal Acc.)

Verbs sometimes have both an internal and an external Object. Verbs meaning 'to divide, to distribute' belong to this group.

τρεῖς μοίρας ὁ Ξέρξης δασάμενος **πάντα τὸν πεζὸν στρατόν**, μίαν αὐτέων ἔταξε παρὰ θάλασσαν ἰέναι ὁμοῦ τῷ ναυτικῷ· (Hdt. 7.121.2.)

*Dividing **all the infantry force** <into> **three parts**, Xerxes appointed one of them to go along the sea<-coast> parallel with the fleet.*

The 'infantry force' existed before the division was made (external Object), but the 'three parts' did not exist until the division was made (internal Object).

37.1.8. Oaths

Verbs of swearing take various Objective constructions:

1. to swear to do something (mostly Intentive/'Fut.' Infin.), or that one is doing something (Imperf. Infin.), or did something (Aor. Infin.), or would have done something (Aor. Infin. with ἄν) or that one has done something (Perf. Infin.). See Lesson 16.3.

2. (a) to swear an oath (internal Acc.).

   τὰς δὲ βασιληίας ἱστίας νόμος Σκύθησι τὰ μάλιστα ἐστὶ τότε ἐπεὰν **τὸν μέγιστον ὅρκον** ἐθέλωσι **ὀμνύναι**. (Hdt. 4.68.2.)

   *And it is the custom for the Scythians generally to swear by the king's hearth(s) then, when(ever) they want **to swear the most serious oath**.*

   (b) to swear to something, to confirm by oath (external Acc.).

   εἰρήνην μὲν γὰρ **ὠμωμόκει**· (D. 9.16.)
   *For **he had sworn to peace**.*

   (c) to swear by someone or something (external Acc.).

   καὶ λέγουσι οὗτοι ὡς τὸ ἐπίπαν μάλιστα τάδε, ὡς **τὰς βασιληίας ἱστίας ἐπιώρκηκε** ὃς καὶ ὅς, λέγοντες τῶν ἀστῶν τὸν ἂν δὴ λέγωσι. (Hdt. 4.68.1.)

   *And these [Scythians] for the most part generally say this, that so and so (stating whoever they actually state of the townsmen) **has sworn falsely by the king's hearth(s)**.*

3. An oath formula may also be used parenthetically in the Accusative. Various positive, negative or neutral particles may precede the oath.

   μὰ τοὺς παρ' Ἅιδῃ νερτέρους ἀλάστορας,
   οὔτοι ποτ' ἔσται τοῦθ', ὅπως ἐχθροῖς ἐγὼ
   παῖδας παρήσω τοὺς ἐμοὺς καθυβρίσαι. (E.Med. 1059–1061.)

   By the avengers below with Hades,
   *this will certainly not ever be, that **I should give up** my own children for my enemies to maltreat.*

37.2. Adverbial Uses of the Accusative

Several uses of the Accusative are more appropriately regarded as adverbial, expressing relationships of space, time, manner, degree and respect.

37.2.1. Accusative of Goal (or 'motion towards')

ἥκω Διὸς παῖς **τήνδε** Θηβαίων **χθόνα** ... (E.*Ba*. 1.)
*I have come the son of Zeus **to this land** of the Thebans ...*

This usage is poetic.

37.2.2. Accusative of Extent of Space

Μενέλαε, μαστεύων σε κιγχάνω μόλις,
πᾶσαν πλανηθεὶς **τήνδε βάρβαρον χθόνα** ... (E.*Hel*. 597–598.)

*Menelaus, in my search I scarcely <manage to> reach you,
after wandering **all over this foreign land** ...*

General area.

ἀπέχει δὲ ἡ Πλάταια τῶν Θηβῶν **σταδίους ἑβδομήκοντα** ... (Th. 2.5.2.)

*And Plataea is distant **seventy stades** from Thebes ...*

Specific distance. (70 stades = c. 13 km.)

37.2.3. Accusative of Extent of Time

... **τὸν** μὲν **πρῶτον ἐνιαυτὸν** ἐν Πειραιεῖ διῃτῶντο· (Lys. 32.8.)
*... they lived **for the first year** in the Piraeus.*

37.2.4. Accusative of Manner

... καὶ ἀντικαταστάντες ταῖς ναυσὶ **τὸν αὐτὸν τρόπον** αὖθις ἐπὶ πολὺ διῆγον τῆς ἡμέρας πειρώμενοι ἀλλήλων ... (Th. 7.39.2.)

*... and taking their stand in opposition with their ships, **in the same way** they again continued for a large part of the day making attempts on each other ...*

37.2.5. Accusative of Degree

Degree is often expressed by the neuter Accusative singular or plural of adjectives of size and number, indefinite adjectives or negative adjectives.

πολὺ δὲ ἐν πλέονι αἰτίᾳ ἡμεῖς μὴ πείσαντες ὑμᾶς ἕξομεν· (Th. 1.35.4.)

*But we shall hold you **much** more at fault if we do not persuade you.*

πολύ (adverbial Acc. of Degree) modifies the Comparative adjective πλέονι.

37.2.6. Accusative of Respect

With verbs used intransitively or in the Passive Voice or with adjectives, the Accusative may denote the respect in which the verb or adjective is defined. The usage ranges from the completely general ('in all respects'), through spheres of activity or attributes, to the body or especially a part of the body.

ἦ **πολλὰ** πολλοῖς εἰμι **διάφορος** βροτῶν. (E.Med. 579.)
*Certainly **in many respects** I am **in disagreement** with many among mortals.*

General; with adjective.

οὐ γὰρ δέσποιν' ἐμὴ
Μήδεια πύργους γῆς ἔπλευσ' Ἰωλκίας
ἔρωτι **θυμὸν ἐκπλαγεῖς**' Ἰάσονος· (E.Med. 6–8.)

*For my mistress Medea
would not have sailed to the ramparts of the land of Iolcus,
struck in her heart with love for Jason.*

Particular; with Pass. Partc.

... ὁ Ἱστιαῖος ... τιτρώσκεται **τὸν μηρὸν** ὑπό τευ τῶν Μιλησίων. (Hdt. 6.5.2.)

*... Histiaeus ... was wounded **in the thigh** by one of the Milesians.*

Here the Accusative of Respect denotes the part of the body of Histiaeus which 'was wounded' (Pass.; Hist. Pres.). Although this usage has been classified as adverbial, it is essentially the Passive form of the Accusative of whole and part (classified as direct Object at §37.1.6 above). The Active form of the present sentence would be: 'One of the Milesians wounded Histiaeus [Acc. of whole] <in> the thigh [Acc. of part]': τῶν Μιλησίων τις τὸν Ἱστιαῖον τιτρώσκει τὸν μηρόν.

37.3. Accusative in Apposition to a Sentence

Sometimes, an Accusative appears to be independent of its sentence and to refer to a phrase, clause or even all the rest of the sentence. For some instances, the rationale of an 'internal Accusative' is plausible. In other instances, the Accusative may be regarded as being in apposition with another Accusative (or Object Infin.). But sometimes these explanations seem strained, except as background to a stereotyped construction.

καὶ **τῶνδ' ἔλεγχον** τοῦτο μὲν Πυθώδ' ἰὼν
πεύθου τὰ χρησθέντ' εἰ σαφῶς ἤγγειλά σοι. (S. *OT* 603–604.)

*And **as proof of this**, first go to Pytho
and inquire, whether I clearly reported the oracle to you.*

Creon is addressing Oedipus. 'This' is Creon's claim that he has no designs on the kingship of Thebes. 'First' translates τοῦτο μέν (an adverbial Acc.). The first item of 'proof' is finding out whether Creon clearly reported the oracle to Oedipus. Thus, the whole content of the sentence after the 'Accusative in apposition' constitutes the 'proof'. ἔλεγχον is not in apposition with any other Accusative in the sentence, and it hardly provides an 'internal Accusative' for any verbal element in the sentence.

References

Smyth (1956), *Greek grammar*, §§985, 991, 1551–1635, 2894 (μά); 2922 (ναί); 2923 (νή).

EXERCISE 37

Translate the following passages. Comment briefly on the function of the Accusative phrases in **bold type** in each passage, for example, direct Object of what verb (citing the form in the text), Accusative in apposition with (the rest of) the sentence.

LESSON 37. ACCUSATIVE CASE

Example

διδάσκουσι δὲ **τοὺς παῖδας** καὶ **σωφροσύνην**·(X.*Cyr.* 1.2.8.)
And they teach their children moderation also.

Double direct Object of διδάσκουσι, person and thing.

1. τί δῆτα χρῄζεις; ἢ **δόμους** στείχειν **ἐμούς**;

2. θανάτῳ γὰρ ἴσον **πάθος** ἐκπεύσῃ.

3. ... τοὺς Ἀσσυρίους **ὑποχειρίους** ἐποιήσαντο πλὴν τῆς Βαβυλωνίης μοίρης.

μοῖρα, -ας (Ionic -ης), ἡ	*province*

4. ... λέξον ἡμῖν πόθεν ἤρξατό **σε** διδάσκειν **τὴν στρατηγίαν**.

πόθεν	*how*

5. ... **τελευτὴν** τοῦ βίου μέλλει τελεῖν ...

μέλλει	*The Subject is masc.*

6. ... ἦσαν **τὴν** πρὸς τὸ ὄρος φέρουσαν **ὁδὸν** ἐς Ἐρυθράς ...

7. σπονδὰς τέμωμεν καὶ διαλλάχθητί μοι.

σπονδή, -ῆς, ἡ (pl.)	*agreement, treaty*
τέμνειν	*to make peace*
διαλλάσσειν (usu. mid.)	*to speak*

8. οἱ δὲ Συρακόσιοι καὶ οἱ ξύμμαχοι προσέκειντο **τὸν αὐτὸν τρόπον** ...

προσκεῖσθαι	*to press hard (upon)* (+ Dat., when expressed)

9. ... ὡς αὐτίκα μάλα **τὰς γνάθους** ἀλγήσετε.

ὡς	*how ...!* (exclamatory with ἀλγήσετε)
γνάθος, -ου, ἡ	*jaw*

10. **Ἕκτορα** δ' αἰνὸν ἄχος πύκασε **φρένας** ἡνιόχοιο.

πυκάζειν	to cover
ἡνίοχος, -ου (-οιο), ὁ	charioteer

11.   ... κούφοις πνεύμασιν βόσκου, νέαν
ψυχὴν ἀτάλλων, μητρὶ τῇδε **χαρμονήν**.

βόσκειν	to feed (here Pass.)
ἀτάλλειν	to nurture, to rear
χαρμονή, -ῆς, ἡ	joy

12. ὅσοι τε **ἵππους** ἀπεστέρηνται, ταχὺ πάλιν ἄλλους ἵππους κτήσονται·

τε	Joins this sentence to the preceding

13. νῦν δ' εἶμι Φθίηνδ', ἐπεὶ ἦ **πολὺ** φέρτερόν ἐστιν
οἴκαδ' ἴμεν σὺν νηυσί ...

Φθίην-δ(ε)	to Phthia
φέρτερος, -α, -ον	better
ἴμεν	= ἰέναι
νηυσί (Epic/Ionic)	ναυσί (Attic)

LESSON 38
Genitive Case 1

38.1. Introduction

This Lesson deals with Genitive phrases which qualify a noun or pronoun; hence, they are sometimes called 'adnominal' Genitives. The function of such phrases is similar to that of an adjective; hence, they are also sometimes called 'adjectival' Genitives. All types of usage in this Lesson are basically Possessive.

38.2. Simple Possessive Genitive

The qualified noun belongs to the person or thing denoted by the Genitive phrase.

ἤδη δὲ τόνδε Θάνατον εἰσορῶ πέλας,
ἱερῆ θανόντων, ὅς νιν εἰς **Ἅιδου** δόμους
μέλλει κατάξειν. (E.Alc. 24–26.)

*And now I see Death here nearby,
priest of the dead, who is going to lead her down
to the house **of Hades**.*

The 'house' belongs to 'Hades'.

38.3. Subjective Genitive

Many Genitive phrases of a generally 'possessive' type may be subdivided as either 'Subjective' or 'Objective'. The Subjective Genitive corresponds to the Subject of a verb equivalent in meaning to the qualified noun.

οὐκ ἤρεσκέ σοι μόρον **Ἀδμήτου**
διακωλῦσαι, ...; (E.Alc. 32–33.)

*Was it not sufficient for you to prevent the fate **of Admetus** ...?*

'Admetus' (Subject) was due to suffer his 'fate'.

38.4. Objective Genitive

The Objective Genitive corresponds to the Object of a verb equivalent in meaning to the qualified noun.

... μετὰ δὲ τὴν **τῶν τυράννων** κατάλυσιν ἐκ τῆς Ἑλλάδος οὐ πολλοῖς ἔτεσιν ὕστερον καὶ ἡ ἐν Μαραθῶνι μάχη Μήδων πρὸς Ἀθηναίους ἐγένετο. (Th. 1.18.1.)

*... and after the removal **of the tyrants** from Greece, not many years later the battle at Marathon of the Persians against the Athenians also took place.*

The Spartans 'removed' 'the tyrants' (Object) from Greece.

38.5. Partitive Genitive

The Partitive Genitive denotes the whole class of which the qualified noun forms a part.

ἦσαν δὲ καὶ τοῖς Κορινθίοις ἐν τῇ ἠπείρῳ πολλοὶ **τῶν βαρβάρων** παραβεβοηθηκότες· (Th. 1.47.3.)

*And many **of the foreigners**, having come to help, were also <available> on the mainland for the Corinthians.*

The 'many' constitute a part of the total number of 'the foreigners'.

38.6. Genitive of Definition (or Apposition)

The Genitive of Definition is a more specific term which defines a more general word. Since both terms refer to the same reality, this usage is also called the Genitive of Apposition.

σπεύσεις **θανάτου** τελευτάν;
μηδὲν τόδε λίσσου. (E.*Med.* 153–154.)

*Will you hasten the end **that is death**?*
Make no prayer for this.

The 'end' is more closely defined as 'death'.

38.7. Genitive of Description (or Quality)

The Genitive of Description or Quality expresses the character or purpose of the qualified noun.

ὦ πατρίς, ὦ δώματα, μὴ
δῆτ' ἄπολις γενοίμαν
τὸν **ἀμηχανίας** ἔχουσα δυσπέρατον αἰῶν(α)... (E.*Med.* 645–648.)

O fatherland, O home, may I certainly
not become city-less,
*having that life **of helplessness**, hard to cross over ...*

'Helplessness' indicates the character of 'that life'.

38.8. Genitive of Material

The Genitive of Material (as also of Measure, and of Price or Value) may be considered a subtype of the Genitive of Description. The Genitive of Material indicates what the qualified noun is made of, or consists of.

... πρῶτοι δὲ ἀνθρώπων τῶν ἡμεῖς ἴδμεν νόμισμα **χρυσοῦ** καὶ **ἀργύρου** κοψάμενοι ἐχρήσαντο, ... (Hdt. 1.94.1.)

*... and they first among men whom we know stamped coinage **of gold** and **of silver** and used it ...*

The material of the 'coinage' is 'gold' and 'silver'. (Ionic τῶν = Attic ὧν, attracted to Case of antecedent. Ionic ἴδμεν = Attic ἴσμεν.)

38.9. Genitive of Measure

The Genitive of Measure describes the qualified noun by indicating its size or duration.

... κίνδυνόν τε τοσόνδε ἀνερρίψαμεν διὰ τῆς ἀλλοτρίας **πολλῶν ἡμερῶν** ὁδὸν ἰόντες καὶ πᾶν τὸ πρόθυμον παρεχόμενοι· (Th. 4.85.4.)

*... we ran so great a risk by travelling on a journey **of many days** through enemy territory and while showing all eagerness.*

The 'many days' indicate how much time the 'journey' takes.

38.10. Genitive of Price or Value

The Genitive of Price or Value describes the cost or worth of the qualified noun.

καίτοι ὁ μὲν ἐμὸς πατὴρ **πέντε καὶ τετταράκοντα μνῶν** μόνων ἑκατέρῳ, ἐμοὶ καὶ τῷ ἀδελφῷ, τὴν οὐσίαν κατέλιπεν ... (D. 42.22.)

*And yet my father bequeathed to each, my brother and me, the estate **of forty-five minae** only ...*

The 'estate' was worth 'forty-five minae'.

References

Smyth (1956), *Greek grammar*, §§1289–1338.

EXERCISE 38

Translate the following passages. Briefly indicate the particular function of the Genitive phrases in **bold** type. For example, Partitive Genitive, Genitive of Material, etc. In passages 2 and 3, the Genitive phrases are either Subjective or Objective; briefly indicate the reason for your choice between these two possibilities.

LESSON 38. GENITIVE CASE 1

1. ἀνέστησαν δὲ καὶ ἐκ τῆς νῦν Ἐορδίας καλουμένης Ἐορδούς, **ὧν** οἱ μὲν πολλοὶ ἐφθάρησαν, βραχὺ δέ τι **αὐτῶν** περὶ Φύσκαν κατῴκηται ...

ἀνιστάναι	*to remove* (people from a place)
βραχὺ ... τι (Nom. adj.)	Understand a noun such as *group*.

2. ... καὶ προῖκα ἐπιδίδωμι Ἀρχίππῃ τάλαντον μὲν τὸ ἐκ Πεπαρήθου, τάλαντον δὲ τὸ αὐτόθεν, συνοικίαν **ἑκατὸν μνῶν** ...

προίξ, προικός, ἡ	*dowry*
Πεπάρηθος, -ου, ἡ	(an Aegean island)
αὐτόθεν (adv.)	*from here* (referring to Athens)
συνοικία, -ας, ἡ	*tenement house*

3. βρόχον κρεμαστὸν **ἀγχόνης** ἀνήψατο.

ἀνήψατο	The implied Subject is fem.

4. ἔκλῃον οὖν τόν τε λιμένα εὐθὺς τὸν μέγαν, ἔχοντα τὸ στόμα **ὀκτὼ σταδίων** μάλιστα, τριήρεσι πλαγίαις καὶ πλοίοις καὶ ἀκάτοις ...

κλῄειν	*to shut up, to block* (here 3rd pers. pl.)
τε	Anticipates a καί (not quoted); need not be translated.
λιμήν, -ένος, ὁ	*harbour*
μάλιστα	*approximately*
πλάγιος, (-α,) -ον	*placed sideways, broadside on*
ἄκατος, -ου, ἡ (ὁ)	*light vessel*

5. ... πάρεισιν **ἀνδρὸς τοῦδε** παῖς τε καὶ γυνή ...

6. τοιάδ' ἐπ' αὐτοῖς ἦλθε συμφορὰ **πάθους**, ...

7. ... πέμπει ἐπὶ τὴν νέα τὴν Ἀδειμάντου τάλαντα **ἀργυρίου** τρία.

πέμπει	Hist. Pres.
ἀργύριον, -ου, τό	*silver*

8. … οὐκ οἶδα **τοιοῦδ' ἀνδρὸς** ἔργα …

9. … ἡ Δεκέλεια … πολλὰ ἔβλαπτε τοὺς Ἀθηναίους, καὶ ἐν τοῖς πρῶτον **χρημάτων** τ' ὀλέθρῳ καὶ **ἀνθρώπων** φθορᾷ ἐκάκωσε τὰ πράγματα.

Δεκέλεια, -ας, ἡ	*Decelea* (place)
πολλά	internal Acc.
ἐν τοῖς πρῶτον	*in the first place*
φθορά, -ᾶς, ἡ	*annihilation*

LESSON 39
Genitive Case 2

39.1. Introduction

This Lesson deals with Genitive constructions which are used with verbs, adjectives and adverbs. The function of such phrases is similar to that of an adverb; hence, they are sometimes called 'adverbial' Genitives. Some of the basically Possessive functions (including Partitive), which were treated in Lesson 38, may also be used predicatively with verbs. In addition, the Genitive of Separation (or Ablatival Gen.) includes a number of other particular functions.

39.2. Possessive Genitive

39.2.1. Complement and Equivalent of Predicate Nominative

The simple Possessive Genitive may be used predicatively as Complement of verbs meaning 'to be', 'to become', 'to seem'; and, as the equivalent of a predicate Nominative, with the Passive of verbs (whose Act. may take a predicate Acc.), such as 'to be called', 'to be considered'. (Cf. Lesson 36.2 and Lesson 36.3.)

… καὶ ἐγένετο Μεσσήνη **Λοκρῶν** τινα χρόνον. (Th. 5.5.1.)
… *and Messene became <the possession>* ***of the Locrians*** *for some time.*

Complement of ἐγένετο.

τίς δ' ἔσθ' ὁ χῶρος; **τοῦ** θεῶν νομίζεται; (S.*OC* 38.)
And which is the place? ***To which*** *of the gods is it regarded <as belonging>?*

Equivalent of predicative Nominative, with the Passive verb νομίζεται.

39.2.2. Complement to an Infinitive Subject

The simple Possessive Genitive may be used predicatively as Complement of the verb 'to be', where the Subject is an Infinitive phrase. This idiom expresses the idea: 'It is the nature/responsibility/habit etc. *of someone* to do something'. (Grammatically: 'To do something is <the nature etc.> of someone'.)

καίτοι τό γ' αἴνιγμ' οὐχὶ **τοὐπιόντος** ἦν **ἀνδρὸς** διειπεῖν, ἀλλὰ μαντείας ἔδει· (S.*OT* 393–394.)

*And yet it was not <the responsibility> **of any man who came along** to expound the riddle, but there was need of prophecy.*

39.2.3. Equivalent of Predicative Accusative

The simple Possessive Genitive may be used with the Active of verbs meaning 'to think', 'to make', 'to appoint', etc. as the equivalent of a predicative Accusative. (Cf. Lesson 37.1.2.)

ὃ δέ μιν προσιδὼν ἀντείρετο εἰ **ἑωυτοῦ** ποιέεται τὸ Κύρου ἔργον. (Hdt. 1.129.2.)

*And he, looking at him, asked in turn whether he regarded the action of Cyrus as **his own**.*

39.2.4. Genitive of Material

The Genitive of Material may modify a verb and indicate what something is made of. The Genitive may be a Complement of the verb 'to be' or the equivalent of a predicative Accusative with verbs such as 'to make'. (Cf. Lessons 36.2 and 37.1.2.)

... συγκειμένου σφι **πωρίνου λίθου** ποιέειν τὸν νηόν, **Παρίου** τὰ ἔμπροσθε αὐτοῦ ἐξεποίησαν. (Hdt. 5.62.3.)

*... although it had been agreed for them to make the temple **of limestone**, they made the front of it **of Parian <marble>**.*

(The adj. πωρίνου may alternatively refer to tufa.)

39.2.5. Genitive of Measure

The Genitive of Measure may be used as Complement of the verb 'to be'. (Cf. Lesson 36.2.)

ξυνέβησάν τε πρῶτα μὲν τὰ μακρὰ τείχη ἑλεῖν Ἀθηναίους (ἦν δὲ **σταδίων** μάλιστα **ὀκτὼ** ἀπὸ τῆς πόλεως ἐπὶ τὴν Νίσαιαν τὸν λιμένα αὐτῶν), … (Th. 4.66.3.)

*And they agreed that first the Athenians should take the long walls (and they were **of** approximately **eight stades** <in length> from the city to Nisaea their harbour), …*

39.2.6. Genitive of Price or Value

The Genitive of Price or Value may be used adverbially with appropriate verbs (such as 'to buy', 'to value') and with adjectives (such as ἄξιος, 'worth', 'worthy of').

κατεγγυῶντος γὰρ Μενεξένου πρὸς τὸν πολέμαρχον τὸν παῖδα, Πασίων αὐτὸν **ἑπτὰ ταλάντων** διηγγυήσατο. (Isoc. 17.14.)

*For when Menexenus required Pasion to give security before the polemarch for the slave, he provided security for him <to the amount> **of seven talents**.*

39.3. Partitive Genitive

As noted in Lesson 38 and in §39.1 above, the Partitive Genitive is properly a subcategory of the Possessive Genitive. The part 'belongs to' the whole.

39.3.1. Complement of the Verb 'to be'

The simple Partitive Genitive may form the Complement of verbs such as 'to be' or 'to become'.

καὶ ἐς οἴκημα οὐ μέγα ὃ ἦν **τοῦ ἱεροῦ** ἐσελθών, ἵνα μὴ ὑπαίθριος ταλαιπωροίη, ἡσύχαζεν. (Th. 1.134.1.)

*And entering a small room which was <**part**> **of the temple**, so that he might not suffer from exposure, he kept quiet.*

39.3.2. With Verbs Meaning 'to have or give a share of'

The simple Partitive Genitive may function as the Object of verbs meaning 'to have or give a share of'. This construction is analogous to the basic use of the Partitive Genitive with nouns. In the adnominal phrase 'one of the citizens', 'one' is the part and 'of the citizens' denotes the whole group (Gen. in Greek). So, in the present example, 'to have a share' or 'to take part' (μετέχειν) is followed by a Genitive phrase denoting the whole group of actions.

… Φείδων αἱρεθεὶς ὑμᾶς διαλλάξαι καὶ καταγαγεῖν **τῶν αὐτῶν ἔργων** Ἐρατοσθένει μετεῖχε … (Lys. 12.58.)

… *Phidon, having been chosen to reconcile you and bring you back, participated* **in the same actions** *as Eratosthenes* …

39.3.3. With Verbs of Perception

Verbs of perception may take a Genitive. For example, the common construction with verbs of hearing is Accusative of the sound, voice, etc. and/or Genitive of the person making the sound or possessing the voice. The sound, voice, etc. is part of the person or of the person's activity.

… εἰκὸς ὑμᾶς καὶ **τῶν κατηγόρων** ἀκροᾶσθαι … (Lys. 14.24.)
… *<it is> reasonable that you should listen also* **to accusers** …

The article τῶν is used generically.

39.3.4. Equivalent to a Direct Object

Sometimes a verb, which otherwise takes a direct Object in the Accusative, may take a Partitive Genitive equivalent to a direct Object. (Cf. Lesson 37.1.1.)

… λέγει ὅτι … ποιήσει ὥστε μήτε **τῶν τειχῶν** διελεῖν μήτε ἄλλο τὴν πόλιν ἐλαττῶσαι μηδέν· (Lys. 13.9.)

… *he said that … he would see to it that neither <would any one> take down* **<part> of the walls**, *nor <would> anything else diminish <the standing of> the city.*

λέγει is Historic Present. The Subject of the Infinitive διελεῖν is not explicit.

39.3.5. Genitive of Limits of Time

The Genitive of Limits of Time is a Partitive Genitive—an action takes place for only part of the time specified by the Genitive phrase.

… ᾤοντο **ὀλίγων ἐτῶν** καθαιρήσειν τὴν τῶν Ἀθηναίων δύναμιν … (Th. 5.14.3.)

*… they thought that **within a few years** they would demolish the power of the Athenians …*

ἔτεος δὲ **ἑκάστου** ἁμάξας πεντήκοντα καὶ ἑκατὸν ἐπινέουσι φρυγάνων· (Hdt. 4.62.2.)

*And [within] **each year** they pile on one hundred and fifty wagon-loads of sticks.*

The Genitive of Limits of Time is commonly used to express frequency.

39.3.6. Genitive of Limits of Space

Similarly, the Genitive of Limits of Space is a Partitive Genitive—an action takes place with reference only to part of the space specified by the Genitive phrase.

θαυμάζω δέ, ὦ ἄνδρες δικασταί, εἴ τις ἀξιοῖ, ἐὰν μέν τις προσιόντων τῶν πολεμίων **τῆς πρώτης τάξεως** τεταγμένος **τῆς δευτέρας** γένηται, τούτου μὲν δειλίαν καταψηφίζεσθαι, ἐὰν δέ τις ἐν τοῖς ὁπλίταις τεταγμένος ἐν τοῖς ἱππεῦσιν ἀναφανῇ, τούτῳ συγγνώμην ἔχειν. (Lys. 14.11.)

*And I am surprised, O men of the jury, that anyone thinks it right, if, as the enemy approaches, someone placed **in the first rank** turns up **in the second rank**, to vote this <man> guilty of cowardice, but if someone placed among the infantry appears among the cavalry, to grant pardon to this <man>.*

The construction with ἐν + Dat. (ἐν τοῖς ὁπλίταις, ἐν τοῖς ἱππεῦσιν) is practically equivalent in meaning to the Genitive construction.

39.3.7. Other Partitive Constructions

The Genitive used with many other verbs (and related adjectives or adverbs) is usually classed as Partitive. The following selected examples show that this classification is not always satisfactory.

In the expressions 'to fill something with water' (verb) or to be 'full of water' (adj.), 'water' regularly appears in the Genitive Case in Greek. The 'Partitive' rationale for this construction is that only some water (not all) is needed for the filling.

ἀλλ' ἐπάμυνε τάχιστα, καὶ ἐμπίμπληθι ῥέεθρα
ὕδατος ἐκ πηγέων, ... (Hom.*Il.* 21.311–312.)

Come, bring assistance very quickly, and fill your streams
with water *from your springs, ...*

River Scamander addresses River Simois.

ταφρὸς μὲν πρῶτά μιν βαθέα τε καὶ εὐρέα καὶ πλέη **ὕδατος** περιθέει, ... (Hdt. 1.178.3.)

First a moat runs round it [= Babylon], *deep and broad and full **of water**, ...*

It is not so clear that a Partitive explanation can be applied to the group of verbs meaning 'to remember, to forget; to care for, to neglect'.

... σὺ δέ, ὦ Νικόμαχε, ... μόνῳ σοὶ τῶν πολιτῶν ἐξεῖναι νομίζεις ἄρχειν πολὺν χρόνον, καὶ μήτε εὐθύνας διδόναι μήτε τοῖς ψηφίσμασι πείθεσθαι μήτε **τῶν νόμων** φροντίζειν ... (Lys. 30.5.)

*... but you, O Nicomachus ... think that it is permissible for you alone of the citizens to hold office for a long time, and neither to submit to an examination, nor to obey the decrees, nor to take notice **of the laws** ...*

φροντίζειν may take a direct Object in the Accusative when it means 'to consider'. When this verb takes a Genitive, it is most often negated and has the sense 'not to worry about'. And from Herodotus onwards, the Genitive may be used with the preposition περί. But it can hardly be said that Nicomachus is 'not worried about' *only some* of the laws. Thus, a Partitive explanation for the construction seems inadequate. Indeed, a Causal explanation seems more plausible: Nicomachus is 'not worried' *because of* the laws. The Causal Genitive is basically a Genitive of Separation (see §39.4.3 below).

The Genitive with adjectives, which are compounded with the negative prefix ἀ-, is usually classed as Partitive.

νέος μὲν καὶ **ἄπειρος δικῶν** ἔγωγε ἔτι, ... (Antipho 1.1.)
*For my part <I am> still young and **without experience of lawsuits**, ...*

Here, the speaker may be regarded as inexperienced 'within the sphere' of lawsuits, in a construction analogous to the Genitive of Limits of Time or Space.

39.4. Genitive of Separation

The Genitive of Separation is used with a wide range of verbs, adjectives and adverbs.

39.4.1. Simple Genitive of Separation

Most simply, the Genitive of Separation is used with verbs meaning 'to be distant from', 'to separate someone (Acc.) from something (Gen.)' or 'to deprive someone (Acc.) of something (Gen.)'.

καὶ νοσφιεῖς με **τοῦδε δευτέρου νεκροῦ**; (E.*Alc.* 43.)
*And will you deprive me **of this second corpse**?*

39.4.2. Genitive of Comparison

The Genitive of Comparison is a particular type of Genitive of Separation.

39.4.2.1. With Comparative Adjectives

The Comparative adjective qualifies the person or thing being compared; the Genitive indicates the standard of comparison. The idea of 'separation' is involved, in that some people may be, for example, more or less numerous or strong in 'departing from' the standard of others.

οὗτοι δὲ τὸ πλῆθος μὲν οὐκ ἐλάσσονες ἦσαν **τῶν Περσέων**, ῥώμῃ δὲ ἥσσονες. (Hdt. 8.113.3.)

*These were not less in number **than the Persians**, but were inferior in strength.*

39.4.2.2. With Verbs Denoting Difference

εἶτ' ἐμὴν ἀψυχίαν
λέγεις, **γυναικός**, ὦ κάκισθ', ἡσσημένος,
ἣ τοῦ καλοῦ σοῦ προύθανεν νεανίου; (E.*Alc.* 696–698.)

*Then do you speak of my faintheartedness, O <you> scoundrel, having become inferior **to your wife**, who died for you, her fine young man?*

39.4.3. Genitive of Cause

The Genitive of Cause is also a particular type of Genitive of Separation.

39.4.3.1. With Verbs of Emotion

The Genitive denotes Cause with verbs of emotion, such as 'to be surprised at' or 'to blame someone (Dat.) for something (Gen.)'. The idea of 'separation' is involved, in that the emotion 'arises from' the thing or person specified in the Genitive.

τιμῆς ἐμέμφθη σωφρονοῦντι δ' ἤχθετο. (E.*Hipp.* 1402.)
She [= Aphrodite] *complained **of the honour** <which you did not show her> and got annoyed with <you> for being restrained.*

39.4.3.2. In Exclamations

The following exclamation presents a standard form: first an interjection ('Oh alas'), then an explanation of the interjection, given in the Genitive. The interjection 'arises from' the matter specified in the Genitive.

ὦ πόποι **κεδνῆς ἀρωγῆς κἀπικουρίας** στρατοῦ. (A.*Pers.* 731.)
*Oh alas **for** our army's **trusty help and defence**!*

39.5. Genitive with Compound Verbs

The Genitive Case is used with some compound verbs, including multiple compounds (with more than one adverbial prefix). The type of Genitive usage depends on the meaning of a particular simple verb and on the meaning of its prefix(es). Legal terms with the prefix κατα– comprise a common group of compound verbs. For example, κατηγορεῖν takes (among other constructions) a Genitive of the person condemned, with or without an Accusative of the charge or crime.

... πολὺ μᾶλλον αὐτοὺς προσήκει **τῶν λιπόντων** τὴν τάξιν κατηγορεῖν ἢ ὑπὲρ τῶν τοιούτων ἀπολογεῖσθαι. (Lys. 14.21.)

*... it is much more appropriate for them to accuse **those who desert** their post than to make a defence on behalf of such people.*

References

Smyth (1956), *Greek grammar*, §§1339–1449.

EXERCISE 39

Translate the following passages. For each passage, briefly indicate the general and particular function of the Genitive phrases in **bold** type, for example, Partitive (general), Limits of Time (particular) and modifying which verb, adjective or adverb.

1. ... πορεύεσθαι διενοεῖτο πρὸς αὐτοὺς ἐπὶ τοῦ Ἑλλησπόντου, ὅπως μέμψηται ... **τῶν** περὶ τὴν Ἄντανδρον **γεγενημένων** ...

διανοεῖσθαι (Mid.)	to intend
περί (+ Acc.)	near

2. ... καὶ πλεύσαντες ἐς Λευκάδα τὴν Κορινθίων ἀποικίαν **τῆς γῆς** ἔτεμον καὶ Κυλλήνην ... ἐνέπρησαν ...

Κυλλήνην	Object of ἐνέπρησαν

3. **σφῷν** γὰρ ἐστερημένη
λυπρὸν διάξω βίοτον ἀλγεινόν τ' ἐμοί·

σφῷν	Gen. dual 2nd pers. pronoun

4. **τοῦ** δ' **ἐπιγιγνομένου θέρους** Πελοποννήσιοι καὶ οἱ ξύμμαχοι ἅμα τῷ σίτῳ ἀκμάζοντι ἐστράτευσαν ἐς τὴν Ἀττικήν ...

ἐπιγίγνεσθαι	to follow (chronologically)
ἅμα (adv.)	at the same time as (+ Dat. with Partc.)
ἀκμάζειν	to be ripe

5. ἐπειρώτεον ὧν οἱ Ἐπιδαύριοι κότερα **χαλκοῦ** ποιέωνται τὰ ἀγάλματα ἢ **λίθου**·

ἐπειρωτέειν (Ionic)	to inquire (here 3rd pers. pl. Past Imperf. Indic. Act.)
ὧν	οὖν (Attic)
κότερα (Ionic)	πότερα (Attic)
ἄγαλμα, -ατος, τό	statue
The two Gen. terms have the same function.	

6. αὐτουργοί τε γάρ εἰσι Πελοποννήσιοι καὶ ... **χρονίων πολέμων καὶ διαποντίων** ἄπειροι ...

αὐτουργός, -όν	self-employed
διαπόντιος, -ον	overseas

7. ὑμεῖς δ', ὦ ἄνδρες Ἀθηναῖοι, Σμίκρῳ **δέκα ταλάντων** ἐτιμήσατε ...

τιμᾶν	to set the penalty

8. ἐπεὶ πλείων χρόνος
ὃν δεῖ μ' ἀρέσκειν τοῖς κάτω **τῶν** ἐνθάδε.

τοῖς, τῶν	masc.

9. ... οὐ μνημονεύεις οὐκέτ' οὐδέν, ἡνίκα **ἑρκέων** ποθ' ὑμᾶς οὗτος ἐγκεκλημένους, ... ἐρρύσατ' ἐλθὼν μοῦνος ...;

οὐδέν	internal Acc. with μνημονεύεις
ἡνίκα ... μοῦνος	noun clause, Object of μνημονεύεις
ἕρκος, -ους, τό	fence, (line of) defence
(ἐ)ρύεσθαι (Mid.)	to rescue

LESSON 40
Dative Case 1

40.1. Introduction

The Dative Case covers two basic functions: denoting the persons whose *interests* are affected by an action or situation, and indicating *accompaniment* in the broadest sense. Lesson 40 treats the Dative of Interest and the Dative of Accompaniment in general. Lesson 41 will treat two further and particular categories of accompaniment: location in place or time, and means or instrument. The functions of the Dative Case are predominantly *adverbial*. However, nouns and adjectives, which are related to verbs, may also take a Dative construction. For example, the verb εὐνοεῖν and the adjective εὔνους used with εἶναι both mean 'to be well disposed (to)' and take a Dative.

40.2. Dative of Interest

40.2.1. Interest in General

A wide range of verbs and related nouns or adjectives take a Dative denoting the persons to or for whom an action is done.

πενθεῖν μέν, εἴ τι **δεσπόταισι** τυγχάνει,
συγγνωστόν· (E.*Alc.* 138–139.)

<*It is*> *pardonable to lament, if something happens* **to one's masters**.

Dative of Interest modifying verb τυγχάνει.

(Grammatically: 'To lament [Subject] <is> pardonable [Complement]'.)

σύνηθες αἰεὶ ταῦτα βαστάζειν **ἐμοί**. (E.*Alc.* 40.)
*<It is> customary **for me** to carry this constantly.*

Dative of Interest modifying adjective σύνηθες.

(Grammatically: 'To carry this constantly [Subject] <is> customary [Complement] for me'.)

40.2.2. Indirect Object

Verbs of saying, giving, etc. commonly take a direct Object in the Accusative and an indirect Object in the Dative.

... δίκας δὲ δώσεις **σοῖσι κηδεσταῖς** ἔτι. (E.*Alc.* 731.)
*... and you will yet give recompense **to your wife's-relatives**.*

40.2.3. Possessive

The Possessive Dative is used with verbs meaning 'to be' or 'to become', where the Subject (concrete or abstract) is or becomes the possession of the person designated by the Dative. A paraphrase with the verbs meaning 'to have' or 'to get' is often used, and the Subject in Greek then becomes the Object in English.

σοὶ δ' ἔστι μὲν νοῦς λεπτός· (E.*Med.* 529.)
*And **you** do have a subtle mind.*

Lit. 'And there exists for you a subtle mind'.

40.2.4. Agent

In classical Greek, the Agent of a Passive verb is usually expressed by ὑπό with Genitive. However, a Dative of Interest is frequently used with Passive verbs in the Perfect Aspect (and rarely with other Tenses). The Dative of Agent is also the normal construction with verbal adjectives ending in -τος and -τέος (Lessons 7.3 and 8.2).

τὰ δὲ χρήματα ἦν ταῦτα μεγάλα, ὡς δεδήλωταί **μοι** ἐν τῷ πρώτῳ τῶν λόγων. (Hdt. 5.36.4.)

*And this treasure was great, as has been made clear **by me** in the first of the books.*

40.2.5. Similarity

A Dative of Interest is used with adjectives and adverbs expressing similarity, including ὁ αὐτός meaning 'the same (as)'.

ἄνακτ' **ἄνακτι** ταὔθ' ὁρῶντ' ἐπίσταμαι
μάλιστα **Φοίβῳ** Τειρεσίαν, ... (S. *OT* 284–285.)

*I know that lord Tiresias generally sees the same things **as lord Phoebus**, ...*

40.2.6. Person Judging (or Reference)

The Dative denotes the person, from whose point of view something is valid. The Dative term may be a Participle only. The usage is common with topographical directions.

πρὸς τὰς μεγίστας δ' οὖν καὶ ἐλαχίστας ναῦς τὸ μέσον **σκοποῦντι** οὐ πολλοὶ φαίνονται ἐλθόντες, ... (Th. 1.10.5.)

*But at any rate **for someone examining** the midpoint* [OR: *average*] *in relation to the largest and the smallest ships, it is clear that not many <men> went, ...*

40.2.7. Purpose

The Dative, especially of abstract nouns, may be used to express the Purpose for which an action is performed.

... χρὴ ... θαρσοῦντας ἰέναι ... ἐς τὸν πόλεμον ... τῆς ἄλλης Ἑλλάδος ἁπάσης ξυναγωνιουμένης τὰ μὲν φόβῳ τὰ δὲ **ὠφελίᾳ**. (Th. 1.123.1.)

*... <we> should ... with high courage go ... into the war ... since all the rest of Greece will join in the struggle partly because of fear and partly **for advantage**.*

(In the context ὠφελία denotes the Purpose of obtaining help or advantage, not the Purpose of helping someone else.)

According to Smyth (1956, §1473), 'For the dative of purpose (*to what end?*), common in Latin with a second dative (*dono dare*), Greek uses a predicate noun: ἡ χώρα δῶρον ἐδόθη *the country was given to him as a* gift' (X.*HG* 3.1.6.). In this Greek example, the 'predicate noun' (δῶρον) is used in the Nominative Case with a Passive verb. But a double Dative may also be used with a Greek Passive verb. In Latin grammars, the 'second dative' is designated 'predicative dative'.

δόσει δέδοταί **μοι** ἐπὶ τῷ μισθῷ. (*Tobit* 2.14 Septuagint.)
*It has been given **to me as a gift** in addition to my pay.*

40.2.8. Ethic

The Dative of the personal pronouns (sg. or pl.) is used to express the interest of the first person or to catch the attention of the second person. (The idiom seldom occurs with the third person.) A paraphrase such as 'please' (1st pers.) or 'I tell you' (2nd pers.) is often appropriate. Typically, the pronoun appears near the beginning of a Main clause and, therefore, tends to 'modify' the whole clause. However, it could sometimes be regarded as modifying the verb of a Main clause, especially an Imperative.

… ἀλλ' ἐμμείνατέ **μοι** οἷς ἐδεήθην ὑμῶν … (Pl.*Ap.* 30 C.)
*… but **please** abide by what I asked of you …*

οἷς = ἐκείνοις ἅ.

40.3. Dative of Accompaniment (or Sociative Dative)

The Dative of Accompaniment in the narrower sense expresses simple accompaniment, attendant circumstances and (with an abstract noun) Manner.

40.3.1. Simple Accompaniment

The Dative may simply express the accompaniment of persons, without any particular nuance.

ἔρρων νυν, αὐτὸς χἠ ξυνοικήσασά **σοι**,
ἄπαιδε παιδὸς ὄντος, ὥσπερ ἄξιοι,
γηράσκετ(ε)· (E.*Alc.* 734–736.)

*Begone then, you yourself and she who came to live **with you**, and grow old childless, as you deserve, although you have a child.*

40.3.2. Attendant Circumstances

Parallel to the expression of personal accompaniment, the Dative may be used to denote attendant circumstances with things both concrete and abstract.

... ἐνταῦθα ἤδη πολλῷ ἔτι **πλέονι βοῇ** τεθαρσηκότες οἱ ψιλοὶ ἐπέκειντο· (Th. 4.35.2.)

*... then straight away **with** even much **more shouting** having taken heart the light-armed troops pressed hard upon <them>.*

40.3.3. Dative of αὐτός *with Noun*

The Dative of αὐτός in agreement with a noun emphasises the inclusion of the Dative phrase in the action of its clause. The Dative phrase may be related to the Subject or the Object of the clause. The Dative of αὐτός usually agrees with a plural noun, and always precedes it in early and classical Greek.

ἆρ' ἂν δυναίμην τὰς Κιθαιρῶνος πτυχὰς
αὐταῖσι βάκχαις τοῖς ἐμοῖς ὤμοις φέρειν; (E.*Ba.* 945–946.)

*Would I be able to carry the mountain-valleys
of Cithaeron on my shoulders, **Bacchants and all**?*

Dative phrase related to Object, 'the mountain-valleys'.

40.3.4. Military Accompaniment

The Dative of Military Accompaniment is merely a particular application of the simple Dative of Accompaniment. It denotes military forces and equipment.

... ἐμὲ δὲ τὸν πανάθλιον
ἔχοντα πλεύσανθ' **ἑπτὰ ναυσὶ** ναυβάτην
ἄτιμον ἔβαλον ... (S.*Ph.* 1026–1028.)

*... but me, completely wretched fellow,
a seaman having set sail willingly **with seven ships**,
they cast <out> dishonoured ...*

40.3.5. Manner

The Dative may denote in what Manner an action is performed. The Dative is typically an abstract noun, which is frequently qualified by an adjective.

οὐ χρὴ σκυθρωπὸν τοῖς ξένοις τὸν πρόσπολον
εἶναι, δέχεσθαι δ' **εὐπροσηγόρῳ φρενί**. (E.*Alc.* 774–775.)

A servant should not be sullen towards guests,
but should receive them ***with courteous attitude****.*

The definite articles (τοῖς, τόν) are used generically.

References

Smyth (1956), *Greek grammar*, §§1450–1502, 1521–1527, 1529, 1544–1545.

EXERCISE 40

Translate the following passages. For each passage, briefly indicate the general function (Interest or Accompaniment) and, where applicable, the particular function (e.g. Possessive or Manner) of the Dative phrases in **bold** type, and state which verb the phrase modifies or how it is otherwise related to its clause.

1. ... συγκαλέσας πάντας τοὺς ξυμμάχους ἀπεδίδου **Πλαταιεῦσι** γῆν καὶ πόλιν τὴν σφετέραν ...

ἀποδιδόναι	*to give back*; here the Imperf. Aspect implies 'proceeded to give back'
Πλαταιεῖς, -έων, οἱ	*Plataeans*

2. ἰδίᾳ δ' ἐκεῖ **Λακεδαιμονίοις** ξυγγίγνεται.

3. σὺ δ' ἄνδρ' ἑταῖρον δεσπότου παρόνθ' ὁρῶν
    στυγνῷ προσώπῳ καὶ συνωφρυωμένῳ
    δέχῃ ...

στυγνός, -ή, -όν	*sullen*
συνωφρυωμένος, -η, -ον	*frowning, scowling* (Perf. Pass. Partc.)

4. καὶ **τῇ** μὲν **πόλει** ἀπὸ τοῦ Γέλα ποταμοῦ τοὔνομα ἐγένετο ...

Γέλας, (Gen.) Γέλα, ἡ	(name of the ποταμός)

5. ... ὑμεῖς καὶ ἔφυτε ἐν τῇ αὐτῇ **ἡμῖν** καὶ ἐτράφητε ...

τῇ αὐτῇ	Understand χώρᾳ.

6. Ἐπίδαμνός ἐστι πόλις ἐν δεξιᾷ **ἐσπλέοντι** τὸν Ἰόνιον κόλπον·

κόλπος, -ου, ὁ	*gulf*

7. καί **μοι** κάλει τούτων τοὺς μάρτυρας.

8. ὅν ποτ' ἐγὼ νύμφαν τ' ἐσίδοιμ' **αὐτοῖς μελάθροις** διακναιομένους ...

ὅν	coordinating relative pronoun
διακναίειν	*to wear away; to destroy*

9. καὶ οἱ μὲν Ἀθηναῖοι ... **ἀτελεῖ τῇ νίκῃ** ἀπὸ τῆς Μιλήτου ἀνέστησαν ...

10. αἱ μὲν δὴ νῆες ἀφικνοῦνται ἐς τὴν Κέρκυραν, οἱ δὲ Κορίνθιοι, ἐπειδὴ **αὐτοῖς** παρεσκεύαστο, ἔπλεον ἐπὶ τὴν Κέρκυραν ναυσὶ πεντήκοντα καὶ ἑκατόν.

μὲν δή ... δέ ...	μὲν δή clause sums up preceding narrative, δέ clause carries narrative forward (Denniston, 1954, p. 258).
ἀφικνοῦνται	Hist. Pres.
παρεσκεύαστο	impersonal Pass.

LESSON 41
Dative Case 2

41.1. Locative

Locative uses of the Dative Case express the meaning 'in' or 'at' a particular place or time.

41.1.1. Place

In classical Attic prose, the Dative denoting location usually requires the preposition ἐν. However, sometimes in prose and frequently in verse a plain Dative is used.

τὸ μὲν γυναῖκα πρῶτον ἄρσενος δίχα
ἧσθαι **δόμοις** ἐρῆμον ἔκπαγλον κακόν … (A.*Ag.* 861–862.)

*In the first place <it is> a terrible problem that a wife should sit **in the house**, deserted, apart from her husband …*

Dative of Place with a common noun in verse; proper nouns also occur in verse.

ταῦτα δὲ ποιεῖν ἐτόλμων … Λακεδαιμόνιοι μὲν ζηλοῦντες τὴν πόλιν τῆς **Μαραθῶνι** μάχης, … (Isoc. 4.91.)

*And they dared to do these things … the Spartans admiring our city for its battle **at Marathon**, …*

Dative of Place with a place name in prose.

Some scholars (including Smyth, 1956, §1534) have claimed that a Locative Dative without preposition is restricted to proper names of places in prose. Even if this commonly occurs in the classical period, the claim seems not to be universally valid.

ἔπειτα δὲ θάπτουσι κατακαύσαντες ἢ ἄλλως **γῇ** κρύψαντες, χῶμα δὲ χέαντες ἀγῶνα τιθεῖσι παντοῖον, ... (Hdt. 5.8.)

*And then they celebrate funeral rites by cremating or otherwise by burying **in the earth**, and after heaping up a mound they conduct every kind of contest, ...*

Dative of Place with a common noun in prose.

41.1.2. Time

The Dative denotes the time *when* something happens. This use of the Dative may be regarded as indicating the 'point of time', provided that allowance is made for the 'point' to be as long as an hour, day, month or year.

τῷ δὲ **πέμπτῳ καὶ δεκάτῳ ἔτει,** ... μετὰ τὴν ἐν Ποτειδαίᾳ μάχην **μηνὶ ἕκτῳ** καὶ **ἅμα ἦρι ἀρχομένῳ** Θηβαίων ἄνδρες ὀλίγῳ πλείους τριακοσίων ... ἐσῆλθον περὶ πρῶτον ὕπνον ξὺν ὅπλοις ἐς Πλάταιαν τῆς Βοιωτίας οὖσαν Ἀθηναίων ξυμμαχίδα. (Th. 2.2.1.)

*But **in the fifteenth year** ... **in the sixth month** after the battle at Potidaea and **just when spring was beginning**, men of the Thebans, a little more than three hundred ... about the first watch entered with weapons into Plataea in Boeotia, when it was in alliance with the Athenians.*

Note the three slightly different Temporal expressions:

1. 'in the fifteenth year'
2. 'in the sixth month after' another event
3. 'simultaneously with spring' plus Participle.

ὦ μελέα ψυχά,
ὃς μηδ' οἰνοχύτου πώματος ἥσθη **δεκέτει χρόνωι,** ...
(S.Ph. 714–715.)

*Oh, the miserable life <of one>,
who did not even enjoy a cup of poured wine **in a ten-year period**, ...*
(R.G. Ussher, 1990)

In English idiom, the Temporal phrase after a negative may be translated '*for* a ten-year period'. But Accusative of Extent of Time in Greek 'would rather suggest that Ph. had not had ten years continuous enjoyment of wine' (Jebb). The present expression is also to be distinguished from the Genitive of Limits of Time—the emphasis is not on the *limits*, but on the fact that Philoctetes did not enjoy a drink at any *point in* the period.

... καὶ **χρόνῳ** ξυνέβησαν καθ' ὁμολογίαν. (Th. 1.98.3.)
... and **after a while** they came to terms.

As in English idiom, so in Greek 'I will do this *in a while*' means 'I will do this *after a while/time*'.

... Ἀθηναῖοι δὲ ναῦς τε τῶν πολεμίων **τῷ χρόνῳ** παραλαβόντες
... καὶ χρήματα τοῖς πᾶσι τάξαντες φέρειν. (Th. 1.19.)

... but the Athenians <controlled their allies> by taking ships from the city-states **in the course of time** ... and by requiring them all to pay money.

This expression is similar to the previous one, but uses the definite article.

41.1.3. Respect

The Dative may indicate in what respect something is the case. This usage is equivalent to the Accusative of Respect. And some nouns may be used idiomatically in either construction—for example, both γένος and γένει may mean 'with regard to birth/family/race'. The construction occurs with verbs, adjectives, adverbs and nouns.

ἦ τἄρα πάντων διαπρέπεις **ἀψυχίᾳ**, ... (E.Alc. 642.)
*Surely then, you are preeminent among all **in faintheartedness**, ...*

The Dative term modifies the verb διαπρέπεις.

οἱ γὰρ κακοὶ **γνώμαισι** τἀγαθὸν χεροῖν
ἔχοντες οὐκ ἴσασι, πρίν τις ἐκβάλῃ. (S.Aj. 964–965.)

*For those who are incompetent **in judgments** do not know that they have the good in their hands, until someone throws it away.*

The Dative term modifies the adjective κακοί.

ἐγὼ μὲν ἧκον φοβούμενος τὸν νόμον καὶ ἐπεδικαζόμην **γένει** ὢν ἐγγυτάτω ... (D. 43.55.)

I *had come revering the law and I was pursuing the case since I was nearest* **in family-relationship** ...

The Dative term modifies the adverb ἐγγυτάτω.

ὁ δὲ δὴ **γένει** πολίτης Ἀθηνόδωρος οὐδὲ βουλεύσεσθαι «ἔμελλεν»· (D. 23.12.)

And Athenodorus indeed, a citizen **by birth**, *<was likely> not even to contemplate <doing so>.*

The Dative term modifies the noun πολίτης.

The Dative of Respect is usually treated as a subcategory of the Instrumental Dative. But the classification is made without positive justification and with the qualification that the Instrumental is used in a transferred or weakened sense.

The Dative of Respect might rather be regarded as a Locative usage, denoting the sphere of action, behaviour or existence. In many instances, the sphere is denoted by an abstract noun. Moreover, already in the classical period ἐν may be used with a Dative of Respect. And this usage becomes more noticeable in the Hellenistic period. ἐν supports a Locative function.

Messenger: ἆρ' οἶσθα δῆτα πρὸς δίκης οὐδὲν τρέμων;
Oedipus: πῶς δ' οὐχί, παῖς γ' εἰ τῶνδε γεννητῶν ἔφυν;
Messenger: ὁθούνεκ' ἦν σοι Πόλυβος οὐδὲν **ἐν γένει**.
(S.*OT* 1014–1016.)

Messenger: *Do you know, then, that you are not rightly fearing anything?*
Oedipus: *But how not, at least if I was born a child of these parents?*
Messenger: *Because Polybus was nothing to you* **with regard to family**.

41.2. Means or Instrument

41.2.1. In General

The Dative Case is widely used to indicate the means or instrument by which an action is performed. The construction occurs both with verbs used transitively and with verbs used intransitively. Many verbs may be used in either way. Either persons or things may implement an action. The construction with a verb used actively is more obvious. But Passive examples occur, where the Dative denotes personal *Means* and not the responsible *Agent*. And when χρῆσθαι ('to use') has a Dative of the *person*, the verb may take a second, predicate Dative. The meaning then tends to shift, for example, from 'use someone as a friend' to 'treat or regard someone as a friend'.

41.2.1.1. With Verbs used Transitively

λέγω σ' ἐγὼ δόλῳ Φιλοκτήτην λαβεῖν. (S.*Ph.* 101.)
I *am saying that you (are to) take Philoctetes by trickery.*

The Infinitive λαβεῖν has a direct Object (Φιλοκτήτην) and a Dative of Means (δόλῳ).

41.2.1.2. With Verbs used Instransitively

... καὶ **ταῖς ὁδοῖς**, ὁποῖαι ἂν ὦσι, **τοιαύταις** ἀνάγκη χρῆσθαι. (X.*Cyr.* 1.6.36.)

... *and <it is> necessary to use **such roads** as there are.*

χρῆσθαι is properly Intr.; lit. 'to make use by means of such roads'.

41.2.1.3. Personal Means

ἐμοί τε λύει **τοῖσι μέλλουσιν τέκνοις**
τὰ ζῶντ' ὀνῆσαι. (E.*Med.* 566–567.)

*And it is expedient for me **by means of the future children**
to benefit those who are living.*

τοῖσι μέλλουσιν τέκνοις is a 'personal' Dative of Means modifying the Active Infinitive ὀνῆσαι.

καὶ μὴν πέλας γε **προσπόλοις** φυλάσσεται. (S.*Aj.* 539.)

Yes indeed, he is being guarded nearby **by means of attendants**.

Tecmessa (the responsible Agent) replies to Ajax's request that he may see his young son. προσπόλοις is personal Dative of Means modifying the Passive verb φυλάσσεται.

41.2.1.4. Personal Means with Predicative Dative

ὡς τοῖς γε σέμνοις καὶ συνωφρυωμένοις
ἅπασίν ἐστιν, ὥς γ' **ἐμοὶ** χρῆσθαι **κρίτῃ**,
οὐ βίος ἀληθῶς ὁ βίος, ἀλλὰ συμφορά. (E.*Alc.* 800–802.)

For to these solemn and frowning people at least,
*all of them, at least to use **me as judge**, life*
is not truly life, but calamity.

χρῆσθαι here is used with a second, predicative Dative, in the sense 'to use/treat/regard as'. (ὡς + Infin. expresses a parenthetical qualification.)

41.2.2. Cause

The Dative may denote the factor, because of which something happens. The usage is very similar to the Causal Genitive, especially since this Dative is likewise often used with verbs of emotion.

ἦ που στενάζει **τοισίδ'** Ἄδμητος **κακοῖς**,
ἐσθλῆς γυναικὸς εἰ στερηθῆναί σφε χρή; (E.*Alc.* 199–200.)

*Is Admetus perhaps groaning **over these troubles**,*
that he should be deprived of his good wife?

(For εἰ meaning 'that' with expressions of emotion, see Lessons 34.2.4 and 34.2.6.)

41.2.3. Degree of Difference

The Dative denotes the degree of difference with Comparative and (less often) Superlative adjectives and adverbs, and also with other expressions implying comparison.

ἢν δὲ ᾖ οὕτερος ὑποδεέστερος **ὀλίγῳ**, τὰς παρείας φιλέονται· ἢν δὲ **πολλῷ** ᾖ οὕτερος ἀγεννέστερος, προσπίπτων προσκυνέει τὸν ἕτερον. (Hdt. 1.134.1.)

*But if the one is inferior <only> **by a little**, they kiss the cheeks; and if the one is **much** more ignoble, he falls before the other and does obeisance to him.*

ὀλίγῳ modifies the Comparative adjective ὑποδεέστερος.

πολλῷ modifies the Comparative adjective ἀγεννέστερος.

ἥκιστα δὲ τοὺς ἑωυτῶν ἑκαστάτω οἰκημένους ἐν τιμῇ ἄγονται, νομίζοντες ἑωυτοὺς εἶναι ἀνθρώπων **μακρῷ** τὰ πάντα ἀρίστους ... (Hdt. 1.134.2.)

*And they hold in least honour those who live furthest from themselves, thinking themselves to be **by far** the best of men in all respects ...*

μακρῷ modifies the Superlative adjective ἀρίστους.

ἐνιαυτῷ δὲ πρότερον τῆς ἁλώσεως ἐνέδειξεν ὡς προδότην τὸν Φιλιστίδην καὶ τοὺς μετ' αὐτοῦ, αἰσθόμενος ἃ πράττουσιν. (D. 9.60.)

*But **a year** before the capture he informed against Philistides as a traitor, as well as his associates, after realising what they were doing.*

In this construction, ἐνιαυτῷ is not a Dative of Time but a Dative of Degree of Difference modifying the Comparative adverb πρότερον and meaning 'earlier *by a year* than the capture'. Other Temporal terms may also be used as Dative of Degree of Difference.

γῆ δὴ πολεμίη τῇδέ τοι καθίσταται· εἰ θέλει τοι μηδὲν ἀντίξοον καταστῆναι, **τοσούτῳ** τοι γίνεται πολεμιωτέρη **ὅσῳ** ἂν προβαίνῃς ἑκαστέρω, τὸ πρόσω αἰεὶ κλεπτόμενος· (Hdt. 7.49.4.)

*And the land becomes hostile to you in this way: if nothing is likely to become adverse for you, <the land> becomes **so much** the more hostile to you, **the** further you progress, being constantly deceived as to what lies ahead.*

τοσούτῳ (demonstrative pronoun), modifying the Comparative adjective πολεμιωτέρη, corresponds to ὅσῳ (relative pronoun, lit. 'by how much'), modifying the Comparative adverb ἑκαστέρω. (Cf. Lesson 43.6.2.)

τοσούτῳ δὲ μᾶλλον προτετίμηται τὸ κάλλος παρ' ἐκείνοις ἢ παρ' ἡμῖν, **ὥστε** καὶ ταῖς γυναιξὶ ταῖς αὐτῶν ὑπὸ τούτου κρατουμέναις συγγνώμην ἔχουσι ... (Isoc. 10.60.)

*And **so much** the more has beauty been preferred among them [= gods] than among us, **that** they pardon even their own wives when they are overcome by it ...*

τοσούτῳ (demonstrative pronoun), modifying the Comparative adverb μᾶλλον, corresponds to ὥστε (relative adverb), introducing the Result clause. (Cf. Lesson 43.6.1.)

References

Smyth (1956), *Greek grammar*, §§1503–1543.

EXERCISE 41

Translate the following passages. For each passage, briefly indicate the general and particular function of the Dative phrases in **bold** type—for example, Locative, Time, modifying which verb; Means, Degree of Difference, modifying which Comparative adjective or adverb.

1. ... καὶ ἐμβοήσαντες ἀθρόοι ὥρμησαν ἐπ' αὐτοὺς καὶ ἔβαλλον **λίθοις** τε καὶ **τοξεύμασι** καὶ **ἀκοντίοις**, ὡς ἕκαστός τι πρόχειρον εἶχεν.

   The three Dative terms comprise a single phrase with a single function.

2. Ἀθηναῖοι δὲ **δευτέρᾳ καὶ ἑξηκοστῇ ἡμέρᾳ** μετὰ τὴν μάχην ἐστράτευσαν ἐς Βοιωτοὺς ...

ἐς (+ Acc. of persons)	into <the territory of>

3. ... καὶ ὅταν τὴν ἐπιστήμην ἐς τὸ ἴσον καταστήσωμεν, **τῇ** γε **εὐψυχίᾳ** δήπου περιεσόμεθα.

ἐπιστήμη, -ης, ἡ	skill
περιεῖναι	to be superior

4. **ὅσῳ** δὲ πλείους ἄνθρωποι ἐν τῇ πόλει εἰσίν ..., **τοσούτῳ** ἂν θᾶττον λιμῷ αὐτοὺς ἡγοῦμαι ἁλῶναι.

LESSON 41. DATIVE CASE 2

5. ... ἐνίκων μαχόμενοι ἅπασαν τὴν δύναμιν τὴν ἐκείνων **τοῖς** ἤδη **ἀπειρηκόσι** καὶ **τοῖς** οὔπω **δυναμένοις** ...

τοῖς ... τοῖς ... + Partc.	masc., referring to persons
ἀπειπεῖν (Aor.)	*to become tired out/exhausted*

6. βέβακε δ' ὅρκων χάρις, οὐδ' ἔτ' αἰδὼς
   Ἑλλάδι τᾷ μεγάλᾳ μένει, ...

χάρις, -ιτος, ἡ	*charm*

7. οἴκτιρε δ', ὦ μῆτέρ, με, μηδὲ **ταῖς ἐμαῖς ἁμαρτίαισι** παῖδα σὸν κατακτάνῃς.

8. ... αὐτῷ δεηθέντι εἶπον χρῆσθαι **ταῖς ναυσὶ ταύταις**, ἣν βούληται, περὶ τὴν Πελοπόννησον.

αὐτῷ	masc.
δεῖσθαι (Mid. and Pass.)	*to request*
εἶπον	3rd pers. pl.

LESSON 42
Prepositions

42.1. Adverbs

In the earliest surviving Greek literature, many words, which are regularly used as prepositions in the classical period, are still being used as adverbs.

ἐπεὶ **πρό** οἱ εἴπομεν ἡμεῖς ... (Hom.*Od.* 1.37.)
*For we told him **beforehand** ...*

42.2. Compound Verbs

When placed immediately before verbs, these adverbs form compound verbs.

αὐτὰρ ὁ τοῖσιν **ἀφείλετο** νόστιμον ἦμαρ. (Hom.*Od.* 1.9.)
*And he **took away** the day of return for them.*

ἀφείλετο = ἀφ' εἵλετο.

42.3. Prepositions

When placed immediately before, in the middle of, or after a noun phrase, these adverbs begin to look like prepositions governing a Case.

... πλάζει δ' **ἀπὸ πατρίδος αἴης**. (Hom.*Od.* 1.75.)
*... but he turns <him> **away from his native land**.*

ἀλλά μοι ἀμφ' Ὀδυσῆϊ δαΐφρονι δαίεται ἦτορ,
δυσμόρῳ, ὅς δὴ δηθὰ **φίλων ἄπο** πήματα πάσχει
νήσῳ ἐν ἀμφιρύτῃ ... (Hom.*Od.* 1.48–50.)

But for me my heart is torn concerning wise Odysseus,
*ill-fated man, who indeed has long been suffering miseries **away from his**
   dear ones*
on an island surrounded by sea ...

42.4. Case Functions

The functions of the Accusative, Genitive and Dative Cases were established before prepositions began to be used with them. In the Lessons and Exercises concerned with those Cases, all the functions of the Cases were expressed without the use of prepositions. In classical Greek, it is often possible to detect the original Case function of a prepositional phrase apart from the preposition itself.

εἴθ᾽ ὤφελ᾽ Ἀργοῦς μὴ διαπτάσθαι σκάφος
Κόλχων **ἐς αἶαν** κυανέας Συμπληγάδας, … (E.*Med.* 1–2.)

If only the ship Argo had not flown through
*the dark Clashing Rocks **to the land** of the Colchians, …*

In the context, αἶαν is clearly an Accusative of Goal, even apart from the use of the preposition ἐς.

However, the original Case function is not always so clear. For example, there are several passages in the tragedy of Sophocles, *Oedipus the King*, where the phrase πρὸς θεῶν is used in an urgent entreaty with second person Imperative or Subjunctive.

πρὸς θεῶν δίδασκέ με. (S.*OT* 1009.)
***By the gods**, instruct me.*

A possible rationale for the prepositional phrase is that it is an elliptical request formula. The request is explicit in the following couplet from Theognis.

χρὴ τολμᾶν χαλεποῖσιν ἐν ἄλγεσι κείμενον ἄνδρα,
 πρός τε **θεῶν αἰτεῖν** ἔκλυσιν **ἀθανάτων**. (Thgn. 555–556.)

A man when involved in difficult sufferings should endure,
 *and **ask from the immortal gods** release.*

Here any response to the *request* (αἰτεῖν) must start *at* (πρός) the gods, but must proceed *from the gods* (θεῶν). The Genitive of Separation would be the appropriate category. Compare δεῖσθαι, προσδεῖσθαι, λίσσεσθαι and χρῄζειν, 'to beg, to entreat, to request (from)', with Genitive of person but no preposition.

The Accusative of Goal without a preposition is limited to phrases denoting Place. However, the Accusative of Goal with a preposition may also express Time.

καὶ τελευτῶντος τοῦ χειμῶνος **πρὸς ἔαρ** ἤδη κλίμακας ἔχοντες οἱ Ἀργεῖοι ἦλθον ἐπὶ τὴν Ἐπίδαυρον, ... (Th. 5.56.5.)

*And as the winter was ending, now **towards spring**, the Argives came with scaling-ladders against Epidaurus, ...*

42.5. Possessive Genitive with Preposition

In an abbreviated construction, a Possessive Genitive may be used with certain prepositions, especially ἐν and εἰς (ἐς) and sometimes ἐκ (ἐξ).

τοῦθ' ὑμῖν Αἴας τοὔπος ὕστατον θροεῖ.
τὰ δ' ἄλλ' **ἐν Ἅιδου** τοῖς κάτω μυθήσομαι. (S.*Aj.* 864–865.)

*Ajax addresses this last word to you,
and for the rest I shall speak **in <the realm> of Hades** to those below.*

... **εἰς ἑνὸς** τῶν διακόνων ἐξέπεμψεν αὐτούς. (X.*HG* 5.4.6.)
*... he sent them off **to <the house> of one** of the servants.*

ἐκ δ' ἄρα **Πεισάνδροιο** Πολυκτορίδαο ἄνακτος
ἴσθμιον ἤνεικεν θεράπων, περικαλλὲς ἄγαλμα.
(Hom.*Od.* 18.299–300.)

*And then **out of <the house> of lord Pisander** son of Polyktor
his assistant brought a necklace, a very beautiful adornment.*

42.6. Compound Verb with Preposition

In classical prose, an adverbial prefix of a verb is often repeated as a preposition with the appropriate Case. However, this usage also occurs in verse. (But in the classical period poets more often than prose writers rely on the established Case functions without a preposition.) The repetition is normally ignored in English translation.

... ἐλέχθη ὑπ' αὐτῶν ὡς οἱ Πελοποννήσιοι φάρμακα **ἐσβεβλήκοιεν ἐς** τὰ φρέατα· (Th. 2.48.2.)

... *it was said by them that the Peloponnesians **had thrown** poison **into** their cisterns.*

Repetition in prose.

... μηδέ ποτ' εἴπηθ'
ὡς Ζεὺς ὑμᾶς **εἰς** ἀπρόοπτον
πῆμ' **εἰσέβαλεν** ... (A.Pr. 1073–1075.)

... *and do not ever say that Zeus **threw** you **into** unforeseen misery ...*

Repetition in verse.

... τὸν ἐσρέοντα διὰ Συμπληγάδων
βοῦς ὑλοφορβοὺς **πόντον εἰσεβάλλομεν**, ... (E.IT 260–261.)

... ***we had been driving*** *our cattle that feed in woodland **into the sea** that flows in through the Clashing Rocks, ...*

No repetition in verse.

42.7. Metaphorical Use of Prepositions

The examples in §42.3 and the first example in §42.4 above use prepositions with the appropriate Cases in a literal sense: ἀπό with Genitive of Separation, ἐν with Dative of Place, ἐς with Accusative of Goal. In the example from Theognis (§42.4), πρός is used with a Genitive of Separation in a metaphorical sense—no literal, physical movement is involved. This metaphorical usage is quite common, especially when a preposition is used with an abstract noun.

ἐτράποντο **πρὸς λῃστείαν** (Th. 1.5.1.)
*they turned **to piracy***

ὑπέστρεφον **ἐπὶ ζήτησιν** τῶν Περσέων (Hdt. 4.140.1.)
*they turned back **to search for** the Persians*

ἐκ τούτου ἐπειρᾶτο Μιθραδάτης διδάσκειν (X.*An.* 3.3.4.)
after this *Mithradates tried to explain*

παρεσκεύασαν τοὺς ἐν τέλει (Th. 3.36.5.)
*they prevailed upon those **in authority***

ἐγὼ ταῦτα τοῦτον ἐποίησα σὺν δίκῃ (Hdt. 1.115.2.)
*I did this to this <man> **with justice***

42.8. Accent and Position of Prepositions

Two-syllable prepositions with oxytone accent (except ἀμφί, ἀντί, διά) become paroxytone when they follow their Case. Note φίλων ἄπο in §42.3 above (second example). In classical prose, περί is the only 'proper' preposition (§42.11 below) which is placed after its Case. ἕνεκα is regularly placed after its Case, and ἄνευ sometimes.

42.9. Adverbial Accusative as Preposition

Some nouns are used adverbially in the Accusative and are qualified by a simple Possessive Genitive. These Accusative nouns virtually have the function of prepositions.

τρόπον αἰγυπιῶν (A.*Ag.* 49.)
in the manner *of vultures*

δίκην τοξότου (Pl.*Leg.* 705 E.)
in the manner *of a bowman*

τόλμας χάριν (S.*Ant.* 371.),
because *of his rashness*

τρέφ' ἀξίως νιν σοῦ τε τήν τ' ἐμὴν χάριν. (E.*Ph.* 762.)
*Look after her properly **for the sake** of yourself and **for** my **sake**.*

In this and other instances there is a mixture of Genitive Case and Possessive adjective with χάριν.

42.10. Pregnant Construction

In a so-called pregnant construction, verbs of rest are sometimes used with εἰς (ἐς) + Accusative when they imply previous motion.

… ἐκ τῆς Μέμφιδος ἐξήλασε τοὺς Ἕλληνας καὶ τέλος **ἐς** Προσωπίτιδα τὴν νῆσον κατέκλησεν· (Th. 1.109.4.)

… *he drove the Greeks out of Memphis and finally shut <them> up **in** the island of Prosopitis.*

Conversely, verbs of motion are sometimes used with ἐν + Dative when they imply subsequent rest.

καίτοι πόθεν κλέος γ' ἂν εὐκλεέστερον
κατέσχον ἢ τὸν αὐτάδελφον **ἐν** τάφῳ
τιθεῖσα; (S.*Ant.* 502–504.)

*And yet from where would I have obtained more glorious glory than by putting my own brother **into** a grave?*

42.11. 'Proper' and 'Improper' Prepositions

The label 'proper' has been applied to prepositions that are used to form compound verbs, and the label 'improper' to prepositions that are not so used. The classification is not very useful. It applies the term 'proper' to the very words which are used in two different ways, either as prepositions or as adverbial prefixes to verbs. It applies the term 'improper' to the very words which are used only as prepositions. It does not apply the term 'improper' to the adverbial Accusative nouns which have the function of prepositions. Nor does it take account of other prepositions which may also originally have been Case forms, such as ἐντός (Ablative) or περί (Locative). See Smyth (1956), §§1647, 1699 and (for a list) 1700–1702.

42.12. Hellenistic and Later Developments

Prepositions are more often used (with the appropriate Cases) than in the classical period.

But the distinction between εἰς + Accusative and ἐν + Dative becomes further blurred.

Fewer prepositions are being used. And their range of meaning is being restricted. By way of compensation, εἰς, ἐν and ἐκ are used more extensively.

The Dative Case is less often used with prepositions. ἀνά, μετά, περί and ὑπό are no longer used with the Dative at all (except ὑπό rarely in Polybius).

There is an increasing tendency for each preposition to be used with one Case only.

The Accusative becomes more generally used as the preferred Case with prepositions. In modern Greek, it is the only Case used with prepositions. And only seven prepositions remain in modern Greek.

References

Leaf & Bayfield (Eds) (1895), *The Iliad of Homer* (Vol. 1), §§33–35.

Smyth (1956), *Greek grammar*, §§1302, 1636–1702.

EXERCISE 42A

1. Translate the following passages.

2. For each prepositional phrase in **bold** type, name the grammatical Case and indicate the particular Case function (apart from the preposition). For the Case functions, see Lessons 37, 38, 39, 40 and 41, and for prepositional expressions of Purpose see Lesson 27.1. Passages for Exercise 42A are selected from Herodotus, Thucydides and Xenophon.

Example

οἱ δ' **ἐν τῇ πόλει** ὄντες Ἐπιδάμνιοι ἐπειδὴ ἐπιέζοντο, πέμπουσιν **ἐς τὴν Κέρκυραν** πρέσβεις ... (Th. 1.24.6.)

*And the Epidamnians who were **in the city**, since they were being hard pressed, sent [Hist. Pres.] ambassadors **to Corcyra** ...*

ἐν τῇ πόλει: Dative, Locative, Place.
ἐς τὴν Κέρκυραν: Accusative, Adverbial, Goal.

1. εἰ οὖν οὗτοι μὴ δώσουσι τὴν ἐσχάτην δίκην, τίς ποτε **πρὸς τὴν πόλιν** θαρρῶν πορεύσεται;

2. τὴν δὲ γῆν δημοσιώσαντες ἀπεμίσθωσαν **ἐπὶ δέκα ἔτη** ...

δημοσιοῦν	*to confiscate*

3. καὶ ἐπειδὴ ἀπέθανεν, **ἐπὶ πλέον** ἔτι ἐγνώσθη ἡ πρόνοια αὐτοῦ ἡ **ἐς τὸν πόλεμον**.

4. ὡς δὲ ὁ κῆρύξ τε ἀπήγγειλεν οὐδὲν εἰρηνεῖον **παρὰ τῶν Κορινθίων** καὶ αἱ νῆες αὐτοῖς ἐπεπλήρωντο ... ἐναυμάχησαν.

5. ἔτυχε γὰρ ταύτῃ τοῖς Μενδαίοις καὶ ἐπικούροις **ἐντὸς τοῦ τείχους** τὰ ὅπλα κείμενα.

ταύτῃ	*here* (Dat. as adv.)
Μενδαῖοι, -ων, οἱ	*Mendaeans, people of Mende*
ἐπίκουρος, -α, -ον	*auxiliary* (esp. of soldiers)

6. ἀφικόμεθα μὲν **ἐπὶ** τῆς πρότερον οὔσης ξυμμαχίας **ἀνανεώσει** ...

7. βουλόμενοι **ἐν τάχει** τὴν ναυμαχίαν ποιῆσαι ... ξυνεκάλεσαν τοὺς στρατιώτας ...

8. τυραννίδες **ἐν ταῖς πόλεσι** καθίσταντο τῶν προσόδων μειζόνων γιγνομένων ...

πρόσοδος, -ου, ἡ	*revenue*

9. ξύμμαχοί τε γὰρ οὐδενός πω **ἐν τῷ** πρὸ τοῦ **χρόνῳ** ἑκούσιοι γενόμενοι, νῦν ἄλλων τοῦτο δεησόμενοι ἥκομεν ...

τε	anticipates a following καί and need not be translated.
τοῦ	*this*

EXERCISE 42B

1. Translate the following passages.
2. For each prepositional phrase in **bold** type, name the grammatical Case and indicate the particular Case function (apart from the preposition). For the Case functions, see Lessons 37, 38, 39, 40 and 41. For prepositional expressions of Purpose see Lesson 27.1. Passages for Exercise 42B are selected from Herodotus, Thucydides and Xenophon.

Example

οἱ δ' **ἐν τῇ πόλει** ὄντες Ἐπιδάμνιοι ἐπειδὴ ἐπιέζοντο, πέμπουσιν **ἐς τὴν Κέρκυραν** πρέσβεις ... (Th. 1.24.6.)

*And the Epidamnians who were **in the city**, since they were being hard pressed, sent* [Hist. Pres.] *ambassadors **to Corcyra** ...*

ἐν τῇ πόλει: Dative, Locative, Place.
ἐς τὴν Κέρκυραν: Accusative, Adverbial, Goal.

1. ταῦτα ὦν ὑμῖν ἀναβάλλομαι κυρώσειν **ἐς τέταρτον μῆνα ἀπὸ τοῦδε**.

ὦν (Ionic)	οὖν (Attic)
ἀναβάλλεσθαι (Mid.)	*to delay* (+ Intentive Infin.)
κυροῦν	*to confirm*

2. καὶ οἱ μὲν αὐτῶν ἐνταῦθα ᾤκησαν, οἱ δὲ ἐσπάρησαν **κατὰ τὴν ἄλλην Ἑλλάδα**.

3. ἔστι δὲ λίθινος ἕτερος τοσοῦτος καὶ ἐν Σάϊ, κείμενος **κατὰ τὸν αὐτὸν τρόπον** τῷ ἐν Μέμφι.

λίθινος, (-α, -ον)	tone (statue) (masc. adj. as noun)
καί	also
Σάϊς	(place name)
τῷ ‹ ... λιθίνῳ›	Dat. with αὐτόν

4. βασιλέϊ τῷ μεγάλῳ **ἐς τροφὴν** αὐτοῦ τε καὶ τῆς στρατιῆς διαραίρηται πάρεξ τοῦ φόρου γῆ πᾶσα ὅσης ἄρχει·

δια-αίρεῖν	to divide up (here Pres. Perf. Pass.)
πάρεξ	apart from (+ Gen.)

5. **ἐντὸς** γὰρ **εἴκοσι ἡμερῶν** ἤγαγε τοὺς ἄνδρας, ὥσπερ ὑπέστη.

ὑφιστάναι	to promise (Mid./Pass. and Intr. Tenses)

6. **πρὸ** γὰρ **τῶν Τρωικῶν** οὐδὲν φαίνεται πρότερον κοινῇ ἐργασαμένη ἡ Ἑλλάς·

φαίνεσθαι (Mid.)	to be clear/obvious (in doing/being) (+ Partc.); often paraphrased as 'It is clear that I (etc.) do/am ...'

7. σῖτόν τε ἐσήγαγον καὶ φρουροὺς ἐγκατέλιπον, τῶν τε ἀνθρώπων τοὺς ἀχρειοτάτους **ξὺν γυναιξὶ καὶ παισὶν** ἐξεκόμισαν.

ἀχρεῖος, (-α,) -ον	unfit

8. οἶδα δὲ τοὺς τοιούτους, καὶ ὅσοι **ἔν** τινος **λαμπρότητι** προέσχον, ἐν μὲν τῷ καθ' αὐτοὺς βίῳ λυπηροὺς ὄντας ...

τινος (neut.)	in any ‹field›, etc.
λαμπρότης, -ητος, ἡ	distinction
προέχειν	to excel
λυπηρός, -ή, -όν	annoying

LESSON 43
Correlative Clauses

43.1. Introduction

Clauses, which are introduced by a relative adjective or adverb, may have as their antecedent the corresponding demonstrative adjective or adverb. The antecedent may appear in the Main clause of a sentence, or in a Subordinate clause or an Infinitive or Participial phrase. The relative term, but not necessarily the demonstrative, always occurs at the beginning of its clause.

43.2. Adjectival Clauses

Most simply, an ordinary demonstrative adjective (ἐκεῖνος, οὗτος or less often ὅδε) is antecedent to the definite or indefinite relative adjective (ὅς or ὅστις) introducing the relative clause. Both demonstrative and relative adjectives may be used as adjectives qualifying a noun or as pronouns without a noun. All adjectival relative clauses may precede, follow or interrupt the demonstrative clause or phrase. Since relative adjectives agree with their antecedent in Number and Gender but take their Case from the syntax of their own clause, they are not necessarily in the same Case as the corresponding demonstrative term.

In addition there are the special demonstrative adjectives and their corresponding relative adjectives.

Category	Demonstrative adjective	Relative adjective
size, number	τόσος, τοσοῦτος, τοσόσδε	ὅσος, ὁπόσος
quality	τοῖος, τοιοῦτος, τοιόσδε	οἷος, ὁποῖος
age, size, status	τηλίκος, τηλικοῦτος, τηλικόσδε	ἡλίκος, ὁπηλίκος

A special demonstrative term may sometimes correspond to an ordinary relative term. And a demonstrative clause may sometimes correspond to an Infinitive construction instead of a clause with a finite verb.

καίτοι γε ὀφειλόμενόν πού ἐστιν **τοῦτο ὃ** παρακατέθετο. (Pl.*R.* 332 A.)

And yet ***this which*** *he entrusted is surely owed.*

τοῦτο (Nom. demonstrative) corresponds to ὅ (Acc. relative). (Cf. Lesson 25.)

ἀλλὰ μὴν ὡμολογοῦμεν, **ᾧ** γε ὅμοιος ἑκάτερος εἴη, **τοιοῦτον** καὶ ἑκάτερον εἶναι. (Pl.*R.* 350 C.)

But in fact we agreed that, ***to*** **what** *each is like,* **such** *also each is.*

τοιοῦτον (Acc. demonstrative of quality) in reported discourse (Acc. and Infin.) corresponds to ᾧ (Dat. ordinary relative).

οὐκοῦν **τοιάνδε τινὰ** φαίνεται ἔχουσα **τὴν δύναμιν, οἵαν**, ᾧ ἂν ἐγγένηται, ... πρῶτον μὲν ἀδύνατον αὐτὸ ποιεῖν πράττειν μεθ' αὑτοῦ διὰ τὸ στασιάζειν καὶ διαφέρεσθαι, ἔτι δ' ἐχθρὸν εἶναι ἑαυτῷ τε καὶ τῷ ἐναντίῳ παντὶ καὶ τῷ δικαίῳ; (Pl.*R.* 351 E–352 A.)

Therefore, does it [= injustice] *not clearly have its power* ***of some such sort***, ***as***, *in whatever it occurs* ... *in the first place it* [= injustice] *makes it impossible for it* [= that in which injustice occurs] *to deal with itself on account of being at odds and quarrelling, and further it is hostile to itself and to every opponent including the just?*

τοιάνδε (Acc. demonstrative) corresponds to οἵαν (Acc. relative with Result Infin. construction). (Cf. Lessons 22 and 28.5.)

43.3. Adverbial Clauses

Parallel to correlative adjectival clauses, some types of adverbial clause may have a demonstrative adverb as antecedent to a relative adverb introducing the relative clause. These relative adverbs may also be viewed as subordinating conjunctions. The relevant types are adverbial clauses of Time (Temporal), Place (Local), Manner (including Comparison) and Result.

43.3.1. Clauses of Time

ὥστε δημιουργὸς ἢ σοφὸς ἢ ἄρχων οὐδεὶς ἁμαρτάνει **τότε ὅταν** ἄρχων ᾖ...; (Pl.*R.* 340 E.)

*And so no craftsman or scientist or ruler makes a mistake **then when** he is ruling...?*

τότε (demonstrative) corresponds to ὅταν (relative).
(Cf. Lessons 30 and 31.)

43.3.2. Clauses of Place

οὗ δ' ἐγὼ μὲν ἀθῷος ἅπασι, ... **ἐνταῦθα** ἀπήντηκας; (D. 18.125.)

*But **where** I <am> immune in all respects, ... **here** you have confronted me?*

ἐνταῦθα (demonstrative) corresponds to οὗ (relative). (Cf. Lesson 33.1.)

43.3.3. Clauses of Manner

ταῦτ' οὖν σκοποῦντες καὶ τἆλλα μνησθέντες, **ᾗ** δίκαιόν ἐστι, **ταύτῃ** ψηφίσασθε. (D. 28.23.)

*Therefore, considering this and recalling the other <points>, **in what way** it is just, **in this way** vote.*

ταύτῃ (demonstrative) corresponds to ᾗ (relative). (Cf. Lesson 33.2.)

43.3.4. Clauses of Comparison

πρὸ πολλοῦ δ' ἂν ἐποιησάμην **οὕτως** αὐτὸν νομίζειν εἶναί με δεινόν, **ὥσπερ** ἐν ὑμῖν εἴρηκεν. (Isoc. 15.15.)

*And I would have regarded it as important, that he should think that I am **so** clever, **as indeed** he has said in your presence.*

οὕτως (demonstrative) corresponds to ὥσπερ (relative). (Cf. Lesson 28.)

43.3.5. Clauses or Phrases of Result

οἴη γὰρ ἄν με, εἶπον, **οὕτω** μανῆναι **ὥστε** ξυρεῖν ἐπιχειρεῖν λέοντα καὶ συκοφαντεῖν Θρασύμαχον; (Pl.*R.* 341 C.)

*'Do you really think that I', I said, 'would become **so** mad **as** to try to beard the lion and outwit Thrasymachus?'*

οὕτω (demonstrative) in reported thought (Acc. and Infin.) corresponds to ὥστε (relative) introducing the relative phrase (also Acc. and Infin.). (Cf. Lesson 22.)

43.4. Interrogative Antecedent

Correlative sentences, which are questions rather than statements, may have an interrogative pronoun instead of a demonstrative pronoun as antecedent.

τίς ἔσθ' ὁ χῶρος δῆτ' ἐν **ᾧ** βεβήκαμεν; (S.*OC* 52.)
What *is the place, then, into **which** we have come?*

43.5. Mixed Adjectival and Adverbial Construction

In §§43.2–3 above, examples have been restricted to sentences either with demonstrative and relative *adjectives* or with demonstrative and relative *adverbs*. However, Result constructions may also have a demonstrative *adjective* as antecedent to the relative *adverb* ὥστε introducing a Result clause or phrase.

ἀλλ' ἐκεῖνος μὲν **τοσαύτην πρόνοιαν** ἔσχεν ὑπὲρ τοῦ μηδὲ φεύγων μηδὲν ἐξαμαρτεῖν εἰς τὴν πόλιν, **ὥστ'** εἰς Ἄργος ἐλθὼν ἡσυχίαν εἶχεν ... (Isoc. 16.9.)

*But that man took **so much care** over doing no wrong against his city even when he was in exile, **that** he went to Argos and kept quiet ...*

(Cf. Lesson 22.1.)

43.6. Pronominal Idioms

43.6.1. Result

A particular Result construction has the form: εἰς τοσοῦτο(ν)/τοῦτο (pronoun) + Partitive Genitive + verb of 'coming' (or similar) + ὥστε with Result clause or phrase. (The construction also occurs without the Gen. term.)

... οἱ δ' **εἰς τοσοῦτον ὕβρεως ἦλθον, ὥστ'** ἔπεισαν ὑμᾶς ἐλαύνειν αὐτὸν ἐξ ἁπάσης τῆς Ἑλλάδος ... (Isoc. 16.9.)

... *but **they came to so great** <a level> **of insolence, that** they persuaded you to drive him out of all Greece* ...

(Cf. Lesson 22.3, first example.)

43.6.2. Dative of Degree of Difference

The Dative of Degree of Difference is a pronominal idiom, and is often but not always used in a correlative construction.

ὥσθ' **ὅσῳ** ἄν τις ἐρρωμενεστέρως ἐπιθυμῇ πείθειν τοὺς ἀκούοντας, **τοσούτῳ** μᾶλλον ἀσκήσει καλὸς κἀγαθὸς εἶναι καὶ παρὰ τοῖς πολίταις εὐδοκιμεῖν. (Isoc. 15.278.)

*And so **the** more strongly any one desires to persuade his hearers, **(so much) the** more he will endeavour to be fine and good and to be in high regard among the citizens.*

τοσούτῳ (demonstrative pronoun) modifying the Comparative adverb μᾶλλον in the leading clause corresponds to ὅσῳ (relative pronoun) modifying the Comparative adverb ἐρρωμενεστέρως in the relative clause. (Cf. Lesson 41.2.3.)

43.7. Note

Since correlative clauses do not receive adequate attention in standard Greek grammars, no references are given for this Lesson.

EXERCISE 43

Translate the following passages.

1. τοῦτο μέν, ἔφην, οὐκ ἀγνοῶ ὃ βούλῃ λέγειν ...

2. ἂν γὰρ ἐμμένῃ τῇ φιλοσοφίᾳ καὶ τοσοῦτον ἐπιδιδῷς ὅσον περ νῦν, ταχέως γενήσῃ τοιοῦτος οἷόν σε προσήκει.

3. ... οὗ δ' ὁ νόμος προσέταττεν, ἐνταῦθα τοῖς σώμασιν αὐτοὶ λῃτουργεῖν ἠξίουν.

λῃτουργεῖν	*to perform public service, to serve* (later λειτουργεῖν)

---

4. σίτῳ μὲν γὰρ τοσούτῳ ἐχρῆτο, ὅσον ἡδέως ἤσθιε·

5. πρὸς θεῶν τίς οὕτως εὐήθης ἐστὶν ὑμῶν ὅστις ἀγνοεῖ τὸν ἐκεῖθεν πόλεμον δεῦρ' ἥξοντα, ἂν ἀμελήσωμεν;

εὐήθης, -ες	*naïve*

---

6. ὅσῳ δ' ἂν εἴπῃς δεινότερα βακχῶν πέρι,
τοσῷδε μᾶλλον τὸν ὑποθέντα τὰς τέχνας
γυναιξὶ τόνδε τῇ δίκῃ προσθήσομεν.

δίκη, -ης, ἡ	*punishment*

---

7. ἐκεῖνος δ' εἰς τοσοῦτον μεγαλοφροσύνης ἦλθεν, ὥστε τὸν ἄλλον χρόνον ἰδιώτης ὤν, ἐπειδὴ φεύγειν ἠναγκάσθη, τυραννεῖν ᾠήθη δεῖν.

8. And they were annoyed then, when *we* thought it right that we should legally have control over certain people.

---

to be annoyed	ἀγανακτεῖν
legally	νομίμως
to have control over	ἐπάρχειν (+ Gen.)

LESSON 43. CORRELATIVE CLAUSES

9. Thus it seems to me at least that, in what way [it is] easiest, in this way also it is best to do this.

thus	οὕτως
easiest	ῥᾷστος, -η, -ον

LESSON 44
Exclamations

44.1. Exclamatory Cries

In the English language, a number of terms are used in isolation to express various emotions. These terms often seem to have no etymology, but are merely grunts, cries, screams and so on: 'wow!', 'whew!', 'aha!', 'ugh!', etc. Similarly, in Greek there are numerous terms expressing a range of emotions. Most simply, the terms stand alone and are marked off by a full stop or colon in modern editions of Ancient Greek writings. Alternatively, such terms may interrupt a Greek sentence at the beginning, middle or end, and may be separated only by commas. It may be difficult to find suitable English equivalents for some of these terms. And sometimes transliteration is a better solution than translation.

The English exclamation mark (!) is not normally used in Greek punctuation. (Occasionally, some modern editors have used it.) In Greek verse texts, some exclamatory cries are 'outside the metre' (*extra metrum*), and may or may not have a line number.

ὀτοτοτοτοῖ.
βαρεῖά γ' ἅδε συμφορά.
οἶ μάλα καὶ τόδ' ἀλγῶ. (A.*Pers.* 1043–1045.)

Otototoi!
This calamity <is> burdensome indeed.
Alas, I am greatly pained at this too.

ὀτοτοτοτοῖ (a cry of pain or grief) stands alone.

ὅδ' ἐγών, **οἰοῖ**, αἰακτὸς
μέλεος γέννᾳ γᾷ τε πατρῴᾳ
κακὸν ἄρ' ἐγενόμαν. (A.*Pers.* 931–933.)

*Here I, **alas**, a lamentable,
wretched <figure>, became a disaster, then,
for my race and my fatherland!*

οἰοῖ (a cry of pain, grief, pity or astonishment) interrupts the sentence.

44.2. A Cry with First Person Singular Pronoun

Reflecting the emotional involvement of an individual speaker, the first person singular pronoun may be combined with a cry. Most often the pronoun is a Dative of Interest (μοι), which may be repeated. Sometimes the Nominative (ἐγώ) is added to the Dative.

ἰώ μοί μοι·
τί φῶ; (E.*Hipp.* 1384–1385.)

Ah me, ah me!
What am I to say?

ἰώ (a cry of grief, suffering or appeal) is used with μοι repeated.

ὤμοι ἐγώ, τί πάθω, τέκνον ἐμόν; (S.*OC* 216.)
Ah me, ah me! *What is to become of me, my child?*

ὤ (a cry of surprise, joy or pain) with μοι (Dat.) and ἐγώ (Nom.).

44.3. An Exclamation with a Causal Genitive

The reason for an exclamation may be expressed by a Causal Genitive phrase. Such Genitive phrases may be added either to a mere cry, or to an exclamatory Nominative phrase. (Cf. Lesson 36.6.)

ὀτοτοῖ, βασιλεῦ, **στρατιᾶς ἀγαθῆς
καὶ περσονόμου τιμῆς μεγάλης,
κόσμου τ' ἀνδρῶν,**
οὓς νῦν δαίμων ἐπέκειρεν. (A.*Pers.* 918–921.)

Ototoi, <O> king, **for the noble army
and for the great honour of Persian rule,
and for the splendour of the men**,
whom now a deity <has> cut down!

The series of Genitive phrases gives the reason for the Chorus's cry, ὀτοτοῖ.

ἰώ,
δύστανος ἐγὼ μελέα τε πόνων,
ἰώ μοί μοι, πῶς ἂν ὀλοίμαν; (E.*Med.* 96–97.)

Ah,
unfortunate <am> I and wretched because of my troubles,
ah me, ah me, may I perish!

The Genitive πόνων gives the reason for Medea's exclamation that she is unfortunate and wretched. (The term '<am>' would be better omitted if English idiom allowed, since the phrase is an exclamatory Nom. rather than a statement.)

44.4. Exclamatory Infinitive Phrases

In English, an exclamation may be expressed in an Infinitive phrase.

Oh, to be in England
Now that April's there ... (R. Browning, *Home Thoughts from Abroad*, lines 1–2.)

Exclamatory Infinitive phrases also occur in classical Greek, mainly in drama. The Infinitive may have an explicit Accusative Subject; otherwise, such a Subject is implied in the context. And the Infinitive may have its own neuter Accusative definite article.

ὦ πλεῖστον ἔχθος ὄνομα Σαλαμῖνος **κλύειν**· (A.*Pers.* 284.)
Oh, <even> ***to hear*** *the name of Salamis, greatest object of hate!*

Infinitive phrase without definite article and without Accusative Subject. The Messenger, who speaks the line, could easily be supplied as Accusative Subject of the Infinitive: 'Oh, that <I> should even hear …!'

τὸ δὲ προσδοκῆσαί σ' – οὐκ ἀνόητον καὶ κενόν; –
ὡς δοῦλος ὢν καὶ θνητὸς Ἀλκμήνης ἔσῃ. (Ar.*Ra.* 530–531.)

And that you should expect *– <is it> not senseless and empty-headed? – that, although you are a slave and a mortal, you will be Alcmena's <son>!*

Infinitive phrase with definite article and with explicit Accusative Subject (σ(ε)). (For the sake of clarity, W. B. Stanford's punctuation has been followed.)

44.5. Exclamatory Sentences Introduced by οἷος, ὅσος or ὡς

Exclamations may be expressed in a phrase or a full sentence which is introduced by the relative adjectives οἷος and ὅσος or by the relative adverb ὡς. οἷος and ὅσος may be used alone as pronouns, or may qualify a noun. ὡς may modify the verb in its sentence, or an adjective or another adverb.

44.5.1. οἷος

οἴμοι μάλ' αὖθις, **οἷα** μ' ἐκκαλῇ, πάτερ,
φονέα γενέσθαι καὶ παλαμναῖον σέθεν. (S. Tr. 1206–1207.)

Alas yet again, **to what** *you do summon me, father,*
to become your murderer and blood-guilty!

οἷα is used as a pronoun.

οἴμοι, τέκνον, πρὸς **οἷα** δουλείας **ζυγὰ**
χωροῦμεν, **οἷοι** νῷν ἐφεστᾶσι **σκοποί**. (S. Aj. 944–945.)

Alas, <my> son, to **what a yoke** *of slavery*
we are going! **What guardians** *stand over us both!*

οἷα qualifies ζυγά, οἷοι qualifies σκοποί.

ἀλλ' **οἷον** τὸν Τηλεφίδην κατενήρατο χαλκῷ,
ἥρω' Εὐρύπυλον· (Hom. Od. 11.519–520.)

But **what** *<a man was> that son of Telephus <whom> he killed with his*
bronze spear,
the hero Eurypylus!

οἷον is used predicatively in reference to τὸν Τηλεφίδην.

44.5.2. ὅσος

ὦ τάλας, **ὅσον κακὸν** ἔχει δόμος· (E. Hipp. 852.)
O wretched <man>, **how great a trouble** *the house contains!*

ὅσον qualifies κακόν.

ὦ πλοῦτε καὶ τυραννὶ καὶ τέχνη τέχνης
ὑπερφέρουσα τῷ πολυζήλῳ βίῳ,
ὅσος παρ' ὑμῖν ὁ φθόνος φυλάσσεται … (S.*OT* 380–382.)

O wealth and royal power and skill surpassing
skill in the greatly-envied life,
how great *<is> the jealousy <that> is fostered among you …!*

ὅσος is used predicatively in reference to ὁ φθόνος.

44.5.3. ὡς

ὦ δῶμ', ὃ πρίν ποτ' εὐτύχεις ἀν' Ἑλλάδα, …
ὥς σε **στενάζω**, δοῦλος ὢν μέν, ἀλλ' ὅμως […](E.*Ba.* 1024, 1027.)

O house, which once in the past were fortunate throughout Greece …
how I, *slave though I am, nevertheless* ***lament*** *for you …*

ὡς modifies the verb στενάζω.

ὡς θρασὺς ὁ βάκχος κοὐκ ἀγύμναστος λόγων. (E.*Ba.* 491.)
How bold *the bacchanal and not unpractised in arguments!*

ὡς modifies the adjective θρασύς.

ὦ δυσπόνητε δαῖμον, **ὡς ἄγαν** βαρὺς
ποδοῖν ἐνήλου παντὶ Περσικῷ γένει. (A.*Pers.* 515–516.)

O troublesome deity, ***how excessively*** *heavily*
you leapt with both feet upon all the Persian race!

ὡς modifies the adverb ἄγαν (which modifies the adj. βαρύς).

44.6. Interrogative Adjective or Adverb

It is sometimes suggested that an interrogative adjective or adverb may introduce an exclamation. However, it seems better to regard such sentences as being rhetorical questions, at least until the end of the classical period. In the Hellenistic period, exclamations may be introduced by an interrogative term. The following examples from early verse, late classical prose and early Hellenistic verse illustrate the usage.

Ἀτρεΐδη, **ποῖόν** σε **ἔπος** φύγεν ἕρκος ὀδόντων;
πῶς δὴ φῂς πολέμοιο μεθιέμεν; (Hom.*Il.* 4.350–351.)

Son of Atreus, ***what word*** *escaped from you <through> the barrier of your teeth?*
How *indeed do you say that <we> are holding back from war?*

Although line 350 has sometimes been treated as an exclamation, it is better understood as a rhetorical question in keeping with line 351. ποῖον ... ἔπος (350) corresponds in meaning to πῶς ... φῄς (351).

πῶς μὲν γὰρ **δυσδιάβατον** τὸ πεδίον, εἰ μὴ νικήσομεν τοὺς ἱππέας; **πῶς** δὲ ἃ διεληλύθαμεν ὄρη, ἢν πελτασταὶ τοσοίδε ἐφέπωνται; ἢν δὲ δὴ καὶ σωθῶμεν ἐπὶ θάλατταν, **πόσον** τι νάπος ὁ Πόντος; (X.*An.* 6.5.19–20.)

For ***how hard to cross*** *<will> the plain <be>, if we do not defeat the cavalry? And* ***how*** *<hard> the mountains which we have passed through, if so many light-armed troops pursue? And if indeed we get safely to the sea, about* ***how big*** *a ravine <is> the Euxine?*

Xenophon, in a speech, is exhorting his troops to battle and arguing that the ravine in front of them is no more difficult or dangerous than the terrain or sea over which they have already passed or will have to pass. The questions, on the borderline between literal and rhetorical, would not make sense as exclamations. Xenophon does *not* want to say: 'How difficult it will be!'

ὦ **πῶς πονηρόν** ἐστιν ἀνθρώπου φύσις
τὸ σύνολον· (Philemo Comicus, *fr.* 2; 4th–3rd century BCE.)

Oh, ***how evil*** *a thing is the nature of man in general!*

Here, the interrogative form πῶς modifies the adjective πονηρόν and is definitely exclamatory, as ὦ (or ὤ: manuscripts vary) helps to confirm.

44.7. Reported Exclamations

Smyth (1956, §§2685–2687) classifies some sentences as 'indirect' or 'dependent' exclamations, while acknowledging that it 'is often difficult to distinguish between indirect exclamations and indirect questions' (§2685). In practice, with one possible exception, all the examples in his §2686 can

LESSON 44. EXCLAMATIONS

be classified as reported questions. And none of the examples in §2687 is a reported exclamation. Instead, there are adjectival clauses (Hom.*Il.* 21.399; Pl.*Phd.* 117 C–D), a direct exclamation (Ar.*Nu.* 1206–1211), an ambivalent adjectival clause or reported question (Pl.*R.* 329 B), a Causal clause (Pl.*Phd.* 58 E) and an adverbial clause of place (Ar.*V.* 1450–1452, metaphorical).

The one possible exception is Pl.*Tht.* 142 B. At this early stage, only Euclides and Terpsion have been involved in the dialogue. Terpsion exclaims:

οἷον ἄνδρα λέγεις ἐν κινδύνῳ εἶναι.
What a man you say is in danger!

The grammatical construction is Accusative and Infinitive of reported speech. And yet, this is not a reported exclamation. For Euclides has *not* said 'What a man!', he has only said, in different words, that Theaetetus 'is in danger', specifically, that he is severely wounded and has dysentery. Terpsion himself, who is not the Subject of λέγεις, is responsible for the exclamatory component of the sentence. The sentence is an abbreviation of the expression 'What a man <he is, who> you say is in danger!' Euclides immediately confirms this general value judgment with the specific phrase καλόν τε καὶ ἀγαθόν.

A comment from the Chorus-leader in the *Trachineae* follows a similar pattern.

ὦ τλῆμον Ἑλλάς, **πένθος οἷον** εἰσορῶ
ἕξουσαν ἀνδρὸς τοῦδέ γ' εἰ σφαλήσεται. (S.*Tr.* 1112–1113.)

O poor Greece, **what grief** *I see*
that it will have if it is (going to be) cheated of this man!

The Vocative phrase is exclamatory, not a genuine address. The following grammatical construction is Accusative Participle of reported mental perception: ἕξουσαν (Acc. fem. sg.) refers to Ἑλλάς, implicitly third person as σφαλήσεται shows.

If the reading ἀλλ' οἷον (rather than ἀλλοῖον) is accepted, then Hom.*Il.* 5.638–639 would already provide another example.

ἀλλ' **οἷόν τινά** φασι βίην Ἡρακληείην
εἶναι ...

But **what a** <man> they say that the strength of Heracles
was ...!

(The phrase 'strength of Heracles' for 'strong Heracles' is a standard idiom; cf. Hom.*Il.* 2.658; 11.690.)

Each of these three examples occurs in a passage of direct speech. The speaker is responsible for the exclamatory component of each sentence, whether she is reporting her own observation (S. *Tr.*), or he is reporting an interlocutor's implied comment (Pl. *Tht.*) or the statements of people in general (Hom.*Il.*). It is not so much that the sentences themselves are reported (or indirect or dependent) exclamations. Rather, the exclamations occur in a subordinate phrase of the sentences: Accusative and Infinitive or Participle.

References

Goodwin (1889), *Syntax of the moods and tenses of the Greek verb*, §§787, 805 (Infinitive).

Smyth (1956), *Greek grammar*, §§2015, 2036, 2575.4, 2681–2687.

EXERCISE 44

Translate the following passages.

1. οἳ 'γὼ τάλαινα διαπεπραγμένου στρατοῦ·
   ὦ νυκτὸς ὄψις ἐμφανῆ ἐνυπνίων,
   ὡς κάρτα μοι σαφῶς ἐδήλωσας κακά.

διαπράσσειν	to bring to an end, to destroy (here Pass.)

2. τὸ οὖν τοιούτων μὲν πέρι πολλὴν σπευδὴν ποιήσασθαι, Ἔρωτα δὲ μηδένα πω ἀνθρώπων τετολμηκέναι εἰς ταυτηνὶ τὴν ἡμέραν ἀξίως ὑμνῆσαι·

οὖν	well then
τοιούτων (neut.) ... πέρι	See Lesson 42.8.

3. ὦ δυστάλαινα, τοιάδ' ἄνδρα χρήσιμον
   φωνεῖν, ἃ πρόσθεν οὗτος οὐκ ἔτλη ποτ' ἄν.

ὦ δυστάλαινα	The speaker addresses herself.

4. εἰ δέ γε δοῦλος ἢ ὑποβολιμαῖος τὰ μὴ προσήκοντ' ἀπώλλυε καὶ ἐλυμαίνετο, Ἡράκλεις ὅσῳ μᾶλλον δεινὸν καὶ ὀργῆς ἄξιον πάντες ἂν ἔφησαν εἶναι.

ὑποβολιμαῖος, -α, -ον	substituted, suppositious (esp. child)
λυμαίνεσθαι (Mid.)	to misuse
Ἡράκλεις	exclamatory Voc.

5. ὦ φίλτατ', ὦ Τρυγαῖ', ὅσ' ἡμᾶς τἀγαθὰ
   δέδρακας εἰρήνην ποιήσας·

6. ὢ ὤ,
   οἷά μ' ἐκέλευσεν ἀναπυθέσθαι σου.

ἐκέλευσεν	The Subject is Peace personified (fem.).

7. φεῦ, τῶν Ἀθηνῶν ὡς στένω μεμνημένος.

8. O men, how pleasant [it is] to see your faces!

9. And how many cities he captured without crossing the ford of the river Halys
   nor rushing off from his hearth…!

ford	πόρος, -ου, ὁ
Halys	Ἅλυς, -υος, ὁ
to rush off	σύεσθαι (Pass.), συθῆναι (Aor.)

Bibliography

Standard References

Goodwin, W. W. (1889). *Syntax of the moods and tenses of the Greek verb* (Rev. ed.). London: Macmillan.

Liddell, H. G. & Scott, R. (1996). *A Greek–English lexicon* (9th ed.). (H. S. Jones & R. McKenzie, Eds.). Oxford: Clarendon Press.

Montanari, F. (2015). *The Brill dictionary of Ancient Greek*. Leiden & Boston: Brill.

Smyth, H. W. (1956). *Greek grammar* (Rev. ed.) (G. M. Messing, Ed.). Cambridge, MA: Harvard University Press.

Other References

Allen, W. S. (1987). *Vox Graeca: A guide to the pronunciation of classical Greek* (3rd ed.). Cambridge: Cambridge University Press.

Denniston, J. D. (1954). *The Greek particles* (2nd ed.). Oxford: Clarendon.

Gildersleeve, B. L. (1900–1911). *Syntax of classical Greek from Homer to Demosthenes* (Vols 1–2). New York: American Book Company.

Hesiod. (1966). *Theogony*. (M. L. West, Ed.). Oxford: Clarendon.

Humbert, J. (1954). *Syntaxe Grecque*. (2nd ed.). Paris: Klincksiek.

Joint Committee on Grammatical Terminology. (1911). *On the terminology of grammar: Being the report of the Joint Committee on Grammatical Terminology*. London: J. Murray.

Kühner, R. (1890–1904). *Ausführliche Grammatik der Griechischen Sprache* (Vols 1–2). (B. Gerth, Ed.). Hanover: Hahnsche Buchhandlung.

Leaf, W. & Bayfield, M. A. (Eds). (1895). *The Iliad of Homer* (Vol. 1, §§33–35). London: Macmillan.

Masterman, K. C. (1962). On grammatical terminology and aspect in particular. *Greece and Rome, 9*, 72–86.

Moorhouse, A. C. (1982). *The syntax of Sophocles* (Mnemosyne Supplement 75). Leiden: Brill.

Paley, F. A. (Ed.). (1883). *The Epics of Hesiod*. London: Whittaker and Bell.

Palmer, L. R. (1980). *The Greek language*. London: Faber and Faber.

Probert, P. (2003). *A new short guide to the accentuation of Ancient Greek*. Bristol: Bristol Classical Press.

Rijksbaron, A. (1994). *The syntax and semantics of the verb in classical Greek* (2nd ed.). Amsterdam: Gieben.

Schwyzer, E. (1950). *Syntax und Syntaktische Stilistik* (*Griechische Grammatik*, vol. 2). (A. Debbruner, Ed.). München: Beck.

Index of Passages Quoted in the Lessons

Abbreviations of the titles of the works of Greek authors follow the usage of H. G. Liddell and R. Scott (1996) *A Greek–English lexicon*. References are made to the Lesson and Section number.

Aeschines		*Pr.* 160–161	17.3
3.2	11.4	*Pr.* 162–163	17.5
3.124	7.3	*Pr.* 173–177	32.3.2.1
		Pr. 211–213	18.4
Aeschylus		*Pr.* 247	17.1
Ag. 49	42.9	*Pr.* 253	17.1
Ag. 861–862	41.1.1	*Pr.* 294–295	18.4
Ag. 1056–1057	27.1	*Pr.* 299–302	17.3
Ch. 195	11.2.1.1	*Pr.* 302–303	17.1
Eu. 611–613	18.3	*Pr.* 377–378	17.1
Eu. 674–675	10.4.1	*Pr.* 485–486	18.4
Pers. 284	44.4	*Pr.* 500–504	17.5
Pers. 515–516	44.5.3	*Pr.* 520	10.3.6
Pers. 731	39.4.3.2	*Pr.* 564–565	18.4
Pers. 742	30.2.2	*Pr.* 616–617	2.3.3
Pers. 918–921	44.3	*Pr.* 648–649	6.2
Pers. 931–933	44.1	*Pr.* 717–718	25.2
Pers. 1043–1045	44.1	*Pr.* 735–737	17.1
Pr. 3–4	25.2	*Pr.* 764–765	7.3
Pr. 29–32	25.5	*Pr.* 825	32.2
Pr. 35	25.4.3	*Pr.* 997	18.1
Pr. 36	17.5	*Pr.* 1073–1075	42.6
Pr. 41	17.1	*Suppl.* 398–399	26.2
Pr. 48	11.2.2.2	*Th.* 247	5.2
Pr. 115	17.3	*Th.* 261	10.3.6
Pr. 135	9.4	*Th.* 550–551	11.1.2
Pr. 153–155	11.2.1.2		

Andocides

1.2	5.1.4		
1.12	5.1.2		
1.12	13.3		
1.14	15.3		
1.17	14.2		
1.19	13.3		
1.28	2.3.1		
1.41	14.2		
1.41	14.3		
1.45	4.3.2		
1.51	2.3.2		
1.55	5.1.5		
1.59	5.1.3		
1.64	13.3		
1.109	5.1.1		
1.136	8.4.1		
1.137	22.1		
1.149	22.7		
3.32	4.3.2		

Antiphon

1.1	39.3.7

Aristophanes

Ach. 221–222	26.2
Ach. 639–640	19.4.3
Ec. 300–301	24.2.1
Ec. 1038–1040	23.1.2
Eq. 36	11.5
Eq. 698–699	20.2.2.2
Lys. 1276–1277	24.5
Nu. 296–297	10.3.5
Nu. 832–833	22.3
Ra. 524–525	10.3.4
Ra. 530–531	44.4
Ra. 748	34.2.2
Ra. 1006–1007	34.2.6
V. 37	2.3.1

Demosthenes

1.3	35.7		
1.12	4.3.2		
3.22	30.3.1		
4.15	29.9		
6.28	8.4.2		
8.53	35.6.1		
9.16	37.1.8		
9.45	24.3.5		
9.60	41.2.3		
15.5	34.2.5		
18.71 (twice)	17.2		
18.125	43.3.2		
18.142	35.4.1		
18.220	22.1		
18.292	34.2.2		
19.99	35.5		
19.179	16.3		
19.316	27.5		
21.221	35.6.4		
22.17	34.2.4		
22.41	23.1.1		
23.12	41.1.3		
23.79	18.3		
24.9	29.6.9		
28.23	43.3.3		
33.11	18.1		
35.26	37.1.4		
37.45	3.5.3		
42.22	38.10		
43.55	41.1.3		
43.61	18.1		
49.17	35.4.1		

Euripides

Alc. 24–26	38.2
Alc. 32–33	38.3
Alc. 40	40.2.1
Alc. 43	39.4.1
Alc. 138–139	40.2.1

INDEX OF PASSAGES QUOTED IN THE LESSONS

Alc. 199–200	41.2.2	*Med.* 96–97	44.3
Alc. 540	19.4.2	*Med.* 153–154	38.6
Alc. 625–627	36.7	*Med.* 269–270	15.4
Alc. 636	36.2	*Med.* 350–351	15.3
Alc. 642	41.1.3	*Med.* 352–354	19.2.1
Alc. 696–698	39.4.2.2	*Med.* 529	40.2.3
Alc. 707	36.7	*Med.* 566–567	41.2.1.3
Alc. 731	40.2.2	*Med.* 579	37.2.6
Alc. 734–736	40.3.1	*Med.* 636	11.1.1
Alc. 774–775	40.3.5	*Med.* 645–648	38.7
Alc. 800–802	41.2.1.4	*Med.* 703	7.3
Alc. 821	36.7	*Med.* 1059–1061	37.1.8
Alc. 1072–1074	11.2.1.1	*Med.* 1169–1170	29.6.3
Andr. 1–6	36.8	*Med.* 1271	17.4
Ba. 1	37.2.1	*Med.* 1306–1307	33.4
Ba. 216–220	25.6	*Med.* 1409–1412	29.4.1
Ba. 341	2.3.2	*Ph.* 263–264	35.4.2
Ba. 491	44.5.3	*Ph.* 762	42.9
Ba. 519–532	36.8	*Ph.* 1174–1176	29.6.7
Ba. 718–721	11.5	*Supp.* 120	27.3
Ba. 945–946	40.3.3	*Tr.* 636–637	3.5.3
Ba. 1024…1027	44.5.3	*Tr.* 1165–1166	25.7
Ba. 1043–1045	31.3.1		
Ba. 1058–1062	12.2	Herodotus	
Hel. 267–268	25.7	1.33	23.2
Hel. 462	7.3	1.50.3	9.3.2
Hel. 597–598	37.2.2	1.65.5	31.3.1
Hipp. 498–499	10.3.4	1.73.3	23.3
Hipp. 518	35.6.1	1.82.7	32.3.2.2
Hipp. 852	44.5.2	1.86.2	29.4.7
Hipp. 1265–1267	29.4.3	1.89.3	25.2
Hipp. 1384–1385	44.2	1.91.1	3.4.1
Hipp. 1402	39.4.3.1	1.94.1	38.8
IA 1467–1469	37.1.5	1.115.2	42.7
IT 157–166	36.8	1.126.5	4.4
IT 260–261	42.6	1.129.2	39.2.3
IT 588–590	27.4	1.134.1	41.2.3
Med. 1–2	42.4	1.134.2	41.2.3
Med. 6–8	37.2.6	1.154	23.3
Med. 95	2.3.3	1.178.3	39.3.7

3.44.2	10.4.1	*Th.* 280–283	23.1.4.
3.72.3	25.4.1	*Th.* 533–534	9.3.4
3.122.3	15.5		
3.135.2	10.4.2	Homer	
3.135.3	35.5	*Il.* 1.35–43	12.1
3.142.5	24.6	*Il.* 2.80–81	20.3.1
4.43.1	35.2	*Il.* 2.527–529	28.5
4.62.2	39.3.5	*Il.* 3.39–40	11.2.2.3
4.68.1	37.1.8	*Il.* 4.350–351	44.6
4.68.2	37.1.8	*Il.* 4.415–416	20.2.2.2
4.140.1	42.7	*Il.* 5.597–600	28.4.3
5.8	41.1.1	*Il.* 5.638–639	44.7
5.15.1, 3	15.5	*Il.* 6.345–347	11.2.2.3
5.36.4	40.2.4	*Il.* 8.477–479	26.3.5
5.49.2	34.2.1	*Il.* 9.165–166	27.4
5.62.3	39.2.4	*Il.* 9.385–387	32.2
5.82.3	22.5	*Il.* 9.697–699	11.2.2.2
5.101.1	29.4.5	*Il.* 11.386–387	20.2.2.2
5.109.2	24.2.1	*Il.* 11.670–672	11.2.3
6.4	9.3.2	*Il.* 12.246	35.7
6.5.2	37.2.6	*Il.* 13.491–493	28.4.2
6.65.1	22.5	*Il.* 15.288–289	16.2
7.8.α.2	24.3.1	*Il.* 16.663–665	3.4.3.1
7.23.4	33.1.2.1	*Il.* 17.70–71	20.3.2
7.49.4	41.2.3	*Il.* 17.556–558	20.2.1
7.107.1	31.3.1	*Il.* 18.107	11.1.3
7.121.2	37.1.7	*Il.* 20.403–404	28.4.3
7.147.1	13.3	*Il.* 21.311–312	39.3.7
8.22.1	22.2	*Il.* 22.86–88	20.2.2.2
8.98.1	29.6.6	*Il.* 23.584–585	16.3
8.108.2	13.3	*Od.* 1.9	42.2
8.113.3	39.4.2.1	*Od.* 1.37	42.1
8.143.3	11.3	*Od.* 1.48–50	42.3
8.144.5	30.3.2	*Od.* 1.75	42.3
9.46.3	35.4.2	*Od.* 1.372–374	27.5
9.117	10.4.2	*Od.* 1.384–385	37.1.3
		Od. 2.372	16.3
Hesiod		*Od.* 4.391–392	20.2.2.2
Op. 363	25.3.2	*Od.* 7.204–206	20.2.2.1
Sc. 5–6	9.3.4	*Od.* 8.221	14.4

Od. 8.479–481	37.1.3	12.112	9.3.4
Od. 11.519–520	44.5.1	12.139–141	29.3.2
Od. 13.128–129	23.1.4	15.15	43.3.4
Od. 13.291–292	26.3.1	15.74	33.2
Od. 13.293–294	26.2	15.83	32.3.1
Od. 14.274–275	11.2.2.3	15.88	31.2.2
Od. 14.331–332	16.3	15.218	22.4
Od. 15.34–35	25.4.1	15.278	43.6.2
Od. 15.341–342	11.1.2	16.5	32.3.2.2
Od. 18.272–273	30.2.1	16.9	43.5
Od. 19.589–590	20.3.3	16.9	43.6.1
Od. 22.27–28	10.3.2	16.22	35.3
		17.14	39.2.6
Isaeus		17.22	35.6.1
2.28	18.5	17.24	34.3.1
8.34	35.4.1	18.17	10.4.1
10.1	11.4	21.16	13.2
18.19	16.3		
		Lysias	
Isocrates		1.21	24.6
2.23	28.3	10.11	15.2
2.49	7.3	12.27	26.3.3
4.91	41.1.1	12.74	21.3
4.129	2.3.2	12.58	39.3.2
4.141	32.2	12.86	11.4
5.123	25.6	13.9	39.3.4
6.40	34.3.1	14.11	39.3.6
6.52	19.4.3	14.21	39.5
6.56	34.3.1	14.24	39.3.3
6.92	8.3	19.32	16.2
7.59	34.3.2	21.12	24.2.4
7.81	34.2.1	23.4	37.1.1
8.19	34.3.2	24.4	14.2
8.53	25.2	24.15	13.2
8.111–112	22.1	25.33	29.5
8.129	34.4	30.5	39.3.7
9.7	8.6	30.32	34.4
10.60	41.2.3	31.15	16.2
11.7	24.3.5	31.31	34.4
12.80	29.5	32.8	37.2.3

Philemo Comicus		*R.* 415 B	10.4.2
fr. 2	44.6	*R.* 526 C	18.2
		Smp. 172 A	4.3.3
Plato		*Smp.* 172 B	12.4
Ap. 17 C	21.2	*Smp.* 172 C	4.3.1
Ap. 19 C	6.2	*Smp.* 173 B–C	22.3
Ap. 20 E	10.2	*Smp.* 173 E	3.4.1
Ap. 21 A	10.2	*Smp.* 173 E–174 A	3.4.2
Ap. 27 A	28.4.2	*Tht.* 142 A	34.4
Ap. 27 C	23.1.1	*Tht.* 142 B	44.7
Ap. 30 C	40.2.8		
Ap. 33 E	22.3	Septuagint	
Ap. 34 C	28.4.1	*Tobit* 2.14	40.2.7
Ap. 35 D	3.5.4		
Ap. 38 C	26.3.1	Sophocles	
Ap. 39 D	3.5.3	*Aj.* 265–267	17.2
Ap. 41 A–B	23.4	*Aj.* 387–391	11.1.4
Cri. 49 D	24.2.2	*Aj.* 539	41.2.1.3
Cri. 51 B–C	8.7	*Aj.* 657–658	33.3
Euthphr. 3 B	27.3	*Aj.* 762–763	36.3
Euthphr. 4 D	34.2.3	*Aj.* 810	33.1.2.2
Euthphr. 10 A	23.1.1	*Aj.* 879–887	11.1.4
Grg. 522 E	35.3	*Aj.* 887–889	3.4.1
Hp.Ma. 282 E	16.1	*Aj.* 944–945	44.5.1
Leg. 705 E	42.9	*Aj.* 964–965	41.1.3
Phd. 59 E	10.4.2	*Ant.* 371	42.9
Phd. 67 A	30.2.2	*Ant.* 453–455	22.1
Phd. 81 D–E	30.4	*Ant.* 502–504	42.10
Phd. 89 C	24.2.3	*Ant.* 678	8.8
Phd. 105 E	17.1	*Ant.* 750–751	4.3.2
Phlb. 27 C	17.1	*Ant.* 752	4.3.2
Prt. 356 C	23.1.4	*Ant.* 885–887	10.3.3
R. 332 A	43.2	*Ant.* 891–894	36.6
R. 340 E	43.3.1	*Ant.* 927–928	11.1.1
R. 341 C	43.3.5	*Ant.* 1087–1088	36.7
R. 350 C	43.2	*El.* 379–381	33.3
R. 351 E–352 A	43.2	*El.* 404	33.1.1
R. 361 B–C	36.2	*El.* 446–448	17.1
R. 377 B–C	25.3.1	*El.* 814–816	17.1
R. 379 B	25.3.2	*El.* 1259	33.1.2.2

El. 1315–1317	22.1	*Ph.* 882–883	4.3.3
El. 1344	5.2	*Ph.* 961–962	32.3.2.1
OC 38	39.2.1	*Ph.* 1026–1028	40.3.4
OC 52	43.4	*Ph.* 1035–1039	23.1.2
OC 216	44.2	*Ph.* 1241	29.4.4
OC 377–381	6.5.1	*Ph.* 1242	29.2.3
OC 656–657	15.3	*Ph.* 1301	37.1.6
OC 791	17.1	*Ph.* 1348–1349	36.5
OC 956	10.3.1	*Ph.* 1469–1471	2.3.2
OC 1486–1487	17.1	*Tr.* 438–439	25.4.1
OT 198–199	20.2.2.1	*Tr.* 445–446	7.3
OT 224–226	25.4.1	*Tr.* 706	15.3
OT 284–285	40.2.5	*Tr.* 903–905	33.3
OT 316–317	33.1.2.2	*Tr.* 1112–1113	44.7
OT 380–382	44.5.2	*Tr.* 1206–1207	44.5.1
OT 393–394	39.2.2	*Tr.* 1227	37.1.7
OT 603–604	37.3		
OT 616	24.5	Theognis	
OT 838	5.2	555–556	42.4
OT 863–865	11.1.3		
OT 1009	42.4	Thucydides	
OT 1014–1016	41.1.3	1.1.1	1.2.2
OT 1216–1218	11.2.1.2	1.5.1	42.7
OT 1255–1257	18.5	1.5.3	9.3.4
OT 1367	18.5	1.6.5	9.3.4
OT 1387–1389	29.6.5	1.7	9.3.4
OT 1442–1443	33.1.1	1.8.3	4.3.2
OT 1455–1456	15.3	1.10.2	5.3
Ph. 45	27.1	1.10.5	40.2.6
Ph. 50–51	27.1	1.11.2	4.3.1
Ph. 58–59	37.1.7	1.18.1	38.4
Ph. 83–85	2.3.1	1.19	41.1.2
Ph. 101	41.2.1.1	1.20.1	6.4
Ph. 118	29.6.4	1.22.3	28.3
Ph. 124	27.5	1.26.2	29.11.3
Ph. 229	2.3.1	1.26.3	21.3
Ph. 302–303	33.4	1.27.2	29.11.2
Ph. 451–452	36.3	1.28.1	6.2
Ph. 714–715	41.1.2	1.31.2	9.3.3
Ph. 734	17.1	1.31.4–1.32.1	12.3

INTERMEDIATE ANCIENT GREEK LANGUAGE

1.35.4	37.2.5	2.84.2	16.2
1.36.4	12.3	2.87.5	3.5.2
1.38.4	19.4.1	2.88.3	4.3.1
1.40.2	26.3.4	2.90.2	27.5
1.47.3	38.5	2.90.4	16.2
1.49.3	31.3.2	2.93.4	3.5.3
1.53.2	29.4.2	2.93.4	14.7
1.57.4	24.3.2	2.99.1	24.3.1
1.64.1	16.1	3.1.2	33.1.3.2
1.66	36.1	3.9.2	19.4.2
1.72.1	8.3	3.22.8	32.3.2.2
1.82.5	24.2.1	3.33.2	35.7
1.86.1	9.3.3	3.34.1	33.1.3.1
1.90.5	34.4	3.36.5	42.7
1.91.5	14.3	3.45.4	8.5
1.98.3	41.1.2	3.60	14.3
1.109.4	42.10	3.81.3	9.3.3
1.123.1	40.2.7	3.96.1	6.3
1.134.1	39.3.1	3.112.6	33.4
1.139.1	6.3	4.17.2	6.4
1.142.1	29.11.1	4.20.3	6.2
1.142.4	29.6.2	4.23.1	14.2
1.143.5	33.1.2.1	4.27.1	35.4.1
1.144.1	3.5.3	4.35.2	40.3.2
2.2.1	41.1.2	4.38.3	12.5
2.5.2	37.2.2	4.55.3	35.4.1
2.5.5	14.6	4.65.3	23.1.3
2.11.5	3.5.5	4.66.3	39.2.5
2.20.1	14.7	4.70.2	32.2
2.20.4	3.4.3.3	4.80.1	21.3
2.44.1	25.7	4.85.4	38.9
2.44.4	3.5.1	4.110.2	15.3
2.48.2	42.6	4.128.2	16.1
2.55.1	33.1.3.1	5.1	28.2
2.59.2	23.3	5.5.1	39.2.1
2.62.2	29.10	5.11.10	15.2
2.67.3	32.2	5.14.3	39.3.5
2.75.1	3.5.3	5.21.3	13.3
2.76.3	35.4.2	5.29.2	8.5
2.81.4	31.4.1	5.34.1	33.1.3.2

INDEX OF PASSAGES QUOTED IN THE LESSONS

5.34.2	4.3.2	*Cyr.* 1.2.6	13.2
5.35.4	31.4.2	*Cyr.* 1.2.10	18.4
5.37.1	37.1.4	*Cyr.* 1.3.8	25.3.1
5.55.1	14.5	*Cyr.* 1.4.17	16.1
5.56.5	42.4	*Cyr.* 1.4.18	5.2
5.63.4	25.2	*Cyr.* 1.4.25	15.4
5.65.3	6.5.2	*Cyr.* 1.5.2	10.4.1
5.83.4	13.3	*Cyr.* 1.5.5	37.1.2
6.10.5	32.3.2.1	*Cyr.* 1.5.13	25.6
6.23.2	4.3.2	*Cyr.* 1.6.36	41.2.1.2
6.34.2	35.7	*Cyr.* 2.1.16	34.3.1
6.36.1	25.4.2	*Cyr.* 2.1.29	24.3.3
6.50.1	37.1.7	*Cyr.* 2.2.8	32.3.2.2
7.39.2	37.2.4	*Cyr.* 2.3.6	35.5
7.47.4	21.4	*Cyr.* 2.4.6	30.2.1
7.48.4	21.5	*Cyr.* 2.4.23	3.5.3
7.56.1	26.3.5	*Cyr.* 2.4.23	29.3.1
7.66.3	30.3.2	*Cyr.* 3.2.13	18.3
7.67.3	35.6.2	*Cyr.* 3.3.18	35.2
7.71.5	32.3.1	*Cyr.* 4.2.22	3.4.3.2
7.77.6	6.3	*Cyr.* 4.5.41	33.1.2.2
8.18.1	29.8	*Cyr.* 5.2.12	18.3
8.68.1	25.4.3	*Cyr.* 5.3.25	31.2.1
		Cyr. 5.4.21	24.6
Xenophon		*Cyr.* 5.5.24	29.6.1
Ages. 1.26	22.3	*Cyr.* 6.2.9	24.3.3
Ages. 1.31	15.2	*Cyr.* 6.2.9	27.1
Ages. 2.8	24.3.3	*Cyr.* 7.1.8	17.1
Ages. 3.5	12.4	*Cyr.* 7.1.10	36.4
Ages. 7.7	24.3.2	*Cyr.* 8.3.8	33.2
An. 1.9.10	21.3	*Eq.* 12.1	11.3
An. 2.1.3	13.4	*Eq.Mag.* 1.3	24.2.2
An. 2.1.4	11.2.2.1	*HG* 1.6.35	29.2.1
An. 2.2.16	24.3.4	*HG* 2.3.13	33.2
An. 3.3.4	42.7	*HG* 3.1.6	40.2.7
An. 3.3.16	29.7.2	*HG* 4.5.18	3.4.3.4
An. 3.5.5	24.5	*HG* 4.8.5	29.4.6
An. 6.5.19–20	44.6	*HG* 6.4.27	35.5
An. 7.2.25	18.1	*HG* 6.5.37	24.3.3
Ap. 5	34.2.7	*HG* 7.2.13	29.7.1

HG 7.4.10	22.5
HG 7.5.24	35.6.3
Hier. 11.11	35.7
Hier. 4.3	27.1
Mem. 1.2.19	13.2
Mem. 1.2.41	16.1
Mem. 2.1.14	27.4
Mem. 4.2.3	29.6.8
Mem. 4.2.10	29.2.2
Oec. 5.11	34.3.1
Oec. 7.38	8.8
Smp. 4.1	15.4
Smp. 4.16	24.2.4
Vect. 4.32	35.6.3

www.ingramcontent.com/pod-product-compliance
Lightning Source LLC
Chambersburg PA
CBHW061251230426
43664CB00025B/2919